INSIDE NEW YORK
2010

An **inside**
NEW YORK
Guidebook

inside NEW YORK

PUBLISHER	Sam Reisman
EDITOR-IN-CHIEF	Nina Pedrad
ASSOCIATE PUBLISHER	Robyn Burgess
DINING EDITOR	Michael Snyder
FEATURES EDITOR	Yin Yin Lu
NEIGHBORHOODS EDITOR	Jia Ahmad
NIGHTLIFE EDITOR	Erin Byrne
ASSOCIATE EDITORS	Morgan Fletcher
	Evan Johnston
LAYOUT EDITOR	Allie Fisher
GRAPHIC DESIGNER	Stephen Davan
PHOTO EDITOR	Kasalina Nabakooza
MAP DESIGNER	Jed Dore
STAFF EDITORS	Alexa Davis
	Erica Drennan
	Marina Galperina
	Alessandra Gotbaum
WEB EDITOR	Jon Hill

STAFF WRITERS
Rowan Buchanan, Kristina Budelis, Sarah Case, Ruthie
Fierberg, Emily Hall, Dasha Jensen, Mary Kohlmann,
John Krauss, Hannah Lepow, Sasha Levine, Jessica
Lewis, Danielle Mandel, Adam May, Laura Mills, Jacob
Rice, Valerie Safronova, Natalie Shibley, Claudia Sosa,
Andrew Wailes, Benjamin Weiner

CONTRIBUTORS
Desiree Brown, Neil Fitzpatrick, Yonatan Gebeheyu,
Halley Hair, Ann Hao, Laura Kleinbaum, Jerry Li,
Zeyynep Memecan, Sarah Pasternack, Eva Peskin, Tess
Russell, Zack Sheppard, Alice Wade, Lauren Zanedis,
Valeria Zhavoronkina

STAFF PHOTOGRAPHERS
Jia Ahmad, Ruoxi Chen, Stephen Davan, Alexa Davis,
Erica Drennan, Maureen Drennan, Marina Galperina,
Alessandra Gotbaum, Ruthie Fierberg, Allie Fisher,
Morgan Fletcher, Yin Yin Lu, Laura Mills, Julienne
Schaer, Claudia Sosa, Andrew Wailes

SALES ACCOUNT MANAGER
Adam May

www.insidenewyork.com
2960 Broadway MC 5727 • New York, NY • 10027
Phone: 212-854-2804 • Fax: 212-663-9398

Printed by: Ripon Printers
656 S. Douglas St.
Ripon, WI 54971-0006

Special thanks to Jared Hecht, Joseph Meyers, Heather Cohen, Syeda
Lewis, Bernadette Maxwell, Patrick Richards, Beth Vanderputten, and the
whole Columbia CCE staff.

Inside New York® and the Inside New York logo are trademarks of Inside
New York, Inc. and Columbia University.

Advertising Disclaimer: Advertisements do not imply endorsements of
products or services by Inside New York and Inside New York does not
vouch for the accuracy of information provided in advertisements.

If you are interested in purchasing advertising space in Inside New York,
contact Inside New York • 2960 Broadway MC 5727 • New York, NY
10027 • 212-854-2804 • ads@insidenewyork.com.

For bulk sales, university sales, corporate sales, or customized editions, please
call 212-854-2804 or email info@insidenewyork.com.

If your bookstore would like to carry Inside New York, please contact
CU Press at 1-800-944-8648.

This is a publication of the Student Enterprises Division of Columbia
University.

Like every other transplant to the City, we grew up on the romance of New York. We fed off the celluloid images of picturesque parks and night skylines ablaze. We heard stories of a city that promised the greatest art, music, food, and nightlife in the world. We thought of 24-hour public transportation and salivated (we're both from LA).

When we started working on this book, we set out to find the real New York. Not the landmarks well-trod by tour groups, but the hidden haunts known only to the natives. Not the "coolest" nightspots, but the most fun—and the easiest on our student budgets. Not tea at the Plaza, but halal on 53rd Street.

Armed with notepads and unlimited MetroCards, our writers explored every borough. We took to the streets, asked the locals for advice, got lost, made mistakes, made discoveries. We even went to Staten Island. We researched, researched, researched, and, eventually, we wrote.

The book in your hands is the result of countless days and nights spent searching for the best this city has to offer.

But the fact is, the best view of Manhattan will be the one you stumble across on your own. The best bar is where the guy behind the counter knows your name. The best NYC pizza—well, that's an extremely personal matter, but once you find it, you'll never veer. There is no "real" New York, save the one you make for yourself.

We've just started finding our New York. Turn the page and hop on a train.

It's time to find yours.

Sam Reisman, Publisher
Nina Pedrad, Editor-in-Chief

TABLE OF CONTENTS

NEIGHBORHOODS

MANHATTAN

1 Washington Heights & Inwood
2 Harlem
3 Morningside Heights
4 Upper West Side
5 Upper East Side
6 Midtown West
7 Midtown East
8 Chelsea
9 Gramercy
10 Greenwich Village
11 East Village
12 SoHo & TriBeCa
13 Chinatown
14 Lower East Side
15 Financial District

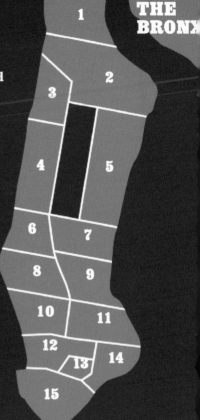

THE BRONX

STATEN ISLAND

*note: map not to scale

QUEENS

Astoria

Jackson
Heights &
Woodside

Flushing

Long
Island
City

Greenpoint

Williamsburg

rooklyn
eights &
UMBO

Fort
Greene

BROOKLYN

Greater
Carroll
Gardens

Park
Slope

Brighton Beach
& Coney Island

ESSENTIALS

V isiting New York City as a tourist is one thing, but living in the metropolis is quite another. To set yourself apart from the camera-laden, fanny pack-toting masses in Times Square, you'll have to know some basic information about how the city operates. That information is encapsulated in the following Essentials—after reading them, you'll be guaranteed to walk, eat, act, read, and feel like a true New Yorker.

First and foremost, you need to be able to navigate the city's bewildering maze of streets. Picking up a subway map isn't enough—**Transportation** provides you with the ins and outs of each train, as well as rundowns of other important modes of travel: walking, buses, commuter rails, taxis, and airplanes. When you're ready to purchase an apartment, read **Settling In** for tips and strategies, as well as places to buy amenities and home furnishings.

City Commerce and **Government and Safety** will fill you in on banking, business hours, taxing, tipping, and bureaucracy. If you're planning on eating out or shopping for groceries, turn to **Dining and Food**.

Student Discounts presents ways to scrimp and save but still enjoy the city's thrilling arts scene. Should you ever need a place to stay at night, check **Hostels** for cheap hotel alternatives. And finally, **Media** is a descriptive listing of New York's popular periodicals, television channels, radio stations and websites.

TRANSPORTATION

With one of the largest subway systems in the world, over 13,000 taxis, reliable train and bus service, and an easily navigable street grid, New York's extensive transportation network offers easy and cheap alternatives to owning a car. So learn the grid, buy a MetroCard, and embrace it—24 hour public transportation is a beautiful thing.

WALKING

With so many stores, restaurants, and office buildings crammed onto every block, sometimes walking is the most convenient method of travel. Thanks to Manhattan's straightforward grid system, even first-time visitors can easily find their way around. North of Houston Street, avenues divide the island vertically and increase in number from east to west (1st to 12th). Streets cross the island horizontally and increase in number from south to north (1st to 220th). There are some exceptions, however:

- Between 5th Ave and 3rd Ave are Madison Ave, Park Ave, and Lexington Ave.
- In Alphabet City, between Houston and 14th St and east of 1st Ave, avenues move up alphabetically from A to D.
- North of 59th St, the avenues between 8th and 11th are now named Central Park West, Columbus, Amsterdam, and West End, respectively.
- Broadway cuts across Manhattan at an angle from northwest to southeast.
- 6th Ave is also known as Avenue of the Americas.
- South of Houston St and in most of the outer boroughs, the rectilinear grid system stops and many streets and avenues have actual names. Here, the easiest way to get around is to find where a place is in relation to a major street, such as Broadway, Bowery, and Delancey.

SUBWAYS

New York City has the largest subway system in the U.S., so it's no wonder that 5.2 million of its visitors and residents travel underground every day. The system's easy access—there are 468 stations scattered throughout the boroughs—and reliable, 24/7 service make hopping on a train a smart and easy choice.

There are 26 interconnected subway routes, grouped by color and divided by letters (A-Z) or numbers (1-7). The subway lines of each color group tend to go the same route, though local trains make more stops than express trains.

DID YOU KNOW?

A **subway party** is when a mass of people gather at a pre-determined station, board the train, and engage in various forms of boisterous merrymaking (often accompanied by blaring music and dancing). They can occur spontaneously, so travel with speakers.

The most popular stations are **Times Square-42nd St**, **Grand Central Terminal**, **34th St-Herald Square**, and **14th St-Union Square**. Find one of them if you ever get lost, because they offer transfers to many different lines. Map out your route on **HopStop.com** before you leave to avoid getting lost—it'll give you the fastest subway and bus routes to take at the time of your departure, and estimate an arrival time.

SUBWAY LINE ESSENTIALS
❶❷❸:
❶ is local in Manhattan
❷ is express in Manhattan, local in Brooklyn (except late nights), and local in the Bronx
❸ is express in Manhattan, and local in Brooklyn (except late nights)

❹❺❻:
❹ is express in Manhattan (except 138th St during peak hours) and Brooklyn, local in the Bronx
❺ is express in the Bronx (in the peak direction), Manhattan, and Brooklyn (except at midday and during the evenings and weekends)

METROCARDS

MetroCards are available for purchase at vending machines in subway stations, from neighborhood vendors, or on MetroCard buses and vans. A one-way ride is $2.25, but there's a 15% bonus for every refillable card that's $8 or more. For express buses, the fare is $5. If you don't want to keep refilling your card, you can buy an unlimited pass (for 1 day, 7 days, 14 days, or 30 days) or try the EasyPayExpress fare option to pay for your ride automatically with your credit card.

Regular cards are accepted on MTA New York City Transit subways, local buses, and express buses. Unlimited cards are only accepted on subways and local buses. Within two hours of using the MetroCard, you can transfer to another bus or subway line for free.

You can also get discounts at participating museums, restaurants, and stores by showing your card. Check www.mta.info for more details.

⑥ is local in Manhattan & express in Brooklyn during midday & rush hours in peak direction

ⒶⒸⒺ:
Ⓐ is express in Manhattan and Brooklyn, local in Queens
Ⓒ is local in Manhattan and Brooklyn (except late nights)
Ⓔ is local during late nights and has limited express stops during rush hours

ⒷⒹⒻⓋ:
Ⓑ is local in the Bronx, express in Brooklyn during rush hours, and local in Manhattan and Brooklyn on weekdays only
Ⓓ is local in the Bronx and express in Manhattan and Brooklyn
Ⓕ is local except for an area in Queens, where it runs express
Ⓥ makes all stops on weekdays only

ⒿⓂⓏ:
Ⓙ and **Ⓜ** are local
Ⓩ is express during rush hours in the peak direction

ⓃⓄⓇⓌ:
Ⓝ is express (except late nights)

Ⓠ is express in Manhattan, local in Brooklyn
Ⓡ is local
Ⓦ is local on weekdays only

❼, Ⓢ, Ⓖ, and Ⓛ:
❼ is local and express in the peak direction
Ⓢ is a special shuttle between Grand Central Terminal & Times Square (except late night)
Ⓖ is express and extended north during evenings, weekends, and late nights
Ⓛ is local

CITY BUSES

New York City also has a bus system, comprised of about 200 local and 40 express routes throughout the five boroughs. The borough in which a local route primarily operates can be identified by one or two letters at the beginning of its name (B=Brooklyn, Bx=Bronx, M=Manhattan, Q=Queens, S=Staten Island), while all express routes begin with "X". Buses can be slow, but they tend to operate in areas far from subway stations. There are also cross-town buses, practically necessary above 59th St because subways don't traverse Manhattan from west to east there. Unlike subways, however, the bus system mostly stops operating after midnight, with the exception of a few late-night buses that

TRANSPORTATION

arrive once an hour on certain routes. But if you are riding between 10pm and 5am, you can get off at any location you want via the Request-A-Stop service, as long as it's safe.

TAXIS

There are over 13,000 cabs in New York City. Though more expensive than taking the subway, taxis are usually faster and more convenient.

How to Hail a Cab:
- Stand on the sidewalk where you are clearly visible from the street.
- Look for lit up numbers on cab roofs—this indicates that they are unoccupied.
- Flag approaching cabs by raising your arm. The driver will pick you up from the curb.
- Let the driver know right away where you're headed. He is obligated to take you to any destination within the five boroughs, Westchester county, and Nassau county.

Tips:
- A cab with "Off Duty" lit on its sign does not usually pick up passengers, but the driver may stop and ask you where're you going. If it's on his way, he'll pick you up.
- If there's more than one person trying to flag a cab, the driver will pick up the first passenger he sees. Be assertive—walk over a block or cross the street.
- If you're catching a cab from the airport, there will be a special cab line outside the terminal.

- Use only the official NYC yellow cabs. Avoid using unmarked (gypsy) cabs, as they are unlicensed and can overcharge.

Standard City Cab Rate:
- $2.50 upon entry.
- $0.40 for every one-fifth of a mile, or every minute spent idle/traveling at less than 12 mph.
- Night surcharge: $0.50 between 8pm and 6am.
- Peak hour weekday surcharge: $1.00 Mon-Fri, between 4pm and 8pm.
- Varying bridge and tunnel tolls.
- A flat fee of $45, plus applicable tolls, from JFK to Manhattan. Newark airport rides to Manhattan are metered, with a $15 surcharge. All other cab rates are metered.
- It is customary to tip 15%-20%.

You can pay with cash or credit card via TaxiTV. If you'd like to know the cost and travel time of your ride in advance, consult either nyccabfare.com or hopstop.com. Make sure you keep your receipt—you'll need it if you leave something behind in the cab. If you happen to be so unfortunate, contact the lost and found at New York's Taxi and Limousine Commission at 212-692-8294.

COMMUTER TRAINS

Whether you're an out-of-state commuter or are just looking to get away for the weekend, take the train! Commuter rails are a reasonably priced, comfortable, and fast mode of transportation (and

New Jersey Transit
- Service to New Jersey from Penn Station; also has buses.
- Rates vary by destination ($15 to Newark Airport).
- njtransit.com

Long Island Railroad
- Service to Long Island from Penn Station.
- Rates vary by destination ($15.25-$25 to the Hamptons).
- mta.info/lirr

Metro-North
- Service to upstate New York and Connecticut from Grand Central or the Harlem 125th St Station (E 125 St and Park Ave).
- Rates vary by destination ($10.21 from Grand Central to Greenwich, CT).
- mta.info/mnr

occasionally come with a scenic view, if you grab a window seat). All depart from Penn Station (33rd St between 7th and 8th Ave, underneath Madison Square Garden) or the Grand Central Terminal (42nd St and Park Ave). These stations are conveniently connected to NYC subway trains—Penn Station to the ACE and 123 lines, Grand Central to the 456 and 7 lines.

Amtrak
- National service from Penn Station.
- Prices are generally lower than airfare, and they offer special discounts online for select trains Tuesday-Friday.
- Amtrak.com, 1-800-USA-RAIL

NATIONAL BUS LINES

For a less expensive, less comfortable escape from the New York City area, opt for a bus ride. Most national buses depart from Port Authority (42nd St and 8th Ave; panynj.gov), just one block west of Times Square in Hell's Kitchen. Local lines to New Jersey also leave from this terminal. If you're willing to compromise your safety to protect your wallet, check out the Chinatown Bus options (chinatown-bus.org).

TRANSPORTATION

Greyhound
- Most popular for national bus service.
- Departs from Port Authority.
- Prices vary by destination; discounts and special rates available ($22 to DC or Baltimore, $20 to Boston).
- Book tickets at greyhound.com or by calling 1-800-231-2222.

Megabus
- Service to Boston, Washington, Philadelphia, Baltimore, Buffalo, Atlantic City, and Toronto.
- Departs near Penn Station, Port Authority, and Pike St.
- Book in advance for tickets as low as $1.
- Purchase tickets at megabus.com.

Popular Chinatown Buses
- Fung Wah Bus (fungwahbus.com) and Lucky Star (luckystarbus.com).
- Hourly service to Boston, Philadelphia, and DC from Bowery Ave and Canal St.

- Tickets are $15, and can be bought online or at the station.

There are three major airports that serve the New York area: John F. Kennedy (JFK), LaGuardia (LGA), and Newark (EWR). Call 1-800-AIR-RIDE for up-to-date travel information.

AIRPORTS

John F. Kennedy (JFK)
- Located in Jamaica, Queens.
- Services all major airlines, international and domestic.
- The most popular airport for overseas flights, but often busy and congested.
- Travel directions:
  - **A E J Z** subway lines or LIRR from Penn Station to Jamaica Station, then AirTrain to and between terminals for $5.
  - Cab for flat rate of $45 plus tolls.

LaGuardia Airport (LGA)
- Located in Flushing, Queens.
- Services domestic flights.
- Smallest airport in the New York metropolitan area.
- Travel directions:
  - New York Airport Service Express Bus from Grand Central, Port Authority (Air Trans Center), or Penn Station for $10.
  - Express Shuttle USA for $13 (call 212-315-3006 or 800-451-0455 for schedule).
  - Super Shuttle from $15-19 (800-BLUE-VAN).
  - M60 bus from between 106th St & Broadway for $2.
  - Cab for metered rates plus tolls.

Newark Airport (EWR)
- Located in Newark, New Jersey.
- Services international and domestic flights.
- Harder to get to but has cheaper fares.
- Travel directions:
  - Express bus from Port Authority or Grand Central for $15.
  - Amtrak or NJ Transit from Penn Station.

UNCONVENTIONAL

There are many alternatives to normal methods of transportation and, with increasing citywide fare hikes and congestion, plenty of reasons to try them. Here are some off-the-beaten-track ways to get around on the beaten path.

Staten Island Ferry
Enjoy a picturesque panorama of the downtown skyline on board this free 30-minute ride across the harbor.
siferry.com. ❶ *to South Ferry.*

New York Water Taxi
Travel on the East or Hudson River for $5-10. On weekends from May to October, sightsee from the water with an all-day Hop-on/Hop-off pass for $20. The Ikea store also offers free rides from Manhattan to their branch in Brooklyn.
nywatertaxi.com.

Bicycle
Race, tour, and commute! Urban bike culture is strong in New York City, so join the movement for green, cheap, and fit adventures.
New York Bicycle Coalition, nybc.net. Bike maps, nycbikemaps.com.

Rickshaw in Times Square
If you're going to do touristy travel, hop on a Times Square rickshaw. Bike-drawn mini-carriages were made to weave through traffic.

The Roosevelt Island Tramway
The aerial tram car from Roosevelt Island descends into Manhattan by way of Queensboro Bridge over the East River, yielding inimitable views of midtown Manhattan. Tickets are $2 and rides are 10 minutes.

Zip Car
Provides day-long car rentals for those over 21.
zipcar.com.

SETTLING IN

Finding the right apartment in New York can take anywhere from one day to three-hundred and sixty-five. Despite plummeting rent prices and increasing vacancy rates in 2009, the real estate market is still notoriously competitive. Be prepared to research, compromise, and pay heftily for a small space. With patience and determination, however, you'll eventually find your own room with a view.

FINDING AN APARTMENT

Identifying Priorities

Set some guidelines before embarking on your search—outline your price range, travel distance expectations, and amenity needs. Then, with this in mind, research some key neighborhoods. Do you want to live close to Central Park, a university campus, or the downtown nightlife scene? Are you willing to move to an outer borough to avoid Manhattan's astronomical costs? If you have kids or pets, search accordingly. A rent-stabilized apartment is always preferable, but often difficult to find.

Timing

Apartments are snatched up as quickly as they become available in New York. Be prepared to act fast before someone else snags your perfect nest, but always make informed decisions. Rents take a slight dip in May and shoot up in mid-to-late summer. Search early and often.

Renting

The available apartments in New York are small in number, but vast in variety—there's everything from tiny, aged singles to deluxe condos. Universities, non-profit organizations, real estate brokers, local publications, and websites all provide listings. Some of the most popular online resources include **FlyRig.com**, **mlx.com**, **CityRealty.com**, **RDNY.com**, **bestaptsnyc.com** and **manhattanapts.com**, while **Craigslist.com**'s extensive and continuously updated openings are great for determined bargain hunters. But browsers beware: fact check and look for scams, hidden fees, neighborhood and size exaggerations ("East Williamsburg" might be Bushwick, "one-bedroom" might be a corner), because even brokers can fabricate a place that doesn't exist by piecing together photos of different apartments, just to get you in the office.

Look for rent-stabilized, no-fee apartments and, if the building is old, renovated kitchens and bathrooms—fixtures can get archaic, especially in pre-war and tenement buildings. Rent-stabilized leases provide tenant rights, landlord service, repairs, protection against unlawful rent increase and eviction, and an option to renew. Don't forget to factor in utilities and the rental company's charges for building repairs, as they can greatly add to the bill.

It's advisable to live near subway stops if you plan to travel to work, especially if you're compromising on neighborhood safety. If concerned, check out the local crime statistics at **nyc.gov**. Be sure to also check out **housingnyc.com** for crucial information and excellent tips.

MOVING SERVICES

While you alone may have picked out your new apartment, packed up all your stuff, and mentally prepared for the move to New York, actually transferring everything from one place to another is not something you can do by yourself—unless you have a big truck and a bevy of pals willing to help. Luckily, there are dozens of moving services in the city, many of which are extremely convenient and won't cost more than your rent. Here are three of the best:

- Rob the Mover (*347-645-3927*)
- Rabbit Movers (*718-852-2352*)
- Man With a Van (*1-888-482-1083*)

Buying

As New York is one of the world's wealthiest cities, it's not surprising that apartment prices are fairly lofty. The average one-bedroom Manhattan condo is between $759 and $950k; high-end condos cost up to $10 million or more. Fortunately, new condominium buildings are popping up all over Manhattan and recently gentrified outer boroughs. These spacious residences are slightly more affordable now, as prices dropped sharply in 2009.

Visiting the Apartment

After calling and setting up a viewing appointment, read up and take safety precautions—know where you're going, how to get there, who you'll be meeting, and bring a friend when you go. Arrive early to take some notes on the neighborhood, nearby supermarkets, laundromats, drug stores, parks, and to get a feel for the area. Check out the building's security, condition, and cleanliness. Ask questions, take a detailed survey of your possible new home, and try to make an impression as a good tenant to increase your chances of becoming one.

Brokers

Brokers have extensive information on apartments for rent not available to the public because they often work with rental companies. They have the resources and agency support to help you with paperwork, personally take you to see homes, and dramatically expand your search options. But big convenience comes at a big price—brokers can charge fees of anything from a month's rent to 12-15% of yearly rent. Find out their fee policies in advance and always ask—many also offer negotiable or no-fee apartments as well. Some apartments are listed with one month free and brokers eager to make the sale may take that in lieu of the sleeper fee.

Drawing up a Lease

As a rule, apartments in New York require a one-year lease contract, sometimes two. Make sure it's legitimate and again, try to obtain a rent-stabilized agreement. Brokers provide extra securities, but in any case, make sure all fees are disclosed and all rental regulations are followed. A signed lease is a legally-binding agreement and requires a security deposit, with sometimes the first and last month's fees up front. They're renewed annually, usually a month before the year is up.

SETTLING IN

AMENITIES

While the city offers an infinite number of exciting events and attractions to explore, sometimes all you feel like doing is watching TV, surfing the web, or chatting on the phone with a friend at home. Luckily, there are dozens of reliable service providers in the city who can help with this—all you have to do is call, and they'll come right to your door and install whatever you need. Though wireless internet, a landline, and cable TV in your apartment can be a costly convenience, many providers offer package deals and special rates (you may find it convenient to get all three amenities from the same company), so make sure to compare prices before purchasing.

Wireless Internet

Almost as important to most New Yorkers than furniture, air conditioning, and probably even food is wireless internet access. Unless you plan on spending most of your time in internet cafés or venturing to free WiFi outdoor areas like Lincoln Square, university campuses or public libraries, installing wireless at your home is a surprisingly convenient necessity. These service providers offer fast internet at good prices depending on your needs, so note that the more expensive plans are likely to include more features:

- **Comcast** (*1-866-937-1750*). $19.99/month.
- **Optimum Online** (*1-866-747-3455*). $29.95/month.
- **Time Warner** (*1-866-924-7257*). $34.95/month.

Phone Services

While nearly everyone has a cell phone these days, not all service providers are equal. Here are those that have the most locations and best service throughout the city, as well as helpful customer assistance. If you're looking to install a landline, these providers can also set you up with a plan that suits your needs:

- **AT&T** (*1-888-333-6651*). From $39.99/month.
- **Verizon** (*800-256-4646*). From $39.99/month.

Roommates and Sublets

Subletting or rooming with others can make finding and paying for your New York City homestead much easier. There are official laws on roommates (check **housingnyc.com**) and roommate resources available online (**nyc.metroroommates.com, newyork.backpage.com**). Make sure to research your possible living companion's background and note that, even if you're staying with friends, you need a formal agreement.

If you're not ready to sign a lease and go Ikea shopping quite yet, look for a sublet in the city. Many permanent New York residents seasonally migrate out of the city or move out but can't break their lease, and so they sublet their apartments, often fully furnished, for weeks or months at a time (listings can be found at **newyorkcity.sublet.com** and **subletinthecity.com**). Subletting requires landlord approval and is a big responsibility. Don't be overwhelmed—by approaching your options and alternatives wisely, you can come out on top.

Cable TV

If you'd rather watch television shows live on a regular screen instead of on Hulu or Youtube, cable TV is the way to go. Prices vary depending on how many channels and add-ons, like HBO and Showtime, you want, so identify your must-see programs before picking a plan:

- **DirecTV** (*1-877-265-9218*). $29.99/month.
- **Optimum** (*1-866-747-3455*). $29.95/month.
- **Time Warner** (*1-866-924-7257*). $49.95/month.

HOME FURNISHINGS

Once you've found your four walls and a roof, you'll need furniture to turn it into a home. While you could scour the streets for your neighbors' junk or take hand-me-downs from your parents and friends, these stores offer stylish, comfortable furnishings at low prices—no more snoozing on the floor!

Furniture

- **Angel Street Thrift Shop** (*118 W 17th St; 212-229-0546*)
- **CB2** (*451 Broadway; 212-219-1454*)
- **Golden Calf** (*319 Wythe Ave, Brooklyn; 718-302-8800*)
- **Ikea** (*1 Beard St, Brooklyn; 718-246-4532*)
- **Salvation Army** (*546 W 46th St; 212-757-2311*)

Kitchen Equipment

- **Bowery Kitchen Supply Equipment** (*460 W 16th St; 212-219-1457*)
- **Broadway Panhandler** (*65 E 8th St; 212-966-3434*)
- **The Brooklyn Kitchen** (*616 Lorimer St; 718-389-2982*)
- **Fishs Eddy** (*889 Broadway at 19th St; 212-420-9020*)
- **Korin** (*57 Warren St; 212-587-7021*)

Light Appliances

- **Green Depot** (*222 Bowery; 212-226-0444*)
- **Lee's Studio** (*220 W 50th St; 212-581-4400*)
- **Lighting and Beyond** (*35 W 14th St; 212-929-2738*)
- **Spectrum Lighting** (*135 Bowery; 212-343-3343*)
- **Surprise! Surprise!** (*91 3rd Ave; 212-777-0990*)

CITY COMMERCE

Citigroup, J.P. Morgan Chase and Company, Verizon, Goldman Sachs, Merrill Lynch, Lehman Brothers… these are only six of the 500 richest U.S. corporations with headquarters in New York City. The towering Manhattan skyline and blindingly massive ads in Times Square are testaments to the sheer magnitude of businesses. With a gross metropolitan product of almost $490 billion, New York well deserves its reputation for being the nation's economic engine. As Joel Grey sang, "Money makes the world go round"—especially in New York.

BANKING

New York is one of the financial capitals of the world, so it's no surprise that over two hundred banks and thousands of ATMs call the city home. Most major banks provide special student packages; do some research to find which benefits best fit your spending style. If you primarily depend on checking or savings accounts, take a look at hidden costs (like the minimum amount you need to keep in your account) to avoid penalties. And be sure to compare interest rates before signing up if plan on using credit.

It's also important to make note of what's in your area—don't pick a bank that's far from your job or apartment, or one that's closed whenever you're free. Also, keep in mind that most banks charge fees for using competitors' ATMs. While a branch of your bank might not be available in

every corner of the city, there's bound to be at least one ATM nearby. And you can always hunt one down in convenience stores, pharmacies, restaurants, and bars. But if you can't find one for your bank, withdraw money from another major company and not from an unaffiliated machine in a seedy area—instances of identity theft are not unheard of.

OPERATING HOURS

New York may be famous for its 24/7 lifestyle, but not everything is open around the clock. The exact hours of each business, however, depend on its location (the following schedules are only approximations):

- **ATMS, transportation:** 24 hours a day, all week.
- **Banks:** 9am-3:30pm during the week. Some stay open later on Fridays; many have Saturday service from 9am-noon.
- **Bars:** Open anywhere from 2-5pm for happy hour and close by 4am.
- **Clubs:** Open between 8 and 10pm and close anytime from 4 to 7am.
- **Museums:** Open between 9 and 11am and close by 5:30pm. Most are closed at least one day per week (usually Monday or Tuesday), and some stay open later on Fridays or Saturdays.
- **Offices:** 9am-6pm, but many have extended hours.
- **Parks:** Usually closed after dusk, although some stay open until midnight.
- **Pharmacies, drugstores:** Some are 24 hours a day, others hold regular business hours.
- **Post offices:** 8am-5pm during the week. Some are open on Saturday until 1pm.
- **Public libraries:** Most 10am-6pm during the week. Restricted hours on weekends.

- **Restaurants:** Expensive ones tend to close for an hour or two between lunch dinner. Most others serve continuously throughout the day, and many diners are open 24 hours.
- **Service-oriented stores** (dry cleaners, salons): Open as early as 7am and often close on or before 9pm.
- **Shops and department stores:** Many are 10am-8pm, though shops in busier areas like Time Square are often open later.

TIPPING

Like everywhere else, paying gratuity in New York is rarely gratuitous, unless your service was absolutely abominable. Here are the workers you should always tip:

- **Bartenders:** $1-2 per drink, or 15-20% of total bill on a tab.
- **Concierges:** $1-2 for hailing a cab; aroud $5 if they help carry luggage.
- **Deliverymen:** 10-15% of the bill; more if the delivery was bigger.
- **Hairdressers/barbers:** 15-20% of base cost.
- **Porters, bellmen, skycaps:** $1-2 per bag; more if the luggage was heavy or fragile.
- **Sommeliers:** 15-20% of wine bill.
- **Taxi drivers:** 10-15% of the fare, but rarely less than $1.
- **Waiters/waitresses:** 15-20% of pretax bill.

TAXES

New York City imposes a sales tax of 4%, the State sales and use tax is 4%, and there is a surcharge of 0.375% that goes to the Metropolitan Transportation Authority, amounting to a total sales and use tax of **8.375%**.

Most **tangible personal property**, such as furniture, cars and electronics, falls under this tax. Many automobile and home services are also taxed (garage parking, gas, electricity, refrigeration, telephone, steam), as well as hotel and motel rooms.

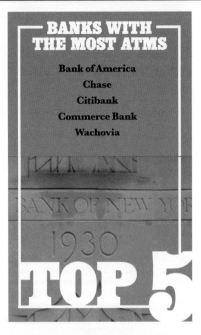

BANKS WITH THE MOST ATMS

Bank of America

Chase

Citibank

Commerce Bank

Wachovia

TOP 5

There are a number of **services uniquely taxed** in New York City, including credit reporting, barbering, cosmetology, tanning, manicures and pedicures, massages, weight control or health salons, and gyms.

Services **exempt from taxes** include visits to a doctor or veterinarian, laundering, dry cleaning and shoe repair. Clothing and footwear under $100 are also exempt, although this does not apply to jewelry, handbags, watches, umbrellas, and other accessories.

With regard to **food and drink**, taxing depends on the location—at a restaurant it's necessary, but at a grocery store it's not. Generally, items considered luxuries (alcohol, tobacco, candy, soda, cosmetics) are taxed, whereas other beverages, drugs, medicine, prosthetic devices, eyeglasses and periodicals are not.

GOVERNMENT & SAFETY

Grime. Corruption. Law and Order. What comes to mind when you think about politics and safety in New York City? With the exception of the latter's film sites, rarely are the above are present in daily city government. Yet City Hall's bureaucracy can be confusing, even to New York natives. Here's a crash course in how to tell the difference between comptroller and borough president, along with some tips on staying safe. And hey, if you're ever bewildered, there's a squadron of armed professionals waiting to help.

CITY OFFICIALS

The metropolis that brought us Alphabet City avoids simplicity like the plague, and, true to form, makes no exception for its government. Over 8.3 million residents are first divided into five boroughs: the **Bronx**, **Queens**, **Manhattan**, **Brooklyn**, and **Staten Island**.

These boroughs are further organized into 51 districts, each of which sends one representative to the legislative **City Council**. Local matters within each district, such as exceptions to zoning restrictions and problems with city services, are handled by public **community board** meetings. Members of the 59 community boards are appointed by the **borough president**, with mandated input from the relevant city councilors.

DID YOU KNOW?

The City of Brooklyn, as it was then called, elected its own mayor between 1834 and 1898.

Regardless of unit placement, all New Yorkers have a say in the selection of their own borough president (BP), and in who holds the handful of other top offices listed below (as of print):
* **Mayor** - Michael Bloomberg
* **Comptroller** - William C. Thompson
* **Public Advocate** - Betsy Gotbaum
* **City Council Speaker**-Christine C. Quinn
* **Bronx BP** - Aldolpho Carrión, Jr.
* **Brooklyn BP** - Marty Markowitz
* **Manhattan BP** - Scott M. Stringer
* **Queens BP** - Helen M. Marshall
* **Staten Island BP** - James P. Molinaro

BUREAUCRACY

Operating under city leaders is an intricate web of offices that comprise New York's bureaucracy. With departments and commissions dealing with everything from cultural celebrations to domestic violence prevention, it influences almost every aspect of New York life. Here are a few of the major channels through which your tax dollars are put to work:
* The **Board of Elections** oversees voter registration, city council elections, and the selection of the mayor.
* The **City University of New York**'s many branches include City College and Hunter College. It's the largest urban university in the world.
* The **Department of Correction** is responsible for the city's inmates. Most are on Riker's Island and Roosevelt Island.
* The **Department of Health and Mental Hygiene** provides free clinics, distributes condoms, and issues regulatory documents like birth certificates.
* The **Department of Sanitation** hauls your trash and handles recycling.
* The **Department of Transportation** manages the city's highway system and renames streets.
* The **Metropolitan Transit Authority**, while technically a public benefit corporation rather than a government branch, runs the subways, buses, some trains, and Staten Island Ferry.
* **NYC TV** broadcasts information and videos of local happenings.
* The **Office of the Mayor** has final say on just about everything city-related.
* The **Taxi and Limousine Commission** regulates how official cabs function and charge their customers.

SAFETY

If you visit New York with someone who lived here in the 80s or early 90s, you'll hear bewildered exclamations of "But it's so *clean*!" and "...Someone just asked if I needed *help*?" While the city may not always seem particularly clean or helpful to you, its transformation is real: in 2007, New York suffered slightly over a third of the overall violent crimes that had affected its 1980 population. Murder, rape, aggravated assault, and most categories of property crime have all seen similar plunges.

The wave of violence and urban decay that swept through New York in the 70s and 80s was unprecedented. Wealthy people left in droves, and underprivileged neighborhoods stagnated in miserable cycles of poverty and crime. After 1991, the city began using a management tool called Comp-Stat, which required increased intra-department communication and systematic analysis of past crime trends. In addition to Comp-Stat, many tie the recent safety success to the surge in the number of police officers on the streets. But even though New York City is a safer and less gritty home than it used to be, certain precautions are still necessary to keep yourself from harm.

The best safety advice here, as with anywhere else, can be boiled down to a tip you'll hear frequently from passing drivers: "Watch where you're going!" Know your route before you leave home. Carry your phone and a small subway map. If you're a student, look into whether your college is among the many (including NYU and Columbia) that offer some form of safety escort at night; if so, enter the service's number into your cell.

The second best tip is to look like a badass. Walk confidently rather than pausing nervously to peer at street signs and you'll appear far less vulnerable. You can also reduce your appeal as a potential target by keeping cash, jewelry, and other valuables hidden while in public. If you are heckled, do not stop or respond. Trust your gut—if you fear you're being followed, enter a store and, if necessary, ask for help.

Although risk is present everywhere—including, as you can point out to your worrying mother, your hometown—certain areas of the city obviously require greater caution than others. For starters, do not stroll through any park after dark. When riding the subway late in the evening, choose a car with plenty of passengers. On a bus, sit near the driver. If you can afford

it, take a taxi. Public buildings, including Port Authority Bus Terminal and Grand Central Terminal, are also best avoided at night—if you need to catch a 2am bus or train, consider bringing a few friends to see you off.

Average safety also vary by district, although guidelines here are more fluid. The area surrounding 120th St and St. Nicholas Ave appeared on a recent list released by the FBI of the nation's most dangerous neighborhoods. Your best bet is to chat with a savvy friend before traveling somewhere new, to make your first visit in the light of day, and use common sense.

PANHANDLING

New York is a city of extremes. There may be dazzling wealth, there's also widespread homelessness. While the vagrant population has fallen slightly over the last several years, many experts worry that the economic recession will spark a reversal.

Not all homeless men and women will ask for or accept money, but for many, panhandling is a primary source of income. If you choose to give,

carry small denominations of cash in an easily accessible pocket.

Some New Yorkers, concerned that monetary gifts could reinforce the drug addictions that often lead to homelessness, instead offer extra food. Others donate to one of many relevant organizations, such as **Picture the Homeless**, the **Coalition for the Homeless**, and **City Harvest**.

DID YOU KNOW?

A 2007 proposal by a city councilman called for an official "pigeon czar" to consolidate government efforts to reduce the birds' numbers and droppings.

Regardless of your financial ability, consider finding a way to help the many New Yorkers who need it. Websites like **volunteermatch. org** will match you to an organization that fits your interests and schedule. It can have a huge impact on the quality of others' lives—and it'll make the city feel more like home.

COUNSELING

It's important to stay mentally healthy in a city known for grinding residents down. Any Woody Allen movie proves that neurosis is as New York as jaywalking. If you're looking for therapy at a less-than-absurd price, here are some options:

- The **New York State Office of Mental Health** (*330 5th Ave, 9th Floor; 1-800-597-8481*) can help you navigate the public health system or find a private provider.
- The **Washington Square Institute** (*41-51 E 11th St; 212-477-2600*) offers a wide variety of services at sliding-scale prices, and matches you with a provider based on a careful compatibility screening.
- At the **National Institute for the Psychotherapies Training Institute** (*250 W 57th St; 212-582-1566*), you can get inexpensive quality care from therapists-in-training.
- **New York-Presbyterian Hospital**'s psychiatry department (*622 W 168th St; 212-305-6001*) has many of the city's highest-ranked doctors and treats everything from schizophrenia to sleep disorders.
- The several branches of **Alcoholics Anonymous** (*307 7th Ave; 212-647-1680*) can help if you're worried that you or a friend's drinking is becoming a problem.
- The **Mood Disorders Support Group** (*P.O. Box 30377, ZC: 1011; 212-533-MDSG*) is a self-help organization for sufferers of depression and their loved ones.
- The **Renfrew Center of New York** (*11 E 36th St; 1-800-RENFREW*) is part of a large network of treatment centers specializing in every level of eating disorder care.
- If you're a student or university affiliate, most **college health centers** offer both short-term counseling and specialized referrals. They can also steer you through the intricacies of finding a provider who takes your insurance.
- If you or someone you know is considering suicide or self-harm, trained members of the **Samaritans of New York** are ready to talk to you 24/7 on their hotline (*212-673-3000*). Please call.

EMERGENCY NUMBERS

911
Emergency Services

311
Government Information and Services

Police Switchboard
646-610-5000

Police Tip Line
800-577-8477

Crime Victims Hotline
212-577-7777

Rape Hotline
212-267-7273

Domestic Violence Report Line
800-621-4673

Crisis Intervention
800-543-3638

Poison Control
212-340-4494

Arson Hotline
718-722-3600

DINING & FOOD

New York's a great place to be if you're hungry—you'll find cuisine from every country around the globe in its illimitable grocery shops, restaurants, cafés, bakeries, and street vendors. From biscuits and gravy to pickled okra, oxtail bruschetta to lentil soup, its cornucopia of eating options is diverse enough to satisfy (and titillate!) every taste bud, budget, and style. It's no wonder that the city's often called the food capital of the America.

EATING OUT

DOING YOUR HOMEWORK

Picking a restaurant in New York City can be an exhausting task, especially since any given block can hold a number of mouth-watering venues! To make this quest easier, conduct some research beforehand so that you know where to go, when to go, and what to expect. Some online resources that provide useful listings and reviews include:

- **Chow.com**
- **Eater.com**
- **Grub Street** (*New York Magazine*'s food blog)
- **Yelp.com**

You can also consult some more acclaimed news outlets and their Wednesday Dining sections:

- *Time Out New York*
- *New York Magazine*
- *The New York Times*

FINDING A DEAL

Prix Fixes. If you want to experience some of the city's finest restaurants without completely blowing your budget, consider trying a prix fixe meal—an appetizer, main dish, and dessert served for a set price (soup and salad usually included). Although your options will be very limited, this is much cheaper (not to mention easier) than ordering each course individually.

Lunch Instead of Dinner. This is another great way to enjoy the city's most expensive cuisine without putting a dent in your wallet. The food is just as good, and the lines are almost always shorter.

Restaurant Week. Twice a year, in January and June/July, over 250 of the city's finest restaurants offer three-course meals at amazing fixed prices—$24 for lunch and $35 for dinner. Visit nycgo.com/RestaurantWeek for a list of

participating venues and dates. Note, however, that for some places it could be a scam, as you won't be paying much less than the normal price.

RESERVATIONS

New Yorkers tend to dine out frequently, both on weekdays and weekends. To accommodate the crowds, nearly all of the city's restaurants accept reservations up to 30 days in advance—in fact, the more popular, mid-to-upscale ones often require them, particularly during prime dinner hours. Places that normally don't allow reservations might take them for large groups.

You can either book your table via phone or **opentable.com**. This website connects to the computerized reservation system of an extensive network of New York restaurants, including some of the busiest and most popular to date.

Make sure you show up on time. If you're going to be late, call the restaurant—there's usually a maximum 15-minute grace period before the table will be released to another customer.

DRESS

Don't unpack your penguin suit quite yet. New York dress code, even in upscale restaurants, has relaxed considerably in recent years. You can generally get away with anything from casual to super fancy, unless regulations are specified on the restaurant's website. When making a reservation you can ask about dress code.

Note, however, that the definition of "casual" is stricter in New York than it is in other places—unless you're visiting your favorite dive or diner, leave your beach bum t-shirt and Rainbow sandals at home. For the most part, men can't go wrong with a nice pair of jeans paired with a jacket and tie, although a button-down shirt has become pretty standard. The same goes for women, though there's more leeway—just be sure to avoid any ripped jeans and overly exposing tanks. In general, it's safer (and more fun) to dress up a bit.

PAYING

Because a significant portion of a waiter's

STREET VENDORS

53rd and 6th Halal Cart
Aka "Chicken & Rice," the "Gyro Spot," or the "Platter"

Antojitos Mexicanos
Roosevelt Ave near 61st St, Woodside

The Endless Summer Taco Truck
North 7th St and Bedford

Huan Ji Rice Noodles
Grand St and Bowery

The Jamaican Dutchy
51st St between 6th and 7th Ave

NY Dosas
Washington Square Park, 4th St. and Sullivan St

Van Leeuwen Artisan Ice Cream Truck
Various locations in Soho. Vanleeuwenicecream.com

Wafels & Dinges Belgian Waffle Truck
Various locations from Financial District to Upper East Side, www.wafelsanddinges.com

TOP 8

DINING & FOOD

TOP 7

salary comes from tips, a **15-20% gratuity** (before tax) is not merely recommended, but necessary—unless, that is, the service was downright awful. On the other hand, if your waiter was exceptionally friendly and helpful, it doesn't hurt to be a little more generous. If you don't want to bother doing the math, calculate an adequate tip (18%) by doubling the sales tax.

Parties larger than five or six will often automatically be charged an 18% gratuity, so no need to tip again if it's already included. Lastly, make sure you know whether or not the restaurant accepts credit or debit before you get the check—some are cash-only, and you don't want to duck out of Peter Luger to track down ATM.

GROCERIES

GREENMARKETS
The best produce in New York comes straight from local farmers. Professional cooks and harried mothers alike congregate at the city's greenmarkets, where stands specializing in everything from bread to fish to vegetables share one characteristic in common: freshness. Go early, as chefs tend to scoop up the best selection in the morning for that night's menu.

The **Union Square Greenmarket** is by far the city's largest (and most famous) open-air market, with hundreds of vendors selling over 1,000 varieties of produce year round. *E 17th St and Broadway.* ❹❺❻❻❶❺❻❻❻ *to 14th St-Union Square. Mon, Wed, Fri, Sat 8am-6pm.*

The less crowded **57th St Greenmarket** is a smaller neighborhood fixture that doesn't have meat or seafood but does offer a plentiful spread of seasonal vegetables. *9th Ave and W 57th St* ❶❹❻❸❻ *to 59th St-Columbus Circle. Wed & Sat 8am-6pm.*

At **Borough Hall Greenmarket**, you'll find an extensive array of flowers, vegetables, cheeses and baked goods. There's even a seafood vendor on Saturdays. *Court St at Montague St, Brooklyn.* ❿❻ *to Court*

St, 4 to Borough Hall. Tue, Sat 8am-4pm year round. Thurs 8am-6pm April-December.

Grand Army Plaza Greenmarket is the Union Square Greenmarket of the outer boroughs. It almost rivals the latter in size and shares some of its vendors.
Prospect Park West and Flatbush Ave ❷❸ to Grand Army Plaza. Sat 8am-4pm.

SUPERMARKETS
Food shopping can't be done at greenmarkets alone. Luckily enough, there are grocery stores to be found on almost every corner of the city, from intimate neighborhood bodegas to brightly lit chains. While the aisles will be smaller than anything suburbanites are used to (use a basket instead of a cart), the selection can't be beat.

Fairway is the king of grocery stores—prices are cheap, and the 132nd St location features a cold room that is an experience unto itself. Grab a jacket and check out the selection of meats, most of which are Kosher.
74th St and Broadway. ❶❷❸ to 72nd St, & 12th Ave at 132nd St (under West Side Highway). ❶ to 125th St.

The ubiquitous, upscale **Whole Foods** is worthwhile for take-out, which includes delectable Indian food, but you may have to wait it out for a free seat among the yuppies and tourists in the café section.
Time Warner Center (at Columbus Circle). ❶❶Ⓐ❶Ⓑ Ⓓto 59th St-Columbus Circle, & 4 Union Square South. ❹❺❻ⒷⓃⓆⓇⓌ to 14th St-Union Square, & 95 E Houston St. FV to 2nd Ave.

Trader Joe's is similar to Whole Foods, but smaller and usually a lot less expensive. Its "Two Buck Chuck" wine is actually three bucks, but who's counting?
142 E 14th St (at Irving Place). ❹❺❻ⒷⓃⓆⓇⓌ to 14th St-Union Square.

Nestled between unlikely neighbors—a restaurant supply store and a sample sale location—the **Manhattan Fruit**

Exchange is a fruit and vegetable haven. Make it past the bakery windows that line Chelsea Market to find an extensive array of conventional and exotic produce.
75 9th Ave (between 15th and 16th St). ❶Ⓐ❸ to 14th St.

Zabar's is a New York institution, and rightfully so. The selection of olives alone is worth marveling over, but head upstairs to discover an army of useful cooking gadgets. It's also a solid destination for Kosher products.
2245 Broadway (at 80th St). ❶ to 79th St.

STUDENT DISCOUNTS

Being a student in New York comes with its perks, and endless, cheap entertainment is one of them. While ticket prices tend to be way outside the typical collegiate budget, hundreds of venues and organizations compensate by offering special discounts. Take advantage of these deals to enjoy New York's performing arts, cinemas, sports and even food at scrimp-worthy prices.

THEATER

The new TKTS "Stairway to Nowhere" structure in Times Square (literally a flight of clear stairs in the middle of the sidewalk) symbolizes the ascent—or comeback, if you will—of New York's theater scene. Take advantage of the following money-savers to see some of the city's most popular plays and musicals.

Subscriptions
Playwrights Horizons *(416 W 42nd St; 212-564-1235)* offers 4-6 show packages for under-35-year-olds at $10 a show, the **Manhattan Theater Company** *(261 W 47th St; 212-239-6200)* has student packages for $30 a show, and **Lincoln Center Theater** *(150 W 65th St; 212-239-6200)* sells $20 student tickets.

Many subscribers choose the **Public Theater** *(425 Lafayette St; 212-260-2400)* or, for Broadway shows, the **Roundabout Theatre** *(212-719-1300)*, which offers $50-60 show subscriptions.

Discount Sites
TKTS' grandfather website, **TDF.org**, has a $28 annual service with 70% discounts for many off-Broadway and Broadway performances. **audienceextras.com** offers $3.50 tickets to various events (mostly theater) for an $85 yearly fee. **Hiptix.com** shells out $20 Roundabout tickets for students with a free subscription.

Student Rush
For Broadway shows, check **Playbill.com** for an updated list of rush policies. Most rush tickets are sold when the box office opens in the morning or a few hours before the show begins, while standing room tickets are usually available two hours before. **Lincoln Center Theater** and Brooklyn's trippy **St. Ann's Warehouse** *(38 Water St; 718-254-8779)* typically have $20 rush tickets up to two hours before the performance. St. Anne's is looking to relocate sometime in the coming year.

Free and Cheap
When the weather is warm, the city's outdoor arenas become stages for a variety of free productions. For tickets to The Public Theater's famous **Shakespeare in the Park**, get up early and stand in line outside Cantral Park's Delacorte Theater *(near West Dr & 81st St)* or sign up for the virtual line lottery at vline.publictheater.org. **The Gorilla Rep** *(363 Tompkins Ave; 212-252-5258)* offers quirky interpretations of classic plays in a variety of parks. Check **CUArts.com** for an exhaustive list of free & student-discounted events.

Many New York repertories and studios provide cheap tickets year round, such as **Soho Rep** *(46 Walker St; 212-941-8632)*, which has 99-cent

Sunday deals. Check **indietheater.org** for further inexpensive alternatives.

MUSIC

Lincoln Center may have undergone a recent quarter-billion-dollar renovation, but it isn't the only source for top-notch performances.

Discount Tickets
If you like classical music, sign up for **Carnegie Hall**'s (*881 7th Ave; 212-247-7800*) mailing list to nab its $10-15 per show student subscription. The **New York Philharmonic** (*10 Lincoln Center Plaza; 212-875-5900*) has $12 tickets up to 10 days in advance on its website, or on the day of the show at the Avery Fisher box office. **Barge Music** (*Fulton Ferry Landing; 718-624-2083*) offers $20 concerts with a beautiful view.

For jazz, **Jazz at Lincoln Center** (*Time Warner Center; 212-258-9800*), home to the Marsalis family and other knock-outs, sells $10 tix at the box office one hour before a performance. Of the smaller venues, the alternative **The Stone** (*Avenue C and 2nd St*) sells $5 teen tickets ($10 for those over 19), without any pesky beverage minimums.

Festivals
Summer in the city means free music galore. The **New York Philharmonic** (*10 Lincoln*

Center Plaza; 212-875-5656) does a dozen or so outdoor concerts from July to August, in parks in all five boroughs. The **River to River Festival** (*rivertorivernyc.com*) hosts a variety of shows in places ranging from Riverside Park to South Street Seaport.

Central Park's **Summer Stage** (*830 5th Ave; 212-360-2756*) presents a program of world music, local artists, and a few big names in benefit concerts that fund the rest—line up early on Fifth Avenue as tickets aren't usually required. The same goes for Prospect Park Bandshell's **Celebrate Brooklyn** (*647 Fulton St; 718-855-7882*), which has captured the borough's spirit with independent music and dance since 1979. The one-day **Siren Music Festival** (*siren.villagevoice.com/siren*) in Coney Island features hot alternative bands.

While space at these venues is technically limited, feel free to bring a blanket and set up camp on the lawn (if there is one) or outside the designated auditorium—you'll still be able to hear (and often see) the performers!

Cheap Venues
The edgy **Arlene's Grocery** (*95 Stanton St; 212-995-1652*) has a mere $8 cover and free Monday night performances. **Le Poisson Rouge** (*158 Bleeker St; 212-505-FISH*) hosts eclectic shows with tickets ranging from free to $20.

STUDENT DISCOUNTS

Some venues, like **Rockwood Music Hall** (*196 Allen St; 212-477-4155*), offer free performances with a one-drink minimum. And most city schools have their own coffeehouses, like Columbia University's legendary **Postcrypt** (*St. Paul's Chapel basement; 212-854-1953*).

MUSEUMS

Young women may be paid to sleep all day at the New Museum (once an actual exhibit), but there are plenty of places to visit for left brain candy—even if your income's not supplemented by sleep money. Many offer discounted hours Thursday-Sunday, others are always free, and some ask for negotiable "suggested donations."

Most art galleries are clustered in Chelsea as well as the Lower and Upper East Sides are free, and showcase everything from late Picasso to melted Barbies. Pick up a gallery guide or check *artinfo.com* as exhibitions change frequently.

Free & Pay-What-You-Wish Times
Thursday
- **Arts and Design** (*2 Columbus Circle; 212-299-7777*). PWYW 6-9pm. Students $12.
- **New Museum** (*235 Bowery; 212-219-1222*). Free 7-9pm. Students $10.

Friday
- **Asia Society** (*725 Park Ave; 212-288-6400*). Free 6-9pm, Sept-June. Students $5.
- **Bronx Museum** (*1040 Grand Concourse; 718-681-6000*). Free 11am-8pm. Students $3.
- **Folk Art Museum** (*45 W 53rd St; 212-265-1040*). Free 5:30-7:30pm, Students $7.
- **MoMA** (*11 W 53rd St; 212-708-9400*). Free 4-8pm, Student $12.
- **The Morgan** (*225 Madison Ave; 212-685-0008*). Free 7-9pm. Students $8.
- **NY Historical Society** (*170 Central Park West; 212-873-3400*). PWYW 6-8pm. Students $6.
- **The Whitney** (*945 Madison Ave; 212-570-3600*). PWYW 6-9pm. Students $10.

Saturday
- **Guggenheim** (*1071 5th Ave; 212-423-3500*).

Free 5:15-7:15pm. Students $15.
- **The Jewish Museum** (*1109 5th Ave; 212-423-3200*). Free 11am-5:45pm. Students $7.50.

Sunday
- **Frick Collecton** (*1 E 70th St; 212-288-0700*). PWYW 11am-1pm. Students $5.

Free Museums and Galleries
- **FIT Museum** (*7th Ave at 27nd St; 212-217-4558*). Fashion yesterday and today. Free is the new black.
- **Gagosian Gallery** (*980 Madison Ave; 212-744-2313*). Big names, beautifully curated.
- **National Museum of the American Indian** (*1 Bowling Green; 212-514-3700*). The price of colonialism.
- **Pace Wildenstein** (*32 East 57th St, 534 West 25th St, 545 W 22nd St; 212-421-3292, 212-929-7000, 212-989-4258*). Epic 20th-century art.

DID YOU KNOW?

A ticket to the Metropolitan Museum of Art also grants free admission to the Cloisters.

SUGGESTED DONATION
- **American Museum of Natural History** (*Central Park West and 79th St; 212-769-5100*) Students $11. Bones and stones.
- **Metropolitan Museum of Art** (*1000 5th Ave; 212-535-7710*). Students $10. The legend.
- **Museum of the City of New York** (*1220 5th Ave; 212-534-1672*). Students $6. The big apple, all sliced.

FILM

A new movie theater in Williamsburg just switched on its crazy LED light display, beckoning us away from YouTube. In the summer, outdoor screenings let you enjoy older films in the open

air. Now's the time to go watch famous people kiss each other without paying $13.

Cinema Deals

- **Cobble Hill Theatre** (*265 Court Street, Brooklyn; 718-596-9113*). $9.50 at night, $6.50 before 5pm on weekdays and before 2pm on weekends. Mainstream flicks.
- **Loews Lincoln Center** (*1998 Broadway; 212-336-5020*). $6 before noon, $10 IMAX.
- **Village East Cinema** (*181-189 2nd Ave; 212-529-6799*). $7 on Tuesdays. Unlimited popcorn.

Festivals

- **Brooklyn Bridge Park** in DUMBO hosts free screenings throughout the summer on Thursday nights.
- The **Celebrate Brooklyn Festival** at the Prospect Park Bandshell offers some silent and live-accompanied free films.
- In late August, **Central Park** screens a free movie a night.
- **River Flicks** in Hudson River Park throws you free popcorn and a film on Wednesday nights, from July to August.
- At the **Rooftop Film Festival** from late May to mid-September, you can enjoy innovative alternative flicks on a gorgeous rooftop (various locations) for $9.

SPORTS

There are plenty of ways to see professional players around New York on a budget. Dust off your foam finger.

Basketball

- **New York Knicks** (*33rd St and 7th Ave; 212-465-6073*) $20-25 student tickets online and at the box office. They won't win, but you might still enjoy yourself.
- **Street Basketball** (*corner of 3rd St and 6th Ave, Houston St and 6th Ave*). Free. More exciting game play and characters, and the home team always wins. Over 70 compete.

Baseball

- **Brooklyn Cyclones** (*1904 Surf Ave, Brooklyn; 718-449-8497*). $8-15 tickets in

Keyspan Park. A fun team, and your only chance for $12 box seats.

- **New York Yankees** (*1 E 61st St, South Bronx; 718-293-4300*). See their website for a variety of discounts, though the usual $15-25 nosebleed tickets aren't bad. Wednesday's games have half-priced grandstand tickets for students at the box office.

Hockey

- **New York Rangers** (*33rd St and 7th Ave; 212-465-6741*). $20-25 student tickets online and at the box office.

FOOD

Ditch the dining hall, use this book, and hunt down cheap eats around the city. Many stores around colleges offer student discounts, such as 10% off sandwiches, soup, and salads at NYU's **Space Market** (*1 University Place; 212-677-0044*). Never be afraid to ask if you can flash your ID for savings.

For restaurants, consider purchasing a deal book like **City Shuffle** (*cityshuffle.com*)—for $30, you'll get $10 off at 52 selected venues.

HOSTELS

For young visitors to the city there's no need to spend your savings on an expensive hotel room. Hostels not only offer a much more affordable alternative, but can also help you meet other young travelers. If you know what to expect (and don't expect too much), staying in one can be a surprisingly pleasant experience.

When checking into a hostel, anticipate shared bathrooms and small living quarters—either a private room for you and your friends (which is usually more expensive) or in a larger dormitory-style room with other guests. If your biggest concern is cleanliness and safety, opt for smaller hostels that give guests more personal attention. The upsides to larger hostels are extra amenities, like rec rooms and laundry facilities, that make for a convenient and fun stay. Before making your reservation, check the hostel's website to see whether or not you should bring your own towels and lock.

Here's a list of the city's best hostels to get you started on your search. Rates are listed per person, per night.

Bowery's Whitehouse Hotel
This bare bones hostel is a good place to stay if you're traveling alone or in a small group, and aren't afraid of a little dirt. For some of the lowest prices in Manhattan, you'll get a bed with clean sheets in an exciting downtown location. Be forewarned that rooms are tiny, with just enough space for your bed and a suitcase, and the walls aren't soundproof—so bring a set of earplugs and plan on spending most of the day in the city. *340 Bowery. 212-477-5623. ❻ to Bleeker St, BDF to Broadway-Lafayette, NR to 8th St. Single rooms $28-30, doubles $54-59, triples $71-82.*

Chelsea Center Hostel–Eastside
This homey hostel is the hip Lower East Side version of its west side sister. In addition to the dorm-style rooms available in the Westside hostel, the Eastside also offers private rooms for small groups. Very clean facilities and décor that scoffs at typically-sparse hostel style make it one of the most attractive options for budget travelers. *83 Essex St. 212-260-0961. ❻❿❶❷ to Delancey St. 6-12 person shared room $35, 2-5 person private room $100.*

Chelsea Center Hostel–Westside
Located in a quiet neighborhood close to both midtown and downtown attractions, this cozy residence is the hostel version of home. Its tiny size makes it easy to get to know the other guests and allows visitors to receive personal attention from the friendly staff. Brightly colored walls and a small garden are added bonuses. Breakfast is included with the price of your room.
313 W 29th St. 212-643-0214. ❶ to 28th St. 6-12 person shared room $35.

Chelsea International Hostel
Situated in a safe and charming neighborhood close to downtown shops, cafés, and art galleries, the Chelsea International is the largest independent hostel in New York City, housing 350 beds. Rooms are basic, but laundry facilities and two separate dining areas and kitchens are convenient for travelers staying for longer periods of time. *251 W 20th St. 212-647-0010. 1 to 18th St, ❸❹ to 23rd St. Dormitory-style room without bathrooms $32, with bathrooms $36, 1-2 person private room $80.*

Gotham Loft 401
This small, easy-to-miss hostel looks gritty on the outside, but is surprisingly clean—and, at only $20 per night, the price can't be beat. Other bonuses are its free breakfast, free WiFi, and proximity to Times Square. Pack lightly, though, because it's on the fourth floor of a building with no elevator. *517 W 45th St. 212-757-3741. ❹❸❹ to 42nd St. 6-person room $20.*

HI New York Hostel
With a gift shop, café, and laundry room, it offers more services than most other hostels. This historical uptown building is close to Central

Park and Columbia University, and a short walk through the park will bring you to Museum Mile. Buy a metro cards right at the front desk and, if you book early with a large group, arrange for a special package of meals and city tours.
891 Amsterdam Ave. 212-932-2300. ❶ *to 103rd St. 10-12 person room $32, 6-8 person room $25, 4-person room $40, 4-person private room with private bathroom $150.*

Jazz on the Park

The first of the five Jazz Hostels now scattered throughout New York City, this hostel remains an excellent and economical choice because of its cleanliness and welcoming staff. Rooms are small, but prices decrease as the number of beds per room increases. A coffee bar and summer barbecues are big draws, but the Union Square location is equally popular for those looking to stay farther downtown. You can find more information about all of the locations on the Jazz Hostels website.
36 W 106th St. 212-932-1600. ⦿ *to 103rd St,* ❶ *to 103rd St. 12-person room $34, 10-person room $37, 8-person room $38, 6-person room $40, 4-person room $40, private room $155-165. jazzhostels.com.*

ZIP112

Nestled in the heart of Williamsburg, ZIP112 is the perfect spot for young travelers looking to live near hip emerging restaurants, stores, and artists. With only two dorm-style, female-only rooms and two private rooms, space is limited, so reserve your room early. Prices are slightly higher than other hostels, but rooms are clean and spacious, and the terrace has a beautiful view of Manhattan.
112 N. 6th St, Brooklyn. 347-403-0577. ❶ *to Bedford Ave. 4-person female shared room $45-$65, 2-person mixed or single sex private room $55-75.*

MEDIA

Everything can change in a New York minute, so keeping up-to-date on the latest news and buzz is crucial. Fortunately (and unsurprisingly), the City is home to one of the largest and most influential media markets in the world. From internationally regarded newspapers to local television stations and event blogs, here's a list of the major news resources that keep New Yorkers informed.

NEWSPAPERS

New York Times *(nytimes.com)*
With "All the News That's Fit to Print," the *Times* is the gold standard for investigative journalism. It features comprehensive daily coverage and a mostly left-leaning editorial page. The Times Media Group recently extended its international pull with the purchase of the *International Herald Tribune*, but the *Times Metro* section still covers everything New York and Tri-State.

Wall Street Journal *(online.wsj.com)*
The business and financial news juggernaut has a prestige that rivals the *Times*, but leans right.

New York Post *(nypost.com)*
Page Six, their storied high-profile gossip section, defines the *Post*. Sure it has plenty of "real" news and a serious sports section, but the *Post* is most notorious for deliciously sensational coverage.

Village Voice *(villagevoice.com)*
A free weekly notable for its local investigative features, extensive reviews, event calendars, sardonic quips, and columns. They also publish some of the best "Best Of" lists for bars, clubs, restaurants, and shops.

New York Observer *(observer.com)*
This salmon (never pink) weekly targets Manhattan's elite. Distributed most widely on the Upper East Side, it publishes a Hamptons issue every summer. *The Observer* is also always the first to report what's going on in real estate, and it has reliable cultural and media coverage.

MAGAZINES

New Yorker *(newyorker.com)*
One of the most prestigious publications for short fiction, poetry and essays, this Condé Nast weekly also features cultural listings in

"Goings On About Town" and short pieces that emphasize city life in "The Talk of the Town." You might not have time to read every article, but a copy on your coffee table makes you seem quite the sophisticate.

New York Magazine *(nymag.com)*
New York Magazine sticks closer to home than the *New Yorker*, trading fiction for articles on maximizing life in all five boroughs—it's your weekly guide to city food, drink, culture, politics, and gossip. And if you want up-to-the-minute reports on all of these check the regularly-updated daily blogs.

Time Out New York *(newyork.timeout.com)*
Yes, there's a *Time Out* magazine for every city you've ever been to, so you know the drill—a weekly chock-full of event listings and reviews for art, books, theater, dance, film, restaurants, shopping, and everything else. Bonus: it speaks to a thriftier audience than *New York Magazine*. Check out their shopping section for a list of the week's sample sales.

El Diario La Prensa *(eldiariony.com)*
The oldest Spanish-language daily in the country, *El Diario* covers both local and world news, with an emphasis on Latin America.

The L Magazine *(thelmagazine.com)*
Akin to *Village Voice*, but smaller and more compact, this free weekly features reviews and information on city events, nightlife, music, culture, and entertainment.

TELEVISION

NY1 (*ny1.com*)
New York's 24-hour cable news station. There are some fairly ridiculous features, like "In the Papers," where a newscaster literally reads headlines from the city's newspapers. They do, however, have some serious outer borough coverage.

Channel 13 (*thirteen.org*)
"All your life is Channel 13," sings Billy Joel. He's talking about New York's PBS affiliate, which covers the usual public television fare. On its website, you'll find city-specific blogs—recent ones include "It's the Economy, New York" and "Green Thirteen."

Manhattan Neighborhood Network (*mnn.org*)
In a city full of up-and-comers, public access channels are understandably packed. MNN, the country's oldest public access network, manages these programs.

RADIO

WNYC (*93.9 FM or 820 AM; wnyc.org*)
National Public Radio's home in New York boasts the largest public radio audience in the country. You'll hear all your favorite nationally syndicated NPR shows, plus WNYC's own fare, some of which is broadcast nationwide ("Studio 360," "RadioLab," "On the Media"). For classical melodies, tune in to Evening Music with Terrance McKnight and David Garland.

WKCR (*89.9 FM; columbia.edu/cu/wkcr*)
Columbia University's noncommercial station is noteworthy for its heavy jazz rotation. The inimitable Phil Schaap, curator of Jazz at Lincoln Center, hosts a daily morning radio program.

WFUV (*90.7 FM; wfuv.org*)
Fordham's radio station, also noncommercial, is well-known for its affiliation with Public Radio International.

WFAN (*660 AM; wfan.com*)
America's first 24/7 sports talk station.

Commercial Stations
Tune in to **WXRK** for alternative (*92.3 FM; krockradio.com*), **WCBS** for classic rock (*101.1 FM; wcbsfm.com*), **WQXR** for classical (*96.3 FM; wqxr. com*), **WQHT** for hip-hop (*97.1 FM; hot97.com*), **WHTZ** (*100.3 FM; z100.com*) for all the hits, and **WSKQ** for Spanish-language tunes (*97.9 FM; lamega.com*).

INTERNET

Gothamist.com
The most popular local blog in New York, Gothamist tracks city life, from the political to the technological to the cultural. Its newsmap plots the location of the latest incidents (fires, robberies, accidents, etc).

Gawker.com
A snarky gossip and media blog that'll keep you posted on any and all celebrity sightings.

HuffingtonPost.com/New-York
"The Internet Newspaper" tested its city-specific coverage with a Chicago page, and has just started one for New York. Reportage is mainly political, with the usual slew of semi-famous columnists editorializing on city issues that interest them.

CityRoom.blogs.nytimes.com
The *Times*' city blog is an online metro section, complete with minute-by-minute updates. Beats include government, crime, and even transportation.

LIFESTYLE

We all know that there are innumerable places to go and things to do in the Big Apple—this guidebook is glutted with them. But before you delve into a particular neighborhood, peruse the following Lifestyle essays for helpful overviews, grouped around the following themes:

Whether you're searching for a Behnaz Sarafpour dress or vintage boots, you'll be able to find it at one of NYC's many **Shopping** venues. **Nightlife** provides a useful breakdown of bars, clubs, and under 21 alternatives, as well as tips on how to "choose your own adventure."

You can't live in the city without visiting the Empire State Building, Times Square, the Brooklyn Bridge, Rockefeller Center, the Statue of Liberty or Ellis Island, and **Iconic New York** explains when to go, in order to save time and money. **Outdoor New York** and **Central Park** are must-reads for the athletically-minded or those desiring a more natural landscape.

Interested in learning how to paint, act, write, dance, play an instrument, or loosen up with yoga? **Classes and Workshops** offers a variety of options for gurus and neophytes alike, from the city's premiere cultural institutions.

If you have rainbow pride, check **LGBT** for suggestions on where to go, shop, dine, or party. Festivals, celebrations, and other exciting annual occurrences that are New York favorites are all listed on the **Events Calendar**.

SHOPPING

*Contrary to popular belief—or at least contrary to what **Sex and the City** would have us believe—shopping in New York is not all glitz and glam. Scouring boutiques, fighting tooth and nail over that perfect pair of shoes, and digging through piles of haphazardly arranged clothes like a ravished raccoon is what the city shopping scene is all about. But nowhere is it easier to dress like a rockstar without breaking the bank.*

UPSCALE

ENTIRE LOOKS
Instead of trekking all over the city to construct the perfect outfit, you can find every component of your ensemble at these posh one-stop shops. Watch out, however, for price inflation.

Keni Valenti Retro Couture is flooded with much-imitated pieces from the 1920s-80s by Chanel, Alaïa, Halston, and Fendi, and also features garments made famous by films, music videos, and celebrities.
155 West 29th St, 3rd Floor - Room C. 917-686-9553.

Bergdorf Goodman is the 5th Ave stop for beautiful people with the bank roll of a royal. Collections from Armani, Dolce & Gabbana, Marc Jacobs, and Yves Saint Laurent line its walls, reeking with fashion consciousness.
754 5th Ave. 212-753-7300.

DRESSES
Throwing a dress on makes you instantly fabulous, sans pressure of pairing a top and bottom. Here's to spending too much money on so little fabric!

Quintessentially feminine and elegant, **Behnaz Sarafpour** offers dresses that will truly last a lifetime—and they better, at a grand a pop. This Chelsea location, amidst dozens of art galleries, reminds you that you are browsing through aesthetic creations as well.
136 W 21st St, 6th Floor. 212-242-2343.

High-quality and superbly chic, **Alice+Olivia** simply dominates on cute, signature frocks and pairs of racy leggings to match. Whether you're looking for an architecturally-structured dress or a loose baby doll, this is the place.
80 W. 40th St. 212-840-0887.

MENSWEAR
Even if you pair blazers with shorts or cowboy boots with oxfords, there is no shortage of men's couture in New York City for special occasions, gifts, or simple purchases for when you have nothing else to spend your trust fund money on.

Chirping parakeets seem to guide your way into the narrow storefront of **Assembly New York,** complete with deeply-recessed, rusticated brick walls. Here, you'll find vintage cowboy boots with rough leather and shiny dress shoes sitting side by side, as well as complete suits hanging from the ceiling.
174 Ludlow St. 212-253-5393.

Far from basic, **Comme des Garcons** has cornered the menswear market in Greenwich Village. The fabrics and colors may seem run-of-the-mill, but the style and cut of the clothes are pleasantly unconventional.
520 W 22nd St. 212-604-9200 & 601 W 26th St #1460. 212-604-0013.

Clark's Register is a store with an eclectic character, described by its owners as "bohemian preppy."
339 W Broadway. 212-334-2444.

SHOES

It doesn't matter if you rock loud-lion platforms or demure kitten heels—the abundance of shoes here will make you wish you were a many-footed centipede.

Was it necessary for **Saks** to create its own zip code for its eighth-floor footwear haven, 10222-SHOE? Of course not, but it deserves it: this multi-level observatory houses every shoe need of New York's well-heeled denizens.
611 5th Ave. 212-753-4000.

As all sneakerheads know, exclusivity is key when it comes to your kicks—and the atmosphere of **Atmos NY**, created from shoe-lined whitewashed walls that fade into the background, will make you want to throw out your ratty old Chucks for a pair of fresh trainers.
203 W 125th St. 212-666-2242.

ACCESSORIES

These alternative places offer accoutrements that will make you reflect in the dark—which may come in handy when you have to turn off your electricity to pay for them. Shine on.

Eye Candy is the stop for countless vintage delicacies, as can be seen from the glass case in front crammed with jewels that rival Queen Victoria's. There are also many chunky and cheesy styles, so you'll be sure to find a piece or six to match any fashion era you're trying to relive.
329 Lafayette St. 212-343-4275.

If, for whatever reason, you are looking for that

one-of-a-kind silver bracelet with Swarovski crystals and purple bows, plunge into **So Good Jewelry** and prepare to dig through piles of rhinestone-encrusted costume jewelry.
496 Broadway. 212-625-9552.

JEANS

The most basic necessity for any wardrobe always causes the most commotion. But there's no more reason to fuss—these shops will fulfill your neverending search for denim dubs.

Scott Morrison's newest step into ultra-sexy denim, **Earnest Sewn**, will, quite earnestly, become your new favorite stop for jeanware. Plus, with the manager's guarantee of lifetime repairs by the store's very own tailor on premises, you'll be hard-pressed to find a more

practical alternative.
821 Washington St. 212-242-3414.

Do you have the premium denim fever? If so, you can satisfy your obsession at **Atrium**, a NoHo boutique with a hot and aloof sales crew. The space may be small, but denim still rules the house, with some hand-painted fedoras and sleek Italian shoes rounding out the collection. Be sure to check out the back sale room for thriftier finds.
644 Broadway. 212-473-9200.

ON THE CHEAP

THRIFT STORES

Clawing, fighting, sweating, and running—all these verbs can be used to describe the battle that is thrift store shopping. Come prepared to lose a limb for other people's discarded clothes.

While you dig through $30 vintage dresses and more Western wear than you'll know what to do with at **No Relation Vintage**, be careful not to step on the rare and unique collection of worn leather boots and retro sneakers.
204 1st Ave. 212-228-5201.

Get ready for a hunt through clothes from every designer, every decade, and every type of denim at **Buffalo Exchange**. This quiet alternative to Beacon's Closet in Williamsburg makes for a more enjoyable shopping experience.
504 Driggs Ave (at 9th St). 718-384-6901 & 332 E 11th St. 212-260-9340.

Tokio 7 is a Japanese company teeming with high-end designer finds. Pick through their vast selection to find Prada pumps or a sweater from Yamamoto.
64 E 7th St. 212-353-8443.

SAMPLE SALES

Because few of us have Anna Wintour sized shopping budgets, we have to find other ways to dress like the editor-in-chief of *Vogue*. The answer: sample sales. Throughout the city on a daily basis, various stores and designers offer overstocked merchandise to the masses with limited-time-only sales of their products. Finding them is no easy task, as there's no huge neon sign with an arrow flashing "Gucci This Way!" You must be diligent—the best way to stay on top of these special occasions is subscribing to *Daily Candy* (dailycandy.com), *Budget Fashionista* (budgetfashionista.com), and *Time Out New York* (newyork.timeout.com).

DEPARTMENT STORES

You'll pay slightly more at these discount superstores, mostly because of organized racks and semi-friendly salespeople.

An absolute must-stop location, **Loehmann's** stocks brands like Free People, Nicole Miller, and Theory at up to 70% off designer prices. Join their savings club to receive additional savings and a birthday discount, for free! *2101 Broadway Ave. 212-882-9990 & 101 7th Ave. 212-352-0856.*

While **Century 21** boasts pieces from high-end labels like Pucci and Marciano, beware—you may be scared away by droves of tourists and rumbling walls from the passing trains. *22 Cortlandt St. 212-227-9092.*

FLEA MARKETS

These are the perfect places to satisfy your craving for cheap designer clothes and a nice tan.

With more than 170 vendors, the **Hell's Kitchen Flea Market** has an abundance of goodies in every imaginable category. *W 39th St (between 9th and 10th Ave). Sat-Sun 9am-6pm.*

Hop on a shuttle from Hell's Kitchen to the **The Garage**, which has been providing locals and tourists alike with prints, jewelry, handbags, fabrics, furniture and fine silver since 1994. *112 W 25th St (between 6th and 7th Ave). 212-243-5343. Sat-Sun 9am-5pm.*

The famous **Brooklyn Flea** has over 150 vendors who peddle their vintage wares in a school parking lot while budding hipsters frolick and DJs spin indie tunes. *357 Clermont Ave (near Greene Ave). Sat 10am-5pm. Brooklyn Bridge Flea Sun 11am-6pm. brownstoner. com/brooklynflea.*

Look forward to leather jackets and other vintage steals at the **SoHo Antiques Fair**. Just don't lose yourself in the jumble. *Grand St and Broadway. 212-682-2000. Sat-Sun 9am-5pm.*

STREET FAIRS

The Earth Awareness Day Festival
Beginning of April. 46th St, from Broadway to 8th Ave

Civic Community Day Fair
Beginning of May. Murray St, from Broadway to Church St

Brooklyn Pride Parade
Beginning of June. 15th St, from Prospect Park West to 7th Ave, Lincoln Pl, Park Slope

The Great July 4th Festival
July 4th. Water St, from Fulton to Broad St.

Celebration of Nations Festival
Mid-July. Madison Ave, from 42nd to 57th St

Summer Seaport Festival
Mid-August. Water St, from Fulton to Broad St

Columbia University Community Block Party
Beginning of September. 120th St, from Broadway to Amsterdam Ave

NYC Oktoberfest
Early October. Lexington Ave, from 42nd to 57nd St

Union Squre Park Holiday Market
Late November-December. Union Square Park at 14th St

TOP 9

NIGHTLIFE

As the city that never sleeps, New York has defined American nightlife. Only here can you find Delirium Tremens on tap, converted warehouses with old-school Pacman, a honky-tonk bar with burlesque and 4 a.m. last calls. But you don't need booze to have an intoxicating experience—besides its goldmine of bars and lounges, New York is also home to some of the world's most buzzed-about comedy shows, jazz clubs, and late-night readings. With subways running 24 hours, you can (and should) hit up different places in one night.

CHOOSE YOUR OWN ADVENTURE

One of the best gifts the city can give you is that of discovery. Don't chain yourself to one lounge or club—wander around the neighborhood you're in with an open mind and travel wherever instinct decides to take you. Your greatest (and shittiest) nights in the city will be those in which you end up someplace completely unexpected.

These famously venue-packed streets will guarantee an epic after-dark adventure:
* Bleecker St, Greenwich Village
* E 7th St (*2nd Ave to Ave A*), East Village
* Ludlow St, Lower East Side
* Amsterdam Ave (*80th to 86th St*), Upper West Side
* Hudson St, Soho/Tribeca
* Bedford Ave, Williamsburg
* Franklin St, Greenpoint
* 5th Ave, Park Slope

BARS & LOUNGES

From adorably grungy local dives to uber-sophisticated cocktail lounges, the city has it all.

Dive Bar
These dark, well-worn, hole-in-the-wall watering holes are often frequented by neighborhood locals. There's something endearing about their crappiness—and drinks are dirt cheap.

Beer Bar
Crowds of avid beer lovers congregrate here to sit, drink, and be merry. The convivial atmosphere is complemented by an enormous number of taps (some have over 70!) and encyclopedic menus that often feature independent American craft brews alongside a respectable foreign selection.

Wine Bar
You won't find plasma TVs blasting football games at these small, warmly-lit, sensual spaces. Come to not only enjoy a glass of wine, but also learn about your drink—the menus are just as detailed and extensive as those at beer bars, and many places encourage tastings before purchases. Perfect for an early night low-key experience.

Cocktail Lounge
New York City defines the classic cocktail, but continues to riff on itself with these swanky, experimental lounges. Prices may be a little steep, but ingredients are fresh and most of the drinks can't be ordered anywhere else. Even if you don't order, it's worth coming just to watch the bartenders squeeze, mix, and pour masterpieces.

Outdoor Bars and Lounges
The only thing better than drinking is drinking al fresco, in the fresh night air. Many bars and lounges have rooftop seating, especially during warmer months. If you're craving something a little more leafy and a little less swanky, swing by a beer garden.

ALTERNATIVE NIGHTLIFE

A night out doesn't need to revolve around drinking. Here are some other ways to have an exhilarating (and by no means milder)

experience. Most of these venues are under 21-friendly but vary by location and show, so be sure to check in advance.

Live Music
The options are virtually limitless—everything from small bars with cleared areas for acoustic performances and open mics to converted warehouse venues where big names book months in advance. The city offers pretty much anything you're looking for, whether it's avant-garde sound art, electro-clash, chamber orchestra, or underground hip-hop. Alcohol can go in tandem with the beat, but it's almost always option and rarely an obligation.

Jazz Clubs
Legends like Duke Ellington and Bille Holiday have lived and played in New York City, so it's no surprise that jazz has a cult following here. The essence of each club is the music; everything else is an accoutrement. Smaller places have no cover, and the cover of more well-known places may be a little steep, but you can stay and listen to people play until 3 or 4 am.

Dance Clubs
Not all of these venues are velvet-rope exclusive, but most are packed, sweaty, and a lot of fun if you come with the right people. There's a spot for every breed of dance lover: you can salsa and swing in a smaller hall, participate in a large-scale, all-night hip-hop or disco-pop marathon, and groove to most anything in between.

Comedy Clubs
Skip the tourist-baiters in Times Square for a black box performance—they're not only cheaper, but will also provide you with bigger laughs. If you're lucky, you might catch a stand-up routine or an improv performance from the likes of Dave Attell, Louis CK, Michael Showalter and Amy Poehler. You should just go for the jokes, but note that some clubs (especially small places) require a drink minimum.

Readings
They're not just at Barnes & Noble and the Strand—bars and cafés also host spoken word events, which can be anything from laid-back talks featuring New York Times bestselling authors to fiercely competitive open mic poetry slams. Most are free, and if there's a cover charge, it's seldom more than $10.

Games
Beyond the basic dartboard, many bars are equipped with foosball, speedball, ping pong, pool tables, and retro arcade or board games for those sober enough to play. If you'd like to flex your brain muscles and win some cash or free booze, sign up for a trivia night.

Bowling
Even going bowling in New York City can be a glamorous experience—popular city alleys have strobe lights, leather booths, and state-of-the-art equipment. To keep you entertained well past midnight, some are even paired with nightclubs, bars, and lounges.

ICONIC NEW YORK

New York has long been a symbol of dreams, excitement, sophistication. Whether your personal conception of the city stems from a lifetime of experience or a handful of Seinfeld episodes, it is inevitably intertwined with images of the city's iconic landmarks. New Yorkers complain that these spots are crowded with tour groups and postcard peddlers, but most will jump at the chance to make a pilgrimage under the guise of "showing a visiting friend."

EMPIRE STATE BUILDING

Yup, it's not to be missed. In fact, bring a date. From the 102nd-floor **observation deck**, you can see as far as 80 miles on a clear day. This view of the city is unrivaled—since 9/11, the Empire State Building is once again the tallest in New York, rising over 1,250 feet.

Consider timing your trip to coincide with the sunset, or right before closing to avoid a line. Even better, visit just after a big snow—the near-

empty observatory and crisp, quiet air is a truly enchanting experience.

Location: Corner of 45th St and 5th Ave
How to Get There: ❻ to 33rd St, ❶❷❸ ❹❸❺❺❺❺❺ to 34th St.
Admission and Hours: The observatory is open all day, every day, from 8am-2am. Last elevators go up at 1:15am. Plan to wait in line for up to an hour, but save some time by buying your tickets online (*esbnyc.com*). They are $18.45.
Nearby Attractions: If you have some cash to spare, wander up **Fifth Ave** and into its sophisticated high-end department stores. A less expensive popular shopping spot, **Herald Square**, is just one block west and contains both the flagship Macy's and the best H&M in the city.

TIMES SQUARE

Once considered a symbol of New York's seediness and corruption, this neon-illuminated spot is now a global landmark, aptly named "The Crossroads of the World." Yes, the lights—especially from the Nasdaq Center—are quite impressive, but there's more to the Square: it's home to the celebrity-studded **Great White Way**, an agglomeration of renowned Broadway theaters. Skip the crowds at the New Year's Eve ball drop and attend one of the lesser-known events, which include "Solstice," an all-day yoga-fest, and "Taste of Times Square," an outdoor food festival with samples from upscale restaurants in the area.

However, Times Square's best attraction is its visitors. Ranging from the naked cowboy to befuddled tourists, the eclectic crowd here makes it a prime spot to people-watch. This activity has become easier than ever since the recent addition of **Broadway Boulevard**,

which the Bloomberg administration has dubbed a "pedestrian living-room." Just south of 42nd and Broadway, part of the street is sectioned off and bordered by large plants, with enough tables, lawn chairs, and umbrellas to fill two pool decks.

Location: From 6th to 8th Ave between 40th and 53rd St.

How to Get There: If all roads lead to Rome, all subways lead to Times Square. Take ❶❷❸ ❼Ⓝ⓪ⓡⓦⓢ to 42nd St, or ❻ⒹⒻⓋ to Bryant Park and walk a block.

Admission and Hours: Free. Times Square never sleeps.

Nearby Attractions: Walk a block east to catch your breath in **Bryant Park** (which also offers free movie screenings in the summer and an ice rink in the winter), or stop by the beautiful main branch of the **New York Public Library** (476 5th Ave). When hunger strikes, walk a few blocks up 8th Ave and explore the many up-and-coming restaurants in **Hell's Kitchen** or head south to **Koreatown** (32nd St, between 5th Ave and Broadway).

DID YOU KNOW?

Lightning strikes the Empire State Building about 100 times a year.

BROOKLYN BRIDGE

In the words of architect Frederick Biehle, this engineering marvel "celebrates the simple act of passage, elevating the commonplace to a ritual." Its 1.13-mile **pedestrian and bike lanes**, perfect for daily commute, offer breathtaking views of Manhattan, especially at night.

As you cross, you'll learn that it was designed by John Roebing and construction begun in 1868. Upon completion, it became the world's longest suspension bridge and a symbol of modernity and optimism. With an intricate, delicate web of cables and striking Gothic piers, it's easy to see why the Bridge has captured the imagination of artists from Georgia O'Keefe to Walt Whitman.

Location: Stretches almost 6,000 feet over the East River, connecting Manhattan and Brooklyn.

How to Get There: ❷❸ to Clark St, ❹❺❻ to Brooklyn Bridge-City Hall, ❹Ⓒ to High St, NR to City Hall. For a good view of the Bridge

itself, head to the South Street Seaport.

Admission and Hours: Free and always open.

Nearby Attractions: On your way to Wall St, consider stopping at **Century 21**, the department store with heaps of discount designer threads, or going north to visit **Chinatown**. Once you get to Brooklyn, you'll probably be hungry, so explore the many bistros on **Mantague St** or head to **Grimaldi's** for one of its deservedly famous pizza pies.

ROCKEFELLER CENTER

Rockefeller Center was conceived by John D. Rockefeller Jr. in 1929 to revitalize the area. It worked. Now this 22-acre marvel of urban design is the largest privately owned complex of its kind, an unusual and arresting blend of art deco and modern architecture (and, inescapably, a symbol of capitalism).

Saturday Night Live, Nightly News with Brian Williams, and NBC's *Today Show* are all broadcast here, and you can check them all out on a studio tour. For a serenely elevated view of the **rink**, snag a table at the **Saks 5th Ave** cafés, and treat yourself to tea and cookies. If you want to skate, go to the quieter Wollman or Bryant Park rinks instead. And be sure to arrive an hour early if you want to be there for the **tree-lighting ceremony** in December.

Location: From 5th to 7th Ave between 47th and 50th St.

How to Get There: ⑧ⒹⒻⓄ to 47th-50th St-Rockefeller Center, ⑥ to 51st St, ① to 50th St.

Admission and Hours: Free! The plazas are open 24/7, but the hours of attractions and shops vary. You can also take tours of NBC studios, the Center itself, or everything combined ($12, $18.50 and $23.50, respectively).

Nearby Attractions: Wander into shiny lobbies to discover tucked-away art pieces, or prowl the many upscale stores nearby—but beware, the prices in this area tend to be steep. Or check out the panoramic skyline on **Top of the Rock**, the observatory deck at 30 Rockefeller Center. Enter on 50th St between 5th and 6th Ave (admission is $17.50). And across the street from 30 Rock you'll find the awe-inspiringly large **St. Patrick's Cathedral** (*460 Madison Ave*), a remarkable gothic structure still open daily for mass.

STATUE OF LIBERTY & ELLIS ISLAND

Liberty and Ellis Islands can only be reached by ferry, and since the ferry goes to both, take advantage your of your ticket purchase by visiting them together. Yes, it sounds like a corny way to spend a day, and yes, you'll be surrounded by tourists, but the views of Manhattan alone are worth the trip.

When you catch the exhilarating sight of the 151-foot, 70-ton Statue of Liberty, you'll understand why it has served as such an iconic symbol of immigration since 1886. To see the regal, massive figure up close, take the elevator up to the pedestal—you'll find a **museum** and a charming collection of Lady Liberty kitsch.

Visiting Ellis Island can be an exciting experience, particularly for those curious about the history of New York. The federal immigration station opened on January 1, 1892 and was closed on November 12, 1954, but not before 12 million immigrants were inspected and let in—roughly 40% of the U.S. population is related to someone who entered the country here. Outside of the main building, there is a **Wall of Honor**, upon which are inscribed the names of immigrants honored by their families with a donation.

DID YOU KNOW?

The Statue of Liberty has a 35-foot waist and a 4½-foot nose.

Enter the re-created processing center through the **Baggage Hall** and proceed up the stairs to the renovated **Registration Room**. The walk is lined with sepia photos of the worn but determined faces that passed through Ellis Island, while audio recordings narrate their humbly heroic stories.

Location: Both are in Lower New York Harbor, slightly over one mile from Lower Manhattan. Ellis Island was the subject of a long-term border dispute between New York and New Jersey—now, it's technically situated predominantly in Jersey City, although a portion of its territory falls within New York's boundaries.
How to Get There: ❶ to South Ferry, ❹❺ to Bowling Green, ❻❼ to Whitehall St.
Admission and Hours: Free, but the ferry ride is $12. Buy tickets at Castle Clinton or online (*statuecruises.com*). Ferries typically depart every 40 minutes from 8:30am to 4:30pm, and the attractions stay open a bit longer.
Nearby Attractions: If you want a free way to get out onto the water and see the Statue from a distance, hop aboard the **Staten Island Ferry**. You don't even have to get off at Staten Island!

OUTDOOR NEW YORK

There's no denying that the city is a mass of steel and concrete, but amidst the sky-scrapers and congested streets lie a wealth of natural areas perfect for outdoor activities. No matter what the season, they'll welcome you to stretch your legs: head to the waterfront in the summer, pick up your skis or skates in the winter, or go running or biking anytime along the city's many paths.

SUMMER

Summer in the city means heat waves, sweaty subway platforms, and uncomfortably crowded streets. While many find themselves longing to escape to Siberia, a simpler solution is to embrace the sun and search for the bearable outdoor spots.

NY BEACHES
Jones Beach
About an hour away, this beach is known for its 6.5-mile stretch of oceanfront and famous Nikon Theater. It also has two pools, a nature center, and a boardwalk. Because of its popularity, the best time to visit is early in the week, when the corporate crowds are in Manhattan.
Ocean Parkway, Wantagh. 516-785-1600. LIRR to Wantagh, $3 shuttle. Dawn-dusk daily.

Coney Island
Although famous in places as far off as California, many New York natives don't come to Coney Island, as they believe it to be too underdeveloped and overrun with families. The beach may not be grand, but after recent renovations, it is cleaner, brighter, and more fun than before. They also have straight-up awesome

rides, attractions, and events.
Surf Ave at Atlantic Shore, Brooklyn. 718-946-1350. ⒷⒹⒻⓃⓇ to Stillwell Ave-Coney Island, ⒹⒻ to W 8th St. 10am-6pm daily.

Brighton Beach
Despite being just a few blocks from Coney Island, this beach attracts a crowd very different from the families that overwhelm Coney's rides. Across the street from Little Odessa, it's a favorite spot amongst Eastern Europeans. There aren't many amenities, but the sand and water are clean.
Brightwater Ave, Brooklyn. 718-946-1350. ⒷⓆ to Brighton Beach or Ocean Pkwy. Dawn-dusk daily.

Long Beach
The town of Long Beach is alive day and night, so it's a great place to escape for an extended visit. Parking here is free, but there's a $10 fee to enter the beach itself. The sand and water are revered by some as "perfect," and the crowd is less rowdy than that of Jones Beach. Long Beach also has also surf rentals and a free concert series during the peak of summer.
Nevada Ave to Maple Blvd. 516-431-3890. LIRR to Long Beach. 9am-6pm daily.

HEALTH CLUBS & GYMS

New York Sports Club
54 locations. 1-800-666-0808.

Reebok Sports Club/NY
160 Columbus Ave. 212-362-6800.

Equinox
22 locations. 212-774-6363.

Crunch Fitness.
7 locations. 888-2-CRUNCH.

Printing House.
421 Hudson St. 212-243-7600.

TOP 5

WATER SPORTS
Prospect Park Boathouse
Rent out paddle boats for $16.50 an hour or take an electric boat ride at $4-8 a ticket.
Prospect Park (near Lincoln Road/Ocean Ave entrance). 718-282-7789.

New York Kayak Company
In the summer they offer many classes and tours for beginner to advanced-level kayakers. While pricey, they're definitely worth it. Participants go to the Piers, the Statue of Liberty, the Boat Basins, and other places with dazzling city views.
Pier 40, South Side (W Houston and West St). 212-924-1327. Classes $50/hour.

Classic Harbor Line
For those looking to relax and let someone else take over the sails, this is the perfect place to go. There are a number of comfortable and luxurious cruises, including the Day Sail, the Sunset Sail, and the Beer and Cheese Sail.
Pier 62 (W 22nd St and the West Side Hwy). 212-627-1825. Cruises $40-155.

WINTER

New York's slushy streets and icy winds may be daunting in the winter, but brave the cold by trying out a few sports. This may not be the Rockies, but there are numerous places to work out those muscles.

SKIING
Mountain Creek
During the winter, NJ Transit runs weekend buses here, though driving is also easy enough. The mountains are of decent size and there's plenty of snow, even when Mother Nature doesn't provide it.
Vernon, NJ. 973-827-2000. $399 season pass.

Windham Mountain
Getting here is easy—take a car, a bus, or Amtrak and you can hit the slopes in less than two hours. There are trails for every level (Upper Wheelchair is a must if you're an expert), and tubing for those who aren't quite ready for skis. Lodging is available in town.

Windham, NY. 518-734-4300. $299 student season pass.

ICE SKATING
Rockefeller Center
World-famous, but expensive and always packed.
5th Ave at 50th St. 212-332-7654. ⓑⓓⓕⓥ to Rockefeller Center, 47-50 St. Admission $9-17, rentals $8.

Wollman Memorial Park
Children and parents flock here on weekends. Visit on a weekday, and be patient with renting and storage—it may get a bit confusing.
Central Park South (enter at 59th St and 5th Ave). 212-439-6900. ⓕ to 57th St, ⓝⓡⓦ to 5th Ave-59th St. Admission $9.50-12, rentals $5.

The Pond at Bryant Park
There are fewer people here than in Central Park, even on weekends. The rink isn't large, but it's cozy and charming in its own way—and admission is free!
42nd St at 6th Ave. 212-661-6640. ⓑⓓⓕⓥ to 42nd St-Bryant Park. Rentals $12.

RUNNING & BIKING

There is no better exercise for the heart than the all-encompassing cardio workouts: biking and running. If you're interested in the former, make sure you wear a helmet and stay off the sidewalks—that's illegal in the city. Here are some of the best paths:

- **Central Park**. Circles the park in its entirety. Various entrances.
- **East River Esplanade**. Runs alongside the highway next to the East River.
- **Fort Washington Park**. On the West Side, near the George Washington Bridge.
- **Harlem River**. Starts at around 145th St near 10th Ave; goes up to Dyckman St in Washington Heights.
- **Brooklyn Bridge**. Starts near City Hall; crosses into Brooklyn.
- **Riverside Park**. Alongside the Hudson River, near Riverside Drive.
- **Chinatown**. Starts in Chinatown; goes across the Williamsburg Bridge.

CENTRAL PARK

New York City has enough imposing metallic skyscrapers and stretches of concrete pavement to leave you craving green. Luckily, Central Park—a verdant paradise that would make even Thoreau proud—is yours to explore for free. Though not the city's largest park, its famously picturesque blend of flora, fauna, architecture, and attractions offer a lush escape from the concrete jungle.

While Central Park architects Frederick Law Olmstead and Calvin Vaux were inspired by London's Hyde Park, this 843-acre expanse of greenery (stretching from 59th to 110th St between 5th and 8th Ave) has become a distinct New York icon. After opening in 1859, it fluctuated through states of robustness and disrepair in the first half of the 20th century, eventually becoming a national landmark in 1966.

59th-68th STREET

Columbus Circle (*59th St at 8th Ave*) and **Grand Army Plaza** (*59th St at 5th Ave*) provide Central Park with the grand gateways it deserves. Nearby is the **Horse-Drawn Carriage Rental Station** where, for a fee, you can take an old-fashioned open-air drive through the park.

The Dairy (*Mid-Park at 65th St*) is the park's main visitor center. If you're in the mood for a traditional board game, walk west to reach the **Chess and Checkers House** (*open Tues-Sun 10am-5pm*).

For skating year-round visit **Wollman Rink** (*East Side at 62nd S*t), a winter ice rink and summer roller rink. **Tavern on the Green** (*West Side at 66th St*) is an award-winning upscale restaurant on prime real estate, and the finish line for the New York Marathon.

Don't miss the rainforest and polar bears at iconic **Central Park Zoo** (*East Side at 65th St*), a small but diverse menagerie of exotic animals divided into three sections: tropical, temperate, and arctic. At its east end is the **Delacorte Music Clock**, with jingles and dancing statues every hour. Another attraction for the kid in you is the **Carousel** (*Mid-Park at 64th St*).

Take advantage of beautiful weather and visit the sprawling **Sheep Meadow** (*West Side between 66th and 69th St*), which traded in its flock of woolly grazers for sunbathers and athletes during the Great Depression. **The Mall** (*Mid-Park at 66th St*) is Central Park's Broadway, cluttered with performers and fodder for people watching.

69th-78th STREET

The Mall ends at the **Bandshell** (*Mid-Park at 72nd St*), the former home of Summerstage. Now it's a wide-open plaza with a dance roller rink and the occasional free concert. Summerstage has moved to the **Rumsey Playfield** (*Mid-Park at 70th St*).

Nearby is **Cherry Hill** (*Mid-Park at 72nd St*), a serene hilltop surrounded by cherry blossoms. It overlooks the **Ramble** (*Mid-Park from 73rd to 79th St*), a natural woodland maze of tiny dirt paths made for getting lost in.

The **Lake** (*Mid-Park between 72nd and 79th St*) boasts one of the best vistas in the park. If you want a more active afternoon, boats and bicycles are available for rent at the **Loeb Boathouse** (*East Side at 74th St*). Head south to reach the famous **Bethesda Terrace and Fountain** (*Mid-Park at 72nd St*), where families, friends, and park performers gather amidst stunning lake views.

For a unique New York sailing experience, visit **Conservatory Water** (*East Side from 72nd to 75th St*), where aspiring captains and pilots breach the waves with model boats.

79th-88th STREET

Central Park's most breathtaking panorama is atop **Belvedere Castle** (*Mid-Park at 79th St*), a granite bastion straight out of a fairy tale. The castle looms over a tranquil body of water named for its most common inhabitants: **Turtle Pond**. It also overlooks **Delacorte Theatre** (*Mid-Park at 80th St*), the stage for the Public

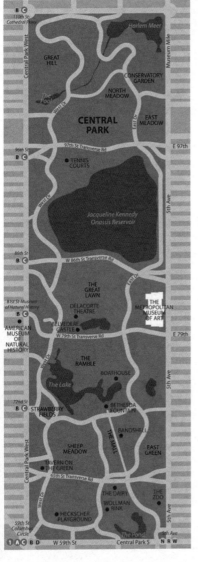

Theater's free summer series, **Shakespeare in the Park**. After watching a performance, head to the nearby **Shakespeare Garden** (*West Side at 79th St*) to find a whole slew flowers and plants the Bard has written about—a tiny plaque of the quote lies next to its mentioned subject matter.

As the largest open field in Central Park, the **Great Lawn** (*Mid-Park between 79th and 85th St*) certainly earns its name. Besides housing many baseball fields, it hosts free concerts by the New York Philharmonic and the Metropolitan Opera house every summer.

89th-98th STREET

The **Jacqueline Kennedy Onassis Reservoir** is the largest body of water in Central Park, covering 106 acres. With a 1.58-mile perimeter, it's a favorite for local joggers.

For more physical activity, you can pop up to the **Tennis Center** (*West Side at 94th St*) to make use of its thirty courts, but make sure you pick up a pass at the **Arsenal** (*East Side at 64th St*) first.

The **North and East Meadows** are a stretch of open fields to the north of the Reservoir, where you can rent sporting equipment for free from the **North Meadow Recreation Center** (*East Side at 97th St*).

99th-110th STREET

Another area of pristine forest is the **North Wood** (*Mid-Park between 102nd and 110th St*), which was designed to give the illusion of untouched nature. As you enter, you'll be surrounded by the sound of running water from its beautiful waterways, which includes a large Pool that connects via the **Loch** to **Lasker Rink** (*Mid-Park at 106th St*).

Nestled further northeast is the **Harlem Meer** (*East Side from 106th to 110th St*), one of the only lakes in the park that allows catch-and-release fishing. Bordering the Meer is the **Conservatory Garden** (*East Side at 104th St*), a manicured floral oasis that replicates several European styles.

CENTRAL PARK 55

LGBT

For LGBT individuals everywhere, finding a place that welcomes nontraditional identities and encourages self expression can seem daunting. Thankfully, New York City is replete with pride and rainbow flags—the veritable East Coast answer to San Francisco. Whether you're searching for support groups, artistic pursuits, or drag queen-run dive bars, you'll find it all here.

NEIGHBORHOODS

The first step to having a great LGBT experience in New York is figuring out where to go. While the whole city is gay-friendly, certain neighborhoods have especially prominent LGBT life.

- **Chelsea** seems to be inhabited and run exclusively by the gay community—gay-owned bistros, pizza shops decorated with rainbow flags, and hordes of muscled men in tanks.
- Once home to gang violence, **Hell's Kitchen** has become the newest destination for New York gays because of its low rents, swanky restaurants, and up-and-coming lounges.
- The **West Village** has a long history of involvement with the New York LGBT scene—it was the site of the 1969 Stonewall Riots, which engendered the American Gay Rights Movement. It's still a stronghold of gay art and culture (not to mention bars) today. Plus, Gay Street is quite literally located there.
- Since the 1960s feminist movement, **Park Slope** has been home to one of the biggest lesbian communities in the city. Located just west of Prospect Park, this center of bohemianism is affectionately nicknamed "Dyke Slope" by its inhabitants.

RESOURCES

It's hard to live in New York without feeling lost at some point. If you want a community network that extends beyond Chelsea, here are some great places and publications to look into.

- With over 6,000 visitors each week, the **LGBT Community Center** (*208 W 13th St; 212-620-7310*) is great to visit not only to become better informed about LBGT life in the city, but also to get involved in cultural and recreational programs, meet a myriad

of passionate people, and promote positive social change.

- While at the Center, be sure to check out information on the **Gay and Lesbian Anti-Violence Project** (*240 W 35th St; 24-hour hotline: 212-714-1141*) and **GLAAD** (*Gay & Lesbian Alliance Against Defamation, 104 W 29th St; 212-629-3322*)—both have tons of volunteering opportunities.
- The **New York Blade**, a free newspaper with a readership of over 100,000, is the city's only gay-owned weekly publication. It covers anything and everything LGBT-related, from politics to profiles of local musicians and dancers.
- **HX Magazine** and **Next Magazine** will keep you up-to-date on the trendiest nightlife and entertainment.

PRIDE EVENTS

While the *5-Boro Dance Challenge* and the *Original GLBT Expo* bring some rainbow hue to the offseason, the city truly comes alive in June, the international month of LGBT pride. Each borough has its own events throughout the month leading up to Manhattan's *NYC Pride* (*nycpride.org*). This weeklong celebration brings countless activities at every LGBT venue in the city, culminating in a Sunday afternoon parade down 5th Ave and a dance of epic proportions on the Chelsea piers.

SHOPPING & DINING

Finding shops and restaurants that are gay-friendly in NYC is easy, but sometimes the more fun ones are gay-owned or themed.

- For fun trinkets, books, and bathing suits check out **Rainbows and Triangles** (*192 8th Ave, 212-627-2166*) in the heart of Chelsea.
- For slightly upscale clothing for any degree of fierceness, visit **Marc by Marc Jacobs** (*382 Bleeker St, 212-929-0304*) in the West Village. Also, check out **Wear Me Out** (*358 W 47th St, 212-333-3047*), a cute Hell's Kitchen boutique with contemporary men's fashion from many well-known designers.
- Hell's Kitchen may be home to "Restaurant Row," but Chelsea has the best LGBT dining options. Go to **Cafeteria** (*119 7th Ave, 212-414-1717*) for a hip crowd, 24-hour diner grub, and celebrity sightings. Just up the street, **Elmo** (*156 7th Ave, 212-337-8000*) holds another hoppin' gay scene with fancy modern décor, trendy diners, and unbeatable American comfort food.
- For an inimitable dining experience, visit **Lips** (*2 Bank St, 212-675-7710*) in the West Village. The food may not be *Gourmet Magazine*-worthy, but drag queen waitresses make up for it with nightly performances and lap dances for the more eager clientele.

NIGHTLIFE

From extravagant clubs with scantily clad go-go dancers to neighborhood dive bars with cobwebbed disco balls, LGBT nightlife in the city runs the gamut of possibilities.

Dance Clubs

For gays new to New York, there is nothing like letting loose to some Gaga and Britney to get the party started. Head to **Club Rush** (*579 6th Ave; 212-243-6100*) for twinky 18+ fun and **Splash Bar** (*50 W 17th St; 212-691-0073*) for an epic night of two-story dancing. For the ladies, there's **Bum Bum Bar** (*6314 Roosevelt Ave, Queens; 718-651-4145*), where lesbians of all ages salsa and meringue to lively Latin beats. There's also **Sugarland** (*221 N 9th St, Brooklyn; 718-599-4044*), the split-level, mixed-crowd alternative to more popular Williamsburg gay destinations.

Lounges

The best lounges in the city are north of downtown glitz. In the heart of Hell's Kitchen is **Therapy** (*348 W 52nd St; 212-397-1700*), a stylish yet comfy bi-level space with cocktails like "Oral Fixation" and "Psychotic Episode." Further uptown is **Brandy's Piano Bar** (*235 E 84th St; 212-744-4949*), where a mixed crowd croons to Broadway showstoppers and jazzy favorites.

Dive Bars

All pretension aside, the true heart and soul of the New York gay community comes out most earnestly in neighborhood dive bars. For Upper West Siders, nothing can beat karaoke at **Suite** (*992 Amsterdam Ave; 212-222-4600*). Over 100 blocks south, **The Cock** (*29 2nd Ave; 212-777-6254*) lives up to its notoriously sleazy reputation with themed after-dark gatherings that are anything but PG.

CLASSES & WORKSHOP

Indulge in your passion for art and enroll in a ceramics workshop. Escape to a tranquil sanctuary for your mind and body through yoga. Always wanted to think funny on your feet? Sign up for an improv class. The city can be a haven of self-enlightenment for novices and experts alike—if you know where to look. Here are some nifty suggestions to start your search.

ACTING

13th Street Repertory Theater
For a more conventional approach, learn time-honored acting techniques based on the teachings of Chekhov and other Russian masters with weekly courses at this renowned Off-Off Broadway company.
50 W 13th St. 212-757-6178. $30 per class. Must commit to 3-month term.

Atlantic Theater Company
The Atlantic Acting School uses the Stanislovsky method of acting in its rigorous part-time and full-time classes, which can go for up to two and a half years. Technique lessons are coupled with voice, speech, and movement training.
76 9th Ave. 212-691-5919. Prices vary.

Upright Citizens' Brigade
Known for its hilarious shows à la ABC's *Whose Line Is It Anyway?*, UCB also offers classes to train and tune your improvisation and sketch comedy skills with experienced gurus.
307 W 26th St. 212-929-8107. 8-week term $325, 4-week term $175.

ART

The Art Studio of New York
Seasoned artists and doodlers alike will find solace in the Art Studio's classes, workshops, and retreats for painting, drawing, acrylics, oils and more. Classes capped at eight students ensure one-on-one attention.
West 96th St. 212-932-8484. Prices vary.

Loop of the Loom
For a taste of Eastern art, try Japanese SAORI weaving at this specialized studio. You'll have a Zen experience—the atmosphere is conducive to healing, self-discovery and individuality.
227 E 87th St (between 2nd and 3rd Ave), Lower Level. 212-722-2686. 2-hour class $45.

CREATIVE WRITING

Gotham Writers' Workshop
Gotham's well-structured workshops are some of the most highly acclaimed and successful in the city. Through 10-week terms, 6-week terms, or single day intensives, writers can study genres (from character development to stand-up comedy) and programs (from nonfiction to poetry).
Multiple Manhattan locations and Online.

Morningside Writers
Advertised as a "community of peers," Morningside Writers functions much like a creative support group for writers of fiction, speculative fiction, memoirs, and screenplays through biweekly meetings.
Morningside Drive (between 7th and Lenox Ave). 646-202-0378. Free, but application required.212-WRITERS. Prices vary.

The Writers Studio
Though sometimes pricey, the Writers Studio has been hailed by the *Times* as one of the most personal writing venues for all levels—students "try on voices" to find their own in its extensive range of fiction and poetry workshops. The Studio also hosts a student works' Reading Series.
272 W 10th St (between Greenwich and Washington) and Online. 212-255-7075. Prices vary.

DANCE

Lotus Music and Dance
Lotus' classes span the entire globe—here you can take a workshop in West African, Native American, and Tahitian dance or try out flamenco, hula and more.
109 W 27th St, 8th floor. 212-627-1076. Prices vary.

Steps on Broadway
A world-renowned dance studio with classes in ballet, jazz, modern, hip hop, tap, and theater,

Steps is unique for its diverse students. Casual enthusiasts and aspiring professionals practice alongside veterans from Broadway, the Met, and major dance companies.
2121 Broadway #3. 212-874-2410. Prices vary.

Elizabeth Streb

Trapeze classes aren't just for Carrie Bradshaw. Learn to fly through the air at Streb's— its PopAction, trampoline, and trapeze classes will challenge you to investigate space with rapid-fire movements that defy gravity.
51 North 1st St, Brooklyn. 718-384-6491. Average Price: $15 per class.

MUSIC

Encore Music Lessons

Lessons from this company, both instrumental and voice, can be conducted in the comfort of your own home. What's more, you can pick your own teacher or have them match one to your schedule and preferences.
Multiple locations. 212-537-6746. Prices vary.

The Kaufman Center

The Merkin Concert Hall, the Special Music School, and the Lucy Moses School joined forces to create the music-lover's paradise. Students of all ages can take instrumental or voice lessons in a group or individual classes, for professional training or pure pleasure.
129 W 67th St. 212-501-3303. Prices vary.

Turtle Bay Music School

With private and group instruction for twenty instruments and voice, Turtle Bay specializes in music outreach programs for all ages and abilities. Don't miss its *Hear It Now! Concert Series*, which promotes music through a plethora of free master classes and education concerts.
244 E 52nd St. 212-753-8811. Prices vary. TRY! Beginner packages: 5 weeks for $175.

YOGA

Bikram Yoga

The signature 105-degree heat of a Bikram Yoga studio allows students of all levels to detox in one room. Though you may leave the 90-minute moving meditation looking like you've just crawled out of a warm pool, its benefits to your health and flexibility are unparalleled.
Multiple Locations in Manhattan, the Bronx, Queens, and Brooklyn. Prices vary.

Laughing Lotus

This laid-back, less traditional yoga studio offers variations on a classic series. Drop by for 7:30 a.m. Sun Celebrations, a mix of Vinyasa and Flow, or upbeat Friday Midnight Yoga Jams to live music.
59 W 19th St, 3rd Floor. 212-414-2903. Prices vary.

Yoga to the People

Inspired by Brian Kest's power yoga, this donation-based studio promotes mind and body strengthening and welcomes all skill levels. Even with four floors classes are always packed, so come at least 10 minutes early to grab prime mat space.
12 St Mark's Place. 917-573-YOGA. Pay what you can; $10 suggested donation.

EVENTS CALENDAR

JANUARY

Arts & Leisure Weekend
Early January
The *New York Times* presents an unbeatable series of panel discussions featuring today's renowned artists, musicians, and writers—from Whoopie Goldberg to Salman Rushdie.
TimesCenter (242 W 41st St, between 7th and 8th Ave). 888-698-1970. artsandleisureweek.com. Most events $30 each.

Three King's Day Parade & Celebration
Early January
Museo Del Barrio sponsors a parade through East Harlem, followed by a presentation of Hispanic theater over the weekend.
Museo Del Barrio (1230 5th Ave, between 104th and 105th St). Parade location varies. 212-831-7272. elmuseo.org. Free.

New York Boat Show
January 20-24
Fishing, sailing, and motoring aficionados gather to buy—or admire—hundreds of nautical beauties, with chances to win amazing prizes.
Jacob K. Javits Convention Center (655 W 34th St, between 11th and 12th Ave). 212-564-2728. nyboatshow.com. $15.

Chinese New Year Splendor
Late January-Early February
The flashy gusto of Radio City Music Hall meets refined Eastern influence in a dazzling display of traditional Chinese music and dance.
Radio City Music Hall (1260 6th Ave, between 50th and 51st St). 888-260-6221. radiocity.com. Prices vary.

Winter Restaurant Week
Late January or Early February
Some of the city's finest and priciest eating establishments open their doors to a more thrift-conscious public, with affordable three-course prix fixe meals for two weeks.
nycgo.com/restaurantweek. $24 lunch, $35 dinner (not including beverages, tax, and tip).

FEBRUARY

Empire State Building Run-Up
Early February
NY Road Runners hosts this mad dash up 1576 steps. The view is worth the 1/5 mile clamber.
350 5th Ave (between 33rd and 34th St). 212-736-3100. nyrr.org. Participation is invitation only.

Winter Jam
Early February
A veritable winter wonderland, featuring a snowboard invitational, a sledding flume, and ice sculpting. Warm up with food, drink, and live music.
East River Park (Houston St and FDR Drive). nycgovparks.org. Free.

Mercedes Benz Fashion Week
Mid-February
World-famous designers and fashionistas gather under the famous white tents at Bryant Park, as the hottest brands showcase their fall looks.
Bryant Park (42nd St at 5th Ave). 646-871-2400. mbfashionweek.com. Prices vary.

Frigid Festival New York
Late February-Early March
A festival of more than 150 independent theater shows and events, at bargain prices.
Location varies. frigidnewyork.info. Most performances $10-20.

Mardi Gras 2nd Ave Stroll
Late February or Early March
Bars join together to provide revelers with cheap drinks, live performances, and miles of beads.
Near 2nd Ave and 53rd St. 800-422-7295. lindypromo. com. $10 with two cans of food, $15 without.

MARCH

St. Patrick's Day Parade
March 17th at 11am
This classic cavalcade transforms 5th Avenue into a valley of shamrocks and green to celebrate Ireland's patron saint.
5th Ave, from 44th St to the Metropolitan Museum of Art. 212-484-1222. Free.

Easter Egg Hunt in Brooklyn Bridge Park
Easter Sunday
Children—and the young at heart—can hunt for eggs, have their faces painted, or listen to live music and stories.
Washing and Main St, Dumbo. 718-802-0603. brooklynbridgepark.org. Free.

Annual Urban Pillow Fight
March 22nd
Feathers fly in Union Square as New Yorkers battle one another in this cathartic, relatively painless experience.
Union Square (14th St at Broadway). newmind-space.com. Free.

Barnum & Bailey Animal Walk
Late March or Early April
In celebration of Barnum & Bailey's annual start-up, ponies, elephants, and other animals of all shapes and sizes make the epic trek from Queens to Madison Square Garden.

Starts at Midtown Tunnel (2nd Ave, between 34th and 36th St). ringling.com. Free.

APRIL

Major League Baseball
Early April
Whether your tickets are in the nosebleeds or behind home plate, grab a team cap and head to the ballgame.
MLB.com.

Antiquarian Booksellers Fair
Early April
You can find a mind numbing variety of dusty tomes at this one-of-a-kind fair—from a 1609 Bible to a first print edition of Dickens.
Park Avenue Armory (643 Park Ave, at 67th St). 212-944-8291. abaa.org. $20/day, $30/two-day pass, $40/three-day pass.

National Tartan Week's Pipefest
Mid-April
Hundreds of bagpipers serenade the city with a cacophonous celebration and nostalgia for the Highlands.
6th Ave, from 45th to 58th St. 212-980-0844. tartanweek.com. Free.

April Coffee & Tea Festival
Mid-April
This annual festival provides much-needed caffeine breaks with free samples of some of the best brands in the country. There are also classes, contests, and how-to demonstrations.
Metropolitan Pavilion (W 18th St, between 6th and 7th Ave). 631-940-7290. coffeeandteafestival.com. $20 to enter.

Tribeca Film Festival
Late April-Early May
This popular festival brings fictional and documentary films of the indie variety to the Triangle Below Canal St.
Various theaters. 212-941-2400. tribecafilmfestival. org. Ticket prices vary.

EVENTS CALENDAR

MAY

Five Borough Bike Tour
Early May
Join more than 30,000 participants for this 42-mile ride. Great for those who have been neglecting exercise—or the outer boroughs.
Starts in lower Manhattan. 212-932-2453. bikenewyork.org. Registration necessary.

Sakura Matsuri Cherry Blossom Festival
Early May
A smorgasbord of activities and performances, from bonsai trimming to samurais dances, all beneath Brooklyn's cherry trees.
Brooklyn Botanical Gardens (900 Washington Ave). 718-623-7200. Students $6 (with ID).

9th Ave International Food Festival
Mid-May
This gastronomic goldmine spans 20 blocks of west midtown, with everything from dim sum to jambalaya.
9th Ave, from 37th to 57th St. 212-581-7217. ninthavenuefoodfestival.com. Free.

Fleet Week
Late May
Whether your patriotism is inspired by hunky sailors or sleek ships, this is New York's grand thank you to the armed forces, with fun events aboard the Intrepid Museum.
Pier 86 (12th Ave and 46th St). 877-957-SHIP. intrepidmuseum.org. Free.

Tattoo Convention
Late May
An art exhibit in flesh, this weekend joins dabblers and those inked from head to toe.
Roseland Ballroom (239 W 52nd St, between Broadway and 8th Ave). nyctattooconvention.com. $18 to enter.

JUNE

Puerto Rican Day Parade
Second Sunday in June
An impressive celebration of Boricua history and culture, often accompanied by the thumping bass of Reggaeton. Watch floats decked out with the lone star drift slowly down 5th Ave.
5th Ave, from 44th to 86th St. 718-401-0404. nationalpuertoricandayparade.org. Free.

Museum Mile
Second Tuesday in June
All nine museums on 5th Avenue are free to the public for this evening—arrive early to avoid long lines.
5th Ave, from 82nd to 105th St. 212-606-2296. museummilefestival.org. Free.

BAMCinemaFest
Mid-June
This self-proclaimed "Brooklyn Style" film festival is a newcomer to the scene. It features 18 films, a night-long movie marathon, and a handful of live performers.
Individual venues vary. Brooklyn Academy of Music. 718.636.4100. bam.org. Tickets to new films $11, $8 for students.

SummerStage
June-August
Operatic recitals, eastern influences, and indie greats participate in this first-come-first-served concert series in Central Park.
Ramsey Playfield (enter at W 72nd St or E 69th St). 212-360-2756. summerstage.org. Free.

River to River Festival
June to Mid-September
A post-9/11 effort to revitalize lower Manhattan with famous live music performances amidst architectural beauties and waterfront vistas.
Venues throughout Lower Manhattan. rivertorivernyc. com. Free.

Shakespeare in the Park
June-September
Performances of star-studded Shakespearian plays take the outdoor stage at Central Park every summer. Be prepared for the wait to score tickets.
Delacorte Theater (west side at 80th St). 212-539-8750. publictheater.org. Free.

2010

JULY

Nathan's Hotdog Eating Competition
July 4th
This stomach-stuffing classic has been a Coney Island staple for more than 90 years.
Nathan's Hot Dogs (King's Plaza at Avenue U). 212-352-8651. nathansfamous.com. Free.

Macy's Fireworks Show
July 4th
A spectacle 55 times more explosive than your average Independence Day event. Prime viewing points are on the banks of the East River.
East River, between Battery Park and 42nd St. Macy's. macys.com. Free.

Summer Restaurant Week
Mid-July
World-famous restaurants offer yet another round of delicious three-course prix fixe meals at jaw-droppingly low prices.
nycgo.com. $24 lunch, $35 dinner (not including beverages, tax and tip).

Lincoln Center Festival
Mid-Late July
Renowned theatrical and musical groups from around the globe perform at this three-week long festival.
Lincoln Center (Columbus Ave at 64th Ave). 212-875-5456. lincolncenter.org. Prices vary.

Warm-Up Festival
July–August
This exciting line-up of DJs and performers takes place in an installation selected from the Young Architects' Program competition.
P.S. 1 Contemporary Arts Center (Jackson Ave at 46th Ave, Queens). ps1.org/warmup. $10.

AUGUST

Hong Kong Dragon Boat Festival
Early August
Rowers celebrate Chinese history and culture in this colorful boat race.
Flushing Meadows Park, Queens. 718-767-1776. hkdbf-ny.org. Free.

Fringe Festival NYC
Mid-August
For two weeks, the Present Company hosts more than 4,500 up-and-coming theater acts to perform for an audience of thousands.
Various venues. 212.279.4488. fringenyc.org. $15.

Harlem Week
All Month
A series of panels, seminars, performances, and fairs showcase this Manhattan neighborhood's rich culture and history.
Venues vary throughout Harlem. 212-862-7200. harlemweek.com. Free or by invitation only.

US Open Tennis
Late August–Early September
The greatest tennis pros in the world descend upon Queens to play in this fourth and final Grand Slam.
US Open Tennis Center (Flushing Meadow Park). 914-696-7000. usopen.org. Ticket prices vary.

EVENTS CALENDAR

SEPTEMBER

West Indian Carnival Festival
Labor Day Weekend
An exuberant celebration of West Indian culture with delicious food, a colorful parade, and performances at the Brooklyn Museum. *Eastern Parkway, Brooklyn. 718-467-1797. wiadca.com. Prices vary.*

Howl! Festival
Early September
This alternative festival celebrates the tradition of downtown art, incorporating everything from painting slams to hip-hop performances. *Various venues in the East Village. howlfestival.com. Free.*

Broadway on Broadway
Mid-September
Some of the greatest Broadway stars perform for an audience of tens of thousands at an enormous outdoor stage in Times Square. *42nd St and Broadway. broadwayonbroadway.com. Free.*

San Gennaro
Mid-September
Street vendors hawking cannolis, sausages, and Tony Soprano t-shirts line the crowded streets of this ten-day feast. *Mulberry St and the surrounding area. 212-768-9320. littleitalynyc.com. Free.*

Fall for Dance
Late September
Ten straight nights of unbeatable dance performances, from famed solo artists to the best ensembles in the world, in every style imaginable. *New York City Center. 130 W 56th St, between 5th and 6th Ave. 212-581-1212. nycitycenter.org. $10 per event.*

New York Film Festival
Late September-October
Features some of the year's best international and domestic films. Actors and directors often hold Q&A sessions after their movie. *Alice Tully Hall. 1941 Broadway, at W 64th St. 212-875-5050. filmlinc.com. Ticket prices vary.*

OCTOBER

Animal Blessing at St. John the Divine
Early October
A parade precedes this ceremony in honor of St. Francis of Assissi, the patron saint of animals. Join the procession or service to catch a glimpse of llamas, camels, monkeys, and more. *1047 Amsterdam Ave, at 112th St. 212-316-7490. stjohnthedivine.org. Free.*

Medieval Festival at the Cloisters
Early October
Lords and vassals from an archaic past visit the vine-laden paths of Fort Tryon Park for food, performances, and even rounds of jousting. *Fort Tryon Park. 212-795-1600. whidc.org/home.html. Free.*

Underground Comedy Festival
Early October
A refreshing alternative to the often dry and predictable New York comedy circuit, featuring major stars alongside many lesser-knowns.

Various venues. 212-501-2089. nyunderground comedyfestival.com. Many free events.

New Yorker Festival
Mid-October
A weekend-long series of fascinating panels and speakers, from the editors of the New Yorker to Stephen Colbert.
Various venues. newyorker.com/festival. Ticket prices vary; sales begin in September.

Greenwich Village Halloween Parade
Oct 31st
The largest in the country and open to anyone with a flair for ostentation. Make your way to the Village to march or watch.
6th Ave, from Spring to 23rd St. halloween-nyc.com. Free.

Procession of the Ghouls
Oct 31st
Silent horror films play at this cavernous institution on Halloween. Afterwards, costumed ghouls float their way up and down the aisles.
St. John the Divine (1047 Amsterdam Ave at 112th St). 212-316-7540. stjohndivine.org. $15.

Chocolate Show
Late October-Early November
The world's best chocolatiers exhibit their wares, demonstrate their craft, and give free samples.
Metropolitan Pavilion (18th St at 6th Ave). chocolateshow.com. Approximately $30 per day.

NOVEMBER

New York City Marathon
Early November
This epic 26.2-mile trek through all five boroughs is open to all, from professional runners to dabbling masochists.
Forts Wortsworth, Staten Island to Central Park. 212-423-2249. nycmarathon.org. $11 application fee, $171 Non-Member Entry Fee.

New York Comedy Festival
Early November
Five days of hilarity and outrageousness as

world-famous stand-up comics take to the stages of New York.
Various venues. nycomedyfestival.com. Ticket prices vary.

Macy's Thanksgiving Day Parade
Thanksgiving Day
A modern marvel of celebrities and gargantuan inflatables take Manhattan by storm.
From Central Park West and W 79th St to Broadway and 34th St. macys.com. Free.

Radio City Christmas Spectacular
Mid-November to December
The young at heart and lovers of the Christmas spirit are sure to enjoy the high-kicking, festive Rockettes at this yearly performance.
Radio City Music Hall (6th Ave at 50th St). 212-307-7171. radiocity.com. Tickets $40-150.

DECEMBER

Tree Lighting at Rockefeller
Early December
Stars appear both at the stage and the top of the tree in this New York City favorite, officially marking the beginning of the holiday season—no matter what Christmas decorations Duane Reade starts selling in October.
Rockefeller Center (5th Ave at 50th St). 212-632-3975. Free.

Menorah Lighting Ceremony
Hanukkah
A cherry picker is necessary to light the 32-foot-tall candelabra on these eight holy nights. Traditional dance and musical performances are also accompanied by belt-busting snacks.
Grand Army Plaza (5th Ave at 59th St). Free.

New Year's Eve
December 31st
Bring your ski goggles and brace yourself for frostbite when waiting for the magic silver ball to drop—the only truly New York way to ring in a new year.
Times Square (42nd St at Broadway). 212-768-1560. timessquarenyc.org. Free.

WALKING TOURS

Make sure you're equipped with a pair of well-worn shoes and an MTA day pass before you embark on one of these custom-designed Walking Tours—they'll each take the greater part of one entire day, and require a lot of dashing about from place to place. And all are accompanied by a map graphic detailing the route, so don't worry about getting lost.

If you're a bibliophile, an aspiring novelist, or an admirer of Holden Caulfield, start with **Literary Landmarks**. You'll visit the stomping grounds of the Beat poets, the room where Dorothea Parker lunched with the "Vicious Circle," *Catcher in the Rye* hotspots, as well as places featured in children's literature.

For those more interested in aesthetics and design, **Public Art and Architecture** showcases New York's breathtaking mansions, Gothic churches, innovative sculptures, towering edifices and exquisite midtown murals.

Cinema buffs and *Gossip Girl* devotees will delight in **TV and Movie Sites**, a romp through the filming locations of shows, classics and blockbusters such as *Seinfeld, Breakfast at Tiffany's, Spiderman* and *Godzilla*—as well as Blair Waldorf's empire.

The **Music** tour traces the footsteps of the greatest rock and roll and jazz legends, covering everything from John Lennon's apartment to the backdrop of Bob Dylan's second studio album to the birthplace of the "Lindy hop."

LITERARY LANDMARKS

You'll notice a trend at New York City parties: a good third of the young people "want to write." This is a city steeped in stories—a walk through New York is a walk through the stomping grounds both of beloved wordsmiths and the characters they penned. With a good pair of shoes, an MTA day pass, and a Moleskin notebook, you can explore the sites that have inspired the likes of Jack Kerouac, Dorothy Parker, and Walt Whitman... and perhaps be inspired yourself.

Begin by taking the 1 train to 150th St and Riverside Drive. Standing across the street from the apartment of the *Invisible Man* author, the **Ralph Ellison Memorial** is an austere six-inch sheet of metal sporting a man-shaped cutout. Come back another time and frame the sunset through it.

Walk south and a bit east to get back on the ❶ at 145th St, and ride it down to 116th and Broadway. **Columbia University** *(2960 Broadway & 116th St)* brims with literary history, but many of the prominent writers who studied there scorned it. Spanish poet and playwright Federico Garcia Lorca lived in **John Jay Hall** *(corner of 114th St & Amsterdam Ave)* and **Furnald Hall** *(corner of 115th St & Broadway)*. He was enrolled in Columbia's School of General Studies, but spent most of his time romping through the city, intoxicated by "its extrahuman architecture, its furious rhythm, its geometry and anguish." Likewise, Langston Hughes spent most of his truncated undergraduate career off campus exploring Harlem.

1940s students Jack Kerouac (who matriculated on a football scholarship and later dropped out) and Allen Ginsberg (who took six years to graduate) drank at 113th and Broadway's **West End** bar, where they talked endlessly to other members of what would become known as the Beat movement. But times change—the iconic dive has been replaced by a Cuban restaurant, **Havana Central at the West End** *(2911 Broadway, btwn 113th & 114th St)*. Kerouac and Ginsberg would likely have groused about this, but don't let that stop you from stopping in for a frita—it's definitely still Beat-worthy.

For dessert, cross one avenue west and walk a couple blocks south to the **Hungarian Pastry Shop** *(1030 Amsterdam Ave & 112th St)*, long the home of many (slightly grimy) young literary men and women. Afterwards, step across the street to the **Cathedral of St. John the Divine** *(1047 Amsterdam Ave & 112th St)* to see the **American Poets' Corner**. Some of the nation's most distinguished writers, including Robert Frost and Gertrude Stein, are honored here with quotations under a stained glass window.

Catch the M4 bus heading east on 110th St and ride it south along the edge of Central Park to the **Frick Collection** *(1 E 70th St & 5th Ave)*. "It's in the Frick," Frank O'Hara wrote, "which thank heavens you haven't gone to yet so we can

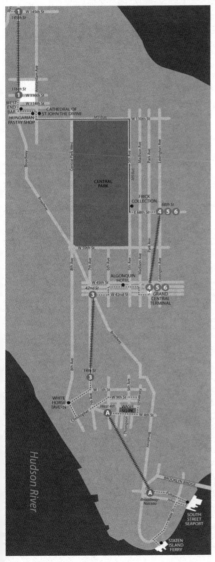

go together the first time." A notable poet in the New York School, O'Hara wrote frequently about the twin gifts of anonymity and community provided by Manhattan's neverending hustle. He worked for a long time at the Museum of Modern Art, but he loved the air of intimacy that immediately envelops visitors of the Frick—a gallery converted from a mansion.

Walk a few blocks east to Lexington Ave, and take the ❹❺ or ❻ south from 68th St to **Grand Central Terminal** (*87 E 42nd St & Park Ave*). Edith Wharton pictured an earlier incarnation of the station when she wrote the opening of *House of Mirth* there, but Grand Central is where the character Lily Bart's free-fall began. Walk a block east and then stroll north along Madison Ave just as Lily and Laurence did.

If your head's spinning by this point, you're not alone—"I might repeat to myself slowly and soothingly, a list of quotations beautiful from minds profound," the ever-quotable Dorothy Parker once said, "if I can remember any of the damn things." Turn left onto 44th St and cleanse your palette of excessive intellectualism with a taste of decadence at the **Algonquin Hotel** (*59 W 44th St, btwn 5th & 6th Ave*). Parker lunched here in the 1920s with the most delightfully bitchy circle of writers that this city may ever have seen. If you're feeling well-heeled, you can grab a meal at its luxurious Round Table room.

Parker's real solution to dilemmas was generally a stiff drink, and you might have better luck finding one of those at the **White Horse Tavern** (*567 Hudson St at 11th St*). Take the ❶❷❸ from Times Square to 14th St, walk a few blocks south on 7th Ave, turn right onto 11th St, and walk two blocks to the intersection with Hudson St. This old-fashioned bar is where Dylan Thomas raged off into his sodden good night in 1953. He fell into a coma on the sidewalk outside after finishing his eighteenth shot of whiskey.

LITERARY LANDMARKS 71

LITERARY LANDMARKS

When you're done, walk south along Hudson St, turn left onto Christopher St, right onto 9th St, and right once more onto University Place. Stroll through the ever-cultured **West Village,** where young writers and bohemians flocked to from the 1940s to the 1970s. A few blocks further south on University Place will take you to the north end of **Washington Square Park**, home to the Henry James novel. Join James by frowning at the Arch, which he considered a gauche intrusion on the public square.

It should be evening now. Hop on the Ⓐ just outside the square, get off at the Broadway-Nassau stop, and walk east on Fulton to watch the **Brooklyn Bridge** light up from the **South Street Seaport**. Everyone from Kerouac to Hart Crane to Marianne Moore has written about it, and if the Brooklyn Ferry is gone it will stand for Walt Whitman as well. Walk south and finish up with a slow round trip on the **Staten Island Ferry**. The MTA quotes Edna St. Vincent Millay's poem on the terminal wall in huge letters, and she really did catch a bit of the city's sparer night-magic when she wrote:

"We were very tired, we were very merry—
We had gone back and forth all night on the ferry.
It was bare and bright, and smelled like a stable—
But we looked into a fire, we leaned across a table,
We lay on a hilltop underneath the moon;
And the whistles kept blowing, and the dawn came soon."

KIDS' LIT MINI-TOUR

Start in **Times Square**. The intersection of 42nd St and Broadway looks strikingly different than it did when *The Cricket in Times Square* was published in 1960, but there's still no better example of New York's magnetic bustle. If, like Chester the cricket, you need a few minutes to absorb everything, take a rest on the pedestrian plaza.

A fifteen-block walk to the north and a two-block walk to the east will take you to the **Plaza Hotel** (*768 5th Ave & Central Park South*), or the home of the inimitable Eloise. The doormen may not let you rush up and down in the elevators like a sassy six-year-old, but you could try. Also, take the time to stop by **F.A.O. Schwartz** (*767 5th Ave, btwn W 58th St & Central Park South*), the toy paradise across the street.

When you're done drooling over the larger-than-life stuffed animals, wander into **Central Park** and walk north along its East Drive. Sit around on some rocks and complain, like Pee-tah and his buddy Jimmy in Judy Blume's *Tales of a Fourth Grade Nothing*. After all, it's really tough when your little brother eats your pet turtle. Around 74th St, at the top of the **Conservatory Pond**, join statues of Alice in Wonderland and her companions for your own unbirthday party.

Emerge onto 5th Ave via the park's 79th St Transverse Road and walk up to 82nd St, where you'll find the imposing **Metropolitan Museum of Art** (*1000 5th Ave at 82nd St*). You'd need a stay as long as that of the Kincaid children in *The Mixed Up Files of Mrs. Basil E. Frankweiler* to see even half of its staggering collection, so you're best off sticking to a few exhibits. Check out the French period rooms at the back of the first floor: wouldn't you like to live here too?

Finally, walk east to Madison Ave and catch the M4 bus up to Madeleine L'Engle's spiritual home, the **Cathedral of St. John the Divine** (*1047 Amsterdam Ave at 112th St*). The author of *A Wrinkle in Time* served as the institution's librarian for thirty years, and it's the setting for most of *The Young Unicorns*. A few minutes of reflection may leave you with some insight into the religious awe that pervades L'Engle's work. And an encounter with the peacocks in the garden may remind you of the joy she took in city's magical quirks.

A DAY IN THE LIFE OF HOLDEN CAULFIELD

So maybe you don't feel comfortable listing it as a favorite book on your Facebook profile any-more—after all, *The Catcher in the Rye* was emo before there was even a word for it—but if you claim it never meant something to you, chances are that you're just being a big "phony," as Holden Caulfield might say. So grab your copy, embrace feelings of disillusionment, and storm your way through the streets that Holden walked. Bonus points if your book's the red version with the sad yellow title font.

Start at **Grand Central Terminal** (*87 E 42nd St & Park Ave*), where Holden himself entered the city. If you arrive at morning rush hour, the mass of glum faces should put you in the right mood.

Head north along 5th Ave and up to 49th St to reach **Rockefeller Center**. You're in luck if it's ice-skating season, although mercifully or tragically they no longer rent out "those darling little skating skirts" that Holden describes.

Take the B train—or a taxi, if you've got some extra dough—up to the **Museum of Natural History** (*Central Park West and 79th St*). Much of the "pottery and straw baskets and stuff like that" is on the first floor, along with vintage dioramas.

Now enter Central Park at 77th St and walk south along its West Drive. Turn right onto the 65th St Transverse Road and head toward the **Central Park Zoo** (here, if you have company, he or she must walk on the opposite side of the street and behave like a miffed ten-year-old). Pay your entry fee and wander around aimlessly. The sea lions are still in their pool and the exhibits make good conversation-starters if you want to strike up a Caulfieldian talk with a stranger.

Walk north along East Drive to the iconic **Central Park Carousel**. You can mount one of its horses for two dollars, although you might find it hard to remain properly depressed. Otherwise, pick out a little girl in a blue coat to watch traveling around and around.

To finish up, walk south to the park's edge and sit down by the **Pond**—yes, that's its official name. Take a deep breath. Chances are that, for now, the ducks are happy right where they are.

PUBLIC ART & ARCHITE

You don't have to visit Museum Mile or go gallery-hopping to see art in NYC—architectural gems, historical monuments, and eye-popping sculptures are on every block. While each neighborhood has its own collection of significant artistic sites, Brooklyn Heights and Lower Manhattan are the perfect places to begin your exploration—from the iconic Brooklyn Bridge to the palatial City Hall, from 1760s tombstones to 20th-century sculptures, here you'll find art from any era in practically any style. And best of all, it's completely free.

Take the ❷ or ❸ to Clark St and exit on Henry St. This is **Brooklyn Heights**, a quiet neighborhood full of 19th-century houses that sit on flower-lined, cobblestone streets. It was declared a historic district by the city in 1965. Stroll down Henry St to see three red-brick **Federal-style townhouses** in a row between Clark and Love St that date back to 1843.

Turn right on Pierrepont St and then left on Hicks St to find many more historical townhouses. On the left, you'll also see **Grace Court Alley**—a mews (row of stables) built for the mansions on Remsen St. While the buggy-sized proportions of the red brick archways don't seem to align with modern sensibilities, tucked in with these openings is a familiar single car garage.

Across the street is **Grace Church** (*254 Hicks St at Grace Ct*). Built in 1847 by Richard Upjohn, this church and its attached school are brownstone Gothic-style masterpieces, bordered by the lush back gardens of nearby mansions.

From Grace Church, backtrack along Hicks St and turn left on Pierrepont, which ends at the **Brooklyn Promenade**, a public walkway that runs over the Brooklyn-Queens Expressway. Stop at a bench for a minute to enjoy the panorama—see the **Statue of Liberty** without waiting in line and get a postcard-perfect view of **Lower Manhattan**.

To reach the **Brooklyn Bridge pedestrian walk**, head up Orange St, and turn left on Henry St. Now turn right on Middagh St, left on Cadman Plaza West, right again on Prospect St, and climb the staircase on Prospect between Cadman Plaza West and East. Take in more breathtaking views of the East River,

the Manhattan Bridge, and the Brooklyn and Manhattan waterfronts as you hike across this national historic landmark.

After a mile of dodging tourists and bicyclists,

head onto the equally bustling Centre St. Turn right on Centre to arrive at the **Municipal Building** (*1 Centre St & Chambers St*). This McKim, Meade, and White skyscraper from 1914 boasts beautiful Renaissance-style outdoor spaces, including a sculpture-decorated central

arch and a forest of white columns and vaulted ceilings. Look up to see **Civic Fame**, the city's second highest sculpture after the Statue of Liberty. The five parapets on the building and five points on the statue's crown celebrate the union of the city's boroughs.

Now cross the street to **City Hall** (*249 Broadway & Murray St*), which bears far more resemblance to a European palace than a New World civic center. Mangin and McComb designed this majestic white structure in 1811, combining French Renaissance and Georgian styles. It stands as the oldest city hall in the country that is still used for its original governmental functions. Visit on a Wednesday and sign up for a tour at the information booth at Broadway and Barclay.

If it's not Wednesday, skip the interior and enjoy the surrounding **City Hall Park**, or the City Common, as it was known in 1700. This sizeable verdant expanse of almost nine acres is a surprisingly pleasant find in the crowded downtown area. Take a moment to sit by the fountain and people-watch—businesspeople come by on lunch break, and if you're lucky you'll glimpse joyful newlyweds emerging from City Hall.

Exit onto Broadway and turn left towards the **Woolworth Building** (*233 Broadway, btwn Barclay St and Park Pl*). Crane your neck as you walk past to appreciate the full grandeur of this intricately-decorated Gothic giant—it stands at almost 800 feet tall.

Continue down Broadway to **St. Paul's Chapel** (*209 Broadway & Fulton St*), Manhattan's only pre-Revolutionary church building. Built in the 1760s in the English Georgian style, St. Paul's may be modest in size, but it's unconventionally constructed and has a formidable history—inside you can see George Washington's pew. The many windows and the white arches inject its small interior with an airy, open feel.

Exit the church into the 240-year-old **cemetery**, another patch of unexpected green in bustling lower Manhattan. And behind the church lies the **Bell of Hope**, cast by the Whitechapel Foundry. It rings every September 11th to honor peacemakers and inspire hope in the face of tragedy.

Continue along Broadway and turn right on Cortlandt St to reach Trinity St. This is **Ground Zero**, the former site of the World Trade Center. The Twin Towers once defined the New York City skyline at 110 stories each, and their absence is just as striking. The area is currently under construction to erect new office buildings and a memorial to the September 11th victims.

Turn left on Liberty St to return to Broadway, then walk along Cedar to reach the **Chase Manhattan building and plaza**, the first large pedestrian court in the Financial District. Take a moment to relax in the shade of Jean Debuffet's massive **Group of Four Trees**, a black and white series of curving planes that is

a marked contrast to its backdrop of rectangular skyscrapers. Finished in 1972, the piece is part of a series called "L'Hourloupe," which, in the words of Debuffet, "evoke[s] something rumbling and threatening with tragic overtones."

Next, cross the plaza, and turn right on Pine St, left on Nassau St, and left again on Wall St. You've reached the **Federal Hall National Memorial** (*26 Wall St & Broad St*), the 1789 inauguration site of George Washington. Today, a statue of him stands approximately where he took the oath of office. The Neoclassical building marries the Greek Parthenon's front temple façade with the Roman Pantheon's dome-shaped interior.

MIDTOWN MURALS

Start by taking the 4, 5, or 6 to **Grand Central Terminal** *(87 E 42nd St & Park Ave)*. The ceiling of the Main Concourse is a massive astronomical mural painted by Paul Cesar Helleu in 1912. Grime from tar and nicotine covered it for years until it was cleaned to reveal the original clear blue color, but there is still a dark patch of sky to remind viewers of the work done for restoration. If you look closely, you'll notice that the section of the sky Helleu painted is actually backwards.

Now exit onto Lexington Ave to reach the **Chrysler Building** *(405 Lexington Ave, btwn 42nd and 43rd St)*. This art-deco beauty was the world's tallest edifice from 1930 to 1931. Look up as you enter the lobby to see **Energy, Result, Workmanship and Transportation**, a mural by Edward Trumbull. One of the world's largest paintings, it is a celebration of how man harnesses energy to solve problems.

When you get back to 42nd St, walk west to 5th Ave, and turn left to arrive at the main branch of the **New York Public Library** *(476 5th Ave & 41st St)*. The outside façade is an impeccable example of Beaux-Arts architecture, but head up to the third floor to discover a myriad of mural masterpieces. Those in the **McGraw Rotunda** were painted by Edward Laning, and depict the story of the recorded word. The 50-foot high ceilings of the **Rose Main Reading Room** are graced with magnificent cloud-filled skies stretching across three large panels.

Finally, exit back onto 5th Ave, and walk north to 50th St. This is **Rockefeller Center** *(45 Rockefeller Plaza and 50th St)*, a collection of office buildings and public artwork. Inside the central art deco GE Building is **Man's Conquests**, a mural by José María Sert. Diego Rivera was originally commissioned to paint it, but he was fired when the Rockefellers realized that one of the main figures he depicted was Lenin. The mural has a man at the center carrying a log over his shoulders. If you look up and watch his knees as you walk under him, he appears to shift his weight from one leg to the other.

Back outside, cross Wall St to reach the **New York Stock Exchange** *(11 Wall St, btwn Broadway and Broad St)*. Another temple-like edifice, this iconic financial center looms in the American psyche as the center of the business world. George B. Post designed the 1903 structure, and Ward and Paul Bartlett made the pediment sculpture, **Integrity Protecting the Works of Man**. Take in the grandeur of the massive, marble American flag, but don't expect a tour—the public is no longer allowed inside.

Now go left down Wall St to reach **Trinity Church**. Its narrow, crocketed spire sticks out from the surrounding financial buildings on Wall St and seems to pierce the sky. Inside you'll find a cavernous assemblage of stained glass and vaulted ceilings which date back to its original construction in 1846.

Venture outside to the church to see the **Trinity Root**, a new sculpture by Steve Tobin. On September 11, 2001, debris from the Two Towers toppled a 100-year-old sycamore tree at one of Trinity's parish chapels. Despite its crowded surroundings, however, the tree didn't knock anything over when it fell. Inspired by this miracle, Tobin created the sculpture for the fourth anniversary of September 11th, using the roots as a metaphor for the community's strength.

PUBLIC ART & ARCHITECTURE 77

TV & MOVIE SITES

Since the 1940s, filmmakers have frequently abandoned the easy gloss of Hollywood and set their cameras on New York to capture the energy and grandeur that can't be matched on any studio backlot. For the traveling film buff, New York City offering a wealth of cinematic hotspots as rich and diverse as the films and television shows in which they were featured.

Begin by taking the ❶ train to 116th and Broadway, enter the **Columbia University** gates, and amble down the beautiful tree-lined College Walk. James Franco, currently a student in the graduate writing program, is not unfamiliar with the campus—his character in *Spiderman* (2002) was dropped off by his father on the steps of Low Memorial Library (to the left of College Walk). These steps are also where Bill Murray, Dan Aykroyd, and Harold Ramis hatched their business plan in *Ghostbusters* (1984).

Walking south on Broadway, you'll pass the **Columbia Bookstore** (*2922 Broadway at W 115th St*). This is the Barnes & Noble where Kate Winslet's character worked as a bookseller in *Eternal Sunshine of the Spotless Mind* (2004).

And three blocks down is **Tom's Restaurant** (*2880 Broadway at W 112th St*), which *Seinfeld* fans will recognize as the exterior of Monk's Café. Though cash only, this inexpensive diner is also a popular late-night spot for the drunk and hungry.

Next, take a right at 112th, and walk west one block to Riverside Drive. Stroll about a mile south on Riverside to the **96th St Bridge**, where jealous ex-girlfriend Cameron Diaz drove herself and Tom Cruise off the bridge and into the wall below in *Vanilla Sky* (2001).

Head into Riverside Park and walk downtown until you reach the **91st St Garden**, the verdant, flowery backdrop of the final scene in *You've Got Mail* (1998). Here "Shopgirl" (Meg Ryan) finally discovered the true identity of her internet love, "NY152" (Tom Hanks). Don't waste time looking for the garden sign in the

movie—a previous fan already snatched it!

Leave the park and walk southeast through the Upper West Side to the **American Museum of Natural History** (*Central Park West at 81st St*). This is the titular setting of *Night at the Museum* (2006),where Ben Stiller plays the museum's newest security guard in for a series of nasty surprises. The museum also includes the Clash of the Titans exhibit in the ocean life wing, which was featured prominently in *The Squid and the Whale* (2006).

At 72nd St and Central Park West, you'll find the historic **Dakota**, built in 1884 as one of the City's first apartment buildings. Its most famous current tenants include Lauren Bacall and Yoko Ono, but for horror buffs, the building itself is the star. The historic structure portrayed the fictional "Bramford" in Roman Polanski's *Rosemary's Baby*, where it acted as a haven for urbanite Satanists.

Enter Central Park at the 72nd St entrance. Walk in until you reach the **Cherry Hill** roundabout where Adam Sandler's character got his son to score him a date with a hot lawyer in *Big Daddy* (1999).

Depart from Cherry Hill and continue to walk along the main road. After a bit you'll reach **Bethesda Fountain** just to your left. The angelic statue at the center was a focal setting for the HBO adaptation of Tony Kushner's *Angels in America* (2003), and it was here that Amy Adams belted "That's How You Know" with a mass of dancing park visitors in Disney's *Enchanted* (2007).

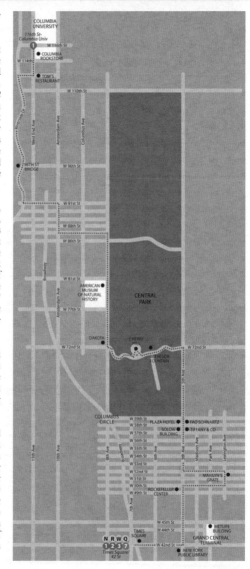

TV & MOVIE SITES

Continue walking east through the park until you reach 5th Ave. Take a right here and head south to 59th St, where you will see the **Plaza Hotel** (*5th Ave at Central Park South*) on your right. It was here Kevin McCallister (Macaulay Culkin) checked in for his solo Christmas vacation in *Home Alone 2: Lost in New York* (1992). During one of his adventures in the city, Kevin hires a limousine to take him to Duncan's Toy Chest, a shop modeled after F.A.O. Schwartz.

To see the real **F.A.O. Schwartz** (*767 5th Ave at W 58th St*), cross 5th Ave to the corner of 58th St. Overzealous Upper East Side parents are known to hire personal shoppers for their budding heirs and heiresses here. Enter, ascend the escalator, and head to the back of the second floor to see the larger-than-life piano that appeared in the Tom Hanks movie *Big* (1988). The piano is always available for the public to play, unless the employees are busy treating audiences to a performance of "Heart and Soul" or "Fur Elise."

After leaving F.A.O. Schwartz, walk south on

5th Ave and look down W 57th St for a glimpse of the 50-story **Solow Building** (*9 West 57th St, between 5th and 6th Ave*). Imagine a colossal letter M perched on top of this monolith of black glass, marble, and steel—it served as the headquarters for the villain Mugatu in *Zoolander* (2001).

Now it's time to put on your best "magnum" model face because the next stop is the **Tiffany & Co.** (*727 5th Ave, between W 57th and W 58th St*) from Audrey Hepburn's now iconic *Breakfast at Tiffany's* (1961). Enter on the southeast corner on 57th and 5th Ave to see the store's 128.54-carat golden icon, the Tiffany Diamond. It has only been worn by two people since it was originally discovered in South Africa in 1878—one of whom was, of course, Hepburn herself.

When you get to 52nd St, walk east to Park Ave. Look downtown and check out the **MetLife Building** (*200 Park Ave, between E 44th and E 45th St*), once the PanAm building, a prominent NYC landmark that was the site of another well-known action movie. Rather than use his strength to help the city like *Spiderman*, however, the monster from *Godzilla* (1998) used it as his playground, demolishing this skyscraper among other large edifices. The MetLife building was also featured in *Coogan's Bluff* (1968) and *Catch Me If You Can* (2002).

Proceed east on 52nd St until you reach Lexington Ave. At first, it may be difficult to see which movie was filmed here. Cross Lexington and walk down the sidewalk between 52nd and 51st St. If a subway happens to be going under you, make sure to keep your skirt from blowing up! Yes, this is the same **subway grate** on which Marilyn Monroe stood in *The Seven Year Itch* (1955), wearing a white halter dress— needless to say, her pose has been preserved in cinematic history.

Walk south on Lexington to 50th St. Turn right and return to 5th Ave, at which point you should walk downtown until you see **Rockefeller Center** on your right between 50th and 49th St. It was there that, after checking into the Plaza Hotel, little Kevin from *Home Alone 2*

GOSSIP GIRL MINI TOUR

Start by taking the ⑥ train to the 96th St station. Walk south on Lexington Ave. At 93rd St, turn right and head west until you reach the **Synod of Bishops** (*74 E 93rd St, between Madison and Park Ave*). This is one of the locations used for Constance Billard/St. Jude's, the school attended by everyone's favorite cast of sexually-charged adolescents. As Blair Waldorf (or Queen B, as she often prefers to be called) rules over her kingdom of (dis)loyal followers, students sneak through the halls taking pictures of anything and everything worth babbling about.

Continue east toward 5th Ave, and head down 5th until you arrive at the **Metropolitan Museum of Art** (*1000 5th Ave at 82nd St*). The front steps leading to museum's entrance is where Blair and her posse sit on a daily basis. Take a seat and relish the fact that you have been granted temporary license to perch on the Queen's most formidable throne.

Head one block east and walk south on Madison Ave. Stroll down this luxurious shopping street with your head held high, past countless boutiques that could easily be home to Eleanor Waldorf Designs. At 61st St, take a quick left to arrive at **Geisha Restaurant** (*33 E 61st St btwen Madison & Park Ave*). This is where, in the pilot episode, Nate takes Blair out for a desperately apologetic sushi dinner.

Walk south on Madison on 59th St. You will pass **Barney's New York** (*660 Madison Ave at E 61st St*), one of the major clothing stores often mentioned in the show. And no wonder—from shoes to dresses to headbands, Barney's has all of the essentials for an up-and-coming Upper East Side princess.

Finally, continue down Madison to 51st St to see the glamorous Van Der Woodsen family residence—**The Palace Hotel** (*455 Madison Ave at E 51st St*). Its courtyard was host to a near fistfight between Chuck and Dan, its lobby was where Dan first asked Serena out on a date, and its **Gilt Restaurant** was where Blair and Serena had their first one-on-one talk after Serena's return to the Upper East Side. Stay as long as you like—if you're there at the right time, you may even see them filming for next season!

(1992) thought to himself that all he wanted for Christmas was to be reunited with his family.

Continue down 5th Ave to 42nd St, where you will see the **New York Public Library** (*476 5th Ave, between W 40th and W 42nd St*) on your right. This was where one of *Spiderman*'s most memorable quotes was uttered—a concerned Uncle Ben told Peter Parker that "with great power comes great responsibility" in a car parked right in front of the 5th Ave entrance.

Finally, turn right on 42nd St and walk east until you reach an impenetrable mass of tourists and a dizzying panoply of digital advertisements—that is, **Times Square**. While the flesh shops and porno theaters have been cleared away, this was a central setting to Martin Scorsese's *Taxi Driver* (1976), and, in a historic first, the entire Square was evacuated to create the haunting opening images of a deserted New York in *Vanilla Sky* (2001). Additionally, ABC's *Good Morning America* and MTV's *Total Request Live* were filmed in studios facing this bustling intersection. The best known show of all would have to be Dick Clark's annual TV special, which documents the New Year's Eve celebration and the over one million people that inundate Times Square each year.

MUSIC: ROCK 'n' ROLL

New York City has played a pivotal role in sculpting both the history and future of Rock 'n' Roll. Bob Dylan, Jimi Hendrix, John Lennon, The Velvet Underground, The Ramones (and many other legendary artists) lived, performed, and composed some of their most memorable songs in the neighborhoods of Manhattan. As Lennon once said, "If I'd lived in Roman times, I'd have lived in Rome. Where else? Today, America is the Roman Empire, and New York is Rome itself."

Begin by heading to the **Dakota Apartments** (*119-121 Central Park West at W 72nd St*). Completed in 1884, this structure is not only one of Manhattan's first apartment buildings, but also where John Lennon lived and died. Across the street in Central Park is **Strawberry Fields** (*West Side between 71st and 74th St*), a memorial to this extraordinary legend that includes a black and white mosaic along a path, detailing the word "Imagine."

Take the ⑧ train down to 7th Ave and head around the block to the **Ed Sullivan Theater** (*1697-1699 Broadway, between W 53rd and W 54th St*). It now houses *The Late Show with David Letterman* but was once home to the *Ed Sullivan Show*. Within this 400-seat theater Elvis Presley hip-thrusted his way into the hearts of American girls, and the Beatles launched their British Invasion.

At 50th St, hop on the ❶ to 23rd St, near which you'll find the renowned **Hotel Chelsea** (*222 W 23rd Street, between 7th and 8th Ave*). As the first building to be preserved by the city as a cultural landmark, it boasts a laundry list of famous guests, including Jimi Hendrix, The Ramones, and Rufus Wainwright. Many popular songs also contain allusions to the hotel, such as Bob Dylan's "Sara" and Joni Mitchell's "Chelsea Morning."

Now take the ❶ down to Christopher St–Sheridan Sq. At the corner of W 4th and Jones St you'll see the backdrop for the cover photo of *The Freewheelin' Bob Dylan* (*161 W 4th St, between 6th and 7th Ave*), the album that established him as one of the greatest songwriters in history. The photo depicts Dylan and his former girlfriend Suze Rotolo huddled together, strolling down snow-covered W 4th St just a couple of blocks away from his Greenwich Village apartment.

It's only a short walk back uptown to **Electric Lady Studios** (*52 West 8th St, between MacDougal St & Ave of the Americas*). Behind the plain stucco walls and black-curtained windows lies one of the most famous recording studios in existence. Built in 1970 for Jimi Hendrix, it was the second personal recording facility ever constructed. Unfortunately, Hendrix died just months after its creation, but since then hundreds of artists have recorded there, including M.I.A., Lil' Wayne, and U2.

Just down MacDougal is **Café Wha?** (*115 Macdougal St between Bleecker and W 3rd St*), distinguished by a bright neon rainbow sign. In its six decades in the East Village, this small but significant cultural landmark has featured knockout, energy-charged performances by artists such as Bob Dylan, Jimi Hendrix, and

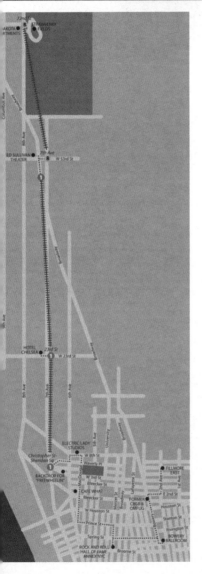

Bruce Springsteen. Comedians Woody Allen and Bill Cosby also made regular appearances during the venue's heyday in the 1960s.

Walk down Macdougal toward Bleeker St, then turn left on Prince St and right on Mercer St to reach the **Rock and Roll Hall of Fame Annex NYC** (*76 Mercer St, between Spring and Broome St*). Though the Hall of Fame itself is in Cleveland, the Annex houses "New York Rocks," a section dedicated to the city's rock history that also displays personal vestiges of rock icons like Billy Joel and John Lennon.

Now turn right onto Spring St, make another right at Bowery St, and turn left at Delancey to catch a show at the **The Bowery Ballroom** (*6 Delancey St, between Bowery and Christie St*). This building was converted into one of New York's smaller venues for indie groups such as The Hold Steady and The Decemberists. Its slightly cramped size creates an intimate vibe (complemented by a velvet-draped lounge and leather chairs) absent from larger venues. And with unbeatable acoustics, it still attracts well-known performers.

Walk back uptown on Bowery to the former site of the iconic club **CBGB & OMFUG** (*315 Bowery at Bleecker St*), often regarded as the birthplace of punk rock. Here, The Ramones and other bands drilled out the melodies that instigated an entire counter-culture in the 1970s. Recently, however, contemporary designer John Varvatos has converted the club into a high-end clothing store, preserving a section of the original wall under glass as a tribute to its former tenants. Visit for the history—a Varvatos t-shirt runs upwards of $60.

Finish by turning right on 2nd St and then left on 2nd Ave to reach another gentrified former venue, **The Fillmore East** (*105 2nd Ave, at 6th St*). Though now a bank, during the three years it was open as a music venue it was a favorite performance spot of classic rock bands including CCR, The Doors, Led Zeppelin, and The Who. Dozens of live albums were recorded here, such as Jimi Hendrix's *Band of Gypsys* (1970).

MUSIC: JAZZ

This city is the homeland of bebop and the herald of the Big Band (swing) period. Ella Fitzgerald, Duke Ellington, Billie Holiday, and other influential icons not only performed in New York City, but also launched their careers and catapulted to fame here. New York has defined jazz as much as jazz has defined New York, and it will continue to be the birthplace of many more legends to come.

Begin at **St. Nick's Pub** (*773 Saint Nicholas Ave, at W 149th St*), where the beat hasn't stopped since its opening in the 1930s. Located in Harlem's celebrated Sugar Hill district, St. Nick's is New York's oldest operating jazz club. In the 1940s, it was owned by Luckey Roberts, Duke Ellington's piano player and a music legend in his own right. Over seven decades later, this historic haunt has managed to stay true to its roots—a cheek-to-cheek crowd of music lovers packs in every day of the week, especially on Monday night for the live jam session.

Head west to illustrious Lenox Avenue, now called Malcolm X Boulevard, and the former site of **The Cotton Club** (*644 Malcolm X Blvd, at W 142nd St*). From its establishment in

1920 to its closing in 1978, the Club hosted a veritable who's who of jazz history, including Ella Fitzgerald, Billie Holiday, and Nat King Cole. Here Duke Ellington, who performed with the house band from 1927 to 1931, garnered widespread recognition from his radio broadcasts. However, the Club's reflection of racist trends tarnished its reputation—the owners constructed sets reminiscent of southern plantations (hence its name) and instructed musicians to compose "jungle music."

Just one block down you'll find a plaque commemorating the **Savoy Ballroom** (*596 Lenox Avenue, between W 140th and W 141st St*). Unlike the Cotton Club, the Savoy permitted both blacks and whites to strut their stuff onstage, begetting trendy dances like the "Lindy hop." In the 1930s, "First Lady of Song" Ella Fitzgerald lent her voluptuous vocals to the House band, which was led by Chick Webb.

Head further downtown to 108 W 139th St, the **former home of Billie Holiday**, and then continue south on Malcolm X Blvd until you reach **Lenox Lounge** (*288 Lenox Ave, between W 124th and W 125th St*). Holiday, Miles Davis, and John Coltrane were all regular performers at this historic art-deco club's renowned Zebra Room. The Lounge also welcomed prominent members of the Harlem community over the years, including Langston Hughes and Malcolm X.

One block west on 125th St looms the glazed white façade of the "Waldorf Astoria of Harlem," **Hotel Theresa** (*2090 7th Ave, between W 124th and W 125th St*). The Hotel rose to prominence during the mid-20th century, when it became the first in Manhattan to permit black guests. Dozens of eminent figures have stayed here over the years, including jazz legends Duke

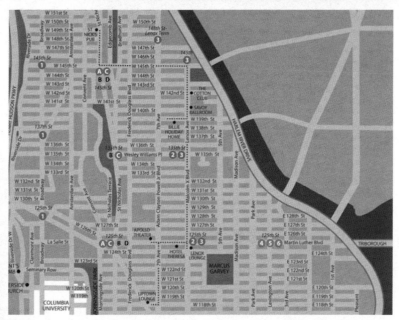

Ellington, Louis Armstrong, and Ray Charles, as well as Muhammad Ali, Jimi Hendrix, Malcolm X, and even Fidel Castro (when he visited the United Nations in 1960). You won't be able to join their ranks, however, because the Hotel was converted into an office building in 1967—it's now the Theresa Towers.

It's a short swing down Martin Luther King Blvd to the **Apollo Theater**, "Where Stars are Born and Legends are Made" (*253 W 125th St, between 7th and 8th Ave*). This concert hall is not only one of the world's most renowned performance spaces and the location of *Showtime at the Apollo*, but also the artistic and cultural stronghold of Harlem. Although it began as a bawdy burlesque theater in 1914, it became a respected music venue in the 1930s with its "Amateur Nights," a tradition that still exists today. It was at this event that Ella Fitzgerald, barely 17 years old first bedazzled audiences.

The Theater also introduced other musical legends to the spotlight, including the Jackson Five, Dionne Warwick, and Jimi Hendrix. Now make a left at 7th Ave, head south until you reach W 118th St, and turn right to reach your final destination, **Uptown Lounge at Minton's Playhouse** (*210 W 118th St, between St. Nicholas and 7th Ave*)—its neon-lighted letters are impossible to miss. In the 1940s, Minton's distinguished itself from other jazz lounges by hosting weekly jam sessions, when musicians took to the stage and ad-lib with the house band, which included Charlie Parker, Kenny Clark, and Thelonious Monk. This open policy was pivotal for the innovation of modern jazz, or be-bop. Recently renovated, Minton's survives as both a historical landmark and an ultra-hip venue—it often hosts popular New York groups like Gerald Hayes and The Qualified Gents, Eli Fontaine and the Organizers, and Patience Higgins' Sugar Hill quartet.

OUTSIDE

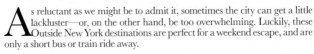

As reluctant as we might be to admit it, sometimes the city can get a little lackluster—or, on the other hand, be too overwhelming. Luckily, these Outside New York destinations are perfect for a weekend escape, and are only a short bus or train ride away.

Hoboken, the "mile-square-city" with more bars than backyards, will give you a fresh dose of suburbia. Go for brunch, spend some time in its parks, wander into cafés, and stay for happy hour before heading on to bars and a concert at night.

It is widely understood by New Yorkers that everyone who's anyone spends their summers in Long Island's **Hampton** towns. But you don't need to own a private yacht to relax at its beaches, participate in its raucous nightlife, and stay overnight—there are plenty of affordable, student-friendly options.

On a sunny day, skip Coney Island to visit the beautiful **Jersey Shore**, home to a combination of college-aged binge drinkers, young families and long-time residents. Belmar's nightclubs draw hordes of vacationers and have earned it the reputation of being a party town. If you're looking for a tamer, family-friendlier crowd, head to Point Pleasant.

Atlantic City is not just a place to hit the jackpot—besides casinos, it boasts shopping areas, high-energy bars and clubs, and a scenic stretch of sand. Before spinning the roulette wheel, get yourself primped at pampered at one of its top-shelf spas.

HOBOKEN

A playground for young families and New Jersey natives who work in the city, Hoboken is the closest suburban substitute for New Yorkers—although its bars outnumber its backyards. Known as the "mile-square-city," you can walk the entire length of the main thoroughfare, Washington St, in less than an hour, but you'll need a lot longer to explore what Hoboken has to offer.

GET THERE

It can take less time to travel to Hoboken via public transit than it does to get from one end of Manhattan to the other. The 10-20 minute **PATH train** is the most convenient way to get across the Hudson, but if you've got the time, hop on the **Ferry** from one of the NY Waterway Terminals for skyline views.

EAT

Food options in Hoboken have grown increasingly diverse and upscale in recent years, but the town still has some solid cheap eats.

At **Re-Juice-A-Nation**, a smoothie and juice bar, you'll find delicious combinations of freshly squeezed fruits missing from your typical chain. The "Got Juice" and "Climax" options are particularly re-juice-a-nating.
64 Newark St (btwn Court and Washington St). 201-792-7200. Mon-Fri 7am-9pm, Sat 9am-7pm, Sun 10am-6pm.

7 Stars Pizzeria is off the beaten path and a favorite spot among locals. Slices are absolutely massive.
342 Garden St (at 4th St). 201-653-7204. Mon-Wed 10am-1am, Thu 10am-3am, Fri-Sat 10am-5am, Sun 10am-Midnight.

Touted by some as the best Cuban food in the state, **La Isla—A Taste of Cuba** is as homey as its food is delicious. Come for their brunch and come back for their dessert—especially their très leches and coconut mango cheesecake.
104 Washington St. 201-659-8197. Mon-Sat 7-10pm, Sun brunch 10am-3pm, dinner 5-9pm.

Bagel Smashery offers a spin—or smush—on a classic by throwing bagels into a panini press until they come out flat.
153 1st St (near Bloomfield St). 201-604-0120. Mon-Sun 11:30am-11:30pm.

Elysian Café, Hoboken's longest-running restaurant and bar, takes the cake on old-time charm. Service can be hit or miss, but when it's a hit, the French bistro food is spot on.
1001 Washington St (at 10th St). 201-798-5898. Mon-Thurs 12-11pm, Fri 12-2pm, Sat 10am-2pm, Sun 10am-11pm.

PLAY

Hoboken boasts the largest number of bars within a square mile in the country, so bar-hopping is necessary—and unavoidable—when you're here. As you move uptown the crowd ages, the venues mellow, and the prices increase.

A neighborhood staple since 1978, **Maxwell's** has hosted some of the punk, grunge, and indie rock greats—from Nirvana to Neutral Milk Hotel—in a more intimate setting than big-name New York venues. The warmly-lit bar, 13 beers on tap, and better-than-bar-food menu make for a fun night.
1039 Washington St (at 11th St). 201-653-1703. Fri-Sat 5pm-1am.

Scotland Yard is the spot for live jazz and blues music—offered six nights a week. The basement bar used to be a prohibition-era speakeasy, but today passerbys can pick it out by the engine-red telephone booth built into the front entrance and the crowds that come for half-off drinks every Thursday.
72 Hudson Street (between Hudson Pl and Newark St). 201-222-9273. Mon-Thurs 4pm-2am, Fri 4pm-3am, Sat 3pm-3am, Sun 12:30pm-2am.

Bin 14 Trattoria, Hoboken's only wine bar, has acquired a crowd of devotees who come to

DID YOU KNOW?

Hoboken is the birthplace of Frank Sinatra, Hostess, and the zipper.

relax at the end of the workday. All dishes are delicious but very small for their price, so grab a more substantial dinner beforehand and stop in for a drink.

1314 Washington St (near 14th St). 201-963-WINE.

A great place for wings and burgers, **Black Bear Bar & Grill** has the best daily food and drink specials in town. In addition to weekday happy hours from 4-8 pm, it offers such tantalizing deals as 6 mini burgers and a 25 oz Sam Adams mug for $8.95, plus $3 pints all night on Wednesdays.

205 Washington St (near 2nd St). 201-656-5511. Dinner Mon-Sat 11am-11pm, Sun 11am-11pm. Bar open Sun-Thurs 11-2am, Fri-Sat 11-3am.

PARKS

Hoboken's waterfront parks are a must see for anyone in town. Jutting out into the Hudson, they offer the most cinematic views of the Manhattan skyline you can get without renting a helicopter. **Pier A Park** (*near 1st St*) is built on formerly notorious mob stomping grounds, but is now home to soccer games, sunbathers, and leashed dogs. Every Wednesday night from June to August, come watch free screenings from the "Movies Under the Stars" series. **Elysian Park** (*near 11th St*) is the last remnant of the Elysian Fields—the site of the first organized baseball game in June 1846. According to local legend, when one side fell behind 23-1 after several innings, both teams called it quits and headed to the local tavern.

THE HAMPTONS

From beach fun and barbecues to deluxe dining and club hopping, the Hamptons are the perfect summer getaway for the young, restless, and excessively wealthy. Expect visiting New Yorkers and celebrities to congregate at the shores, bars, nightclubs and restaurants of its luxurious towns—Southampton, Bridgehampton, Sag Harbor, East Hampton, Amagansett, and Montauk. Peak visiting season is late May to September.

GET THERE

The **LIRR Montauk Line** makes three to five daily trips from Penn Station (2 hrs 40 min to Southampton or 3 hrs 20 min to Montauk). For those who want to arrive by happy hour, LIRR's premier express train, the **Cannonball**, leaves Penn Station at 3:58pm on Fridays and arrives by 6pm.

Bus travel to the Hamptons is more luxurious, but can take up to three and a half hours. The most popular line among New Yorkers is the **Hampton Jitney**. Those who value first-class comfort opt for the **Hampton Luxury Liner**.

SLEEP

Though Hamptons overnight accommodations are notoriously expensive, don't assume that you have to head home at the end of the day—there are many places that will host you at an affordable price, if you follow a few simple rules.

Book in advance. Lodgings tend to fill up fast, especially in the summer. If you're on a budget, opt for a less-scenic inn. Note that many require minimum weekend stays (two or more nights).

Most rooms can fit two to four people, so bring friends to split the fare. Average rates are listed below as per room, per night.

- **White Sands Resort**. *28 Shore Rd, Amagansett. 631-267-3350. Off-Peak $115. Peak $195.*
- **Enclave Inn**. *2668 Montauk Highway, Bridgehampton. 631-537-2900. $100.*
- **The Mill House Inn**. *31 North Main St, East Hampton. 631-324-9766. $275.*
- **Ocean Beach Resorts**. *108 South Emerson Ave, Montauk. 631-668-4000. Off-Peak: $85. Peak: $175.*
- **Baron's Cove Inn**. *31 West Water St, Sag Harbor. 631-725-2100. Off-Peak: $125. Peak: $250.*
- **Southampton Village Motel**. *315 Hampton Rd, Southampton. 631-283-3034. Off-Peak: $135. Peak: $250.*

EAT

Many Hamptons vacationers prefer to spend evenings hosting dinner parties. After all, why go out to eat when you can grill seafood with your friends in your own backyard? Go to the **Seafood Shop** (*356 Montauk Hwy, Wainscott; 631-537-0633*) for the freshest fish in the area, and stop by **Citerella** for other groceries (*2209 Montauk Hwy, Bridgehampton; 631-537-5990*).

If you're looking to eat out, your options aren't cheap. There are, however, a few spots that serve quality food at more affordable prices.

Rowdy Hall serves classic English Pub food to a boisterous crowd.
10 Main St, East Hampton. 631-824-3555. Lunch Mon-Sun 12pm-3:30pm. Dinner Sun-Thurs 5pm-10pm, Fri-Sat 5pm-11pm.

For a fresh and creative spin on sushi, try **Suki Zuki**. It's also famous for its rabata (Japanese open-fire grill) dishes.
668 Montauk Hwy, Watermill. 631-726-4600. Mon-Fri 12pm-9:30pm, Sat-Sun 6pm-9:30pm.

Since 1947, **Gosman's Dock** has served Hamptonites some of the best seafood around. Drop by the restaurant for lunch or dinner, or the clam bar for an afternoon snack.
500 West Lake Dr, Montauk. 631-668-2549. Mon-Sun 12pm-10pm.

PLAY

Whether you're hoping for a night of table dancing, bar hopping, and celebrity sightings or just looking for some cheap fun with friends, the Hamptons' nightlife has what you're looking for.

If your destination club is high-profile, you can

 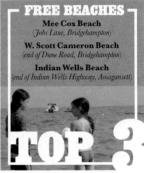

reserve a table to guarantee entry. Also, since it's unlikely that any venue you visit will be within walking distance of where you're staying, look up the numbers for shuttle services.

For celebrity sightings, head to the hyper-trendy **Lily Pond**. It hosts over-the-top Saturday night dance parties and has both inside and outside bars for easy ordering.
44 Three Mile Harbor Rd, East Hampton. 631-324-3332. Sat 10pm-4am.

For those who want to dance until dawn sans paparazzi, long lines, and steep prices, hit up the **Harbor Club** for a wild, up-scale evening.
964 Bridgehampton/Sag Harbor Turnpike, Bridgehampton. 631-537-6060. Mon-Sun 7pm-1am.

If casual bars are more your speed, **Stephen Talkhouse** is a must. With tons of live music—including blues, hip-hop, rock and reggae—it's a popular, casual beer spot.
161 Main St, Amagansett. 631-267-3117. Mon-Sun 7pm-4am. Open at 3pm daily from Dec-March.

Southampton Publick House also offers live performances and DJs. This busy brewhouse is perfect for beer-drinkers and tipsy hip swayers.
52 North Sea Rd, Southampton, 631-283-2800. Mon-Thurs 11:30am-10pm, Fri-Sat 11:30am-11pm, Sun 12pm-9pm. Mon-Fri Happy Hour 4-7pm.

If you prefer to have your beer with a beachside view and movie screening, the "Outdoor Surf Cinema" at **The Surf Lodge** is the spot for you. It also hosts the occasional concert and art series.
183 Edgemere St, Montauk. 631-668-3284. Mon, Wed-Sun 5pm-12am.

THE JERSEY SHORE

While New Yorkers may scoff at bridge-and-tunnel commuters that clog highways on their way to Manhattan, Jersey residents take pride in at least one draw of the Garden State: the Jersey Shore. Stretches of beaches, fresh seafood, and raucous nightlife make it a prime warm-weather spot for "bennys" (shore-speak for non-natives).

BELMAR

A sun-drenched haven for beach volleyball, greasy food, and clubbing, Belmar has all the essentials for a college student's dream vacation. The mile-long beach is home to bronzed revelers and surfing competitions.

GET THERE
Take an **NJ Transit bus** from Port Authority or the **North Jersey Coast Line** from Penn Station to Long Branch, then transfer to the local Belmar train. The trip is about two hours.

EAT
Nautically-themed **Boathouse Bar & Grill** is famous for its delectable pub grub (order burgers, not fish), live music, and nightlife.
1309 Main St. 732-681-5221. Mon-Sat 11am-2am, Sun 12pm-2am.

Named after a Dublin train station, **Connolly Station** serves Irish pub fare and sushi. At night, it morphs into a bar with live music.
711 Main St. 732-280-2266. Mon-Sun 11am-2am.

PLAY
Belmar's famous for its busy, often seedy nightlife. While stereotypes of over-tanned, scantily clad, and extremely intoxicated twenty-somethings may be exaggerated, there is a fair amount of fist-pumping and dirty dancing at clubs.

Bar Anticipation is packed—even with a capacity of 3,000. Loud music, volleyball games, and drink specials draw in the crowds.
703 16th Ave, Lake Como. 732-681-7422. Mon-Sun 10am-12am.

By day a beachside snack shack, **D'Jais Bar** offers a dance club atmosphere and gorgeous oceanfront views.
1801 Ocean Ave (at 18th Ave). 732-681-5055. Mon-Sat 11am-2am, Sun 11am-12am.

With an outdoor patio, flat-screen TVs, live entertainment, two bars, and classic American food, **507 Main** is both a bustling after-dark locale and a casual post-tanning hangout.
507 Main St. 732-681-6301. Mon-Fri 4pm-2am, Sat-Sun 3pm-2am.

EXPLORE
Located less than half a mile away from the shore, the **Belmar Marina** offers boat rentals, deep-sea fishing gear, and a cute coffee shop.
Route 35 and 10th Ave. 732-681-2266.

Enjoy a variety of nautical activities like crabbing, fishing, or kayaking in the Shark River at Belmar's popular **Maclearie Park**, which also has tennis courts, a boardwalk, and perfect picknicking scenery.
Off River Rd and L St.

POINT PLEASANT

Known more for wholesome family fun than rowdy drinking games, Point Pleasant is the perfect getaway for those seeking respite from the Shore's party scene. A slew of attractions (including the famous Boardwalk), prime beaches, and even some trendy nightclubs keep it crowded with visitors of all ages.

GET THERE
Take an **NJ Transit bus** from Port Authority or the **North Jersey Coast Line** from Penn Station to Point Pleasant Beach.

EAT
Located right on the waterfront, **Red's Lobster Pot** serves the elusive combination of freshly-caught, reasonably priced lobster.
57 Inlet Dr. 732-295-6622. Lunch Mon-Sun 12pm-4:30 pm. Dinner Mon-Sun 5pm-9pm.

Jack Baker's Wharfside & Patio Bar is a lovely seafood restaurant with a great view of the

DID YOU KNOW?

Bruce Springsteen's "E Street Band" is named after Belmar's "E" Street.

ocean and an excellent raw bar menu.
101 Channel Dr. 732-892-9100. Mon-Sun 11:30am-9:30pm.

Europa South has Spanish and Portuguese food and periodic live entertainment from a one-man band.
521 Arnold Ave. 732-295-1500. Tue-Thurs 4pm-10pm, Fri-Sat 4pm-11pm, Sun 11:30am-10pm.

PLAY

While Point Pleasant may be more family-oriented than its Jersey Shore counterparts, there are still a number of hotspots that light up the boardwalk once the kids are asleep.

Located right on the beach, **Jenk's Nightclub** has live music, DJs, cover bands, and drunken debauchery.
300 Ocean Ave. 732-899-0569. Sun-Mon 9pm-2am. $10 cover charge after 9pm.

With its exotic mixed drinks and full sushi menu, **Martell's Tiki Bar** is a laid-back alternative to Jenk's. But don't expect it to be quiet—live music and a thirsty crowd ensure that no night here is mild.
308 Boardwalk. 732-892-0131. Open until 2am.

EXPLORE

While the rides at **Jenkinson's South Amusement Park** may not rival Six Flags' adrenaline rushes, they are still crowd-pleasing. Bring money for scrumptious funnel cakes and churros.
500 Boardwalk. 732-295-4334.

Kids and adults love watching "feeding time" at **Jenkinson's Aquarium**, a two-floor aquatic playhouse that includes a petting tank, fossil room and exotic fish.
300 Boardwalk. 732-899-1212. Mon-Fri 9:30am-5pm, Sat-Sun 10am-5pm.

ATLANTIC CITY

You may know it as a casino town, but this former 19th-century resort haven is changing. Although the slots are still there—and continue to be the main attraction— Las Vegas' Mid-Atlantic cousin is going back to its roots. Resort amenities like golf courses, prime beaches, and just about every available 21st-century luxury suggest that this one-time refuge for day-tripping blue hairs is looking to the future, and to a younger crowd.

GET THERE

Take a bus from **Port Authority** or the new weekend express train from **Penn Station**. Both trips are about two and a half hours. If you're driving, take the **Garden State Parkway** south to Exit 38 and merge onto the **Atlantic City Expressway East**.

SHOP

There are three main shopping areas in Atlantic City. They comprise an assortment of outlets, retail stores, souvenir shops, and boutiques that will please fashionistas and thrift-seekers alike.

The Walk has around 80 major brand outlet shops, ranging from Banana Republic to Converse to the Disney Store. It was voted the 2008 Best Shopping Center in *South Jersey Magazine*, and is open seven days a week year round.
1931 Atlantic Ave. 609-872-7002. Mon-Sat 10am-8pm, Sun 10am-6pm. Summer: Mon-Sat 9am-9pm, Sun 10am-8pm.

The Pier Shops at Caesars is Atlantic City's newest shopping district. Located on a pier just off the boardwalk and connected to Caesars Palace Casino by a sky bridge, it's a higher-end version of the Walk with an equally great selection.
1 Atlantic Ocean. 609-345-3100. Mon-Thurs 11am-9pm.

Billed as a taste of "Old Havana," **The Quarter at Tropicana** is built to resemble the palm tree-lined streets of the Cuban city. It has around thirty notable names in retail, including smaller boutiques like Tahari and larger chains like Brookstone.
2831 Boardwalk. 609-340-0092. Store hours vary, some open daily until 11pm.

PLAY

Nightlife and Atlantic City are almost synonymous. Every casino has its own collection of bars, clubs, and the obvious late-night gambling. Here are a few notable spots for nocturnal fun.

Borgata Comedy Club @ The Music Box's nightly acts are a lighthearted alternative to the club scene.

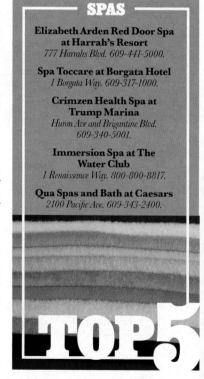

SPAS

Elizabeth Arden Red Door Spa at Harrah's Resort
777 Harrahs Blvd. 609-441-5000.

Spa Toccare at Borgata Hotel
1 Borgata Way. 609-317-1000.

Crimzen Health Spa at Trump Marina
Huron Ave and Brigantine Blvd. 609-340-5001.

Immersion Spa at The Water Club
1 Renaissance Way. 800-800-8817.

Qua Spas and Bath at Caesars
2100 Pacific Ave. 609-343-2400.

TOP 5

1 Borgata Way. 866-692-6742. Shows: Mon-Sun 9pm. Average cover $20.

Bally's Bikini Beach Bar is a casual venue, open seasonally, that provides live entertainment all day. Most nights are themed, like Karoke Tuesdays and 80s Wednesdays.
Park Pl and the Boardwalk. 609-340-2000. Mon-Sun 11:30am-2am. Happy Hour Sun-Fri 5pm-7pm.

The "hottest new nightclub" in town, **Providence Atlantic City** has bottle service and two DJs. Groups and Bachelor/Bachelorette parties are encouraged.
2801 Pacific Ave #304. 609-345-7800. Thurs-Fri 11pm-4am, Sat 10pm-4am. Cover free-$20. Average drink $10-$14.

Besides nightly live music, the East Coast's largest selection of Tequila is at **Gypsy Bar at the Borgata**. Jimmy Fallon and Dave Navarro have performed here in the past, but lesser-known rock bands are the norm.
1 Borgata Way. 609-317-1000. Mon, Wed 5pm-1am, Tue 11am-1am, Thurs 5pm-2am, Fri 5pm-3am, Sat 2pm-3am, Sun 2pm-1am. Average Drink $8-$10.

GAMBLE

Atlantic City would be not be Atlantic City without these mammoth emporiums for adult fun. Think world-class luxury hotels built on top of sprawling gambling casinos, with the occasional mall, bar, or theater thrown in.

Located at the Marina, the Tuscan-inspired

Borgata is the newest and most popular casino resort in Atlantic City.
1 Borgata Way. 1-866-692-6742.

A favorite among tourists, **Trump Taj Mahal** is worth a visit simply for the spectacle.
1000 Boardwalk. 609-449-1000.

The Ancient Rome-themed **Caesars Atlantic City**'s biggest draw— aside from gambling—is its pier shopping.
2100 Pacific Ave. 609-348-4411.

Resorts Atlantic City was the first casino in Atlantic City, and therefore the first on the East Coast. It boasts the largest standard guest rooms of all the hotels in the area.
1133 Boardwalk. 1-800-336-6378.

With a 640-slip marina and an exclusive heliport on the roof, **Trump Marina** is for the highest of rollers.

BEACHES

Huron Ave and Brigantine Blvd. 609-441-2000.
Few come to Atlantic City simply for the beaches, but they are free, which is unusual on the Jersey Shore. **Crystal Beach**, **Delaware Ave Beach**, and **Downtown Beach** at Raleigh Ave are great for surfing, and kayaking and windsurfing are allowed at **Jackson Ave Beach**. Fishing is permitted along Oriental and Maine Ave on the **Jetties**. You can rent bikes and beach chairs from **B&K Bicycle Rentals** and **Sunnyside Up Beach Rental**, both of which have multiple locations along the Boardwalk.

MANHATTAN

WASHINGTON
HEIGHTS & INWOOD

At the tip of Manhattan, a yuppie wine shop opens its doors next to a street vendor hawking fruit on sticks while the George Washington Bridge stands in the distance. That's Washington Heights and Inwood for you—simultaneously a comfortable residential area and a bustling urban neighborhood with enough shoreline to provide plenty of picturesque views. The neighborhood is most visibly shaped by the heavy Latin influence, mostly from Cuban and Dominican immigrants who arrived in the latter half of the 20th century.

The land was settled by the Dutch in the 17th century, and the deal by which Manhattan was transferred into European hands was (according to legend) brokered in what is now Inwood Hill Park. As the Dutch gave way to British colonists, this land, being the highest geographical point on the island, became a crucial strategic position in the Revolutionary War. The area remained primarily rural for decades after the Revolution—and the rolling hills of Inwood evoke a pre-developed Manhattan to this day. The 19th century brought some commerce to the ample coast, though these relics of industry and maritime trade have all but disappeared. It was the 20th Century that truly changed the atmosphere of the neighborhood, with the influx of immigrant populations.

Although plagued by crime in the 80s and 90s, the neighborhood has, in recent years, undergone a great deal of urban renewal. (Apartment hunters will be delighted to know that this has created some great deals in a now not-so-crime-riddled neighborhood.) This gentrification has been centered on the western side of Broadway, where you're more likely to take a pleasant stroll among the charming pre-war residences than push through crowds. The eastern side has a more distinctly urban feel, with crowds, vendors, and the odd mural bursting in vital color off an otherwise shabby brick wall. Stroll along the sidewalks and duck into a Latin restaurant or the odd Irish pub. Whether you're looking for high-end, low-end, residential, urban, or almost pastoral, you'll find it all within a couple blocks in Washington Heights and Inwood.

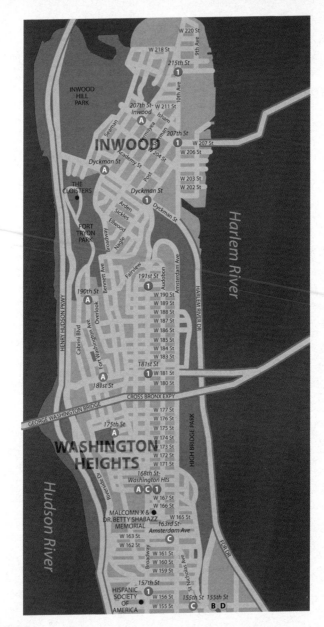

EXPLORE

The Cloisters

Hidden high within Fort Tryon Park in the northernmost corner of Manhattan, this offshoot of the Metropolitan Museum of Art is much more than your average museum. The lush gardens and neo-medieval architecture—complete with stone walls, tiled roofs, and glorious vaults—whisk visitors away from modern New York to the Dark Ages. Kneel at the chapel—which was transported across the Atlantic—admire the world-famous tapestries, or take a seat in the garden and sip some tea from the snack bar. Free gallery and garden tours are regularly held for history aficionados, but even if you don't come for the scoop on Boccaccio's love life, you'll find this picturesque spot overlooking the Hudson a welcome respite from the honking horns and sirens of the rest of the island.

99 Margaret Corbin Dr
212-923-3700
Tues-Sun (March-Oct)
9:30am-5:15pm, (Nov-Feb)
9:30am-4:45pm
Ⓐ to 190th St
M4 to The Cloisters (last stop)

DAY TO DAY

Community Board 12: 711 W 168th Street, Ground Floor, 212-568-8500.

Dry Cleaners: Heights French Cleaners, 812 W 181st St, 212-928-6923.

Groceries: C-Town, 4918 Broadway, 212-567-4881.

Gym: Planet Fitness, 82 W 225th St, 718-933-9300.

Hospitals: New York-Presbyterian, 622 W 168th St #137, 212-305-2500. Allen Pavilion, 5141 Broadway, 212-932-5000. Milstein Hospital, 177 Ft. Washington Ave, 212-305-6905.

Laundromats: Boogaloo Bubbles, 89 Cooper St, 212-304-8438.

Libraries: Washington Heights Library, 1000 Saint Nicholas Ave, 212-923-6054. Inwood Branch Library, 4790 Broadway, 212-942-2445.

Media: *Washington Heights and Inwood Online*, washington-heights.us. *Inwoodite*, inwoodite.com.

Volunteer Opportunities: Friends of Payson Avenue, 73 Payson Avenue, 646-427-9665. Washington Heights Youth Center, Intermediate School 164, 401 W 164th St, 914-217-6208.

The Hispanic Society of America

This museum houses the most comprehensive collection of art and literature of the Hispanic diaspora outside Spain and Latin America. The molded terracotta arches are an unconventional setting for their sculpture collection, which includes both Islamic and Christian work. The library boasts first editions of significant Spanish works, including *Don Quixote*. Tucked away in a corner of the upstairs gallery, find paintings by El Greco—several portraits and a Sagrada Familia—that exemplify the elongated faces and bright pallor of the painter's stranger work. But the biggest museum draw is the Goya collection, which contains almost all of his prints as well as the famous 1797 Portrait of the Duchess of Alba, in which Goya demonstrates some of his Zaragozan arrogance and wit.

613 West 155th
(near Broadway)
212-926-2234
Main gallery open Tues-Sat
10am-4:30pm, Sun 1-4pm,
Mon closed
❶ to 157th St
Free with suggested donation

Inwood Hill Park   *Park*

With over 190 acres of rolling greenery, Inwood Hill Park is the most authentically bucolic destination on the island. Located on the northernmost tip of Manhattan, it boasts arresting views of the Hudson and feels worlds removed from the chaos of Times Square only a subway ride away. The heavily wooded scenery is dotted with hawks, owls, eagles, and a resident birdwatcher or two. Warm weekends find children playing soccer and baseball on the fields, while families picnic in the shade and bikers ride along the paths. Summer also brings the annual Inwood Shakespeare Festival, so pack up picnics and blankets to enjoy free music and theater in the park.

> Dyckman St & Payson Ave to 218th St (along Hudson River)
> **A** to Dyckman St or 207th St-Inwood, **1** to 215th St

Morris-Jumel Mansion

The oldest house in Manhattan, the Morris-Jumel Mansion looks just as it did when it was George Washington's headquarters during the Battle of Harlem Heights in 1776. Built on Mount Morris, the island's highest naturally occurring point, the house boasts impressive views of both rivers, Long Island Sound, and the city skyline. Visitors can peek into the room where Aaron Burr proposed to his second wife, and then go up the creaky staircase to see where Alexander Hamilton (Burr's rival and subsequent casualty) dined as Washington's guest. The period furnishings offer a bizarre glimpse into the conveniences of our forefathers, including an adaptable mirror designed for the large and small and an unapologetic armchair commode with a hole cut out of the seat.

> 65 Jumel Terrace (near 160th St)
> 212-923-8008
> Wed-Sun 10am-4pm, Mon-Tues by appointment only.
> **C** to 163rd St
> Admission $5, Students $4

SHOP

Scavengers

	600 W 218th St
	(near Indian Rd)
	212-569-8343
	Thurs 3pm-7pm,
	Sat-Sun 10am-5:30pm
	❶ to 125th St

Neighbored by the sprawling greens of Inwood Hill Park, this modest antique shop has all the charm of your grandmother's house—without the cat and strange smell. Behind the shabby brick storefront, oil paintings of stoic strangers line what wall space hasn't allready been filled by free-standing chests and shelves overflowing with rare books, kitten lamps, and ornate costume jewelry. As you inch your way through timeless evening dresses and coats, Dyckman Farmhouse note cards, and dainty china, you're guaranteed to stumble upon the perfect bauble for your room. Though some of the larger items can be costly, smaller pieces tend to run between $10-$30. Navigate the narrow aisles of this tiny shop and you might be rewarded with a modest treasure.

Probus

	714 W 181st St
	(near Bennett Ave)
	212-923-9153
	Mon-Sat 10:30am-7pm,
	Sun 12pm-7pm
	Ⓐ or ❶ to 181 St

Specializing in hi-end men's street wear, the mentality behind this shop is that music plus art equals fashion. The exposed brick store is decorated with its designer clothes and Probus' own line of urban wear—a colorful collection of graphic tees. Diesel blue jeans in varying washes and detailings hang on racks throughout the store. The store also carries a well-edited selection of over-sized tees, many with quirky lines like "Oh Snap!" Rounding out their stock of goods are hoodies, colorful skytop sneakers by Supra, and watches and sunglasses by brands like G-Shock and Paul Frank.

EAT

El Malecon *Latin American, Caribbean*

The overwhelming menu at this Dominican neighborhood favorite is conveniently written in both Spanish and English, but you probably won't need it. You could order the deliciously sweet and spicy chorizo, but chances are

you've come for the famous roasted chicken—crisp and richly spiced on the outside, each tender, juicy bite practically

	4141 Broadway
	(btwn 175th & 176th St)
	212-927-3812
	Mon-Sun 7am-12am
	Ⓐ to 175th St
	Mains $7-15

dissolves in the mouth. Each dish comes with a massive serving of separately plated rice and beans, which, along with a whole chicken, could easily feed three people. A working knowledge of Spanish is almost a prerequisite for ordering, and waiters are happy to chat with anyone who remembers a few words from high school, but non-speakers can convey their enjoyment by returning completely clear plates to the efficient kitchen.

El Presidente *Dominican*

	3938 Broadway (at 165th St)
	212-927-7011
	Daily 24 hours
	❶ⒶⒸ to 168th St
	Appetizers $7-11,
	Entrees $6-18

The only thing in English at this Washington Heights Dominican joint is the menu. Everything from the *Televisión Dominicana* to the faster-than-light waiters exudes

Caribbean warmth, and the kitchen, though boasting Italian and Mexican offerings, does best with traditional island grub (go for the perfectly moist chicken and plantain mofongo). Generous $5 lunch specials, which come zipping from the kitchen with a side of rice and beans, are perfect for anyone on a tight budget or schedule. If you can't make up your mind between the Ropa Vieja (beef stew) or the maduros rellenos (stuffed plantains), head to the lunch buffet where more than 100 different dishes a day are yours for only $4.99 a pound.

Genesis
Ecuadorian

538 W 207th St
(near Sherman Ave)
212-942-1222
Daily 10am-10pm
❶ ❹ to 206th St
Soups & Salads $3-8,
Entrees $9-15

The doors of this family-run spot open onto a scene straight out of Quito. Employees rush to-and-fro serving up some of the best Ecuadorian fare New York has to offer. Regulars chat away in Spanish under the proprietress's matriarchal gaze. Choose your meal from the bright picture menu, which features flavorful dishes like the avocado salad, beef tripe stew, and fried plantains side. Enjoy a sweet-tart glass of their fresh-squeezed blackberry juice to wash down the generously portioned grub. All food comes alongside wonderfully spicy homemade salsa that pairs well with plates. The flowers may be fake and the yellow tablecloths' plastic, but everything about the food at Genesis is authentic. Genesis serves no alcohol, so don't plan on a cold cerveza with your dinner.

Indian Road Café and Market
Café, New American

600 W 218th St (at Indian Rd)
212-942-7451
Mon-Thurs 7am-10:30pm, Fri 7am-11:30pm, Sat 7am-11pm, Sun 8am-10pm
❶ to 215th S
Appetizer $6-11, Entrees $13-27

This rustic café is a neighborhood place through and through, with organic ingredients sourced from local green markets and baked goods purchased from the nearby bakeries on Arthur Ave. This love of all things local and non-corporate pays off: the fair trade coffee won best in the neighborhood in 2008, and the food is consistently fresh and flavorful. Inventive sandwiches and salads predominate on the menu—a proscuitto and fig panino is a popular choice among regulars. Brick walls, orange-yellow accents, and giant windows overlooking the park

warm up this cozy, eclectic hangout, which hosts a Monday night knitting club, and weekly jazz and folk musicians. Settle into the worn wood chairs and wile away an afternoon—or, if you're a local, every afternoon.

Jou Jou Café
Café, Sandwiches

603 W 168th St (at Broadway)
212-781-2222
Daily 24 hours
❶ ❹ ❻ to 168th St
Baked goods $2-4,
Sandwiches & Salads $4-7
Cash Only

Lanterns hang from the ceiling and coffee cup patterns decorate the sunshine yellow walls—Jou Jou is as chipper as its name suggests. The lavish

UNDER $20

WASHINGTON HTS & INWOOD

Assuming you don't spend the entire of your $20 (students $10) on a tick to the **Cloisters** (*99 Margaret Corb Drive, Fort Tryon Park*), start your day the **Little Red Lighthouse** (*benea George Washington Bridge*) for son breathtaking—and delightfully free-views of the Hudson River. Up 181 St, break for $6.50 iced coffee and so du jour in the backyard of **Emilou Café** (*827 West 181st St*), or try a pipi hot calzone at **Fivo's Pizza** (*804 W 187th St*). Then walk down Broadwa

bounty of homemade pastries and sandwiches boast plenty of vegan, organic, whole wheat, and low fat options that appeal to carb lovers and health nuts alike. Turkey avocado on sourdough, chicken ratouille on ciabatta, and the multitude of berry muffins are particularly delectable. Free WiFi and proximity to the Columbia University Medical Center make the café a popular study spot, with a cozy back nook perfect for settling in with a laptop. And because Jou Jou never sleeps, hard-working students can satisfy midnight munchies or 3am caffeine cravings at the Espresso Bar, which serves fresh-brewed Danesi blends sure to re*jou*venate.

Mamajuana Café *Nuevo Latino*

247 Dyckman St
(near Seamen Ave)
212-304-0140
Daily 5pm-12am, Sun Brunch 11am-3pm
A to Dyckman St
Brunch buffet $19, Small plates $8-18, Entrees $12-30

Near the northern end of Fort Tryon Park sits a sexy restaurant that combines downtown vibes with the distinct styles and flavors of

for near endless $5 shopping: **Gem Story** *(Broadway at 180th St)* is full of glam accessories like costume jewelry and headbands. The **street market** *(at 177th St)* offers über-cheap newsboy caps and porkpies. You can purchase toys, tatami mats, and bizarre knickknacks at the **770 Discount 99¢ Store** *(724 West 181st St)*. On your way home, stop by the Russian grocery store **Moscow on the Hudson** *(801 West 181st St)* and pick up a rich tiramisu Chanticlaire for a cool $2.99.

Latin America. Named for a liquor fermented by the Taino Indians, native to the Caribbean islands, Mamajuana integrates Spanish-colonial design elements like stone walls, vaulted ceilings, and wrought iron detailing, with tropical orchids and pre-Columbian artifacts. Chef Ricardo Cardona strikes a similar balance, using tropical ingredients to liven traditional Spanish preparations. A plantain starter with cod puree

quite literally injects a tropical ingredient with a Mediterranean standard, while larger plates like Paella draw more from the eastern side of the Atlantic. Some entrees run steep, but a lively and mostly local clientele ensures that Mamajauna retains the spirit of its neighborhood.

PLAY

Keenan's Piano Bar *Pub, Open Mic*

4878 Broadway
(near 204th St)
212-567-9016
Daily 11am-3:30am
A **1** to 207th St
Average Drink $6
Happy Hour: 4pm-7pm, $2 Domestic drafts

Keenan's Piano Bar looks like a Midwest small-town bar circa 1975—old-time slot machines crowd the corners, wooden panels cover the walls, and a square-shaped wood bar dominates the main room. Despite the name, there's no piano. Locals are perched on nondescript bar stools or watching TV in the back of this brown-toned lounge. Cheap beer and Monday open mics draw everyone from bearded men in cowboy hats to skinny Spanish-speaking goth boys. The bar is well-stocked and straightforward—knock back a $2 Bud at Happy Hour, stick around for live entertainment on Tuesday "Jam Night," or shoot some pool. They don't serve food, but customers are welcome to bring snacks from the deli across the street.

No Parking *LGBT*

4168 Broadway
(near 177th St)
212-923-8700
Mon-Fri 6pm-4am, Sat-Sun 7pm-4am
A to 175th St, **1** to 181st St
Average Drink $7
Happy Hour: Daily until 10pm

Zebra print walls, draped ceilings, and hanging beach balls make for modern aesthetic chaos at this boisterous gay pub. But, as the name suggests, you'll be dancing too much to notice. From Wednesday to Saturday the dimly lit space transforms into a jam-packed, sweaty party. Go-go boys parade across the surface of the horseshoe bar while a DJ spins salsa beats, and Kelly Clarkson videos play on mute in the background. Take a break on one of the black and gray fur-covered stools to sip Bud Light from a plastic cup and marvel at the hanging chandelier. Come on Thursdays and catch Peppermint, their much-loved drag queen, entertaining droves of drunken, merry revelers.

HARLEM

In the late 18th century, this area emerged as an elegant getaway for wealthy urbanites. But the difficulty of traveling downtown and the infertile soil diminished property value, and much of the land was auctioned off cheaply and forgotten. The extension of elevated railroads into Harlem in 1880 brought accessibility and a succession of immigrants—Jews, Irish, Italian, and, beginning in the early 1900s, blacks. The last group migrated en masse from the southern states and rallied together, taking heart in the solidarity and sense of activism that the neighborhood enabled. By 1910, the neighborhood was known as the "black capital of America."

History and legends of Harlem abound, but its most famous period was in the 1920s. Then it was the center of the Harlem Renaissance, a prolific outpouring of black culture driven by artists including Langston Hughes, Countee Cullen, Dorothy West, and Zora Neale Hurston. But as Harlem's culture soared to new heights, Harlem itself began to deteriorate as an increasingly poor population became riddled with crime and drug addiction.

Finally, in the 1990s, drastic steps were taken to remedy Harlem's problems. The Upper Manhattan Empowerment Zone began to funnel money into new developments, and former Mayor Guiliani vigorously cleaned up the many housing projects. Property values soared by 300% that decade and, as the story goes, rapid gentrification followed, ushering in lowered crime rate, Starbucks, and the offices of Bill Clinton. Yet despite its new edge, the area has maintained its lively cultural aura. Harlem still boasts some of the best jazz and soul food in the city, and Wednesday nights, when it's showtime at the Apollo Theater, you can still pop in to see the next big star.

Apollo Theater

With a marquee declaring, "The Apollo Theater: Where Stars are Born and Legends Are Made," this historic theater proudly marks its territory as one of Harlem's greatest landmarks. Founded in 1914, the Apollo is known for launching the careers of some of the greatest African American performers of the 20th century, like Ella Fitzgerald, Billie Holiday, and Aretha Franklin.

253 W 125th St
(btwn Adam Clayton Powell &
Frederick Douglass Blvd)
212-531-5300
Shows start at 7:30pm or 8pm
② ③ to 125th St,
Ⓐ Ⓒ Ⓑ Ⓓ to 125th St
Ticket price varies by show,
Amateur Night $17-27

The beautiful theater, featuring deep red seats, regal chandeliers and elegant wood paneling, hosts historic tours, a summer concert series, and community outreach programs. Come for the famous Amateur Night on Wednesdays at 7:30, where groups like the Jackson Five got their start, and see if you can spot the next Michael Jackson sliding across the stage.

The Conservatory Gardens

At the edge of Central park this garden flourishes with charming trees and flowers, well-manicured lawns, and gurgling fountains. Styled after European gardens, it has a regal, old-fashioned air that distinguishes it from the cutting-edge garden designs downtown. The Gardens offer

105th Street at 5th Ave
⑥ to 103rd St

a beautiful wisteria canopy, perfect for a picnic with friends or some alone time with a favorite read. Stop by in the summer to lounge under the flowers in full bloom, and return in fall for the vibrant autumn metamorphosis. Unlike other parks in the city, the Gardens are not nearly large or popular enough to be polluted with tourists, bikers, and endless strollers—and the relative obscurity allows this spot to maintain its peaceful atmosphere.

Graffiti Hall of Fame

It wasn't too long ago that graffiti was considered by many to be simple property

106th St (near Park Ave)
Daily 24 hours
6 to 103rd or 110th St

destruction, a hoodlum activity. Luckily, that perception has changed. In recent years, graffiti has become widely recognized as a legitimate form of expression, and Harlem's Graffiti Hall of Fame is the most visible celebration of this. Located on the walls surrounding a school on 106th Street, the Hall of Fame is practically a museum—except it doesn't have a roof, curators, or guards. The work featured is incredibly detailed and bright, and it possesses a depth that's difficult to achieve with the spray can medium. If street art interests you, this is the place to see the best of it.

DAY TO DAY

Community Board 10: 215 West 125th Street, 212-749-3105.

Groceries: Fairway, 2328 12th Avenue, 212-234-3883.

Gym: Bally Total Fitness, 1915 Third Ave.

Hospital: Harlem Hospital Center, 506 Lenox Ave.

Library: NYPL Harlem Branch, 9 West 124th Street, 212-348-5620.

Media: *The Harlem Citizen,* theharlemcitizen.org. *East Harlem News,* east-harlem.com. *Harlem Online,* harlemonline.com.

Volunteer Opportunities: foodbanknyc.org. Harlem YMCA, 180 W 135th St, 212-283-8570, ymcanyc.org.

Harlem Stage

This two-venue performing arts center is dedicated to supporting up-and-coming artists

150 Convent Ave
(at W 135th St)
212-281-9240
1 to 137th St,
A C B D to 125th St

of color. Special focus is given to community projects, spotlighting the theater's surroundings and its people. The flagship location is the Gatehouse, a gorgeous old masonry structure used initially as an aqueduct for the area in the 1800s. Aaron Davis Hall, the secondary venue, is a three-theater complex built at The City College of New York. The two locations are within blocks of one another, providing Hamilton Heights and the rest of Harlem with a theater district in miniature. There are several series of performances playing at any given time, and the stage also hosts a number of traveling events. In addition to live musical and theatrical performances, Harlem Stage hosts myriad community events, festivals, classes, and workshops throughout the week.

Marcus Garvey Park

This 20-acre park in East Harlem has two names: Mount Morris Park, the original name given when the park was opened in 1840, and Marcus Garvey Park, the 1973 name given in honor of the black nationalist who resided in the neighborhood for several years. Locals are split on which name to use. Real estate near the park is in high demand as wealthy individuals vie for the brownstones of the Mount Morris Park Historic District, which counts Maya Angelou among its residents. The park's facilities include a baseball field, basketball courts, playgrounds, a community recreation center, an amphitheater, and dog runs, as well as an 1857 cast-iron fire watchtower, the sole surviving tower of several that were erected throughout the city at the time. On Saturdays, a group of drummers gather in the tradition of an African drum circle and pound out rhythms, much to the consternation of the park's neighbors, who frequently complain about the noise level.

Madison Ave
(btwn 120th St & 124th St)
❷ ❸ to 125th St,
❹ ❺ ❻ to 125th St

Mural Row

The murals of East Harlem encapsulate the passion, anger, and spirit of El Barrio, glorifying local and national heroes while condemning inequality and racism with colors so vibrant entire blocks pulsate to the rhythm of salsa or bachata. The real masterpiece of Mural row is the four-story Spirit of East Harlem Mural, created in 1973 by Hank Prussing and renovated by his apprentice Manny Vega in 1997. The mural is dedicated to

E 104th St & surrounding area
❻ to 103rd St

SPANISH HARLEM

Known just a century ago as Italian Harlem, this pocket of Manhattan, north of 96th street from the East River to Central Park, was completely transformed by a wave of Puerto Rican immigration following the First World War. Recast as Spanish Harlem—El Barrio to the locals—the area was wrought with poverty-related violence, drug abuse, and race riots throughout the 60s and 70s. While safer now, many in Spanish Harlem still live in low-income housing, but a wave of gentrification is extending Upper East Side price tags to the area. Still, Tito Puente's birthplace is a lively neighborhood where salsa and mambo play on the streets as residents chat on stoops, calling out to passersby. **El Museo del Barrio**, at 104th Street on Museum Mile, continues to celebrate the Three Kings Day Parade each January. Colorful murals by guerilla artist James de la Vegas and his contemporaries cover the walls of E 116th St as the tantalizing aroma of chicarrones and pastels from street carts wafts through the air. The area is rapidly changing, so come shop at **La Marqueta**, explore the botanicas, and admire the graffiti art before it's all gone.

the residents of El Barrio and includes many of the people who inhabited the very building it is painted on. As you continue toward 116th Street, note how personal graffiti—look particularly for one dedicated to "Papote"—stand alongside politically fervent portraits of Che Guevara and the like. This mix of musical, historical, and personal references captures the energy of East Harlem better than any museum could.

El Museo del Barrio

El Museo has ex-panded significantly since activists and artists founded it, aiming to celebrate Puerto Rican culture. Its new location on Museum Mile includes a sizable collection of Latin American and Caribbean works. It's not uncommon for these expansive exhibits to spill into the muse-um's hallways. Those looking to admire famous works of Latin American artists can browse works by Frida Kahlo, Jorge Soto, and Marcos Dimmas, as well as a permanent exhibit of pho-tographs documenting the migration of Latinos to East Harlem. Also renowned for its remark-able collection of Pre-Columbian artifacts, El

1230 5th Ave (at 104th St)
212-831-727
Wed-Sun 11am-5pm,
Mon-Tues closed
❷❸ to 110th St,
❻ to 103rd St
Suggested Donation:
Adults $6, Students $4

Museo makes for a culturally rich exploration of Spanish Harlem.

National Black Theater

Just a few blocks away from the Apollo Theater, this smaller establishment strad-dling the border of East and West

2031 5th Ave
(btwn 125th & 126th St)
212-722-3800
❷❸ to 125th St,
❹❺❻ to 125th St
Ticket prices vary

Harlem has been providing quality African American theater to the public since 1968. The building, sleekly decorated with African art, contains several small and cozy performance halls providing a rich, intimate experience. The performances often fuse traditional theater with cultural components of the African diaspora by incorporating percussion, voice, and dance. The theater, however, is not merely for those who want to be entertained. Aside from its numerous performances, workshops, and symposia, NBT also rents out spaces for receptions and events, giving local residents a place where they themselves can put on a show.

The New York Mosque

On the southern border of Spanish Harlem lies the

1711 3rd Ave (at 96th St)
❻ to 96th St

largest center of worship for Muslims in the city. Built through a joint effort by the governments of Libya, Saudi Arabia, and Kuwait, the mosque was the first to be built in New York City and took almost 30 years to complete. The mosque's architecture is distinctive for its incorporation of modern features into medieval elements traditional to mosque design. Even those who do not practice Islam will find it a remarkable experience to enter this building, where over 4,000 people come to worship on Fridays.

The Studio Museum

Created in 1968 to pay due homage to African-American artists, the Studio Museum showcases edgy exhibits about interactions between art and society. Having expanded

144 W 125th St
(near Adam Clayton Powell Jr)
212-864-4500
Sun & Wed-Fri 12pm-6pm, Sat
10am-6pm, Mon-Tues closed
❷❸ to 125th St,
❹❺❻ to 125th St
Suggested Donation:
Adults $7, Students $3

its scope to include African and Caribbean objects, this small museum provides a voice for black culture. Rotating exhibits—and yearly re-interpretations of the permanent collection—ensure that no two trips there are alike. 2009 marked the exhibit opening of "We Come with Beautiful Things," in which students juxtaposed their modern pieces with James VanDerZee's photographs from the permanent collection. Be sure to visit the small sculpture garden, as it holds some of the museum's outdoor treasures.

SHOP

Atmos

On a street lined with competing shoe stores, this sleek, ultra-modern sneakers shop reigns king. Blasting music and cooler-than-thou

203 W 125th St
(at Adam Clayton Powell Blvd)
212-666-2242
Mon-Sat 11am-8pm,
Sun 12pm-7pm
❷❸ to 125th St,
❹❻❽❹ to 125th St

employees only contribute to the street cred of this Harlem institution, where simple classics like Converses or Pumas line the mirrored display shelves next to far funkier kicks. The store even collaborated with major brands like New Balance and Nike to release exclusive sneaker designs in flashy metallic hues and unexpected Jolly-

Rancher-neon color combinations. Most shelf space is devoted to footwear, but they also have a sizable selection of jackets, jeans, and t-shirts—moderately priced at $20-40—with eye-catching graphics. And be sure to browse the accessories, from funky bags to retro Casio G watches.

Malcolm Shabazz Harlem Market

Under the arched, colorful cover of this flea market, dozens of vendors set up to sell traditional African wares. Stalls feature

52 W 115th St (btwn
Malcolm X Blvd & 5th Ave)
212-987-8131
Mon-Sun 10am-8pm
❷❸ to 116th St

UNDER $20

HARLEM Begin your visit to this histor[ic] neighborhood at the memorial dedicate[d] to Invisible Man author **Ralph Elliso[n]** (*Riverside Drive at 150th St*), or at t[he] home of founding father **Alexand[er] Hamilton** (*287 Convent Avenue*). The[n] head to the **Studio Museum** (*144 [W] 125th St*) for works by African America[n] artists. If you're early (or lucky), y[ou] can score $12 rush tickets to **Amateu[r] Night at the Apollo** (*253 W 125th S[t]*) where you could catch the next Maria[h] Carey launch her career. With or witho[ut] tickets in tote, stop by the independe[nt]

brightly colored dresses and other textiles, intricately beaded jewelry, woodcarvings, hair braiding service, and music, as well as foods from Ghana, Nigeria, and other West African countries. Visit the different kiosks for home decorations and furnishings, one-of-a-kind bracelets, or super hydrating shea butter body lotions. Chat with eager vendors about the stories behind their wares, or just haggle them down to the right price. And if the promise of unusual goods doesn't lure you back soon, the friendly, chatty atmosphere, different dialects, and delicious aromas of West African food will.

Swing

As the nascent brainchild of world traveler Helena Greene, this shop packs carefully selected clothing and furnishings that reflect Greene's quirky personality and far-flung

1960 Adam Clayton Powell Jr (at 118th St)
212-222-5802
Wed-Fri 12pm-8pm, Sat 11am-7pm, Sun 10am-6pm
②③ to 116th St
⑧⑥ to 116th St

travels. Hindu-inspired décor coexists with handmade Belgian wine decanters converted into makeshift vases. Well-crafted purses with comfy over-sized shoulder straps hold silk scarf clutches hidden inside. Natural light floods the bright, open space, and paintings and photographs from local artists decorate cheery white walls—check out one of Michael Jackson and various Jazz bigwigs. The shop also carries vintage accessories

like bags by London-based company Lie Down I Think I Love You. Their selection of women's clothing veers toward the simple and classy—breezy summer dresses and wide-brimmed Italian hats hang on hand-painted furniture.

EAT

Africa Kiné — Senegalese

After recently relocating to an expansive second story space, this inexpensive-but-upscale restaurant remains the crown jewel of Little

256 W 116th St (near Frederick Douglass Blvd)
212-666-9400
②③ to 116th St,
⑧⑥ to 116th St
Lunch Entrees $10, Dinner Entrees $10-15
Daily 12pm-12am

Senegal. Juicy grilled meats and seafood, robust curries, and mounds of steaming rice make up the majority of their signature West African plates. The national dish of fish, rice, and vegetables, Thiebu Djeun, comes with a flavorful tomato sauce—but it's only served at lunch. Dinner options exhibit greater French influence, like Brochette Crevettes (savory grilled shrimp skewers). Wait staff in typical Senegalese dress, music from Dakar, and above all, patronage from the local Senegalese community ensure Kiné's authenticity. Service can be slow, but a BYOB policy and a speedy first-floor takeout window easily compensate. Be sure to bring cash—they charge 5% on your bill to use a credit card.

Amy Ruth's — Soul Food

Named for owner Carl Redding's grandmother and culling from a long tradition of home-style Southern comfort foods, this Harlem mainstay is old-fashioned and friendly to its core.

113 W 116th St (near Lenox Ave)
212-280-8779
Mon 11:30am-11pm, Tue-Thurs 8:30am-11pm, Fri 8:30am-5:30am, Sat 7:30am-5:30am, Sun 7:30am-11pm
②③ to 116th St,
⑧⑥ to 116th St
Breakfast $5-13, Dinner $12-19

Painted in cheerful yellow, with a large front window, Amy Ruth's is warm and bright inside—just the right casual, comfortable environment to enjoy Southern staples. Crisp fried chicken is amazingly moist inside, and when honey-dipped is gooey, crunchy, and altogether amazing. All entrees, however decadent in themselves, come

Hue Man Bookstore Café *(2319 Frederick Douglas Blvd)* for titles by African American writers, book signings, and events. Hungry? Chow down on soul food from the founder of Amy Ruth's at **Doc's** *(1902 Adam Clayton Powell Jr. Blvd)*, devour the thiebou diene at traditional Senegalese haunt **Keur Sokhna** *(225 W 116 St)*, or munch on the $10 lunch menu at vegetarian joint **Raw Soul** *(348 W 145 St)*. Work off the meal with a stroll down the **Graffiti Hall of Fame** *(106 St at Park Ave)* or at the Conservatory Gardens in Central Park.

LITTLE SENEGAL

A three block slice of Dakar in Central Harlem, Little Senegal is the main social and shopping enclave for Harlem's West African immigrants. Stroll down W 116th St between Frederick Douglass Boulevard and St. Nicholas Ave and you'll hear snippets of conversation in French and Wolof, see passersby decked in traditional garb, and smell the aroma of Senegalese fare wafting out of packed restaurants. The Harlem of jazz greats and the Apollo Theater is worlds away and replaced by TVs blaring Senegalese news in French and radios blasting MC Solaar and Le Raam Daan. Order the thiebu djen, (fish stew that comes with carrots, eggplants, cassava root, and couscous) or the yassa ginaar (confit-like chicken that has been stewed for hours in lemon-onion sauce) at **Africa Kine Restaurant** *(256 W 116th St)*, which acts as the unofficial embassy for the immigrant community—every day expats meet up in its spacious, elegant dining room to enjoy a sizeable taste of home.

with a choice of two sides, among which the mac and cheese, grits, and okra are particularly delicious. More than ten years after its opening, Amy Ruth's has gone from the new kid on the block to the perpetually packed go-to for comfort foods on cold winter days. That's a success story to make any grandmother proud.

Dinosaur BBQ
BBQ

This disheveled country roadhouse is home to some of the best damn barbecue you're likely to find in Manhattan. On weekends, expect to wait hours at the

646 W 131st St (at 12th Ave)
212-694-1777
Mon-Thurs 11:30am-11pm,
Fri-Sat 11:30am-12am, Sunday
12pm-10pm
❶ to 125th St
App $4-11, Platters $14-24,
Sandwhiches $8-12

boisterous bar, where you can sip a stiff drink or tap beer and munch on Dino Apps—try the impeccably crispy fried green tomatoes or spicy shrimp "cooked in a raging boil of beer and cayenne." Good as these small bits may be, save room for what you came for: ribs. Slow cooked over a wood pit, Dino's succulent ribs, pulled pork, and brisket come in a variety of sizes, combos, and sampler platters. Most entrees are smothered in Dino's house BBQ sauce (available in bottles for purchase) and come with a choice of sides, including gingered applesauce, mac 'n' cheese, and sweet simmered greens. As the sign out front says, "If you leave hungry, it's your fault."

MoBay
Caribbean

This pleasant, swanky surprise in the bustling heart of Harlem is, as owner Sheron Chin-Barnes puts it, the kind of restaurant "Harlem deserves." The boisterous but

17 W 125th St (btwn 5th Ave
& Malcolm X Blvd)
212-876-9300
Mon-Wed 11am-11pm,
Thurs-Sat 11am-12:30am,
Sun 11am-10pm
❷❸❹❺❻ to 125th St
Appetizers $6-14,
Entrees $15-24

relaxed local crowd, sultry orange lighting, and sleek décor set the tone for the stylish, inventive meals that draw their influences from around the globe. Much of the menu marries the flavors of the American South and the Caribbean, like the complimentary corn bread served with coconut pineapple butter, or MoBay's Famous Rummy Rum Cake. Savory, soul food staples like macaroni and cheese and candied yams should not be snubbed, while Caribbean standards like jerk chicken are spiced up with ingredients and techniques borrowed from Ms. Chin-Barnes' Chinese background. Cool down after a spicy entree with one of the many house cocktails while listening to live music from local performers.

Patisserie de Ambassades — *Bakery, Café*

2200 Frederick Douglass Blvd
(near 119th)
212-666-0078
Mon-Thurs 7am-2am, Fri 7am-3am, Sat-Sun 8am-3am
❷❸ to 116th St,
❽❾ to 116th St
Brunch & Pastries $2-12,
Lunch & Dinner $7-13

The kitchen staff is Senegalese, the décor is vaguely North African, and the food draws inspiration from the diverse cuisines of Vietnam, Italy, India, and Lebanon. Heaping portions of flavorful, multi-ethnic spins on French fare are served from breakfast through dinner at this unassuming spot. The popular Robespierre sandwich packs succulent grilled chicken or lamb with fresh mixed greens, sautéed onions, tomatoes, mayonnaise, and fries in a foot-long baguette. Diners can also graze on appetizers like deep-fried spring rolls while using free WiFi. A display case holds pastries, tarts, and other mouth-watering desserts, all for $5 and under. Regulars flock for weekend brunches, so prepare to wait for the coveted leather couch alcove in the back. Or avoid the masses and come on a weekday afternoon to enjoy a cool Vimto soda and practice your French with the wait staff.

Strictly Roots — *Vegan*

2058 Adam Clayton Powell Jr
(at 123th St)
212-864-8699
Mon-Fri 8am-10pm, Sat
11am-10pm, Sun 12pm-8pm
❷❸ to 125th St,
❹❻❽❾ to 125th St
All dishes $5 and under

Around the corner from the Apollo Theater, this vegan food shop serves up cheap, satisfying, healthy grub with a Caribbean twist. "Nothing that crawls, walks, swims, or flies," the slogan claims, its earthy style underlining its "one with nature" philosophy. The humble café offers a small but constantly rotating buffet of hot foods priced from $1-$3.50. Selections include brown rice with beans or lentils, tender steamed cabbage, savory stews, spaghetti, greens, yams, fried tofu, dumplings, and juicy plantains, generously heaped cafeteria-style onto your plate. We recommend the fresh-from-the-grill veggie burger, and the texture of the veggie chicken (flavored with BBQ or curry) is

NATIVE'S PICK

Melba's — *Comfort Food*

300 W 114th St
(near Frederick Douglas Blvd)
212-864-7777
Tues-Fri 5pm-11pm Sat-Sun
10am-3pm & 5pm-11pm
❽ ❾ to 116th
Appetizers $7-9, Entrees $9-17

With black subway tiling, dark wood, low lighting, and mirrors all around, this Harlem hangout is effortlessly cool and popular with young, local professionals. Smooth jazz plays in the background and the drink menu includes stiff cocktails, fine wines, and Harlem's own Sugar Hill beer. Melba's waffle batter has eggnog mixed in, making for smoother, richer waffles, unlike any others in town. They come served with fried chicken or on their own with sweet strawberry butter and natural maple syrup. Other old-fashioned dishes are perfected with similar creativity, like catfish livened by a complex chipotle mayo. Recognizing the changed identity of New Harlem, Melba's refers to its cuisine as American comfort food instead of soul food—but there's nothing new about a smooth, fruity sweet potato pie that tastes just like grandma's.

surprisingly authentic. Finish off with a home-made cake-slice of bread with fruits and spices, an herbal tea, a non-alcoholic ginger beer, or a fresh juice mix, like the signature badman shake of bananas, nuts, protein, and moss.

Talay
Latin, Thai

701 W 135th St
(near 12th Ave)
212-491-8300
Brunch Sun 11am-4pm,
by reservation only
Dinner Mon-Thurs 5pm-12am, Fri-Sun 5pm-1am
1 to 137th St
Appetizers $8-12,
Entrees $12-25

A steep flight of steps down from Riverside Park, this cavernous Thai-Latin spot feels as though it has fallen off the edge of Manhattan. By night, the indoor space is a two-floor, neon-lit lounge and restaurant, while on Sundays Talay hosts brunch with live jazz played in the front room or outdoor patio facing Riverside Park. Dinner consists of small plates, with Thai chicken satay offered alongside distinctly Latin dishes like chicken flautas. Sunday brunch options lean more toward the New World, with fluffy, delicate pancakes, and sweet, smooth mangu (a traditional dish of mashed plantains and sauteed onions) topped with a fresh, subtle salsa verde. With unlimited mimosas and sangria, you may find yourself lazing the afternoon away, listening to the world whiz by far overhead on Riverside Drive.

PLAY

Nectar
Wine Bar

2235 Frederick Douglass
Blvd (at 121st St)
212-961-9622
Mon-Sun 4pm-1am
B C to 116th,
B D A C 125th
Average Drink $9

This cheerful, contemporary, cream-colored space is Harlem's first wine bar, opened a few years ago by the owners of the wine shop next door. Discover your new favorite go-to wine from Nectar's selection with a 'flight'—a taster of three wines starting at only $3 each—and mix-and-match them with complimentary cheeses and charcuterie. A final course with dessert wines or liqueurs with chocolate by Jacques Torres offers a sweet finish to the night. Nameless club remixes dominate the sound system but play soft enough to encourage conversation, if not also a club-like atmosphere. Sit at a table with a few friends or chat up the knowledgeable sommeliers around their trendy O-shaped bar.

NATIVE'S PICK

St. Nick's Pub
Jazz

773 Saint Nicholas Ave
(btwn 148th & 149th St)
212-283-9728
Daily 1pm-4pm
1 A C B D to 145th St
Average Drink $7
Happy Hour: Daily 4pm-8pm

The uptown favorite of locals and jazz enthusiasts alike, this Sugar Hill gem carries on a legendary jazz legacy with its fantastic nightly jam sessions. The exposed white brick walls graffitied with eighth notes, tattered seats, and plastic tablecloths suggest that St. Nick's hasn't been redecorated since Duke Ellington's piano player owned the joint, but the haphazard décor only adds to the atmosphere. Sit up close to the stage with the regulars and watch beads of sweat drip down the saxophonist's temple as he dives into his last solo, or strike up a chat with the friendly bartender in the back and enjoy the toe-tapping tunes from afar. You'll find great musicians—with a few famous names thrown into the mix—starting their sessions around 8pm nightly. Come early to avoid the crowds—grab a seat and get a piping hot plate of soul food for only $10.

MORNINGSIDE HEIGHTS

In the midst of chaotic urban sprawl, Morningside Heights is a serene pocket of Manhattan—a college town in the middle of the City. Bounded by 110th and 125th Streets on the western side of the island, the neighborhood boasts a rich culture steeped in the histories of the institutions that call it home.

For much of the 1800s, Morningside Heights was home to the Bloomingdale Insane Asylum. Towards the end of the century, the asylum's land was parceled off to developers to build St. John the Divine Cathedral, St. Luke's Hospital, and most notably, Columbia University. The influx of new institutions helped relieve the developmental stigma that had previously surrounded the area, but also raised rents and displaced much of the area's former population. Development remains an issue of neighborhood contention, as Columbia's imminent northern expansion into Manhattanville sparked a flurry of ongoing debate among students and locals alike.

These days, Morningside Heights bustles with students from Columbia, Barnard College, Manhattan School of Music, Union and Jewish Theological Seminaries, among other schools. Its green parks, iconic architecture, and famous filming locations make it a tourist destination and popular neighborhood for young families. You probably won't find George and Kramer dining in Tom's Restaurant or Barack Obama admiring the neoclassical facades of his alma mater, but you will find Morningside Heights teeming with highly caffeinated collegiate energy. Rows of used book tables on Broadway testify to the neighborhood's academic pedigree, and most bars and restaurants in the area cater to student tastes and budgets.

A quiet part of the city, Morningside Heights is probably a better place to take your family to brunch than your friends for a night on the town. Any lazy Saturday is perfect for tossing a Frisbee in Riverside Park or watching toddlers waddle around Columbia's campus. Finish off the day with dinner on a sidewalk café or take a seat at the Hungarian Pastry Shop and catch up on your Pynchon.

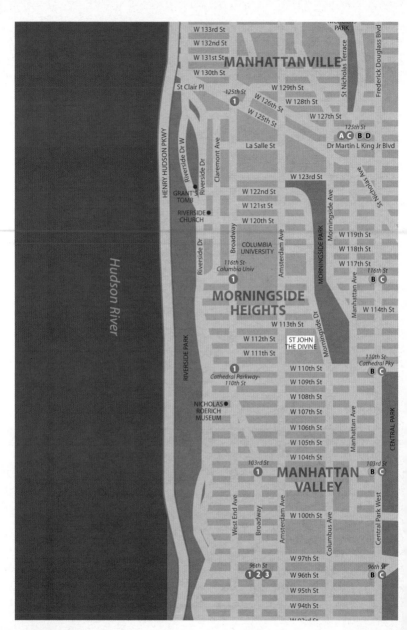

EXPLORE

Columbia University

A picturesque anomaly in Manhattan's chaotic landscape, Columbia University's self-contained campus boasts sweeping neoclassical architecture, expansive green lawns, and bookish students. New York's iconic Ivy League academic institution has been around since 1754, when it was founded as King's College by a charter from England's George II. Visitors can stroll down College Walk, the pedestrian-only artery through campus created by former university president Dwight Eisenhower, or lounge on the steps of Low Library with bespectacled academics and hookah smokers alike. Come during warmer months and you may catch one of the campus's dance troupes performing in the plaza, neighborhood toddlers waddling around the lawns, or you might even witness the latest student protest.

114th St to 120th St (btwn Broadway & Amsterdam Ave)
1 to 116th St-Columbia University
Tours available Mon-Fri 1pm in 203 Low Memorial Library

El Taller Latino Americano

This cultural arts center invites enthusiasts from all backgrounds to come together and learn about Latin American arts, language, and customs. Its fun, interactive Spanish classes—capped at ten students and focusing on conversational skills and Latin American culture—are some of the best in the city. El Taller also offers dance classes, art workshops, musical performances, and exhibitions year-round. Learn salsa at their weekly lessons, check out local artists' photography installations, or enjoy a live Afro-Peruvian musical performance. The staff works hard to provide a warm, welcoming atmosphere for regulars and newcomers alike.

2710 Broadway (at 104th St)
212-665-9460
1 to 103rd St

Grant's Tomb

No one's sure how it started, but "Who's buried in Grant's tomb?" is one of the country's most-told jokes. The answer

Riverside Dr (at 122nd St)
212-666-1640
(for group reservations)
Daily 9am-5pm
1 to 125th St

isn't quite as obvious as you'd think—turns out both Ulysses and his wife Julia were laid to rest here, the largest tomb in North America and the biggest landmark in Riverside Park. It now serves as a meeting spot, most notably for a unicycle club. While the mausoleum fell into disrepair in the 1970s and 80s, recent renovations have restored the building to its original condition. Come in the summer to hear live music—free weekly jazz concerts draw throngs of locals armed with folding chairs. While the landmark lacks many actual exhibits, it does have civil war memorabilia, a circular map room that charts the battles of General Grant, and a modest gift shop well worth the visit.

Riverside Park

Stretching four miles from 72nd St to 158th St along the Hudson River, Riverside Park offers some of Manhattan's most stunning waterfront views. Frederick Law Olmsted designed the tree-lined boulevard that dominates the middle of the park, where bibliophile bench sitters share the space with cyclists, joggers, and power walkers. Upper West Side families can be seen daily at the three dog runs, the Boat Basin at 79th St, the garden at 91st St, and the ever-exciting Dinosaur Playground

72nd St to 158th St
(along Hudson River)
1 2 3 to stops btwn 72nd St & 125th St

and architects since 1892—as a result, its architecture reflects the varied history of this city's urban design. Each of the seven chapels represents one of the primary ethnic groups that came to New York City via Ellis Island, which opened the same year that construction on the cathedral began. Although a five-alarm fire destroyed the Cathedral's north transept in 2001, the entire interior was reopened to the public in November 2008 with a re-dedication service. Be sure to visit the surrounding gardens and the Peace Fountain, decorated with whimsical bronze statuettes made by local children—linger long enough and you might even catch a glimpse of the resident white peacock.

SHOP

Book Culture

Formerly named Labyrinth Books, this independent shop's multi-floored collection is a maze of towering shelves that easily disorients even the most focused of shoppers. More Columbia's bookstore than the official campus bookstore in the university's student center, Book Culture carries an extensive selection of titles not readily found in mainstream mega-chains and is the go-to store for course material. Casual browsers can find books, niche magazines, and moleskins on the user-friendly ground floor—titles are organized by categories like history and philosophy—but serious shoppers in search of an adventure should head upstairs to search for more obscure titles. Keep an eye out for author readings and other in-store events—and if you're a student, be sure to take a look at the store's generous buyback offer, membership card, and special requests policy.

536 W 112th St (btwn Broadway & Amsterdam Ave)
212-865-1588
Mon-Fri 9am-10pm, Sat 10am-8pm, Sun 11am-7pm
1 to 110th St-Cathedral Pkwy

at 95th St. For the more athletically inclined, the park offers tennis, volleyball, soccer, and basketball courts, as well as the Manhattan Waterfront Greenway, the West Side's bike path. The truly adventurous can try to sneak into the Amtrack railway tunnels at 86th St and 125th St. Abandoned for years, these tunnels were once occupied by the homeless and graffiti artists but have since been revived for use. For the more historically inclined, the park houses the Eleanor Roosevelt Monument at 72nd St, the Soldiers and Sailors Monument at 86th St, and Joan of Arc statue at 93rd St.

Saint John the Divine

As long as two football fields and as tall as the Statue of Liberty, the still-unfinished Saint John is, by some accounts, the largest cathedral in the world. The cathedral's walls have been crafted by successive generations of contractors

1047 Amsterdam Ave (btwn 110th St & 113th St)
212-316-7441
Mon-Sat 7am-6pm, Sun 7am-7pm
1 to 110th St-Cathedral Pkwy
B C to 110th St

Liberty House

Splurge on colorful clothing and handmade jewelry at this den of a store. The clothing, strewn about the store, is mostly geared to older women, but the beautiful, natural fiber cloth is

2878A Broadway (at 112th St)
212-932-1950
Mon-Wed 10am-6:45pm, Thurs 10am-8:45pm, Fri-Sat 10am-6:45pm, Sun 12pm-5:45pm
1 to 110th St

worth a feel. Richly colored scarves in luscious fabrics, flowing skirts, and feathered hats are compromises for younger crowds. The center of the store houses an impressive display of beautiful jewelry made with semi-precious stones or crafted silver and worth the higher price tags. You're right to pick up on an old timey vibe here—during the Civil Rights Movement, Liberty House was a group of stores that sold goods made by craft cooperatives in Jackson, Mississippi and then returned the profits to the community. And its charitable history makes shelling out for handcrafted necklaces a little easier.

EAT

A Cafe
Caribbean, French

Al, the owner/ waiter/ chef, finds time to smile at customers between packing in another patient couple and torching a crème brûlée. Masterfully executed French classics like juicy escargots, and Caribbean-inflected fare like grilled avocado suggest a kitchen full of accomplished chefs—but a peek behind the bamboo screen in the back of the room reveals a closet-sized kitchen, where Al, and Al alone, lovingly crafts his food. Dishes like a succulent duck confit distract from the humble décor, and substance handily makes up for any shortcomings in style. The BYOB policy and $20 prix fixe menu make A Morningside's best gourmet bargain. Come for elegantly plated, richly favored dishes like the spice pear with gorgonzola. Just be prepared to wait—half the neighborhood's there too.

973 Columbus Ave
(near 108th St)
212-222-2033
Tue-Sat 6-11pm
B C to 103rd St
Appetizer $14-12, Entrees $14-20
BYOB

Awash
Ethiopian

On a stretch of Amsterdam Avenue crammed with Mexican and Dominican restaurants, this charming Ethiopian spot makes for

947 Amsterdam Ave
(btwn 106th St & 107th St)
212-961-1416
Mon-Thurs 1pm-11pm,
Sat-Sun, 12pm-12am
1 to 110th St-Cathedral Pkwy
Appetizers $5-8,
Entrees $10-15
Happy Hour: Daily 4-8pm

NATIVE'S PICK

Kitchenette
Brunch

The sunny digs of this brunch spot are ideal for down-home comfort food and draw consistent weekend crowds. With ink accents, mismatched furniture, and mason jars for cups, Kitchenette feels like an urban pastiche of country-style shabby chic—but there's no kitsch in their honest, hearty cooking. Egg dishes come with massive, pillowy buttermilk biscuits and your choice of scrumptious cheese grits or home fries. Sweet dishes are equally satisfying, like a seasonally-changing baked French toast, as luscious and dense as bread pudding. Combined with sides of house-made turkey sausage or perfectly cooked bacon, their brunch is enough to put even the heartiest of diners in a Sunday morning food coma. Thankfully, bottomless coffee will put you on your feet again.

1272 Amsterdam Ave
(near 123rd St)
212-531-7600
Mon-Fri 8am-11pm, Brunch
Sat-Sun 9am-4:30pm, Dinner
Sat-Sun 5pm-11pm
1 to 125th St
Average Brunch $10

a surprising change of pace. Portraits of Ethiopian greats gaze serenely from the walls, and bartenders mix stiff cocktails as diners dig into richly spiced meats and vegetables. House specialties like butter-soft kitfo (Ethiopian raw beef), and a creditable doro wat (chicken stew with boiled egg) are scooped up with chunks of injera, the spongy, vaguely vinegary flat-bread that serves as the only utensil in Ethiopian dining. All entrees come with stewed lentils, carrots, and beets on the side, so if menu prices seem steep at first (most entrees cost near $15), keep in mind that three mains will easily suffice for five, making Awash an ideal destination for group dining, and a far better bargain than you might expect.

Community Food and Juice *American*

Easily the coolest restaurant in Morningside, this farm-to-table spot is also the only green-certified eatery in the neighborhood, working with local farmers, using recycled glassware, and composting trash at the end of the day. Community serves contemporary American food using local, seasonal, and organic ingredients in comfortable, stylish surroundings, combining a sleek, industrial aesthetic with elements of farmhouse warmth. The food reflects the same

2893 Broadway
(btwn 112th & 113th St)
212-665-2800
Mon-Thurs 8am-10pm,
Fri-Sat 8am-11pm,
Brunch Sat-Sun 9am-3:30pm
❶ to 110th St-Cathedral Pkwy
Brunch $8-20,
Dinner Appetizers $8-12,
Entrees $12-26

sensibility: a simple bowl of vegetables is elevated by farm fresh ingredients and black truffle oil, an outstanding burger made with grass-fed beef, caramelized onions, and Vermont Cheddar. Come for the beloved brunch to feast on the hearty farmhouse breakfast, buttery blueberry pancakes, or a massive serving of banana-topped French Toast. Weekend mornings can be maddening with the onslaught of the stroller set, so come a little later to enjoy your genuine country breakfast in lazy, Manhattan style.

Haakon's Hall *American*

Milk and cookies, PB&J, and a daily rotating selection of TV dinner-style entrees lend a homey feel to the exposed brick walls and posh décor of this new Morningside Heights establishment. From the Yankee Pot Roast to the Ugly Tomato Salad, chef James Lenzi offers American classics with casual elegance. There's free WiFi, ample plush seating, and late hours for sleep-deprived undergraduates, but Haakon's serves far more than the Columbia crowd. With flat-screen TVs, an entertainment space for cooking classes, live music, poetry readings, and a lengthy international wine list, Haakon's serves Mom's cooking in a dynamic urban dining room. And Mom makes a damn good burger.

1187 Amsterdam Ave.,
between 118th & 119th
212-300-4166
❶ to 116th St-
Columbia University
Daily 11am-4am
Appetisers $4-9, Entrees
$9-15, Dessert: $4-6

Hungarian Pastry Shop & P&W Sandwhich Shop
Café — Sandwhiches

1030 Amsterdam Ave
(btwn 110th & 111th St)
212-866-4230
Mon-Fri 7:30am-11:30pm,
Sat 8:30am-11:30pm,
Sun 8:30am-10:30pm
🚇 to 110th St-Cathedral Pkwy
Desserts $2.25, Coffee $2.25,
Sandwiches $3-6

A Morningside institution, the Hungarian—as it's affectionately known by the regulars—is a sought after spot for locals in search of bottomless cups of coffee, tea, or a nice place to read. Day and night, this dimly-lit, thirty-year-old coffee shop houses local students cramming for finals, scholars engrossed in books and conversation, and the most erudite bathroom graffiti in New York. If you're hoping for some fresh air, grab a chair outside and enjoy the view of the Cathedral of St. John the Divine. For more savory sustenance, stop next door at the Hungarian's sister shop, P&W, and order a delicious and reasonable sandwich or salad to consume in either location. The Hungarian may not serve the most nuanced cup of coffee or the most delectable pastry, but an independent neighborhood spot as atmospheric as this is truly one in a million.

Koronet Pizza
Pizza

2848 Broadway
(btwn 110th & 111th St)
212-222-1566
Sun-Wed 10am-2am, Thurs-Sat 10am-4am
🚇 to 110th St-Cathedral Pkwy
Jumbo cheese slice $3.25

While this pizza parlor doesn't offer much in the way of charm, seating, or variety, what they do have is a cheese slice the size of a boogie board. Koronet's signature jumbo slice is the stuff of local legend: immense, incredibly satisfying, and dripping with grease. Every weekend until 4am, local collegians stagger over from nearby bars and line up out the door for a $3.25 continent of cheese, sauce, and crust. Purists may decry its overly bready dough and toppings that are undercooked and overpriced. Leave the purists to their puny pocket-sized slices, we say. The staff is no-nonsense and the pizza is hot, fresh, and damn good—and if you're lucky enough to grab a seat on a Saturday night, you're sure to see just about everyone you know in the neighborhood drop by.

Max SoHa
Italian

This Italian nook is perpetually packed, and adored by students and neighborhood residents alike for serving hearty portions of perfectly sauced pastas at prices that befit a collegian's budget. While a no-reservations policy

1274 Amsterdam Ave
(at 123rd St)
212-531-2221
Daily 12pm-12am
🚇 to 125th St
Appetizers $5-10, Entrees $10-17

and limited seating may have you waiting in line for a table, the cozy brick-walled space, with its candlelight and sparse decorations, makes for a romantic setting, and provides a sense of having discovered that elusive, perfect neighborhood Italian. Hearty, cheese-laden pasta dishes like rigatoni and gnocchi—cooked to perfection and served with tomato sauce, basil, and melted homemade mozzarella—can warm up even the coldest winter night. And fish entrees like the roasted cod and grilled filet of salmon are lighter alternatives for a summer lunch, especially pleasant while people-watching from the outdoor patio.

Pisticci
Italian

This simple, elegant trattoria is the perfect place for outstanding Italian classics in a quaint, casual atmosphere. Adorned with candles, chandeliers, and locally-produced art, Pisticci is warm and intimate, despite being fairly large. Though

the menu stays the same year round, Pisticci's numerous daily specials make use of fresh, seasonal ingredients. It is impossible to go wrong on this menu, but the simple Pisticci penne is about as pure and flavorful a pasta preparation as you could hope to find. Accompany your meal with a bottle of wine, and let yourself go: fresh, delicious food at fair prices combined with the trattoria's 100% carbon neutral practices ensure that a meal at Pisticci will do as little damage to your wallet as it does to the environment.

125 La Salle St (btwn Broadway & Claremont Ave)
212-932-3500
Mon 11am-11pm, Tues-Thurs 11am-11pm Fri-Sat 11am-1am, Sun 11am-12am
❶ to 125th St
Appetizers $5-11, Entrees $8-16

Sookk   *Thai*

This well-kept neighborhood secret serves bold, enticing dishes inspired by the best of Bangkok street food. The extensive menu goes beyond run-of-the-mill Thai standards to include items like cinnamon duck and Yaowarat beef soup. Forego pad Thai for spicy basil noodles—flat rice noodles loaded with basil, onions, bell peppers, and tomatoes sautéed in a sharp, sweet sauce. Pumpkin and butternut squash add warm, nutty depth to the pumpkin chicken, a creative twist on Thai red curry. Dishes will leave your eyes watering, throat burning, and nose running—thankfully, a pitcher Sookk's lychee sangria is as refreshing and cool as it is delicious. Generous dinner portions arrive at your table within

2686 Broadway (btwn 102nd & 103rd)
212-870-0253
Sun-Thurs 11:30-11:00, Fri-Sat 11:30-11:30
❶ to 103rd St
Appetizers $4-8, Entrees $9-3

minutes, and the $7, two-course lunch special is one of the best deals in Morningside.

Taqueria y Fonda la Mexicana   *Mexican*

This fluorescent-lit hole in the wall is a real find for any burrito connoisseur. Bowls of deliciously crisp chips and a triumvirate of superior salsas are continuously refilled, helping to stave off hunger pangs brought on by the open kitchen—two broad frying surfaces next to the cash register. Spicy and moist meats, poultry, fish, and vegetables are stuffed into football-sized burritos or petite, grilled corn tortillas for tacos, all of which can be washed down with a Modelo, Horchata, or a glass of Sangria. When choosing your food, know that the more obscure the protein, the better—the chorizo sausage, beef tongue, goat meat, and pork ear make for some of the most flavorful options. When the handful of tables are occupied, opt for the reliable take-out or delivery.

968 Amsterdam Ave (btwn 107th & 108th St)
212-531-0383
Mon-Sun 11:30am-12am
❶ to 110th St-Cathedral Pkwy
Entrees $11-13,
Tacos & Tostadas $3-5,
Quesadillas & Burritos $5-9

Toast   *American, Burgers*

Masterful burgers make this self-proclaimed "truckstop gourmet" a neighborhood favorite. Toast is most famous for its burgers, all served on—you guessed it—toasted buns. The

3157 Broadway (near Tiemann Pl)
212-662-1144
Mon-Wed 11am-11pm, Thurs-Fri 11am-12am, Sat 10am-12am, Sun 10am-11pm
❶ to 125th St
Appetizers $5-9,
Burgers & Sandwiches $8-12,
Entrees $11-17

standard burger sits on the menu next to specialties like the Danish (stuffed with blue cheese) and the lamb burger (only at the 103rd St location) stuffed with feta and rosemary and topped with pesto spread. Beyond burgers, Toast smokes its own pork and cures its own salmon in true gourmet style. Teal plastic ceiling canopies, faded wallpaper, and timeworn wooden floors contribute to a happily divey atmosphere, belied by the fresh, high quality ingredients used to produce the generously portioned meals.   A stocked bar with a popular happy hour (daily from 5-7 pm), and prices that err thankfully on the side of 'truckstop' rather than 'gourmet', ensure that Toast remains the honest, casual neighborhood joint it was always meant to be.

PLAY

1020 *Dive*

The de facto Columbia University bar, 1020 is an endearingly unremarkable dive packed nightly with students and locals. Scoring a seat is near-impossible, and on weekends even standing room is hard to come by. And the décor of this worn-out former barbershop is simply bizarre: a coat of arms, a disco ball (never used), vintage street signs and tin beer ads, and a barber's chair for the bouncer. The spectacularly ill-placed dartboard has players shooting pointed projectiles across the bar's entrance-way. What little floorspace is left is consumed by a disastrously inconvenient pool table, splotched with continents of beer stains. At the coveted back mezzanine, new couples guzzle Gin and Tonics and canoodle on busted leather couches. Two TV screens and a projector show a motley collection of cable flicks, but most visitors prefer to solicit hookups and knock over each other's Brooklyn Lagers. Fortunately, the booze is cheap, so there's no reason to cry over spilt beer.

1020 Amsterdam Ave
(at 110th St)
212-531-3468
Mon-Sun 4pm-4am
❶ to 110th St-Cathedral Pkwy
Average Drink $4
Happy Hour: Mon-Sun 4-7pm

The Abbey *Pub, Dive*

Stained glass windows and pew-like booths form this holiest of holy places: a cozy pub full of beer, old friends, and a sinful brownie to die for. Antique lamps cast dim light on the brick space, where couples and solo riders spanning multiple

Ding-Dong Lounge *Dive*

This spacious, barely lit dive was built in the remains of a vacated crack den and has defiantly retained much of its seedy Lower East Side vibe in the face of neighborhood evolution. The draught levers are guitar handles, and the mahogany bar was—according to lore—bankrolled by selling pornography left behind by the former owners. Grungy bartenders serve a mixed crowd of neighborhood regulars and Columbia students seeking asylum from the overcrowded campus dives. Concert posters, graffitied bathrooms, and live DJs every night give Ding-Dong a punk rock feel. Ultimately more of a place to hang out than head bang, the perennially available plush chairs and candlelit tables offer a welcome retreat. Feel free to test your skills at the pool table or vintage Ms. PacMan/Galaga set.

929 Columbus Ave
(btwn 105th & 106th)
212-663-2600
Mon-Sun 4pm-4am
❶ to 103rd St, Ⓑ Ⓒ to 110th St
Average Drink $6
Happy Hour: Daily 4-8pm,
All draft beers $3,
Cocktails $4

generations sit at the bar, while groups of old friends compete for the wooden booths in the back. The crowd is a mix of professionals after work, Columbia students, and locals with decades of loyal patronage. Burgers, soups, and nachos come out hot and fresh from the kitchen, which is open past 1am on the weekends. Come for classic rock and great beer from the constantly changing, extensive list, and stay for the three flavors of chicken wings and the ever-present, always passionate sports talk.

237 W 105th St
(near Broadway)
212-222-8713
Mon-Sat 4pm-4am, Sun
12pm-4am
❶ to 103rd St
Average Beer $5

The Heights

Rooftop Bar

2867 Broadway
(btwn 111th & 112th St)
On the 2nd floor
212-866-7035
Mon-Fri, 11:30am-4am,
Sat-Sun 11am-4am
❶ to 110th St-Cathedral Pkwy
Average Drink $6
Happy Hour: Twice Daily
4pm-7pm Pints &
Margaritas $4, Mon-Wed
& Sun 11pm-4am Pints,
Margaritas, & Well drinks $4

This second-floor watering hole is best known for its massive burrito, its after-work and late-night happy hours, and its shockingly potent frozen margarita. During warm months, the glass roof of the third-story patio opens to patrons, offering less in the way of views than fresh air. In cooler weather bar-hopping Columbia undergrads and diners in search of decent, inexpensive bar grub share the strangely-shaped main room, with its odd mix of collegiate memorabilia and WPA-style labor murals. After a couple of massive margaritas—one of which is easily sweet enough to induce a diabetic coma—the fuzzy design concept will hardly be a concern. Navigating your way down the steep, narrow stairs to the street, however, might be.

The Underground Lounge

Live Music, Comedy

955 West End Ave
(at 107th St)
212-531-4759
Daily 4pm-4am
Sat-Sun 2pm-4am
❶ to 103rd or 110th St-
Cathedral Pkwy
Average Drink $6
Happy Hour: Daily 4-8pm

Depending on the night of the week, the Underground is either a comedy club, fratty party spot, or laid back blues lounge. This chameleonic venue seems to have as many personalities as it does rooms. Like most bars in the neighborhood, it houses its fair share of Columbia students, especially on Thursdays, but in general the Underground welcomes a slightly older crowd than the nearby bars. Grab a table in the front room if you want a view of the daily sports game, or head to the adjoining pool area for a round and new company. On show nights the back lounge fills up with happy onlookers there to support the local musicians and comedians. But beware: with such cheap drink specials, that small flight of stairs in may begin to look a little riskier on the way out.

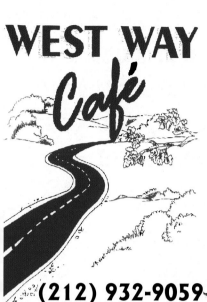

CU IT

COLUMBIA UNIVERSITY
INFORMATION TECHNOLOGY

The CUIT Helpdesk

http://askcuit.columbia.edu

》 by email
askcuit@columbia.edu

》 by phone
212.854.1919

》in person
202 Philosphy Hal

The Center for Student Advising (CSA)

CSA provides support for students throughout their undergraduate years.
Your advisor will assist you with:

- Questions about course selection and course load
- Helping you map out a '4-year plan'
- Pre-professional advising for pre-law, premed, or pre-business
- Questions about AP/IB/GCE credits
- Questions about Columbia College & SEAS deadlines, policies, and procedures
- Questions about major selection and facilitating connections to academic
  departments & faculty

To schedule an advising appointment, please call (212) 854-6378.

CSA website: www.studentaffairs.columbia.edu/csa/

Crêpes on Columbus
New York

Café
Crêperie
Ice Cream

Enjoy!

990 Columbus Avenue, New York, NY 10025
(between 108th & 109th streets)
(212) 222-0259 www.crepesoncolumbus.com
Major Credit Cards Accepted
8am–10pm Daily   Free Delivery

TAP-A-KEG

2731 BROADWAY
BET. 104th & 105th STS
INTERNET JUKEBOX
FREE WIFI
POOL TABLE   DARTS
12 BEERS ON TAP

WE HAVE NO KITCHEN SO BRING YOUR OWN
OR HAVE IT DELIVERED
HAPPY HOUR EVERDAY 12 NOON UNTIL 7PM
OPEN 7 DAYS FROM 12 NOON TO 4AM
212-749-1734

UPPER WEST SIDE

Playing the quirky socialist to the Upper East Side's rich Republican stalwart, the Upper West Side has for decades housed the City's artistic and cultural elite. It's also home to premier performing arts centers and museums like Lincoln Center and the Natural History Museum.

Originally called the Bloomingdale District, it was mostly farmland until the turn of the 20th century, when the swelling island population pushed middle class residences uptown. The pastoral neighborhood quickly urbanized with the the completion of the 9th Avenue elevated train in the late 1800s, and soon the neighborhood's landed class was replaced by barflies and boarders. After World War II, the neighborhood was snatched from their hands and gifted again to a bourgeois elite, drawn by the Lincoln Center Renewal Project and the growing theater scene.

Today, the Lincoln Center sprawls out over 16 acres, encompassing numerous theaters, the Metropolitan Opera House, and Jazz at Lincoln Center. The neighborhood draws tuxes and pearls from all over the city on opening nights, but on most other days the scene is decidedly less ostentatious.

Blocks liberally peppered with supermarkets, laundromats, and family-friendly restaurants cater to liberal young families and yuppies alike. Wealthy, young, and progressively minded parents appreciate the neighborhood's proximity to both Riverside and Central Parks. And the yuppie classes flock for trendy boutiques, gourmet specialty shops, and a buzzing nightlife scene on Amsterdam Avenue between 80th and 86th Streets—aptly titled Beer Row.

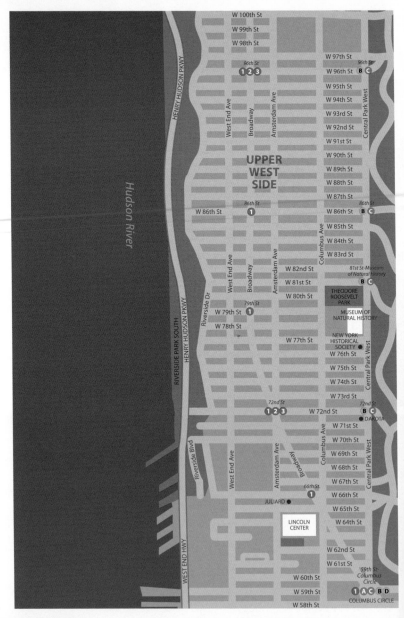

EXPLORE

American Museum of Natural History

No matter how touristy, crowded, or overpriced it may be, the American Museum of Natural History is one of the most fun experiences in the city, and every true New Yorker should go at least once. From lions, tigers, and bears to quetzals, dodos, and giant squids, this massive museum is filled to the brim with breathtaking exhibits. Some may be a little tacky, especially the replicas of actual people, but that's part of the charm. Although everything is worth seeing, be sure to check out the dinosaur fossils in the gorgeous Theodore Roosevelt Rotunda, the planetarium shows at the sleek new Rose Center for Air and Space, and the mammoth overhanging squid and whale model in the hall of biodiversity.

> 79th St (at Central Park West)
> 212-769-5100
> Mon-Sun 10am-5:45pm
> **B C** to 81st-Museum of Natural History
> Suggested Donation Adults $16, Students $12

The Dakota

At this opulent brown castle on Central Park West, iron dragons and stern bearded men glare below epic fire burning sconces. A steady flow of tourists gazes up at the terra-cotta panels, balconies, and corner pavilions dating back to the 1880s. Peek through the gates on 72nd and 73rd (the guards will not let you in) to steal a glimpse of the gorgeous courtyard, or you can try to spy into one of the $20 million apartments from across the street. The palace has been the home of musicians John Lennon and Yoko Oko, author Carson McCullers, and impresario Leonard Bernstein. Movie buffs should note that the Dakota was featured prominently in Roman Polanski's classic horror film *Rosemary's Baby*.

> 1 W 72nd Street
> (at Central Park West)
> **1 2 3** to 72nd St,
> **B C** to 72nd St

New-York Historical Society

The city's oldest museum is housed in this distinguished research institution, featuring an exhaustive collection spanning four centuries of artifacts, artwork, and documents indispensable for any scholar of American culture. Galleries on the second floor showcase a rotating selection of

DAY TO DAY

Community Board 7: 250 W 87th St, 212-362-4008.

Copy Services: Global Copy, 2578 Broadway, 212-222-2679.

Dry Cleaner: Drop Spot Cleaners, 20 W 76th St, 212-721-2480.

Grocery: Fairway Market, 2127 Broadway, 212-595-1888.

Gym: Crunch Fitness, 162 W 83rd St, 212-875-1902.

Hospital: St. Luke's Roosevelt Hospital, 1000 Tenth Ave.

Laundromat: West 79th Laundromat, 218 W 79th St, 212-595-8776.

Library: Riverside Branch Library, 127 Amsterdam Ave.

Volunteer Opportunities: nyccares.org

paintings, while on the fourth floor the Henry Luce Center houses thousands of sculptures, pieces of furniture, decorative objects, glass work, Tiffany lamps, silverware, ceramics, textiles, accessories, toys, coins, buttons, badges, and other ephemera. When your head has finished reeling, stagger back downstairs to the library and reading room. Here, in the shadow of Ionic columns, researchers and the general public alike can burrow through over four million books, maps, newspapers, broadsides, photographs, and architectural drawings, all relating to American history.

170 Central Park West (btwn 76th & 77th St) Tues-Thurs, Sat 10am-6pm, Fri 10am-8pm, Sun 11am-5:45pm, Library Tues-Sat 10am-5pm, 212-873-3400 **Ⓑ Ⓒ** to 81st-Museum of Natural History Admission: Adults $10, Students (with ID) $6

The Vivian Beaumont Theatre

Following Lincoln Center founder John D. Rockefeller's mandate—"the arts not for the privileged few, but for the many"—the Vivian Beaumont has grown to become the largest not-for-profit theater in America. While tickets at other Broadway venues cost upwards of $100, a regular ticket for a show

150 W 65th St (near Broadway) 212-362-7600 Events every Tues 7pm, Wed-Sat 2pm-8pm, Sun 3pm **❶** to 66th St-Lincoln Center

here can go for as little as $32. Though far from the Great White Way, Vivian Beaumont is surrounded by the landmarks of Lincoln Center: the Metropolitan Opera House, Julliard, and Avery Fischer Hall, among others. Another advantage of watching a show at the Vivian Beaumont is that its relative modernity gives it architectural advantages over older Broadway venues. For instance, the aisles are wide and the balcony is only a couple of rows deep, assuring everyone a great view.

Walter Reade Theater

In the 40 years since it opened, The Film Society of Lincoln Center at the Walter Reade Theater first introduced Fassbinder,

165 W 65th St (Upper Level) 212-875-5600 **❶** to 66th St-Lincoln Center Adults $11, Members/Children/ Students $7, Seniors $8

Godard, and Scorsese to American audiences through its two annual film festivals (New York Film Festival and New Directors/New Films). It continues to support emerging and major directors with events, retrospectives, appearances, and premiere screenings and publishes the respected film journal *Film Comment*. The theater regularly offers a prime selection of American and foreign films, along with tasty pound cakes and popcorn. Young art lovers should take advantage of the $7 student tickets to catch some truly stellar pictures.

LINCOLN CENTER

Located at the foot of the Upper West Side on 66th St, Lincoln Center has served as New York's major performing arts center for over half a century. The conception of this cultural epicenter dates back to the 1950s, when a consortium of local leaders assembled by John D. Rockefeller III sought to construct a central performing arts complex as part of Robert Moses' widespread urban renewal project. Since the realization of this project in the 1960s, Lincoln Center has lived up to its aim, providing a dazzling home to 12 of New York's finest performing arts organizations, including the New York Philharmonic, the Metropolitan Opera, the New York City Opera, the New York City Ballet, the Juilliard School, Film Society of Lincoln Center, and Lincoln Center Theater.

Unfortunately, if you're strapped for cash, events at Lincoln Center can prove to be excessively costly. Regular prices run into the hundreds, so check out Lincoln Center's website (*www.lincolncenter.org*) for a host of student discounts for almost every act, including the student rush program, which provides day-of-event tickets for a fraction of the original price. Still, there's no better deal than zero—and that's exactly how much you'll pay for one of the Juilliard School's free concerts, which offer a wide array of presentations. While they may lack the lauded status of their professional counterparts, these free concerts yield just as superb a show while leaving your wallet as full as when you entered. Other highlights of the Center include the New York Film Festival, hosted by the Film Society each fall, and the Lincoln Center Festival, which provides the summer scene with a variety of events every July.

SHOP

Portrait Bug

Part portrait studio, part crafts store, and part party venue, Portrait Bug is a triple threat for anyone looking to create a

2466 Broadway
(btwn 91st & 92nd)
212-600-4457
Mon-Sat 10am-8pm,
Sun 11am-6pm
① ② ③ to 96th St

unique gift or just have some fun. Owner and Upper West Sider Kim Brooks conceived the idea when she couldn't find a place in Manhattan to get a reasonably priced portrait of her young daughter. This bright and cheery store enables parents, friends, and even pet owners to have their loved ones professionally photographed for under $100. If you'd like a creative twist on your new portrait (or a picture you already have), choose from thousands of decorative items like ribbons, stickers, lettering, flowers, buttons, and paint. Gather some goods and craft your photo in the back room—which also hosts birthday parties, and baby and bridal showers—to transform your photo into a personalized work of art.

Toga Bike Shop

Looking for a greener way to travel to work? Eager to test your skills at dirt-track racing? No matter what your cycling needs, the city's oldest and largest bike shop will fulfill them. Floor and ceiling racks are laden with road, mountain, commuter, cross, triathlete, and

110 West End Ave
(at W 64th St)
212-799-9625
Mon & Wed-Fri 11am-7pm,
Thurs 11am-8pm, Sat 10am-6pm, Sun 11am-6pm
① to 66th St

even kids' bikes from premium brands like Cannondale, Giant, Bianchi, Guru, and Independent Fabrications. Cutting-edge accessories and equipment cram the shelves, along with a vast assortment of bike wear. Toga Bikes is also known for its experienced and accommodating staff—proprietor Luis Vieira personally assists customers. Expert mechanics are also on hand to provide free lifetime tune-up services for any bike you buy there. And if you just want a bike for the day, the store rents out hybrids for $30.

Uptown Birds

A cacophony of ear-splitting chirps and a whirlwind of bright colors welcomes visitors to this avian paradise. Birds of

522-526 Amsterdam Ave
(btwn W 86th & W 85th St)
212-877-BIRD (2473)
Mon-Fri 11am-7pm,
Sun 11am-6pm, Tues closed
① to 86th St

all different feathers flock together here, from cockatoos and finches to eclectuses, conures, and lorikeets. They also sell an equally exotic

menagerie of fish, reptiles, and amphibians from around the world. Most people fly to Uptown Birds for its premium quality products: there are cages, terrariums, toys, bedding, heating and lighting supplies, and gourmet bird food—with flavors like Caribbean Crunch, Veggie Delight, and Gardenflora Blend. Prices may be expensive—most parrots cost from $500 to $1000, and rare species like the hyacinth macaw are $15,000!—but it's worth coming just to check out the animals, many of which can't be found anywhere else in Manhattan.

Zabar's

This family-run gourmet and kosher market takes up nearly an entire city block—but its size	2245 Broadway (at 80th St) 212-787-2000 Mon-Fri 8am-7:30pm, Sat 8am-8pm, Sun 9am-6pm ❶ to 79th St

does little to betray the market's nearly century-old tradition of quality products. Just ask any of the 35,000 weekly visitors, who come from all over the island to buy home-roasted coffee, hand-picked smoked salmon, and olives from their extensive bar. Shoppers crowd at the cheese counter to pick from over a hundred cheeses and seek the foodie advice of sagacious staff. An indie market bereft of name brands, Zabar's prides itself on providing high-quality and hard-to-find goods at (mostly) affordable prices, so even those on a tight budget can enjoy delicious, fresh-market fare at this famous destination.

EAT

Bar Boulud

French

A display case of aged sausages by the first-come-first-serve bar, plain wooden tables, and a casual weekend crowd removes just about all traces of pretension	1900 Broadway (btwn 63rd & 64th) 212-595-0303 Mon-Fri 12pm-2:30pm & 5pm-11pm, Sat 11am-2:30pm & 5pm-11pm, Sun 11am-2:30pm and 5pm-10pm ❶ to 66th St Charcuterie $10-15, Entrees $25-28

from renowned chef Daniel Boulud's casual wine and charcuterie bar. Modeled after a wine cellar (albeit one with cream walls, limestone, and track lighting), Bar Boulud specializes in the humble peasant fare of pâtés, meats, wines, and cheeses that constitute classic French charcuterie. Stop by with a friend and split the silky cheese terrine, paired expertly by the approachable sommelier. For something more substantial, try the pre-theater prix fixe, or select entrees from a seasonally changing menu (the wonderful house-made sausages are a safe bet). Windows open onto a breezy outdoor patio during summer months, while inside clinking glasses and friendly chatter ensure that Bar Boulud is as fun as it is refined.

Dovetail

New American

In a neighborhood littered with sleek upscale dining options, the home of French Laundry alum Chef John Fraser sets the new standard. Seasonal ingredients, classic technique, masterful execution, and the spirit of haute cuisine	103 W 77th St (near Columbus Ave) 212-362-3800 Brunch Sat-Sun 11:30am-2:30pm, Lunch Wed-Fri 12pm-2:30pm, Dinner Mon-Sat 5:30pm-11pm, Sunday "Suppa" 5:30pm-11:00pm ❶ to 79th St, ❽❿ to 81st St Brunch $28, Lunch prix fixe $24, Dinner tasting $88, Appetizers $12-26, Entrees $26-43, Sunday "Suppa" $38

produce inspired dishes like sautéed foie gras with graham crackers and huckleberries, and halibut confit with tender sweet peas and maitake mushrooms. The impressive show of savories is followed by an inventive array of desserts, including their popular brioche bread pudding with bacon brittle and rum ice cream. A minimal-but-warm design keeps the focus on the food. Expect the standard clean lines, exposed brick, and tucked-away track lighting of modern establishments, without any of the pretension. Waiters are attentive without suffocating, and will happily help navigate the extensive wine list, made accessible by its "under $75" section.

H & H Bagels

Bagels

Bagel-loving New Yorkers flock to H&H at all hours to pick up some of New York's best bagels	2239 Broadway (at 80th St) 212-595-8003 Daily 24 hours ❶ to 79th St Bagels $1.40

straight from the oven. H&H seems to have everthing: blueberry, poppyseed, whole wheat, plain, cinnamon raisin, onion, salt, garlic, sesame, sourdough, or pumpernickel. You can eat your bagel on the spot or, if you can resist, take home a dozen for later. The refrigerators

NATIVE'S PICK

Barney Greengrass
Deli, Brunch

Famed for excellent fish and shareable portions, this grease-stained landmark has provided quintessentially New York sustenance for over 100 years. The deli-fare crafted by "The Sturgeon King," includes salty Nova Scotia lox and egg scrambles, a slew of hot meat sandwiches, whitefish and sardine specials, smoked fish platters, and triple-decker sandwiches large enough to feed four. Cheese blintzes, matza brei with fresh preserves, and sticky-sweet challah French toast are sensational. The service is friendly and quick—necessarily because the restaurant floods with hungry brunch crowds every weekend. If it's busy there can be a near endless wait for coveted table space, so if you're craving a fresh bagel and schmear on a busy morning, head to the counter for speedy pick-up.

541 Amsterdam Ave
(btwn 86th & 87th)
212-724-4707
Tues-Sun 8:30am-5pm
1 to 86th St, **B C** to 81st St
Sandwiches $5-21
Cash Only

---

that line the walls of the no-frills UWS shop are equipped with all essential bagel toppings from lox to cream cheese to homemade jams. There's no seating here, so H&H isn't exactly a place to linger. Instead, pop in and grab a steaming hot, doughy specimen of New York's best, comforted with the knowledge that, should you ever leave the City, H&H ships all over the world, bringing a little taste of New York just about anywhere.

Hampton Chutney Company
Indian

There's an indescribable pleasure in devouring something that is filling, under 200 calories, and nearly the length of your arm. That something is a dosa at Hampton Chutney Co., where the traditional South Indian snack gets the American treatment, stuffed in thirteen variations from the traditional masala dosa, (a blend of potato and South Indian spices),

464 Amsterdam Ave
(btwn 82nd & 83rd St)
212-362-5050
Mon-Sun 10am-10pm
1 to 79th St
Dosas $8-12, Sandwiches $6-9
BYOB

to a Californian mélange of avocado, arugula, tomatoes, and jack cheese. Each dosa comes with your choice of five signature chutneys: cilantro, curry, mango, tomato, and peanut. All dosas can also be ordered as uttapams, made from the same batter cooked as a thick, doughy pancake rather than a thin crispy dosa. Cleanse your palate with a mango lassi or cardamom coffee, and rest assured that a burrito will never taste the same again.

The Mermaid Inn
Seafood

The siren song of this stylish, romantic reimagining of a New England fish shack lures in Upper West Siders with traditional seafood dishes rendered with aplomb. A simple, concise menu eschews fashionably overwrought preparations for classically robust flavor and style. Seemingly tired dishes are given a refined

568 Amsterdam Ave #1
(btwn 87th & 88th St)
212-799-7400
Brunch Sat-Sun 10am-3pm
10am-3pm, Dinner Fri-Sat
5pm-12am, Sun 5pm-10pm
1 to 86th St, **B C** to 81st St
Appetizers $7-12,
Entrees $17-26

resuscitation, like the now-famous lobster sandwich. Decadent chunks of lobster meat come served in a light, creamy dressing nestled between two pieces of buttery toasted brioche, served alongside a heaping mound of fries redolent of Old Bay seasoning. With nautical maps on the walls and dim candlelight, The Mermaid Inn is traditional without being dull, stylish without being pretentious, and intimate without being cramped. By the time your complimentary demitasse cup of chocolate pudding arrives, the Mermaid's seduction is complete. Alas, so is your meal.

Ouest
New American

All taste and no pretension, Ouest serves innovative plates that expand your palette and satisfy your stomach. Large circular booths and the

2315 Broadway
(btwn 83rd & 84th St)
212-580-8700
Brunch Sun 11am-2pm
Sun-Tues 5-9:30pm, Wed-Thurs 5-10:30pm, Fri-Sat 5-11pm,
❶ to 86th St
Appetizers $9-17, Entrée $24-39

sounds of an open kitchen make for a cozy dining experience rare among upscale eateries. It pays to be adventurous when choosing from the menu, as celebrated chef Tom Valenti specializes in subtle and unexpected flavor combinations. His truffled omelet soufflé—airy egg with slivers of mushroom and a rich mousseline sauce—is a favorite appetizer among regulars. The standout entree is new chef Derrick Styczek's roasted rabbit. Stuffed with brioche and pancetta, and served over a bed of garlic orzo, it's sure to induce a state of culinary bliss. Hold onto that feeling a while longer by ordering the orange-mascarpone cheesecake with candied orange peel, a sweet and tart concoction of well-balanced flavors.

Levain Bakery
Bakery

The bakery's founders first bonded over a love of triathlons—ironic, given that Levain's claim to fame is its enormous, decadent cookie. Their six-

167 W 74th St
(near Amsterdam Ave)
212-874-6080
Mon-Sat 8am-7pm,
Sun 9am-7pm
❶❷❸ to 72nd St
Pastries & Cookies $2-4,
Breads $4-6, Pizzas & Sandwhiches $7

ounce, saucer-sized sweets are the stuff of legends—the secret recipe is often imitated, but never duplicated. The chocolate chip walnut packs enough sugary, gooey goodness to satisfy even die-hard chocoholics. And pastry lovers all over the island come to sample freshly baked favorites like the baguette with butter and raspberry jam and chocolate chip brioche. Should you want to impress friends with homemade treats, Levain's website offers tips and instructions for recreating some of their signature selections, like the cinnamon raisin country bread and oatmeal raisin scones.

Pinch and S'mac
Comfort Food, Pizza

Though their décor seems inspired by a junior high cafeteria, Pinch and S'mac plates new twists on childhood faves. This is no kiddie snack spot—the

474 Columbus Ave
(btwn 82nd & 83rd)
646-438-9494
Sun–Thurs 11am - 10pm,
Fri - Sat 11am-11pm
❶ to 79th St, ❽ ❾ to 81st S
Mac & cheese $5-11,
Plain pizza 55¢ per inch

selection of cheeses (gorgonzola, pecorino), meats (chorizo, grilled shrimp), and vegetables (grilled eggplant, sundried tomatoes) modernize classic kiddie comfort food for older crowds. Twelve variations on mac and cheese fill the billboard-sized menu—popular are the rich Parisienne with brie, figs, shiitake mushrooms, and rosemary, and the spicy Cajun with pepperjack cheese and andouille sausage. Add any number of toppings to pizzas and pay by the inch. Health-conscious diners—presumably dragged here against their wills—can choose from a decent selection of salads instead of the cheesy main show. Nostalgia never tasted so grown up.

Salumeria Rosi Parmacotto
Italian

As though plucked from Parma and plopped onto Amsterdam Ave, this Italian joint is a shrine to salumi—traditional

283 Amsterdam Ave
(btwn 73rd & 74th St)
212-877-4800
Mon-Sun 11am-11pm
❶❷❸ to 72nd St
Entrees $5-9 (5 per meal),
Salumi $2.75-9.25 (¼ lb)

Italian cured meats. A row of hefty prosciutto haunches dangles behind the meat counter, which displays everything from parmacotto (cooked ham) to mortadella (finely ground pork sausage) to cacciatorino (pocket-sized salame), plus specialty beans, cheeses, and prepared foods. The tasting menu's modestly-sized portions boast rich flavor sure to linger on your palate long after the meal. Supplement these with the signature salad, a luxurious blend of soft scrambled eggs, pancetta, and mesclun, or the creamy, slow-cooked orzotto with zucchini and pesto. If you're jonesing for indulgence, try the pancia, a vinegar-soaked slab of melt-in-your-mouth pork belly served over dandelion greens. With so many ways to swine and dine, who needs chicken?

PLAY

Barcibo Enoteca — *Wine Bar*

2020 Broadway (at 70th St)
212-595-2805
1 2 3 to 72nd St
Mon-Fri, 4:30pm-2am; Sat-Sun, 3:30pm-2am

The tall marble-topped tables and high stools provide an elegant setting for good times shared over great wine, and Barcibo knows great wine. This wine bar houses an impressive selection of over 130 Italian wines to choose from, 40 of which are available by the glass. Go for a glass of the Montepulciano or Valpolicella, and you can always count on the staff to make knowledgeable suggestions if you're unfamiliar with Italian varietals. Pair your wine with something form the equally extensive tapas selection, like the shrimp risotto, the marinated octopus, or calamari salad. Perfect for a pre-theater drink, Barcibo beckons patrons to give free reign to the connoisseur inside.

Bourbon St — *College Bar*

405 Amsterdam Ave
(btwn 79th & 80th St)
212-721-1332
Daily 12pm-4am, Sun 12pm-12am
1 to 79th St
Average Drink $5
Happy Hour: Daily 4-8pm

Lit by neon signs, red lights, and alligator-head lamps, this New Orleans-themed bar fills to capacity with college students and twenty-somethings looking to dance on the bar and down cheap drinks. A Big Easy frat party transplanted to the Upper West Side,

Jake's Dilemna — *Dive Bar*

430 Amsterdam Ave
(near 81st St)
212-580-0556
Mon-Fri 5pm-4am,
Sat-Sun 2pm-4am
1 to 79th St
Average Drink $5
Happy Hour: Mon-Thurs 4-8pm, Fri 3-8pm

Jake's Dilemna is like a nostalgic throwback to those staples of college drinking: beer pong and alcohol-fueled lit discussions. Upstairs there's a rowdy, rock- and R&B-infused singles scene, with friendly bartenders, a decent beer selection, and a rollicking crowd of mostly locals and the occasional out-of-towner on the prowl. The almost daily drink specials encourage hoarse throats, spilled beer, and hazy memories the next morning. For a break from the raucous partying, head downstairs to The Oak Room, where exposed brick, bookshelves, and intense conversation instead of thudding bass-lines might make you think you've stumbled out of a frat house and into Hemingway's den. But when the buzz that was stoking your passionate Rawls debate has run out, head back up the stairs into the fray to grab another cheap screwdriver.

Bourbon St is decorated primarily by Mardi Gras beads. Hundreds of bras hang above the bar, undoubtedly surrendered by drunken college girls looking to add a few more beads to their collection. Specials like 50-cent Bud drafts from 9-11pm on Beat-the-Clock Thursdays, and $3 Blue Moon pints on Saturdays make Bourbon St the pregame destination of the west 80s. If you're looking for a slightly less raucous drinking experience, head to the back of the bar to play video games, pool, or darts.

Cleopatra's Needle
Jazz, Live Music

2485 Broadway (at 92nd St)
212-769-6969
Daily 11am-11:30pm
❶❷❸ to 96th St
Average Drink $6
Happy Hour: Daily
4-7:30pm, Half-Priced
Martinis and wine

Serving a Mediterranean medley of couscous and kebab—with American extras like French fries and chicken wings—this eatery and bar hosts live jazz every night of the week. The bar swallows most of the space, serving Happy Hour specials for about three-and-a-half "happy" hours every day. But the best thing about this Upper West Side spot isn't the menu or the twinkly light décor: it's the free cover charge for music. There is, however, a ten-dollar per person minimum—so the exodus of your cash inevitable.

Prohibition
Lounge

503 Columbus Ave (btwn
84th & 85th St)
212-579-3100
Mon-Wed 5pm-2am,
Thurs-Sat 5pm-4am, Sun
12pm-2am
❶ to 86th St, ❸❿ to 81st St
Average Drink $10

The front windows and loud live music belie this lounge's namesake, which conjures misleading images of speakeasy back rooms accessed only by password. The bricked space is dimly lit, outfitted with leather furniture, and always bustling. The crowd is a heterogeneous mix of young couples loitering after dinner, fresh-from-the-office yuppies, and recent grads upgrading from college dives to a more sophisticated locale. Their long and diverse drink menu includes signature martinis perfect for pairing with the late-night New American cuisine. Nightly live music ensures a pleasant variety of genres: a group of shaggy-haired, twenty-something musicians covering 90s rock hits one night and a jazz trio the next.

UPPER EAST SIDE

Woody Allen immortalized it, Tom Wolfe parodied it, *Sex and the City* reveled in it, and the tell-all book *The Nanny Diaries* scandalized it. The Upper East Side is the first and last word in old money, style, and aristocracy.

Of course, an area as large as the Upper East Side couldn't be homogeneous—sprawling over nine avenues and almost 40 blocks, the neighborhood includes both palatial luxury townhouses and cramped studios. A few blocks from the duplexes overlooking Central Park lie the bars, burrito joints, and high-rises that line Second, Third, and Lexington Avenues.

As with most of Upper Manhattan, there wasn't much to see here until Central Park opened to the public in the 1860s. The eastern section of the region developed quickly as the Second and Third Avenue elevated lines eased transportation between the urban center and its outlying regions. The development that would earn the Upper East Side its elite reputation, however, was construction along Fifth, Madison, and Park Avenues. From Astor to Tiffany, New York's wealthiest barons erected mansion after mansion facing the new park. While the penthouses pass hands in wealthy families generation after generation, the northeasternmost part of the neighborhood is witnessing a new population trickle in. Still nursing hangovers from graduation, frat-friendly investment bankers and their cohorts are coming in droves, attracted by dirt cheap rents and a bar scene reminiscent of their their midwestern college towns.

Today, the Upper East Side is a top cultural destination, drawing crowds to museums like the Met, the Whitney, and the Frick Collection. The neighborhood's galleries are among the city's most esteemed, offering Picassos, Braques, and Chagalls to a public that could actually afford to put them on their walls. But don't let exclusivity of this community intimidate you—the only thing you need to appreciate it is your eyes.

EXPLORE

Asia Society Museum

The crowd-free museum at the Asia Society offers salvation to those who wish to avoid the noise, bustle, and hype suffered at the city's more traditional artistic

725 Park Ave (at 70th St)
212-288-6400
Tues-Sun 11am-6pm, Fri
11am-9pm except July 4th-
Labor Day, Mon closed
6 to 68th St, **F** to 63rd St
Admission $ 10, Students $5,
Free Fri 6pm-11pm

attractions. Featuring up to three exhibitions at a time, the museum includes in its collections art from Iran to India to Korea, from the Han to the Hu Jintao empires. Despite its bulky exterior, the museum's interior is delicate and modest, with one floor devoted to exhibitions of drawings, paintings, and sculptures. A second floor houses film exhibitions—a maze of barren, interconnected projection rooms that play video installations by contemporary Asian video artists. Admission is free during their extended hours, which are Fridays from 6pm-9pm, Labor Day through July 4th.

Cooper-Hewitt

This museum includes over 250,000 objects and an extensive library showcasing both the history of design

2 E 91st St (5th Ave)
212-849-8400
Mon-Fri 10am-5pm, Sat
10am-6pm, Sun 12pm-6pm
456 to 86th St
Adults $15, Students $10

and contemporary projects. Situated in the old Carnegie Mansion, it is the only museum in the country dedicated entirely to design. There are approximately 40,000 art objects dating from classical antiquity to present day. Objects range from Soviet porcelains to Japanese tsuba (sword fittings). Cooper-Hewitt is also committed to education, offering programs for all levels and ages—from youth programs to a Masters of Arts. They offer free daily tours of the museum and special design events.

The Frick Collection

Formerly the private residence and personal collection of Henry Clay Frick, this Fifth Avenue mansion is now a

1 East 70th Street (at 5th Ave)
212-288-0700
Tues-Sat 10am-6pm, Sun
11am-5pm, Mon closed
6 to 68th St
Adults $15, students $5

public museum. The building itself is a work of art—flaunting shiny marble floors, beautiful

DAY TO DAY

Community Board 8: 505 Park Ave, 212-758-4340.

Dry Cleaner: C88 Cleaners, 1689 1st Ave, 212-289-8147.

Groceries: Gristedes, 1365 3rd Ave, 212-535-8449.

Gym: 92nd Street Y, 1395 Lexington Ave, 212-415-5500.

Hospital: Mount Sinai Hospital, 1190 5th Ave, 212-241-6500.

Library: New York Public Library, 112 E 96th St, 212-289-0908. Also 328 E 67th St, 212-734-1717.

Media: uppereast.com. uppereastsideinformer.blogspot.com.

Volunteer Opportunities: nyccares.org

wood ceilings, and exquisitely molded walls— and the impressive collection includes paintings, sculptures, rugs, porcelains, and furniture. The works are displayed without explanatory plaques, so get the free audio guide if you want to know what you're looking at. The majority of their collection is permanent, but they often also have a few small, temporary exhibitions. Unlike its institutionalized counterparts, the Frick offers a uniquely elegant museum experience enhanced by the intimacy and serenity of the home setting—a home that houses Renoir and Rembrandt art, that is.

The Metropolitan Museum of Art

This world famous museum stretches almost four city blocks, nearly quarter of a mile long. The neoclassical lobby of warm white stone only hints at the enormous

1000 5th Ave (at 82nd St)
212-535-7710
Tues-Thurs & Sun 9:30am-
5:30, Fri-Sat 9:30am-9pm,
Mon closed
6 to Nassau Ave
Adults $20 suggested,
Students (with ID) Free

permanent collection that lies in its wings. Greco-Roman statues share the building with Byzantine art and Matisse paintings. The Arms and Armor collection even has spears and gauntlets sure to enthrall the most stubborn of five-year-olds. Equally impressive is the ever-popular Temple of

Dendur, transported in its entirety from Egypt to the first floor of the Met. Fuel for the visit can be found in one of the public restaurants in the main building, and on nicer days, at the street vendors parked by the front steps. Avoid crowds and visit Friday or Saturday evening, when the museum's open until 9pm.

The Museum of the City of New York

Unlike Manhattan's more glamorously stylized museums, the Museum of the City of New York showcases both the glorious and the gritty.

1220 5th Ave (at 103rd St)
212-534-1672
Tues-Sun 10am-5pm,
Mon closed
❷❸ to 110th St-Central Park North, ❻ to 103rd St
Suggested: Adults $10,
Students $6

This spectacular neo-Georgian building boasts more than 1.5 million objects—from antique furniture to 20th-century street photography—that collectively tell the the rich history of New York. Natives and tourists alike go to appreciate era-defining pictures by Jacob Riis, peer into the recreated rooms of John D. Rockefeller, or peruse original copies of Eugene O'Neill's manuscripts. Among its exhibits are the New York City Toy Collection, an archive of 10,000 toys, some of which date back to the colonial period, the New York Fashion Exhibit, a collection of textiles worn by 17th century city-dwellers, and the Theater and Broadway Collection, which houses costumes

and props from throughout Broadway's history. With all this at your fingertips for an extremely affordable suggested donation, you can feel free to revisit the history of this great city any time like.

Neue Galerie

This sumptuous Upper East Side mansion, only a few blocks north of the Metropolitan,

1048 5th Ave (at 86th St)
212-628-6200
11am-6pm, Tues & Wed closed
❹❺❻ to 86th St
Admission $15, Students $10

houses the greatest concentration of 20th-century German and Austrian art in New York. Three floors of exhibition space display art ranging from Jugendstil to Bauhaus to Expressionism, with masterworks by Klimt and Kirchner, among others, squeezed into two compact floors of galleries. With fine arts, decorative arts, and applied arts all given equal treatment, the Neue Galerie demonstrates the same spirit of modernity as its 1923 Viennese namesake. For those as yet unfamiliar with this period in art history, the first floor is arranged as a primer. A design store, a book store, and two lauded cafés all on the premises make the Neue Galerie one of the densest and most rewarding arts destinations in New York.

Solomon R. Guggenheim Museum

Like an extraterrestrial drill burrowing into Fifth Avenue, Frank Lloyd Wright's iconic

masterpiece boldly marks its territory on the Upper East Side. Seven floors of sloping white walls, a massive, ornate skylight, and sunlit nooks house modern and contemporary international art installations, encompassing works from the mid-19th-century to the present. While touting an impressive permanent collection with works from Picasso, Van Gough, and Kandinsky, the museum gives ample room to the sculptures, paintings, and video installations of its temporary exhibits, seamlessly integrating them along its coiling walkway. Brave the crowds and come on Saturday nights between 5:45 and 7:45 when admission is pay what you can. Or come the first Friday night of the month to check out Gaugin while getting your groove on—the Art After Dark events offer drinks and DJs till 1am.

1071 5th Ave (at 89th St)
212-423-3500
Sun-Wed 10am-5:45pm,
Fri 10am-5:45pm,
Sat 10am-7:45pm, Thurs closed
4 5 6 to 86th St
Adults $18, Students $15,
Art After Dark $25

Sotheby's

The only North American location of this international institution, Sotheby's offers famed auctions and ten floors of free public gallery space. During the peak spring and fall seasons, international visitors come to buy and sell every type of art imaginable. From rare wines and 19th-century paintings to Chinese ceramics and 20th century furnishings, this place runs the gamut of possible art forms. Come by to see world renowned pieces before they're auctioned off—they're typically on display the week before. Be sure to check out the huge gallery space on the tenth floor, and stop by their rooftop café for soups, sandwiches, and the like. No matter what you're looking for, so long as you have an appreciation for art, you'll find it here at Sotheby's.

1334 York Ave (at 72nd St)
212-606-7000
6 to 68th St-Hunter College

Whitney Museum of American Art

From painting and sculpture to photography and video, this five-floor museum offers an impressive representation of 20th-century American art. The

945 Madison Ave
(at 75th St)
212-570-3600
Wed-Thurs 11am-6pm,
Fri 1pm-9pm, Sat-Sun 11am-
6pm, Mon-Tues Closed
6 to 77th St
Adults $15, Students $10,
Friday 6pm–9pm
Pay-what-you-wish admission

building itself—constructed in 1966—is a modern structure that stands out amongst its more subdued neighbors on Madison Ave, properly reflecting the "artist's museum" ethos originally intended by Mrs. Whitney. The second, third, and fourth floors house temporary exhibits that change frequently, and the fifth floor is given over to a jaw-dropping permanent collection of works by Hopper, O'Keeffe, Rothko, Calder, and Pollock. The Whitney Biennial opens the celebrated galleries to works by emerging American artists every other year and should not be missed.

SHOP

The Corner Bookstore

Cozy, bright, and crammed full of books, the tiny shop that inspired Meg Ryan's store in the film *You've Got Mail*

1313 Madison Ave (at 93rd St)
212-831-3554
Mon-Fri 10am-7pm,
Sat 10:30am-6pm,
Sun 11am-6pm
6 to 96th St

is everything an independent bookstore ought to be. There isn't much space to spare on the wooden shelves that line this former turn-of-the-century pharmacy. Trust that each book you see has been researched, and likely read, by at least one person on shift. Still deliberating? Seek help from the knowledgeable staff, happy to give you their true opinions of the books and authors—don't be surprised if one says, "I think he's a terrible writer, honestly." An ancient 1890s cash register at the counter adds to the old-time charm. This picturesque bookstore is the perfect place to wile away an afternoon perusing sections and curling up on a bench by the windows with your new favorite read.

Dylan's Candy Bar

The board game Candyland manifest, Dylan's Candy Bar devotes three floors to all that is sweet. From the music selection— "Chocolate Girl" and

1011 3rd Ave (near 60th St)
646-735-0078
Mon-Thurs 10am-10pm,
Fri-Sat 10am-11pm,
Sun 10am-9pm
4 5 6 N Q R W to
Lexington Ave-59th St

"I Want Candy" ring from the speakers—to the shelves supported by 8-foot candy canes, everything here seems coated in sugar. And then, of course, there's the candy itself: brightly colored lollipops bigger than a kid's head fan out enticingly

MUSEUM MILE

Best known for its art world giants like the Met, Guggenheim, and Frick, this stretch of Fifth Avenue conceals lesser-known gems just a short walk uptown. Check out these museums for impressive collections with a fraction of the weekend crowds. One day a year, the street is closed to traffic and all the museums open their doors for free for the Museum Mile Festival.

The **National Academy Museum** (*at 89th St*) houses one of the largest national collections of 19th- and 20th-century pieces with the class of a European salon. Founded by professional artists in 1825, it offers visitors an inspiring display of new works during its Annual Exhibition

As the only design-centric museum in the US, the **Cooper-Hewitt National Design Museum** (*at 91st St*) explores the balance between aesthetics and functionality in early print media, object design, and architectural drawings. It also exhibits work by contemporary artists with environmental and humanitarian themes.

The Jewish Museum (*btwn 92nd St & 93rd St*) aims to spark thought-provoking social questions through its exhibits of Jewish art and cultural shows.

The wide-ranging exhibitions at the **Museum of the City of New York** (*btwn 103rd St & 104th St*) explore and celebrate of the history of the city. Come see urban photography, a tour of NYC theater, and architectural plans for past and future New Yorks.

from countless stands, plastic dispensers of penny candies sit on nearly every ground floor shelf, and containers of Jelly Bellys and M&M's cover the upstairs walls. True to its name, Dylan's Candy Bar serves as much as sells—there's a chocolate and fudge bar open for chocoholics, and a third-floor café with sundaes and other sit-down treats. As the gummy-filled stairs declare, "May each step you take be sweet."

standards, hard to find imported teas, and unique blends like Lavender Earl Grey. With over 140 varieties to peruse, the tea menu can leave you a bit blurry eyed, but knowledgeable wait staff will help shrink it down to a manageable size—no "drink me" bottle required.

EAT

Alice's Tea Cup—Chapter III   *Café, Tea*

Tea devotees and young birthday girls alike spend afternoons sipping from mismatched porcelain teacups and nibbling at tiny sandwiches (crustless,

220 E 81st St (near 3rd Ave)
212-734-4832
Daily 8am-8pm,
Brunch Sat & Sun until 3pm
⑥ to 77th St
Scones & Tea $10, Brunch
$20-25, Lunch $20-25,
Afternoon Tea $22-30

of course) at this quirky teashop of Wonderland fame. Freshly-baked scones come in a variety of flavors, both sweet and savory, and are served with classic clotted cream and jam. The popular pumpkin scones are worth a try, but even better are the mixed berry or ham and cheese. Alice's awe-inspiring collection of teas includes café

Café Mingala   *Burmese*

With influences from Thai, Indian, and Chinese cooking, Burmese cuisine is difficult to capture in all its complexity,

1393 #B 2nd Ave (at 73rd St)
212-744-8008
Sun-Thurs 11:30am-11pm,
Fri-Sat 11:30am-12am
⑥ to 68th St-Hunter College
Appetizers $5-9, Entrees $10-17

and often overwhelms with an excess of flavors. This is not the case at Café Mingala. Here, images of Burmese cities cover all the walls, setting the scene for clean, creative, and delicious cooking. Mains featuring chicken, pork, duck, beef, seafood, and vegetables are all well prepared and seasoned, but it is Café Mingala's appetizers and salads that stand apart. Order the assorted appetizers delight for a sampling of lentil fritters, golden triangles, shrimp spring rolls, golden fingers, and fried tofu, or the mango salad for something light and fresh. Café Mingala also offers an irresistible lunch special, with entrees at half price from 11:30am to 3:30pm.

Café Sabarsky

Austrian

This café dishes delicately crispy wiener schnitzel and decadent apple strudel to patrons of the Neue Galerie Museum. Inspired by the turn-of-the-century Viennese cafés that nurtured artists and intellectuals, Sabarsky's high ceilings and mirrored walls create a lofty space prime for discussing the surrounding German and Austrian artwork. Regional staples like goulash, spätzle, and knackwurst are prepared with inventive twists, like the delicious smoked trout-filled crêpes accompanied by horseradish crème fraiche. To finish off your meal, sample a cup of their rich and flavorful coffee—exclusively imported from Austria and served on a silver platter—before wishing "auf Wiedersehen" to the polite, friendly, and mostly Austrian staff.

> 1048 5th Ave (86th St)
> 212-288-0665
> Mon & Wed 9am-6pm,
> Thurs-Sun 9am-9pm,
> Tues closed
> ④⑤⑥ to 86th St
> Breakfast $6-21, Dinner $12-28

Daniel

French

Dinner at Daniel is about as close to a perfect dining experience you'll find in New York. It begins the moment you walk in: lithe, focused servers perform a veritable ballet as they guide you through one of the several seasonal tasting menus. Dishes are uniformly magnificent. A whole roasted Portuguese dorade is filleted tableside and served with an ethereal fig compote. Refreshing cucumber gazpacho tempers a snapper ceviche. And in the sunken central dining room, bordered by an elegantly embroidered white colonnade, you'll find rarefied surroundings that only enhance the dining experience. Truth be told, it hardly matters what dishes you order. The level of quality is so uniform, and ingredients treated with such reverence, that the entire dining experience at Daniel is dreamlike and transporting. The best you can do is enjoy the ride.

> 60 E 65th St
> (btwn Madison & Park Ave)
> 212-288-0033
> Mon-Thurs 5:45pm-11pm,
> Fri-Sat 5:30pm-11pm,
> Sun closed
> ⑥ to 68th St-Hunter College
> Prix fixe menus $105-175

Serendipity 3

Café, Dessert

It's serendipitous to get a table at this unbelievably popular ice cream shop and restaurant— everyone from little girls to famous celebs come to indulge for an afternoon.

> 225 E 60th St
> (btwn 2nd & 3rd Ave)
> 212-838-3531
> Sun-Thurs 11:30am-12am,
> Fri 11:30am-1am,
> Sat 11:30am-2am
> ⑥ to 59th St-Lexington Ave
> Desserts $7-$22, Appetizers
> $4-$12.50, Entrees $12.50-$23

Fashioned like an old-time soda shop, the airy space of Serendipity 3 is filled with Tiffany lamps, marble-topped tables, and butterfly mirrors. Their most popular offering is the signature Frrrozen Hot Chocolate: served in a huge glass bowl made for sharing, this dessert drink is a glorious mixture of thick chocolatey-cold goodness and the unmistakable grainy taste of hot cocoa mix. If you aren't too full, order another dessert off the massive newspaper-fashioned menu: the Forbidden Broadway Sundae, a hot fudge sundae with chocolate blackout cake, and the gigantic banana split are definite crowd pleasers—and you'll need a crowd to help finish them.

Sfoglia
Italian

1402 Lexington Ave
(near 92nd St)
212-831-1402
Lunch Tues-Sat 12pm-2:30pm,
Dinner Mon-Sun 5:30pm-11pm
6 to 96th St
Appetizers $12-18,
Entrees $22-32

With wooden tables, hanging tapestries, an open pantry, and fresh field flower centerpieces, this discrete Italian spot resembles a romantic Tuscan villa. Sfoglia is a neighborhood mainstay and much-loved destination for gourmands seeking exceptional food in a space designed for quiet comfort and pleasure. Delicately spicy wild mussels or tender fava beans with candied walnuts are excellent starters. The fresh papardelle alla Bolognese is rich and buttery, and the housemade potato gnocci delicate and supple. Their signature chicken al mattone is cooked traditionally under a brick, leaving it crisp and juicy. Handcrafted pastries, gelati, and sorbetti round out the carefully crafted dessert menu. Wine connoisseurs will not find classic, budget-busting bottles—their wines are exclusively from small, Italian family vineyards.

Yorkville Creperie
French

1586 York Ave (at 84th St)
212-570-5445
Mon-Thurs 8am-9pm, Fri-Sat
8am-11pm, Sun 9am-8pm
456 to 86th St
Crepes $5-9

Comfortable couches and a pretty, bistro-like interior make this Upper East Side crepêrie an ideal place to enjoy a leisurely breakfast, lunch, or dinner. Breakfast lovers prefer the classic morning crêpe with bacon, egg, and Swiss cheese, while those with a sweet tooth, if they dare, indulge in the decadent bubba crêpe, stuffed with Snickers, Reeses cups, Nutella, strawberry jelly, and topped with vanilla ice cream and whipped cream. Should none of the varieties on offer pique your fancy, you can create your own from the considerable selection of fillings on hand. If crêpes aren't your style, you may be better served dining someplace else, though the comparatively small selection of panini is also quite tasty. A full bar, wine list, and comfortable bar seating complete the delightfully Gallic picture.

PLAY

The Big Easy
College Bar, Dive

1768 2nd Ave (92nd St)
212-348-0879
Mon-Fri 5pm-4am, Sat
12pm-4am, Sun 1pm-2am
6 to 96th St
Average Drink $3
Happy Hour: Daily 5-8pm

You'll run into the crowd—and the smell—of this rowdy joint before you've cleared the sidewalk. Inside is a frat boy's dream: bras decorate one full wall, simple concrete outfits the floors, and a hot, all-female wait staff wearing smiles bigger than their skimpy uniforms give The Big Easy an anything goes spirit. Careful not to spill your warm, slightly stale beer or unidentifiable mixed drink as you navigate through hordes of happy bros. Take your glass to the cavernous backspace and play a game of pong—there's an entire fleet of tables. Fridays boast the $20 open bar special, aptly named "Road to Rehab." So brush up on your Journey sing-along skills, warm up your throwing arm, and kick back with approximately half of Jersey's male population.

Cavatappo Wine Bar
Wine Bar

1728 2nd Ave (near 90th)
212-426-0919
Mon-Thurs 5pm-12am,
Fri-Sat 5pm-1am, Sun
4pm-11pm
456 to 86th St
Average Glass $9

A tiny red and blue awning, small patio, and narrow room define one of the most enjoyable and romantic spots on the UES. The gregarious sommelier will chat you up as he fills your glass, recommending his favorite cheese to accompany your selection. The list of bottles (mostly under $40) are categorized by their sensuous characteristics like "soft and supple" and "full-bodied, robust." Pair with some Foxy cheese fondue or hand-pressed finger sandwiches—food specials change almost daily and are worth sharing. Visit on Sunday to buy cheap bottles

Pyramida

Middle Eastern

Only slightly more spacious than a walk-in closet, Pyramida may be the archetypal hole-in-the-wall eatery—but a dingy dive it's not. This neat, brightly-painted falafel shop serves up fresh Middle Eastern cuisine so fresh and satisfying you'll wonder how it possibly came out of a tiny kitchen. The reliable falafel sandwich packs its ingredients into a pita sturdy enough not to crumble in your hands, so you can enjoy your meal down to the last warm, crispy bite. Make sure to order the hummus, with hints of garlic and welcome chunks of chickpea, either on the side or in your sandwich. Wash it down with their popular freshly squeezed lemonade. It'll run you a bit steep at $4.50 a cup, but the cool drink is intensely citrusy, sweet, and pulpy—immediately refreshing in any weather.

401 E 78th St (near 1st Ave)
212-472-5855
Daily 11am-11pm
6 to 77th St
Appetizers $5-8, Entrees $5-15
Cash only

and build your knowledge of global wines—the weekend's opened reds are sold half-off until they're gone.

Stir

Lounge

Stir is a little black dress amid a sea of polos, valiantly breathing life into the frat-boy abyss that is the Upper East Side bar scene. While it may occasionally come off as trying too hard—with an affected downtown vibe and a fussy drinks list—Stir definitely has its perks: the crowd is diverse and the music is a danceable melange of hip-hop and funk. Sleek, dark, and minimalist décor dresses the bar area. In the back, charming candlelit banquettes offer perfect first date seating. Enjoy signature martinis like the Temptation, a blueberry mojito Stoli muddled with fresh blueberries, lime, and mint, or sip on the Passion, a genteel Southern peach tea cocktail. Just be prepared to share the

1363 1st Ave
(btwn 72nd & 73rd St)
212-744-7190
Mon-Wed 5pm-1am, Thurs
5pm-2am, Fri 5pm-4am, Sat
8pm-4am, Sun closed
6 to 68th St or 77th St
Average Drink $6
Happy Hour: Mon-Thurs
5pm-8pm, Fri 5pm-9pm:

space with raucous birthday and bachelorette parties on weekends.

Swig

Dive

This cozy and amiable neighborhood pub offers an enthusiastic sports environment, Tuesday trivia nights, and a generally low-key good time befitting the clean-cut, yuppie crowd. Irish and Scottish bartenders and wait staff unafraid to milk their accents for all they're worth pleasantly undercut the post-college vibe. Their respectable beer menu, which varies from Bud Light to quirky imports like Delirium Tremens, strikes the right balance between the divey atmosphere and the authentic pub feel. As the night goes on, you'll spy many tipsy, devoid-of-all-dance-skill-white-boy types trying to get their groove on. But with the sweet throwback music, a competent kitchen that doesn't close until midnight, and a friendly crowd, it's easy to walk in and swig a pint of your favorite beer.

1629 2nd Ave (at 85th St)
212-628-2364
Mon-Fri 2pm-4am,
Sat-Sun 12pm-4am
4 5 6 to 86th St
Average Drink $5
Happy Hour: Daily before 8pm

MIDTOWN WEST

Nowhere else are New Yorkers so closely pitted against tourists than in Midtown West. The nine-to-five home of corporate armies and media hawks alike, Midtown West also serves as the permanent stomping ground for camera-carrying tourists seeking shots of Big Apple icons like Times Square, and Rockefeller Center.

But the glittering, behemoth attractions and business bustle of the district belie the neighborhood's seedy past. The Great White Way was once plagued with drug-trafficking and sordid adult businesses, but a massive cleanup effort polished it anew and transformed it into a family-friendly attraction. Likewise, 8th Avenue marks the western boundary for Hell's Kitchen, the neighborhood immortalized in *West Side Story* that was once home to immigrant strongholds, machine bloc votes, and organized crime. Following extensive redevelopment and gentrification in the 1990s, real estate agents now pimp the neighborhood as "Clinton" to a moneyed creative class that brings with it pricey boutiques, restaurants, and nightlife. Other changes are afoot in Hudson Yards, the far Western portion of the area and a current hotbed of development. Proposals include replacing much of its working-class housing and warehouse infrastructure with an extension of the 7 train, a new Penn Station and Madison Square Garden, tax-abated high-rises, a convention center, and a rezoned business district.

The recently revitalized Theater District is also leaking westward. Companies like the New Dramatists draw audiences to independent off-Broadway theaters. Koreatown's many karaoke bars lure drunken belting crowds from all around the island. Even Times Square now merits a visit: Mayor Bloomberg's decision to ban cars on Broadway between 42nd and 47th has made it into a peculiar pedestrian promenade.

There is a dual landscape here—one both magnetic and repellent. It is home to some of the most satisfying and exciting food and theater in the world, but also to garish commercialization perpetuating a snow globe image of the city.

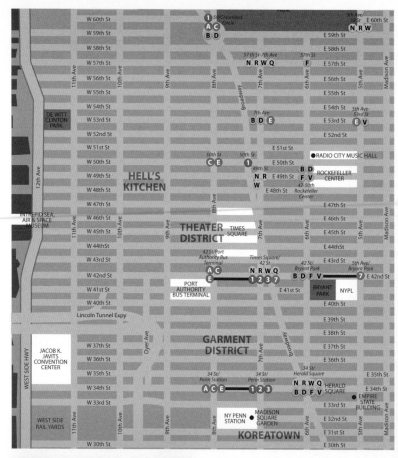

EXPLORE

American Folk Art Museum

This popular art museum houses a plethora of American folk culture within its fiberglass and stone walls. The eight-story architectural beauty hosts various workshops in

45 W 53rd St
(btwn 5th & 6th Ave)
212-265-1040
Tues-Sun 10:30am-5pm, Fri
10:30am-7:30pm, Mon Closed
E V to 5th Ave-53rd St,
B D E to 7th Ave
Adults $9, Students & Seniors $7
Fridays 5:30pm-7:30pm Free

traditional arts, like quilt making, and offers free admission and live music every Friday. Particularly worth seeing is the Henry Darger collection, an exhibit of over 20 paintings and four manuscripts from the enigmatic Chicagoan outsider artist. The museum is small—one can probably tour the entirety in about two hours. But don't let the neighboring MOMA eclipse this smaller museum and its wealth of American history.

Herald Square

Welcome to the commuter hub of New York City:

with close proximity to over 10 subway lines and Penn Station, Herald Square teems with tourists and bridge-and-tunnelers year-round. Named in honor of the New York Herald newspaper, the triangular park in the middle of the intersection is surrounded by iconic attractions like the Empire State Building and Madison Square Gardens. Sit and enjoy the crowds with a cup of coffee from the nearby restaurant 'wichcraft or explore one of the most concentrated shopping centers in the world—the titanic Macy's store, self-proclaimed as "the biggest store in the world," sits comfortably on an entire city block just minutes away from Manhattan Mall. Don't miss its annual Flower Show and Thanksgiving Day Parade, a balloon-bearing national institution that ends in Herald Square before a crowd that regularly exceeds 3 million.

34th St (at Broadway)
Ⓑ Ⓓ Ⓕ Ⓥ Ⓝ Ⓠ Ⓡ Ⓦ to
34th St-Herald Sq

International Center of Photography
The stark white walls of this internationally-recognized museum, founded by photojournalist Cornell Capa in 1974, provide an emphatic contrast to the ever-rotating exhibitions on display—which have featured everything from 19th-century tintypes to fashion portraits to quantum dot technology. Die-hard photography geeks and history fiends will revel in its permanent collection of over 150,000 original prints, housed in the adjoining Print Study Room (but an appointment is necessary for access). Make sure you drop by the museum store to browse through thousands of limited edition photography titles, monographs, camera

paraphernalia, and more. And since the two floors of galleries won't take you all day to peruse, you'll have time afterwards to see the student exhibitions at the ICP school just across the street, before plunging back into the maelstrom of Times Square.

1133 6th Ave
(btwn 43rd & 44th St)
212-857-0000
Tue-Thurs, Sat-Sun 10am-6pm, Fri 10am-8pm
①②③⑦Ⓝ Ⓠ Ⓡ Ⓦ Ⓢ to Times Square-42nd St,
ⒷⒹⒻⓋ to 42nd St-Bryant Park
Adults $12, Students $8

Madison Square Garden

Home to the New York Liberty, Knicks, and Rangers, Madison Square Garden is truly "The

7th Ave (btwn 31st & 33rd St)
①②③ⒶⒸⒺ to 34th St-Penn Station
Ticket prices vary

World's Most Famous Arena." Any sports fan will be thrilled by the intense competition on the court, rink, or ring, where viewing angles are clear from every price level. Halftimes and timeouts keep the crowds' spirits high with performances, contests, t-shirt giveaways, and celebrity sightings. For music enthusiasts, the arena's set-up allows it to be restructured for massive, high-end concerts from the likes of Green Day, Beyoncé, and John Legend. Up to 19,000 screaming fans can fit in The Garden, for an exhilarating concert experience. Take the All-Access Tour to learn intriguing trivia about what is, in fact, the fourth Madison Square Garden building, and sign up for the MSG Insider e-mail newsletter for great ticket discounts.

NASDAQ Market Site

The lifeblood of the world economy pulses through the LED lights of this cylindrical

4 Times Square
(btwn 42nd & 43rd)
①②③⑦Ⓝ Ⓠ Ⓡ Ⓦ Ⓢ to Times Square-42nd St

monument to the free market. Ebbing crowds of tourists and businessmen are led to Times Square by the 24-hour lighthouse of up-to-the-second economic news. Inside its walls, the masses are welcome to hob-knob with the world's financial leaders and attend the opening and closing ceremonies at 9 am and 3:30 pm respectively. The "big board" inside is updated every second and simulcast to over 100 media stations through the state-of-the-art broadcast studio. To accompany the pervading scent of commerce, the Market Site hosts product launches, press conferences, and many other events. The building itself is also home to both the Good Morning America studio and Condé Nast publications.

New Dramatists

Set in the sacred halls of an old cathedral-like tower, New Dramatists protects the sanctity of theatrical artistry. As

424 W 44th St
(btwn 9th & 10th Ave)
212-757-6960
Sept-June: Mon-Fri 10am-6pm
A C E to 42nd St-
Port Authority

the oldest non-profit center for the development of playwriting talent, New Dramatists currently houses 48 resident playwrights who are granted a safe space to hone their craft through readings, workshops, and career support. Members have won numerous Tony Awards, Pulitzer Prizes, and Obie Awards, and the center itself received a Special Tony Honor for Excellence in 2001. Unique to New Dramatists is their script library open weekdays from September to June by appointment. Always welcoming new talent to all divisions, New Dramatists also offers an internship program for those exploring theater, non-profit work, and art.

The Paris Theatre

This 60-year-old, 586-seat landmark art-house, with its single movie screen and absence of advertisements, offers a purity that

4 West 58th Street
212-688-3800
Showtimes vary
F to 57th St, **N R W** to 5th
Ave, **E V** to 5th Ave-53rd St
Tickets Adults $12,
Students (with ID) $8

is hard to find in the often commercial clamor of New York City. The films screened are often filmed in the city of lights from which the theater takes its name. In addition to the French retrospectives and premieres, the Paris also gives screentime to modern Hollywood, as long as the films have artistic merit and cultural significance. The reserved, elegant décor and balcony recall movie palaces of old, and it's all the same price as your friendly neighborhood multiplex. Its film program may offer limited choices, but the experience is worth the price of admission all on its own.

Playwrights Horizons

Dedicated to fostering new theatrical work, Playwrights Horizons sheds light on the artistic visions of up-and-coming and accomplished

416 W 42nd St
(btwn 9th & 10th Ave)
212-564-1235
Box office daily 12pm-8pm,
Performance schedule varies
A C E to 42nd St-
Port Authority

playwrights, composers, and lyricists. In

its effort to encourage talent, Playwrights awards several commissions each year and accommodates about 20 readings for works in progress. The cozy 198-seat Mainstage Theater presents six productions a season with an up-close-and-personal vantage point, and the smaller Peter Jay Sharp Theater hosts two musicals or plays each season. Also devoted to obliging theatergoers of all budgets, Playwrights features a slew of ways to get cheap tickets, including student subscriptions ($10 ticket per show), student rush, $5 online lottery rush tickets, and HotTix ($20 for patrons 30 years and younger).

Radio City Music Hall

Live music, the Rockettes, and the annual Christmas Spectacular—these are only a few of

4 Penn Plaza (at 7th Ave)
Contact radiocity.com
1 2 3 A C E to
34th St-Penn Station

the reasons to go to Radio City Music Hall. The supernova of performance spaces, J.D.

Rockefeller's Depression-era masterpiece is the largest indoor theater in the world—the marquee itself is a full city block long. And the venue is as spectacular as its shows. The interior designer, Donald Deskey, created Radio City Music hall so it would fit the title "The Palace of the People." The Grand Foyer is regal with deep red and gold hues, drapery, and glittering chandeliers, and there are eight lounges and smoking rooms, each with its own motif. In the last six decades artists like Ella Fitzgerald and Frank Sinatra have performed on The Great Stage, which is framed by a golden, shimmering curtain, and since 1997, the Tony Awards have called the venue home. Swallow your jaded New Yorker pride and take a trip to this beautiful NYC showplace.

SHOP

30th Street Guitars

The caterwauling of electric guitars rings from this extensively-stocked store. Real guitar heroes can try their

236 W 30th St (near 8th Ave)
212-868-2660
Mon-Wed & Fri 11am-5pm,
Thurs 11am-8pm, Sun closed
❶❷❸Ⓐ©Ⓔ to 34th St-
Penn Station

fingers on one of the glittering vintage guitars. Covering the walls are four tiers of guitars, ranging from the classic electrics—Les Pauls, Fenders, and Gibsons—to beautifully crafted acoustic guitars. Goods overflow onto the balcony, where rare finds like glass guitars are perched on an alcove. The store also carries necessities like straps, pedals, amps, and picks in various colors and designs. If your guitar needs fixinvg, weave past guitar-strumming dudes and massive amps to visit the experienced repair staff. Knowledgeable and friendly, they're able to do most major repairs for a reasonable price.

Midtown Comics

This two floor comic book heaven offers an enormous selection of graphic novels and comics both mainstream

200 W 40th St (at 7th Ave)
212-302-8192
Mon-Sat 11am-9pm,
Sun 12pm-7pm
❶❷❸❼ⓃⓆⓇⓦⓈ to
Times Square-42nd St

and alternative. Titles by DC, Marvel, and independent comics are arranged neatly on the huge shelves. Come here to grab back issues like Archie, Anna Mercury, and Fantastic Four Vol. 3, and check in often—the stock changes regularly. If you're coming in on new-comic book day to round off your collection, be ready to duke

HELL'S KITCHEN

Once populated by poor, working-class immigrant families crammed into dilapidated tenements, this historically seedy Manhattan neighborhood often saw tense ethnic conflicts on its streets. But the district that inspired *West Side Story* is no longer known for its resident ruffians. Just steps away from the Theater District, the modern day Hell's Kitchen is like the cheaper, northern extension of Chelsea. Low rents and new high-rises have drawn artists and the LGBT community. Intimate off-Broadway houses like the **Beckett Theater** and **Acorn Theater** (*both are at 410 W 42nd St*) invite drama-loving crowds, but you can hear A Little Night Music at jazz haunts **Birdland** (*315 W 44th St*) and **Swing 46** (*349 W 46th St*). The sheer number of fantastic, cheap, diverse eateries on 9th Avenue ensures that each visit yields a new favorite. Try the special Thai menu at **Wondee Siam II** (*813 9th Ave*), one of the standout Asian joints in the area, stuff yourself with kabuli pulao at **Afghan Kebab House** (*649 9th Ave*), eat traditional Greek fare at **Uncle Nick's** (*747 9th Ave*), or gorge on some grilled cheese and tomato soup at **Say Cheese** (*649 9th Ave*). Less crime, younger crowds, and a burgeoning LGBT scene have recently spawned a dynamic nightlife landscape: local bars like **The Snug** (*751 9th Ave*) and **Vlada** (*331 W 51st St*)—a gay community favorite that boasts an expansive flavored vodka selection—bustle with regulars throughout the week.

---

it out over the rarities. Luckily, Midtown offers a subscription service to avoid epic customer battles. They also carry DVDs, magazines, collectible action figures, and t-shirts sporting familiar superhero faces.

Rizzoli Bookstore

If you're a Europhile, an aesthete, or a sophisticate, this three-floor Italian bookshop is your nirvana.

31 W 57th St
(btwn 5th & 6th Ave)
212-759-2424
Mon-Fri 10am-7:30pm, Sat
10:30am-7pm, Sun 11am-7pm
🄵 to 57th St

Since 1964, Rizzoli has been known for its unbeatable selection of fine art, architecture, and fashion books, foreign language titles, and rare collection of international music. The bookstore's décor gracefully accents the glossy, coffee-table-bound merchandise: wrought-iron chandeliers dangle from every ceiling, electric candles cast a soft glow upon rich wood-paneled shelves, and an ornate railing wraps around the center atrium on the second floor. Granted, such elegance comes with a hefty price tag, but there is an annual summer sale, and you won't find most of Rizzoli's selections anywhere else—well, except across the pond. But who needs London, Paris, or Rome, when you can be in all three places at once?

EAT

Amy's Bread

Bread

Tucked away in the heart of Hell's Kitchen—that homey haven from the mega-pixeled chaos of Times Square—Amy's Bread attracts passers-by with the strong scent of baking

672 Ninth Ave
(btwn 46th & 47th St)
212-977-2670
Mon-Fri 7:30am-11pm, Sat
8am-11pm, Sun 9am-6pm
❶ to 50th St-Broadway,
🄲🄴 to 50th St-8th Ave,
🄽🄡🅆 to 49th St-7th Ave
Pastries $3-5,
Sandwiches & Salads $4-8

sourdough and whole wheat bread emanating from its small back kitchen. Once you've braved the sometimes-lengthy lines, expect slightly stressed (or maybe just claustrophobic) bakers doling out bargain loafs and baguettes, while snackers munch on sweet and savory "twists" of chocolate, semolina, Parmesan, and prosciutto, all priced at around a dollar. The cheese biscuits are decadent but not too heavy, and the small sandwiches feature fresh vegetables and meats to complement the just-baked breads. Staple beverages and soups (the mushroom barley is a favorite) complete a lovely meal, which you can enjoy at a table in the back—that is, if there's room. The success of

KOREATOWN

The blocks bounded by W 32nd and W 35th Sts between Broadway and 5th Ave tightly pack in more frenzied activity than exists in entire neighborhoods. Fluent Korean speakers will have no trouble finding travel agents, acupuncturists, saunas, commercial banks, churches, grocery stores, bookstores, and even two galleries on these streets— **Lee Young Hee Museum** (*2 W 32nd St*) displays traditional Korean dress and **Hun Gallery** (*12 W 32nd St*) exhibits contemporary works by Korean artists. Weekend nights find twenty-somethings cavorting from restaurant to bar to karaoke room, slurping down boiling clay-pot stews and quaffing soju, a traditional Korean spirit. Try the cocktails at **Maru** (*11 W 32nd St*) and then stagger upstairs to belt pop tunes in their posh karaoke rooms, or head to **Forte Baden Baden** (*28 W 32nd St*) to guzzle beer while munching on their unbeatable garlic chicken wings. For a toothsome fare any time of day, restaurants like **Kang Suh** (*1250 Broadway*) and **Chung Mu Ro** (*10 W 32nd St*), offer a wealth of traditional high-quality menu items. For particular specialties, try **Cho Dang Gol** (*55 W 35th St*) for house-made tofu and **Hyo Dong Gak** (*51 W 35th St*) for jja jang myun, or noodles in black bean sauce invented in Korea by Chinese immigrants hundreds of years ago.

the original location has led to the opening of two more Amy's shops, one in Chelsea Market, the other in Greenwich Village.

Anthos — *New Greek*

Greek food attracts relatively few followers in the world of haute cuisine. The obvious exception is renowned chef Michael Psilakis' midtown shrine to Greek gastronomy, where Psilakis attends to his ancestral cuisine with masterly ritual, ingenuity, and skill. Even seemingly innocuous dishes like yellowfin tartare surprise the palate with distinctly Eastern Mediterranean flavors like mint, feta, olive, and dill. Though plated with precision and artistry, dishes like the stunning house-smoked octopus and lush ricotta dumplings are never too precious to be consumed with relish. The all-but-blank white space is surprisingly formal, but a menu of traditional tapas is served upstairs in less rarefied surroundings. And youthful, professional staff keep things lively in both spaces.

36 W 52nd St (5th Ave)
212-582-6900
Lunch Mon-Fri 12pm-2:30pm,
Dinner Mon-Thurs 5pm-10:30pm, Fri-Sat 5pm-11pm
E V to 5th Ave-53rd St
Appetizers $16-19,
Entrees $29-38

Azuri Cafe — *Israeli*

This tiny Middle Eastern favorite is closed for Shabbat, but when open it serves some of the best falafel in town. The run-down interior is tremendously cramped, with tables shoved right up against the deli counter where food is dispensed, but any traces of discomfort will be forgotten with the first crispy bite of the sensationally flavorful falafel sandwich. The large platters pair bright, fresh salads with tender, richly-seasoned shwarma and shish kebab. Refreshing Israeli soft drinks make an ideal accompaniment to the fragrant food, and the thick, strong Turkish coffee, served in a proper demitasse cup if the famously curmudgeonly owner is in the right mood, makes a perfect conclusion to your Middle Eastern feast.

465 W 51st St
(btwn 9th & 10th Ave)
212-262-2920
Sun-Thurs 10am-9pm, Fri 9am-4pm
1 to 50th St-Broadway,
C E to 50th St-8th Ave
Appetizers $2-5, Entrees $8-12
Cash only

Bouchon Bakery & Café — *French*

10 Columbus Circle (near Broadway)
212-823-9363
Mon-Sat 11:30am-9pm, Sun 11:30am-7pm
❶❹❸❻❼ to 59th St-Columbus Circle
Sandwiches $10-16, Salads $12-16

With this classic boulangerie, former French Laundry and Per Se chef Thomas Keller brings the more affordable end of his gourmet empire to Manhattan. Tomato soup, the most popular selection, is creamy and light, coupled with grilled milk bread oozing with Fontina and Gruyère. A gourmet rendition of the fluffernutter, a juvenile staple, squeezes marshmallow cream, pecan butter, Italian meringue, and bananas between two golden-brown slices of toasted brioche, and comes served with a side of nutella pudding. For dessert, the signature chocolate bouchons are an adorable trifecta of cork-shaped, sugar-dusted brownies with caramel ice cream and peanut nougatine. If you don't have time to sit and enjoy impressive views from the café's perch on the Time Warner Center's third floor, their adjacent bakery sells a variety of delectable baked goods to go.

Burger Joint — *Burgers*

119 W 56th (btwn 6th & 7th Ave)
212-245-5000
Sun-Tues 11:30am-11:30pm, Fri-Sat 11:30am-12am
❻ to 57th St, ❶ to 59th
Burgers $7-8, Sides $2-4

An unlikely haven for the best burgers in town, this down-and-dirty burger dive is tucked behind the pristine pleated curtains of Le Parker Meridien hotel. At Burger Joint, the weathered wooden panels, graffitied walls, giant jars of pickles, and oldies playlist take over where the marble floors and high ceilings left off. Burgers (and the vegetarian grilled cheese sandwich) are the only items listed on the makeshift cardboard menu that dangles above the charred grill. 'The Works,' the signature burger, is flipped to perfection, and dripping with melted cheese that oozes onto the paper wrapping (your plate). The accompanying fries live up to the messy delight of the burger without being excessively greasy or salty. Milkshakes, almost too thick to drink from a straw, complete this practically flawless fast food trifecta.

Café Forant — *Bistro, French*

The staff treats customers like family at this tiny family-run café, where fresh ingredients and old-fashioned French favorites are served in humble, homey surrounds. Chef Lea Forant owns the restaurant with partner Carolyn Montgomery, who runs the tiny dining room with all the care and patience of a mother, chatting amiably with diners. Ever-changing specials, inspired by whatever fresh produce is available, supplement bistro mainstays like French onion soup and flank steak. TLC cooking ensures that dishes leave the kitchen as warm, fresh, and flavorful as home-cooked meals. And diners are treated with the same love and care, which could help explain the number of repeat visitors.

449 W 51st St (near 10th Ave)
212-245-4214
Mon-Fri 7am-7pm, Sat-Sun 7am-7pm
❻❸ to 50th St-8th Ave
Starters $6-9, Mains $8-22

Casellula — *New American, Cheese*

401 W 52nd St (near 9th Ave)
212-247-8137
Daily 5pm-2am
❶ to 50th St-Broadway,
❻❸ to 50th St-8th Ave
❻❸❼ to 49th St
Small and large plates $9-16, Cheeses $6 each

One visit to Casellula will turn the mildest love for cheese into a ripe obsession. With its carefully selected wine list and easy intimacy, Casellula might well be mistaken for a Californian wine-tasting room. Casually charming waiters easily navigate the worn, honey-colored floor crammed with small, candlelit tables, which are set only with forks and cheese knives: the bare essentials for the meal to come. The cheese plate is, of course, the highlight of a visit to Casellula, with over 40 varieties from around the world, ranging from subtle, fresh goat to sharp mimolette to tangy buffalo blue. An in-house fromager will compose a "flight" from these, pairing each with a unique garnish, such as mustard or toffee marshmallow. The menu of large and small plates also gives pride of place to cheese in dishes like the fresh, filling roasted beet salad with mozzarella and the fluffy ricotta crostini drizzled with honey and topped with lemon zest and hazelnuts. Though such a single minded approach might render another restaurant inaccessible, Casellula excels at presenting quality cheese without the slightest hint of pretension.

Estiatorio Milos — *Greek*

Finding a good meal amidst the tourist traffic of midtown can seem a near-impossible task: until you enter Estiatorio Milos. Fresh fish rules the day at this Greek seafood restaurant, which specializes in simply prepared seafood served in elegant, breezy surroundings. While breading and frying may be fine for cheap frozen filets, Milos' range of exceptionally fresh fish—flown in daily from the Mediterranean—needs little more than a brushing of olive, a few minutes on the grill, and a squeeze of lemon. Choose from grilled loup de mer (a house specialty), lavraki, pompano, or any of the dozen others, and savor their unadulterated flavor. Appetizers and desserts are similarly stark in preparation—whether calamari or baklava, Milos lets the high-quality ingredients speak for themselves.

125 W 55th St
(btwn 6th & 7th Ave)
212-245-7400
Lunch Mon-Fri 12pm-2:45pm,
Dinner Mon-Fri 5:30pm-
11:30pm, Sat-Sun 5:30pm-
10:45pm
N Q R W to 57th St
Prix fixe $49,
Appetizers $14-28,
Entrees $39.50-44

Gazala Place   *Middle Eastern*

From the sidewalk, you can peer through the narrow front window to watch Chef Halabi Gazala making her signature Druze sagg. A crêpe-like flatbread unique to the Druze religious community (a minority group in Israel, Lebanon, and Syria), sagg is quite different from the doughy pita pockets normally associated with Middle Eastern cuisine. Order the mezze platter for a sampling of falafel, kibbe, houmus, babaganush, and labanee, which alone is nearly enough to feed two for dinner. If you're still hungry, the lamb kabab entree is tender and flavorful, and the baked breads and pies—stuffed or topped with cheese or meat—are crispy on the outside and moist within. Their tiny room can only seat 20 people, so expect to bump elbows with fellow diners at this tiny, affordable, and unique Hell's Kitchen outpost.

709 9th Ave
(btwn 48th & 49th St)
212-245-0709
Sun-Thurs 11am-11pm,
Fri-Sat 11am-12am
1 to 50th St-Broadway,
C E to 50th St-8th Ave
N R W to 49th St-7th Ave
Appetizers $7-10, Entrees $8-9
BYOB

Kyotofu   *Dessert, Japanese, Tofu*

A sweet spoonful of sesame tofu with a light drizzling of green tea honey is but one of many delicate bits offered at this dessert bar-cum-restaurant. More traditional treats like the miso chocolate cake always arrive with a creative flourish like green tea cream and candied violets.

705 9th Ave
(btwn 48th & 49th St)
212-974-6012
Lunch & Brunch Tues-Sun
12pm-5:20pm, Dinner &
Dessert Bar Sun, Tues, Wed
5:30pm-12:30am, Thurs-Sat
5:30pm-1:30am
1 to 50th St-Broadway,
C E to 50th St-8th Ave,
N R W to 49th St-7th Ave
Dessert Bar $7-17,
Lunch & Brunch $6-16

For the indecisive or the intrepid, Kyotofu offers a prix fixe tasting that includes the signature sweet tofu, rhubarb-strawberry cobbler, and miso chocolate cake. Whether ordered in the tasting or à la carte, each dessert can also be paired with one of Kyotofu's many wines and sakes. Small and impeccable, Kyotofu is divided into a tiny bar up front and a slightly larger room in the back that can be reserved for larger parties. The space is cheekily decorated in pink and white, done up in a minimal Japanese aesthetic that highlights the exquisite preparations and platings of these small tofu treasures.

Landmarc

New American

10 Columbus Circle
(at 60th St), 3rd Floor
212-823-6123
Sun-Mon 7am-2am
1 A C E D to 59th St-
Columbus Circle
Brunch $5-14,
Dinner Appetizers $9-15,
Entrees $18-35

The younger uptown sibling of the original TriBeCa location, this larger Landmarc (located in the Time Warner Center) can fit nearly 300 people, and often fills with shoppers from surrounding stores and foodies from around town. Though the industrial-chic aesthetic leaves the cavernous room impersonal and cold, an extensive menu of updated classics and a bold, eclectic wine list are sure to warm you up. Among the appetizers, tried-and-true favorites like crisp fried calamari stack up well against more sophisticated creations, like satisfyingly greasy smoked mozzarella and ricotta fritters. The same can be said of the mains, where Landmarc's signature hamburger might actually outshine the flavorful filet mignon. For smaller crowds and stunning views of Columbus Circle, come in the morning, snag a seat by the window, and enjoy expertly prepared breakfasts like the massive pain perdu (essentially French Toast) and eggs Benedict.

Mandoo Bar

Korean

2 W 32nd St (near 5th Ave)
212-279-3075
Daily 11am-11pm
B D F V N O R W
to 34th St-Herald Sq,
6 to 33rd St
Average Meal $11

This simple dumpling spot stands out amidst other, more intimidating K-town restaurants by offering extraordinary renderings of one subtly spiced Korean dish: dumplings. Hardworking dumpling matrons toil away in plain sight, often drawing crowds

of curious visitors. Their creations all contain scallions and a slightly toned down profile of Korean spices. Pan-fried or in soup, the dumplings come in a variety of flavors, like seafood and kimchi, the notoriously spicy pickled cabbage that's a staple of Korean cooking. Though these mandoo are the heart of the menu, dishes like Bibimbap and Japchae (the Korean equivalent of Thai and Vietnamese glass noodles) are also on offer. Enjoy your plate in Mandoo Bar's minimalist metal and wood space, fitting given their refreshingly simple menu.

Norma's

Brunch

119 W 56th St
(btwn 6th & 7th Ave)
212-708-7460
Mon-Sun 7am-3pm
N Q R W to 57th St,
B D E to 7th Ave
Brunch $15-25

In the lobby of the Parker Méridien Hotel the most underappreciated meal of the day is not just "done right"— it's done decadent. Indulge in a $100 caviar frittata, or more traditional (and reasonable) breakfast classics with a twist—French toast drenched in Valhrona chocolate sauce and coated with strawberries, pistachios, and Devonshire cream, for example. The signature Waz-Za, a waffle containing diced mangoes, papayas, and berries, crowned with a delightfully sweet, lightly brûléed hollandaise sauce, a ring of banana slices, and a glistening mound of sugary blueberries, is as transcendent as it is unique. Wash down these delectable bites with freshly squeezed orange juice and a free sampling of the daily smoothie. Prices may be lofty, but the food is made to order and the servings are generous. Best of all, late-risers can wallow in gastronomical breakfast delights until the restaurant closes at 3 pm. Dinner has never felt so overrated.

Pam Real Thai
Thai

Near the tourist din of Times Square and the watered-down Asian restaurants that crowd Hell's Kitchen is Chef Pam Panyasiri's authentic Bangkok eatery. The cherry wood booths, gray paint, and aging tile

404 W 49th St
(btwn 9th & 10th Ave)
212-333-7500
Mon-Thurs, Fri-Sat 11:30am-11:30pm, Sun 11:30am-11pm
① ⑥ ⑥ to 50th St,
⑪ ⑬ ⑭ to 49th St
Appetizers $4-10, Entrees $6-20

floors may not have much character, but the food has more than enough flavor to compensate. Begin with the spicy som yum (shredded green papaya salad) or the fried calamari with sweet chili sauce, perfectly crisp and virtually greaseless. Classic curries like panang are reliably delicious, but spice lovers should try the crispy, piquant duck chili sauce. The noodle dishes are perfectly cooked, abundantly seasoned with fresh herbs and savory fish sauce, and large enough to share. Brusque, no-frills service rounds out Pam Real Thai as the perfect place for a quick meal.

Xie Xie
Asian, Sandwiches

A step up from your average neighborhood deli, Xie Xie (which means 'thank you' in Mandarin) will be sure to earn your gratitude with its

645 9th Ave (near 45th St)
212-265-2975
Daily 11:30am-8:30pm
① ② ③ ⑦ ⑪ ⑬ ⑭ Ⓢ to Times Square-42nd St
Ⓐ Ⓒ Ⓔ to 42nd St-Port Authority
Sandwiches $9-14

creatively composed sandwiches, tempting desserts, and unusual drink options. Despite its concise menu, picking a sandwich at this lunchtime hotspot is a matter for lengthy deliberation. Choose between options like the cha ca la vong (grilled fish) with onion jam and

spicy mayonnaise, the Asian lobster roll with Kewpie mayo, crunchy shallots, and tarragon, or the sweet glazed pork on a Chinese bun with sweet and sour sauce. Any of the above will do. Wash down your meal with a lemon peel and ginger root soda or soda pop sake, or opt to sip Sophia sparkling wine from a juice box. For dessert, indulge in the "1000 year old" ice cream sandwich, full of gooey caramel.

PLAY

123 Burger Shot Beer *Sports Bar*

On the outskirts of the theater district lies a sports haven where waitresses serve dirt cheap sliders and the shots pour for $2. A fleet of flat screen TVs means any seat affords a front-row view of ESPN. With twelve beers on tap and six more bottled, there's little reason to venture into the more expensive drinks. Instead, order a $3 plate of their Angus beef mini-burgers and $3 sweet potato fries. If you're sharing don't expect to fill up on one round of food, so take advantage of the late night kitchen that's open till

738 10th Ave (near 50th St)
212-315-0123
Daily 11am-4am
1 C E to 50th St
Average Drink $3
Happy Hour: Daily 11am-8pm

closing. Game nights are the ideal time to go—a young, after-work crowd packs the sleek bar with keg party enthusiasm. The bar mellows after the final buzzer, so stick around, spread out at a picnic table in the outdoor patio, and end your night on a relaxed note.

Leisure Time Bowl *Bowling*

A bouncer and red-velvet rope flank the entrance of this bowling alley across from Port Authority as if it were an exclusive club—and it kind of is. Multi-colored club lighting, plush couches, and a bar that serves strong martinis put Leisure Time Bowl a world away from neighborhood lanes. The kitchen even serves filet mignon as part of a party package. Come for DJ spun pop tracks, midnight bowling, and surprisingly inexpensive rates. Though the crowd is largely bridge-and-tunnel, this swankified alley delivers as a fun place to bowl and drink your early evening away. If you're committed to partying, order a beer tower with your pizza to enjoy amidst strikes and strobe lighting.

625 8th Ave (near 42nd St)
212-268-6909
Sun 11am-11pm, Mon-Wed 10am-12am, Thurs 10am-2am, Fri-Sat 10am-3am
1 2 3 7 N Q R W S to Times Square-42nd St
A C E to 42nd St-Port Authority
Average Game $9 per person

Terminal 5

Live Music

This tri-level, all-ages venue boasts one of the largest and best spacesforexperiencing brand-name indie acts. Despite the 3,000+ capacity, Terminal 5's superior sound system makes it feel intimate. The main floor is the easiest place to snag a spot, but avoid it on sold-out nights when mobility is nearly impossible—aim for a railing spot on one of the three balconies and take advantage of excellent sightlines and crowd watching while sampling a snack from the Empanada Mama cart on the third level. In addition to the four bars dotting the enormous space, the new, fully stocked rooftop lounge, resembling an airplane hanger (an homage to the venue's namesake), is now open for all your overpriced, watered-down drinking needs.

610 W 56th St
(btwn 11th & 12th Ave)
212-582-6600
Hours vary by performance,
check website or box office
1 A C B D to 59th
St-Columbus Circle
Average Drink $6
Tickets $25-$35

Move with a crowd after the show, as late-night public transportation is limited.

Therapy

LGBT

Bright wood paneling on the walls, dark stone floors, and minimalist, modern decor make this spacious bar ideal for the after-work crowd seeking therapeutic indulgences. The stylish two level bar offers daily drink specials and coyly-named cocktails like the Gender Bender and Freudian Sip, in addition to a full bar menu that includes wild mushroom dumplings and steak skewers. The downstairs lounge is perfect for charming a date and the upstairs cabaret-style stage hosts nightly shows—next to plenty of table seating and a dance floor where you can enjoy live

348 W 52nd St
(btwn 8th & 9th Ave)
212-397-1700
Sun-Thurs 5pm-2am, Fri-Sat
5pm-4am
1 C E to 50th
Average Drink $7
Happy Hour: Daily 5pm-
8pm, 2-for-1 Draft Beer &
Well Drinks

NATIVE'S PICK

Hudson Terrace

Rooftop Bar

The crowd is appropriately swanky at this gorgeous rooftop lounge perched above the West Side Highway. With the Manhattan skyline in the background, the terrace, outfitted with an ivy-covered lattice, leather couches, and miniature palm trees, feels like a hidden oasis. Once past the red velvet ropes, ascend to the roof where scantily dressed twenty-somethings dance under the open sky to the pulsing bass of rotating Top-40 remixes. The friendly, attentive staff keeps your champagne glass filled to the brim as you take in the breathtaking views. Stop by after work for the signature pineapple mojito and oddly delicious caviar-topped nachos, or head over after 10pm for a younger crowd.

621 W 46th St
(near West Side Highway)
212-315-9400
Tues-Fri 5pm-4am, Sat
9pm-4am, Sun Brunch
2pm-9pm
1 C E to 50th St
Average Drink $14
Happy Hour: Tue-Fri 5pm-
10pm, 2 for 1 specialty
drinks and Bud Lights,
20% off all bottles

DJs, comedy, and sexy spins with a new friend. Therapy's most popular show is Wednesday night's "Cattle Call" hosted by famed drag queen Peppermint, who pits three contestants against each other in a raunchy singing contest for cash prizes.

Vintage

Cocktail Lounge

With 80 beers and a bible of cocktails, this dive is a little bit of heaven in Hell's Kitchen—if heaven served up over 201 specialty martinis. Choosing a drink can seem like a challenge, so jump mouth-first into a candy-named martini like the Caramel Apple or Tootsie Roll. A solid stream of 80s tunes caters to the after-work crowd while weekends tend to draw younger droves. Because of its location, Vintage is also popular with the after-theater set, and a few Broadway stars even stop by its dimly lit bar and dark wood tables. Bring friends, sample several cocktails, and share the nachos— this unbelievably massive mess of melted cheese is the perfect salty pairing for your sweet sip.

753 9th Ave (at 51st St)
212-581-4655
Daily 5pm-4am
① ⓒ ⓔ to 50th St
Average Drink $10
Happy Hour: Daily 4-8pm

Limited Engagement

"Don't think twice— just go!"
−London Evening Standard

Photo by Lindsay Hebberd

BURN THE FLOOR®

Ballroom. Reinvented.

ON BROADWAY

Visit Telecharge.com or call 212-239-6200 ♿ Longacre Theatre, 220 W 48 St   burnthefloor.com

Student Rush available day of only at the box office   Limit 2 tickets per student with valid I.D.   Subject to availability

New York's Most Horrifying Haunted House

NIGHTMARE:
VAMPIRES

CREATED BY TIMOTHY HASKELL

"**SICK.** Deliciously, awesomely **SICK.**"
-Time Out New York

Sept. 25th - Nov. 7th

NIGHTMARENEWYORK.COM
TICKETS: 212-352-3101 ⊙ GROUPS: 212-929-2963

Truth, justice, porn.

THE DEEP THROAT SEX SCANDAL

A sinfully entertaining play about freedom.

Who gets to decide what's obscene in America? In 1972, it was 12 jurors in a Tennessee courtroom.

DeepThroat**ThePlay**.com

follow us on twitter

MIDTOWN EAST

While its neighbor to the west has more familiar, engaging environs, the landscape of Midtown East has a strange, uneasy blend of historical landmarks and cold steel skyscrapers. During the day, streets are packed with power suits hustling to work on Lexington and Park Avenues, well-heeled ladies lunching on Madison, and tourists blocking pedestrian traffic on Fifth. Further uptown is the quiet, secluded, and very exclusive residential enclave Sutton Place. This pricey neighborhood, where the homes overlook the East River, may be the only place in Manhattan you can find houses with driveways.

Above 42nd Street, you'll see remnants of New York's Gilded Age past—or, today's old-money haunts: the Plaza Hotel, Waldorf-Astoria Hotel, and Bergdorf Goodman department store. Going downtown along Fifth, you'll run into attractions like the first Saks Fifth Avenue, F.A.O. Schwartz, New York Public Library, Grand Central Terminal, Chrysler Building, Empire State Building, and the original Macy's, as well as the flagship retail stores for Apple, Disney, and Gap, among others. Tourists keep this shrine to consumerism, dubbed "the most expensive street in the world," buzzing into the night, but the other avenues of Midtown East are quiet and deserted after work.

Once happy hour ends, the area becomes distinctly silent as offices close shop, commercial districts shut down, and residents return to their brownstones and converted high-rises in tucked-away areas like Tudor City and Turtle Bay. It's worth the effort to drop by and see the noteworthy structures—like St. Patrick's Cathedral—drool over the upscale restaurants, or sample happy hours at various watering holes, but it goes without saying that nighttime revelries should take place elsewhere. Whenever you stop by, come prepared with plastic since most things worth purchasing come at an inflated price.

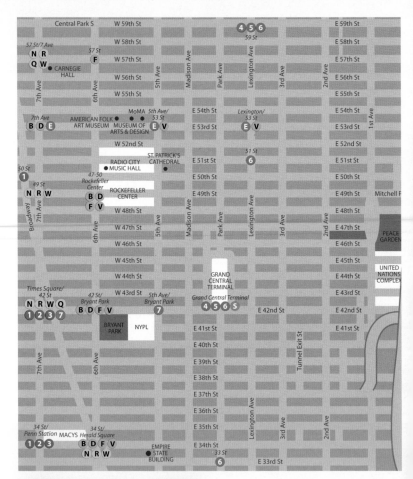

EXPLORE

Bryant Park

"Manhattan's Town Square" doesn't provide much relief from the city crowd—because of its proximity

42nd St (at 6th Ave)
Hours vary seasonally
B D F V to 42nd St-Bryant Park, **7** to 5th Ave

to Times Square, 20,000 people flood in every day when the weather's pleasant. But Bryant Park encloses a splendor of outdoor charms, including tree-lined gravel paths, an army of dark green tables and movable chairs, a picturesque fountain, a carousel, six flowerbeds, and an aptly-named Great Lawn. Free WiFi attracts businesspeople on lunch breaks, but those unarmed with laptops should still drop by to grab a snack from one of the four 'wichcraft kiosks (be sure to sample their three flavors of hot chocolate offered in colder months). Come during Fashion Week to catch a glimpse of mingling models and designers, or take advantage of free movie screenings during the HBO Summer Film Festival.

Carnegie Hall

Built in 1890 by steel giant Andrew Carnegie, this venue quickly grew to host some of the most talented musicians and brightest lecturers around the world. Audiences aren't just blue-haired old ladies going to hear symphonies—the program at Carnegie Hall grew beyond classical musicians to include jazz, popular music, theater, and dance. Three beautiful stages comprise Carnegie Hall: the Isaac Stern Auditorium/Ronald O. Perelman Stage, the premier American performance venue in for classical music since 1891; Weill Recital Hall, a more intimate space that seats 268 listeners; and Zankel Hall, which seats 599 guests for performances and educational events. Shows are available year round, but orchestral season runs from late September to mid-March.

881 7th Ave (at 57th St)
212-632-0540
Hours Vary
N Q R W to 57th St-7th Ave,
F to 7th Ave, **1 A C B D**
to 59th St-Columbus Circle

Grand Central Terminal

Opened in 1913, Grand Central is one of city's last truly beautiful transportation centers. Over 100,000 daily

87 E 42nd St (at Park Ave)
For tours call 212-340-2345
4 5 6 7 S to Grand
Central-42nd St

DAY TO DAY

Community Board 6: 866 UN Plaza, Suite 308, 212-319-3750.

Dry Cleaner: Alpian's Garment Care, 325 E 48th St, 646-755-9429.

Groceries: Katagiri, 244 E 59th St, 212-755-3566.

Gym: MonQi Fitness NYC, 201 E 67th St, 646-755-9411.

Hospital: NYU Medical Center, 550 1st Ave, 212-263-7300.

Laundromat: East 51 Street Launderette, 305 E 51st St, 212-759-5430.

Libraries: New York Public Library 58th St Branch, 127 E 58th St, 212-759-7358.

Media: Turtle Bay Association, turtlebay-nyc.org. Digital Murray Hill, murrayhill.gc.cuny.edu.

Volunteer Opportunities: Big Brothers Big Sisters of NYC, 223 E 30th St, 212-686-2042. bigsnyc.org. Salvation Army, 221 E 52nd St, 212-758-0763, salvationarmyusa.org. Bideawee Volunteers & Education, 410 E 38th St, 212-532-4968, bideawee.org.

commuters pass through this cathedral to industry without a thought to its aesthetics, but first time visitors tend to gape at the endless marble of the main concourse. A rich green, vaulted ceiling with scattered gold constellations from the night sky and the famous four-faced clock on the centered information booth are just a few intricacies of this iconic terminal. Come at rush hour for the full, harried experience, or enjoy the cavernous relative quiet of the terminal's off-hours. Then again, Grand Central takes in thousands of visitors daily, so don't expect to be alone.

Museum of Modern Art

Just blocks away from Central Park, MoMA is not only an internationally known art museum but also one of the most remarkable architectural structures in the city. Redesigned by Yoshio Taniguchi in 2004, the building has clean lines, open, airy spaces, and floor-to-ceiling windows with views of nearby brownstones and skyscrapers—itself a masterpiece. Besides its permanent collection from modern masters like Dalí, Picasso, Van Gogh, Mondrian, and Warhol, the museum also features a large-scale (and often overwhelming) sculptural exhibit in its atrium, as well as rotating

11 W 53rd St (near 6th Ave)
212-708-9400
Wed-Mon 10:30am-5:30pm,
Fri 10:30am-8pm,
Tues closed
E V to 5th Ave-53rd St,
B D F V to 47th St-50th St-
Rockefeller Center
Adults $20, Students (with ID) $12

cutting-edge exhibits by renowned artists. For cinema lovers, there are contemporary and international film screenings. And during warmer months, drop by the hushed sculpture garden on the ground level for a pleasant respite from exhibit-browsing.

New York Public Library

Polymaths and plebeians alike make the pilgrimage to this "Splendid Temple of the Mind." As the NYPL's central research center, it comprises a vast network of divisions that contain over 15 million items in 1,200 languages, ranging from historical documents and rare books to maps and photographs. The autographed manuscript of Washington's Farewell Address and a copy of the Gutenberg Bible are some of its most distinguished treasures. Moreover, this building is not only a feast for the mind, but also one for the eyes—it is a Beaux-Arts masterpiece, inside and out. Its marble-floored hallways are graced with rococo ceilings, from which dangle elaborate glass-orbed chandeliers. On the third floor, don't miss the murals in the McGraw Rotunda or on the ceiling of the Rose Reading Room.

476 5th Ave (at E 42nd St)
Mon & Thurs-Sat 11am-6pm,
Tues-Wed 11am-7:30pm,
Sun 1-5pm
917-ASK-NYPL (275-6995)
1 2 3 N Q R W to 42nd
St- **B D F V** to 42nd St-
Bryant Park, **7** to 5th Ave,
4 5 6 7 S to Grand
Central-42nd St
Free tours conducted
Mon-Sat 12:30pm & 2:30pm,
Sun at 3:30pm

Paley Center for Media

Formerly known as the Museum of Television and Radio, the Paley Center was founded in 1975 to examine the cultural significance of those two media. Today it is a leader of discussions on the intersection between media and society, but also preserves a part of our cultural heritage as it is expressed through television and radio. The permanent media collection includes nearly 150,000 programs and advertisements, which you can spend a day browsing through and listening to at individual consoles. The center also hosts daily screenings in its two full-sized theaters, and sponsors frequent seminars and panel discussions with notable figures from the media industry. Various classes and workshops for visitors of all ages (including "Muppets and Puppets" and "Faster than a Speeding Bullet: Superheroes on Radio") are offered as well.

25 W 52nd St
(btwn 5th & 6th Ave)
212-621-6600
Wed & Fri-Sun 12pm-6pm,
Thurs 12pm-8pm
Adults $10, Students $6
E V to 5th Ave-53rd St,
N R W to 49th St-7th Ave,
B D F V to 47th St-50th St-
Rockefeller Center

St. Patrick's Cathedral

Construction on this Neo-Gothic giant began in 1858 and finished 20 years later, after a building hiatus during the Civil War. Today the Cathedral seems out of place amongst the glass and steel skyscrapers of midtown, but once inside this quiet sanctuary all the bustle dies away. Besides serving as the seat of New York's Roman Catholic Archdiocese, St. Patrick's remains a fully functioning church with daily masses and the odd choir practice session. But the landmark's chief visitors are not worshippers: flocks of tourists stroll below its vaulted ceilings, and among its massive columns everyday. Outside, necks crane to take in the exquisite detail of the towering facade and conical spires. It may not be the tallest building on 5th Avenue anymore, but it remains easily among the most awe-inspiring.

460 Madison Ave
(btwn 50th St & 51st St)
212-753-2261
Daily 6:30am-8:45pm, Masses
begin 7am-5:30pm
6 to 51st St, **E V** to 5th Ave-
53rd St, **B D F V** to 47th St-
50th St-Rockefeller Center

United Nations

On the boarder of the East River lies this working monument to peace. Designed by a team of international architects including Le Corbusier, the four buildings that comprise the UN headquarters sit on international

United Nations Plaza, 1st Ave
(btwn 42nd & 48th St)
212-963-8687
Tours Mon-Fri 9:30am-4:45pm
4 5 6 S to Grand Central
Adults $12.50,
Students (with ID) $8

territory. Pass through the flags of the 192 member nations that trace the perimeter to check out free art exhibits and take a guided tour of the complex—the council chambers and 1,800-seat General Assembly Hall are notable highlights. Inside, gifts from member nations stand as symbols of peace and admiration. Loiter in their Public Concourse, which offers a coffee shop, a bookstore, and a gift shop that sells everything from international jewelry to shot glasses. Should you want to dress up, the reservation-only Delegates Dining room is open weekdays for lunch. Be sure to visit the UN post office—you can send a postcard only mailable from the UN to anywhere in the world.

SHOP

Book-Off *Bookstore*

Visit this used bookshop for simply unbeatable prices—half of its English-language titles are $1. The Book-Off chain is wildly popular in Japan, but

14 E 41st St
(btwn 5th & Madison Ave)
212-685-1410
Daily 10am-8pm
4 5 6 7 S to Grand Central-42nd St, **7** to 5th Ave

its New York location is one of just a handful of overseas stores. The Japanese-language sections are full of Manga fans absorbed in the next Naruto volume and more serious bookies browsing classics by Yukio Mishima. The English selection has a bit of everything, including romance novels, biographies, and a fiction section heavily consisting of popular beach reads—no Hemingway here. The store also buys and sells media, and is a great place to find cheap DVDs, video games, or the Titanic soundtrack for a buck or two.

EAT

Artisanal *French*

Done up with the requisite mirrors, dark mahogany paneling, Art Deco posters, and wicker chairs of a classic Parisian bistro, Artisanal surpasses the standard with exceptional food. The menu changes seasonally, but Chef Terrance

2 Park Avenue (33rd St)
212-725-8585
Mon-Fri 11:45 am-11pm,
Sat 10:30am-11pm,
Sun10:30am-10:00 pm
6 to 33rd St,
N R W to 23rd St
Appetizers & Charcuterie
$11-16, Entrees $20-27

Brennan's perennial favorites are the best bets. Succulent hanger steak is perfectly marinated and tenderly cooked, and comes with crisp, golden fries. The skate, served with a sweet, tangy blood orange grenobloise, and pureed cauliflower, is a light but satisfying dish. A meal at Artisanal isn't complete without Brennan's pet predilection: cheese. The resident frommagier will happily arrange a flight straight from the immense cheese cave at the back of restaurant, where you can stop by after your meal for to pick up an assorted basket of cheese, charcuterie, and other gourmet delicacies to enjoy at home.

Boi to Go   *Sandwiches, Vietnamese*

Local businessmen line up at this popular sandwich shop to sate their banh mi cravings. While the interior is unremarkable—little

> 800 2nd Ave (near 43rd St)
> 212-681-1122
> Mon-Fri 11am-5pm
> ❹❺❻❼❽ to Grand
> Central-42nd St
> Lunch boxes $7-8,
> Small bites $3-6

more than a long counter stocked with fresh vegetables—the long list of delicious sandwiches is reason enough to visit. Traditional banh mi comes in variations to suit any diet pick from several choices of meats (the slightly sweet pork and the curried chicken balls are both good options), fish, and vegetables, all topped with slices of avocado. If you're not in the mood for a sandwich, instructions above the counter help customers to build their own "lunch boxes," all of which are served with fresh vegetables and herbs. These noodle or rice bowls, burritos, salads, and wraps can be made with a choice of meats and homemade specialty sauces.

Dawat   *Indian, Vegetarian*

While the elegantly-dressed waitstaff and refined décor alone would warrant its haute cuisine title, the food is what distinguishes Dawat. And Dawat delivers, spectacularly so. The recipes of renowned

> 210 E 58th St (near 3rd Ave)
> 212-355-7555
> Mon-Sat 11:30am-11pm,
> Sun 5:30-11pm,
> Closed Daily 3-5:30pm
> ❹❺❻ ⓃⓇⓌ to 59th St-
> Lexington Ave,
> ⒻF to Lexington Ave-63rd St
> Appetizers $7-12, Entrees $15-
> 25, Tasting menus $45-75

chef and author Madhur Jaffrey warm the palate with expert spice blends, worlds apart from overly-seasoned curries of dime-a-dozen neighborhood joints. Gloriously robust raan (leg of lamb) and savory Chilean sea bass from the tandoor oven epitomize their upscale

truffle butter. The meat and fish entrees possess a similarly deft, rustic sensibility, but Chef Psilakis best demonstrates his playful, unforced skill with the pastas —all available in reasonably priced full- and appetizer-sized portions. Co-owner Donatella Arpaia brings her urbane style to the space, which is designed to feel like a private home— it's divided into a lively lounge up front, a cozy "living room" in the middle, and a peaceful, handsome dining room in the back. Tied together with pale wood and black and white accents, the space is as modestly chic as the food served within it.

206 E 58th St
(btwn 2nd & 3rd Ave)
212-750-8170
Brunch Sun 12pm-3pm,
Lunch Mon-Fri 12pm-2:30pm,
Dinner Mon-Thurs 5pm-
10pm, Fri-Sat 5pm-10:30pm,
Sun 5pm-9:30pm,
4 5 6 N R W to 59th St-
Lexington Ave
Appetizers $9-14, Entrees $16-26

Oms/b
Japanese

156 E 45th St
(btwn Lexington & 3rd Ave)
212-922-9788
Mon-Fri 8am-7:30pm,
Sat 11am-5:30pm
4 5 6 7 S to Grand
Central-42nd St
Rice balls $2-4, Appetizers
50¢-$3, Noodles $5-9

Though this tiny café benefits little from its location on a falafel cart-packed midtown street, the unusual Japanese snacks inside keep regulars coming back. Oms/b is known for making over 40 varieties of omusubi, or rice balls—order that and skip the lackluster sushi. A traditional Japanese snack, an omusubi is essentially dried seaweed wrapped around flavor-infused rice and topped off with a garnish. Those on offer at Oms/b range from more traditional flavors like sesame to unique varieties like the bacon and-egg. Try the salmon for its subtle saltiness, or the pickled plum for its uniquely salty-sour flavor profile. Shrimp rice balls are crunchy, delicious, and a favorite among customers. Special set meals are a considerable value, and include several rice balls with appetizers and soup.

Tea Box Café
Japanese, Tea

693 5th Ave (near 54th St)
212-350-0180
Mon-Sat 11:45am-2:45pm,
3pm-5:30pm
E V to 5th Ave-53rd St,
B D F V to 47th St-
Sandwiches $7, Tea sets $8-18

Tucked away in the basement of the upscale Japanese department store Takashimaya, this peaceful enclave is an ideal escape from noisy Fifth Avenue. The understated décor of

renderings of sub-continent staples. Explore different Indian cuisines through less familiar dishes like the Baghari Jhinga—succulent shrimp cooked with garlic, mustard seeds, and curry leaves. Just make sure to heed the servers' recommendations and box your leftovers, as time in the fridge intensifies flavors for even the most subtle dishes.

Mia Dona
Italian

Simple elegance is the key to this Midtown haven, where chef Michael Psilakis pulls off inventive preparations of classic Italian dishes with considerable finesse. An appetizer of mussels with pesto, couscous, and ricotta is delicately satiating. The ricotta gnudi are small, pillowy wonders served with mushrooms, proscuitto, and light wooden furnishings and glazed ceramic pottery is typically Japanese in its minimal elegance. The serene hush of the room is unbroken even by the amiable staff who serve the light, refreshing lunches and afternoon teas to guests seated on the café's pillow-lined benches. Early afternoon diners can enjoy the tea box, a bento box filled with the chef's selection of small dishes. Those arriving after 3pm should bring a friend and share the east-west afternoon tea, which comes with finger sandwiches, pastries, fresh fruit, and, of course, your choice of a pot of tea from the extensive list.

PLAY

Rattle N Hum   *Beer Bar*
The bar's covered in neglected coasters and empty glasses, the ceiling's decorated with remnants of old draught taps, and the regulars sit elbow to elbow at this narrow beer spot. They have forty brews on tap every night—mostly American craft beers, with some European fare and a couple casks thrown in for good measure. The beer menu, updated daily, includes drinking instructions carefully crafted by connoisseurs. Though the extensive selection may intimidate dilettantes, helpful staff is eager to explain the difference between the Elysian Immortal IPA and the Prometheus IPA. Grab a food menu, which boasts familiar, greasy fare, and pair burgers or wings with your cold Circus Boy.

14 E 33rd St
(btwn 5th & Madison Ave)
212-481-1586
Mon-Wed 10am-2am,
Thurs-Sat 10am-4am,
Sun 11am-2am
Ⓝ Ⓠ Ⓡ Ⓦ to 34th St
Average Beer $7
Happy Hour: Mon-Fri:
10am-6pm & 11pm-1am

NATIVE'S PICK

The Ginger Man   *Beer Bar*
The impressive selection of nearly 70 draughts and bottled varieties gives true brew fanatics a chance to branch out, pick the brains of the extensively trained, thoroughly knowledgeable staff, and find a new favorite. The exhaustive options are organized by country and type: beer connoisseurs can tour the menu without sipping the same style twice. Luckily, the bar's large enough to accommodate the weekend pilgrims that flock to this beer mecca. Past the long, dark wood bar and row of booths is the back lounge, which looks like a gentleman's scotch room and holds relics of beer taverns past encased with museum-like veneration for refined drinking. Savor a robust Southampton Abbey Dubbel or pair a flight of four draught samples with the special house hot dog wrapped in bacon and doused in melted cheddar.

11 E 36th St
(near Madison Ave.)
212-532-3740
Mon-Thurs 11:30am-2am,
Fri 11:30-4am, Sat 12:30am-
4am, Sun 3pm-12am
Ⓑ Ⓓ Ⓕ Ⓥ Ⓝ Ⓠ Ⓡ Ⓦ to
34th St Herald Sq, ⑥ to 33rd St
Average Beer $9

MIDTOWN EAST 189

CHELSEA

Avenues with towering skyscrapers crisscross cozy brownstone-lined streets, trendy vintage boutiques neighbor an Old Navy megastore, and decades-old Italian diners decorate windows with bright rainbow flags.

Although it's largely associated with the bronzed, gym-loving, look-at-me-not-looking-at-you gay men who call it home, Chelsea's streets also boast glamorous fashionistas toting designer bags, wrinkled women arguing in Spanish, and art aficionados shouldering oversized egos.

The neighborhood wasn't always so polished. When the Chelsea Piers opened in 1910, they became the prime docking space for both passenger and military ships. After being used as cargo terminals in the 50s and 60s, they fell into disrepair and were deemed a blemish on the skyline. In the 90s, the piers were finally overhauled and rebuilt, and reopened as a state-of-the-art entertainment and sporting facility.

Chelsea also boasts a rich history of artistic movements. Throughout the 20th century, the Chelsea Hotel was home to some of the modern era's greatest writers, actors, and musicians including Bob Dylan, Janis Joplin, and Tennessee Williams. The 90s art boom saw an influx of studios and galleries move into the neighborhood, as artists were priced out of more traditional visual art enclaves such as Soho. Today, Chelsea's 350-plus galleries are a key destination not just for haughty curators, critics, and creators, but also for international tourists and neighboring students.

Today, amid the relics of Chelsea's industrial past, New Yorkers wine, dine, and unwind in the area's many coffee shops, chic lounges, and nouveau restaurants. Perhaps no monument marries the neighborhood's present with its past better than the newly re-opened High Line. Stretching from the Meatpacking District to Chelsea, this elevated railway that once hauled freight between factories now exists as a brand new park, where eco-friendly landscaping shares space with the rusted tracks of old.

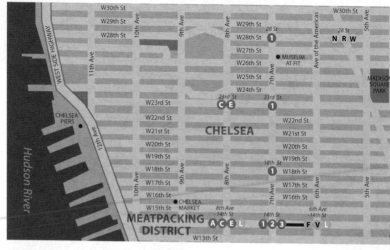

Atlantic Theater Company

With two large theaters, an acting school, and an active production center, the Atlantic Theater Company is an innovative, award-winning performance center that has propelled shows like Spring Awakening

Linda Gross Theater: 336 W 20th St (btwn 8th & 9th Ave), & Atlantic Stage 2: 330 W 16th St (btwn 8th & 9th Ave)
212-691-5919
Call box office for specific show times and prices.
1 to 18th St, **C E** to 23rd St, **A C E L** to 14th St-8th Ave
Admission varies by show, Student & member discounts may be available.

to nationwide success and fame. Founded by influential playwright David Mamet and acclaimed actor William H. Macy, the company is comprised of the two founders and their colleagues and friends, including Desperate Housewives star Felicity Huffman. Past seasons have included new works by Woody Allen, Mamet, and filmmaker Ethan Coen. The Atlantic keeps well-heeled drama buffs coming, but students on a budget can rush tickets two hours before the show for ten bucks or opt to see up-and-coming actors and playwrights on Atlantic Stage 2.

Chelsea Art Museum

This 30,000-square-foot exhibition space offers a unique contribution to the Chelsea Art District and the New York art scene with its emphasis on "contextual" art. The focus at CAM is the cultural, political,

556 W 22nd St (at 11th Ave)
212-255-0719
Tues-Sat 11am-6pm, Thurs 11am-8pm, Sun-Mon closed
C E to 23rd St,
Adults $8, Students $4

and social background of the artist and its impact on his or her work. The museum presents underexposed artists of the 20th and 21st centuries and their commentary on a variety of global issues, ranging from Queer culture in Iran to conflicts in Darfur, Uganda, and the Sudan. Along with such rotating exhibits, the museum also hosts the Miotte Foundation, dedicated to preserving the work of Jean Miotte, a French abstract painter of the post-WWII era who helped pioneer "L'Art Informel." Miotte's bold use of heavy, unrefined strokes and contrasting colors helped break away from the traditional emphasis on figure, warranting his work a look for both its historical and aesthetic value.

Chelsea Piers

Created from four abandoned piers and $120 million, this state-of-the-art sports facility boasts

23rd St (at the Hudson River)
212-336-6666
Hours and prices vary by pier
M23 and M14 buses to the Hudson River

everything from a regulation-sized boxing ring to a skating rink. Beach volleyball, swimming, weight lifting, gymnastics, rock climbing, golfing, bowling, dancing, you name it—every imaginable physical activity can be found on its 28 acres. With four restaurants, a brewery, and a physical therapy group, Chelsea Piers is a veritable adult playground (the exceptions being piers 59, 60, 61, and 62, where children are also welcome). And its convenient location near the cycling and running track on the West Side Highway makes it a magnet for sports enthusiasts, athletes, and families alike. If you can't afford to pay top dollar to use the premium equipment, though, plan to do your sit-ups at home.

David Zwirner Galleries

David Zwirner Galleries has grown exponentially since its opening, which is no surprise considering its infallibility in showcasing contemporary art's heavy-hitters—think Luc Tuymans and Neo Rauch—when they are just up-and-comers. Having ditched their Soho outpost in 2002 for more spacious accommodations in Chelsea, the gallery now measures over 30,000 square feet (or 80 percent of its 19th St block). This monumental space is

525 W 19th St (near 10th Ave)
212-727-2070
Tues-Sat 10am-6pm
C E to 23rd St
A C E L to 14th St-8th Ave,

DAY TO DAY

Community Board 4: 330 W 42nd St, 26th Floor, 212-736-4536, info@manhattancb4.org.

Dry Cleaners: Belle Claire Dry Cleaners, 156 8th Ave, 212-242-3577.

Groceries: Gristede's Supermarket, 221 8th Ave, 646-486-7310.

Gyms: The Sports Center at Chelsea Piers, 60 Chelsea Piers, 212-336-6000.

Hospitals: New York Foundling Hospital, 590 6th Ave, 212-633-9300.

Libraries: Muhlenberg Library, 209 W 23rd St, 212-924-1585.

Laundromats: Well More, 204 8th Ave, 212-366-9764.

Media: *Chelsea Click Your Block,* Chelsea.clickyourblock.com. *Destination Chelsea,* destinationchelsea.org. *Chelsea Now,* chelseanow.com.

Volunteer Opportunities: Youth Opportunity Centers, 247 W 54th St, 2nd Floor, 212-621-0790, www.labor.state.ny.us.

NATIVE'S PICK

The High Line
Park

Mon-Sun 7am-10pm
212-500-6035
A C E to 14th St-8th Ave,
C E to 23rd St, **L** to 8th Ave,
1 2 3 to 14th St-7th Ave,
1 to 18th St

Spanning from Gansevoort Street in the Meatpacking District to West 30th Street in Hell's Kitchen, the long-defunct High Line Railroad seamlessly combines its elevated rails with sleek wooden benches and chic glass alcoves to create a beautiful new park. Finally open to the public after three years of construction, the award-winning design displays public art installations and offers fantastic views of the Hudson and the distinctive architecture of the area. Check out Friends of the High Line, the non-profit organization which advocated for the High Line's restoration and maintenance—they often offer cool events like tours of the park and gallery hops in Chelsea (order tickets in advance online if you want to go, as they tend to sell out). Alternatively, peruse a book on the benches, observe the pedestrians and traffic whiz by underneath you, or just meander about the rails on this elevated garden by the Hudson.

large enough to fit three full-scale exhibitions simultaneously, so it's the closest thing to a free art museum you're ever going to find in New York City. The spotless white rooms will be less packed than more renowned museums, but the quality of the artwork (which rotates every 2-3 months) is guaranteed to be no less mind-blowing.

Trapeze School of New York

The graceful, toned figures who fly through the air with ease were once as burdened by gravity as you—but here at the Trapeze School is where they perfected their high-flying skills. Excellently trained instructors will teach beginners of all ages the ropes to the flying trapeze, with additional classes in silks and rope, static trapeze and lyra, trampoline, and aerial conditioning. Feel the adrenaline rush as you stand atop a 23-foot-high platform, waiting to embark on your flight. The

Pier 40 (West St at Houston St)
212-242-8769
❶ to Houston St
Classes $50-70

outdoor facilities offer an incredibly supportive atmosphere for nervous students. Whether you're looking for an intense workout or a short thrill, the Trapeze School is your best bet for action. They also have a second, indoor location on 30th Street between 10th and 11th Avenues.

SHOP

The Garage

The early bird gets the goods at this upscale flea market. On weekends, the two-level garage is filled not with vehicles but with bustling New Yorkers scouring 100 packed booths for the perfect artifact. The wares are as varied as the people, who show up at sunrise in everything from bouffant wigs to heavy makeup. Antique furniture, high-quality vintage clothing

112 W 25th St (near 6th Ave)
212-243-534
Sat & Sun Sunrise-Sunset
❻ ❼ to 23rd St

MEATPACKING DISTRICT

Long before it became one of the trendiest hotspots in Manhattan, the Meatpacking District really did sell meat. In the early 1900s, 250 slaughterhouses and packing plants made up the region known as Gransevoort Market. It evolved throughout the 20th century, and by the 80s the district became well known for its outrageous nightspots and underground BDSM culture.

Filled with trendier-than-thou nightclubs, cutting-edge restaurants, and glitzy designer stores, the area retains some humility with randomly placed reminders of its past such as cobblestone streets and signs announcing the presence of "Meat Market #25."

For those interested in getting to know the district after dark, the lively nightlife scene is as chic and exclusive as it is expensive. For an updated take on the Roman architectural tradition, try **Kiss and Fly** (*409 W 13th St*), a hot nightclub that may have you waiting in line for longer than you'd like. To try out the best of the basement lounges, head over to **APT** (*419 W 13th St*), a secretive club that plays beats as late as 6 am.

Myriad options for both fine dining and delicious cheap snacks will have foodies feeling right at home. For chic French bistro food, check out **Pastis** (*9 9th Ave*) or, if you're in the mood for Mediterranean, head over to **Fig & Olive** (*420 W 13th St*), a restaurant known for its abundant use of olive oil in many of the dishes.

For shopaholics, Meatpacking offers both innovative and traditional options—some of the edgiest boutiques and designers put up their new creations in stores along the worn-out streets. For clothing that is alternately frightening and astounding, check out **Shelly Steffee** (*34 Gansevoort St*), or go the opposite route and head over to **Vince** (*833 Washington St*) for classic cuts and comfortable style.

Those looking for activities more intellectually stimulating than shopping, partying, or eating, should take a look at some of the District's galleries. **Heller Gallery** (*420 W 14th St*) features artists who use glass as their medium, while the **Ground Zero Museum Workshop** (*420 W 14th St*) offers private tours of the images and artifacts from the WTC site. And for a dose of the Warhol era, check out **Wooster Projects** (*418 W 15th St*).

delicate necklaces, and home furnishings (which include mounted antlers and vivid framed paintings) pile on tables throughout the open space. Don't be surprised if you bump into a celebrity, model, or designer while you're browsing through a box of old records and beautifully crafted masks—creative types flock for inspiration. The Garage feels like your suburban yard sale on high-end speed.

Rainbows and Triangles

This quirky gay-pride shop is the perfect place to pick up party favors, masculine sterling silver jewelry, or suggestive (and skin-tight) graphic tees and tanks by Ruff Riders. Browse the racks for swimsuits, underwear, and clothing knickknacks, or check out the exhaustive literature section. As the largest gay bookstore in Manhattan, they have

192 8th Ave # 1
(btwn 19th & 20th St)
212-627-2166
Mon-Sat 11am-10pm, Sun 12pm-9pm
C E to 23rd St

endless shelves of books on art, photography, travel, cooking, and gay and lesbian issues—plus a whole slew of glossy magazines. Find greeting cards more hilarious than anything Hallmark prints, or head to their DVD collection for movies like Funny Girl and Some Like It Hot.

EAT

Brgr

A brick building with flourishes of warm reds and oranges, Brgr resembles an uber-trendy McDonald's. While prices are easily double those of its fast food counterparts, the food is worth the extra cash. Brgr burgers come with a plethora of

Burgers

287 7th Ave
(btwn 26th & 27th St)
212-488-7500
Mon-Fri 11am-11pm, Sat 11am-12am, Sun 11am-9pm
1 to 28th St
Burgers $8-10, Sides $2, Shakes $6

toppings from the standard lettuce and tomato to Gruyère and Roquefort to sweet onion marmalade and fried egg. Regardless of what you put on them, the grass-fed and steroid-free burgers are juicy, if a bit small, and packed with flavor. Though you might be tempted by the exotic-sounding onion hay and sweet potato fries, go with the classic russet fries—you won't be disappointed. Finish off your all-American meal with one of Brgr's famous milkshakes, including an award-winning blueberry pomegranate shake that will knock your socks off.

Donut Pub

American, Bakery
203 W 14th St (near 7th Ave)
212-929-0126
Daily 24 Hours, Fridays closed
①②③ to 14th St,
Ⓐ Ⓒ Ⓔ Ⓛ to 8th Ave-14th St,
Ⓕ Ⓥ Ⓛ to 6th Ave-14th St
Pastries & Donuts $1-2

This so-called Pub seems more inspired by classic 50s diners than grimy drinking holes. Chrome bar stools sit in a row under the counter and a perky neon sign lights up after dark. But it's Donut Pub's full window display of tasty muffins and donuts in every conceivable flavor that lures curious first-timers into this sugary sweet emporium. The wall space is a veritable shrine to the carbohydrate, with everything from Boston Cream donuts to Oreo muffins. Even connoisseurs might be surprised by some of the shop's more unusual donuts, like pineapple, blueberry, and vanilla jelly varieties. Relish in the sugary splendor of each delicious bite and order a coffee to wash it all down. Since the store's open 24 hours, it's sure to sate your sweet tooth—day or night.

The Green Table

American
75 9th Ave
(inside Chelsea Market, across
from the waterfall)
212-741-6623
Mon-Sat 12am-10pm, Sun
11am-5pm
Ⓐ Ⓒ Ⓔ Ⓛ to 14th St-8th Ave
Appetizers $6-9
Entrees $10-22

Squeezed snuggly into a tiny space deep in the heart of Chelsea Market, this all-sustainable eatery serves up moderately priced American classics prepared entirely from local, organic produce. Barely two tiny rooms large, The Green Table overlooks the main artery of the market and is outfitted in warm, autumnal hues with mismatched furniture that evokes an

Tía Pol

Spanish
205 10th Ave (near 22nd St)
212-675-8805
Brunch Sat-Sun 11am-3pm,
Lunch Tues-Fri 12pm-3pm,
Dinner Mon-Thurs 5:30pm-
11pm, Fri 5:30-12am,
Sat 6pm-12am,
Sun 6pm-10:30pm
Ⓒ Ⓔ to 23rd
Small plates $4-15
(3-4 per person)

Come early to nab a stool at this tiny, traditional tapas bar. A front bar fills up the sliver of a main room and a long, brick hallway connects to the small back room lined with high tables and stools. Using tapas bars in Spain as its model, Tía Pol offers an authentic menu of tried-and-true preparations supplemented by daily changing specials—don't miss the blistered pimientos if they're available. Familiar ham croquettes surprise with hot, creamy interiors flavored with the slightest hint of truffle, and even a dish as simple as Pan con Tomate is made extraordinary by its trio of spreads. An all-Spanish wine list completes the dining experience, and after a few bottles you may step outside and be surprised to find yourself in Manhattan rather than Madrid.

appropriately farmhouse-like setting. The menu changes daily according to the local greens market, with fresh, seasonal salads and soups joined by entrees inspired by old-fashioned American recipes, like mac and cheese and pot pie. Though menu prices can range rather high, the half grilled cheese sandwich (made with local cheese and apples), served with a cup of soup, for $10 is as good for the environment as it is for your wallet.

La Taza de Oro — *Puerto Rican*

Wood-paneled walls, hand-stenciled menus, and aging red-and-gold décor will have you wondering

96 8th Ave (near 15th St)
212-243-9946
Mon-Sat 6am-10:30pm
A C E L to 8th Ave-14th St
Dishes $4-13

what happened to Chelsea, but it's precisely the old-school charm of this Eighth Avenue dive that keeps regulars coming back. The estimable, daily-rotating menu of traditional, no-fuss Puerto Rican food is nothing fancy, but the crispy fried pork chops are hot and enjoyable, the squid and rice marvelously redolent of the sea, and the rice and beans hearty and filling. Each generous dish, from the familiar to the more unusual, is simple, rich, and exactly as it should be. No Puerto Rican meal would be complete without sides like the avocado salad or fried plantains to add color and sweetness—and be sure to leave room for the flan tempting you from behind the counter.

Murray's Bagels — *Bagels*

"We don't toast," this bagel shop proudly asserts with a typically endearing dash of curmudgeonliness, and indeed they don't have to. Crunchy on the outside, meltingly soft and slightly sweet inside, the bagels come with spread

242 8th Ave
(btwn 22nd & 23rd St)
212-462-2830
Mon-Fri 6am-9pm,
Sat-Sun 6am-8pm
1 to 23rd St, **C E** to 23rd St
Bagel with Spread: $3-5

options ranging from maple raisin walnut to sundried tomato with roasted garlic. The small café is a mess of food, decorations, and crowds, with the menu listed on chalkboards, and an odd array of artwork—from haphazard sketches to classic photographs—adorning the brick walls. Don't miss the lox and cream cheese combination, which is done to perfection here. The profusion of cream cheese on the bagel makes finger-licking inevitable, and the salted lox packs the appropriate salty, fishy punch. Though crowds are often overwhelming, particularly during the breakfast rush, don't be intimidated—the bagels are well worth the wait.

Ronnybrook Milk Bar — *Ice Cream*

Consistent praise turned this once-tiny stand, begun 13 years ago by the owners of Ronnybrook Farm upstate, into the Chelsea Market

75 9th Ave (at 16th St)
212-741-6455
Mon-Fri 8:30am-8pm,
Sat-Sun 10am-7pm
1 to 18th St
A C E L to 8th Ave-14th St,
Brunch $3-9, Lunch $3-10,
Ice Cream and Shakes $2-6

restaurant that now serves brunch and lunch in addition to its signature dairy concoctions. The current space resembles something between a farmhouse and an old-fashioned

CHELSEA GALLERY HOPPING

As you walk further west through Chelsea, streets become quieter and the boisterous city activity dwindles to a near stop. Amid these brownstones, cement alleys, and industrial buildings lie upwards of 350 galleries, nestled between 16th and 27th Streets and 10th and 11th Avenues. A walk through Chelsea's gallery row provides a look at work by the world's boldest modern artists. Any wanderer ought to find a novel aesthetic pleasure, whether from the contemporary works at **Yvon Lambert** (*550 W 21st St*) and **Tanya Bonakdar** (*521 W 21st St*) or futuristic furniture at **Sebastian & Barquet** (*544 W 24th St*). While nothing is conventional about any of the listed galleries, Tanya Bonakdar stands out for shock value—previous works include spicy-scented stockings transformed into a glob and dinosaur-shaped chairs with electrical sockets for the heads and tails. **The Gagosian Gallery** (*located at both 555 W 24th St and 522 W 21st St*), presents works from such renowned artists as Andy Warhol and Damien Hirst. Fine art lovers should check out neighboring galleries **DJT Fine Art** (*231 Tenth Ave*) and **Max Lang** (*229 Tenth Ave*). The online calendar at **chelseaartgalleries.com** lists all exhibits and their duration and announces opening receptions, art fairs, and auctions. Gallery hopping in Chelsea is a must for any art lover and a signature New York experience for anyone.

soda fountain, with stools at the counter in the center of the room, cream colored walls, and old wooden milk crates as the primary decorative motif. In addition to meals and milkshakes, Ronnybrook sells milk, eggs, yogurts, and pints of ice cream, all sourced from the farm. While all of the food is tasty, the ice cream easily steals the show, with classic flavors like strawberry, chocolate, and vanilla, as well as inventive flavors like ginger crème brûlée for the more adventurous. And since all the dairy products come straight from the cows upstate, the offerings at Ronnybrook Milk Bar are a sweet and unbeatably fresh indulgence.

Scarpetta

Italian

In a sea of excessively posh restaurants, Scarpetta's modest white brick facade floats like a life preserver of minimalism.

355 W 14th St (at 9th Ave)
212-691-0555
Dinner Mon-Thurs 5:30pm-1am
A C E L to 8th Ave-14th St
Appetizers $13-22,
Pastas $23-28, Entrees $26-37,
Late night small plates $9-15

Inside the airy restaurant, Chef Scott Conant deftly prepares Italian dishes both luxuriously creative and classically straightforward. The simple spaghetti (menu description: "tomato,

basil") stands as a testament to the power of high quality, fresh ingredients, and careful preparation. A late night menu of small plates provides fertile ground for experimentation: tender pork belly with flavorful grain mustard and raw yellowtail accented with ginger oil and baked sea salt. The chatter of the impeccably-dressed clientele may overwhelm faint strains of Radiohead in the background and distract from your company's attempts at conversation, but don't worry—once the food arrives, you won't be talking much anyway.

The Standard Grill

New American

Tucked under the tracks of the High Line, the restaurant at the Standard Hotel marries old-school New York style with contemporary chic. Outdoor seating and a light-filled

848 Washington St
(near Little W 12th St)
212-645-4100
Sun-Wed 5:30pm-12am,
Thurs-Sun 5:30pm-1am
A C E L to 8th Ave-14th St,
Charcuterie $6-15,
Appetizers $8-16,
Entrees $15-32

bar offer a classically casual setting, while the more formal back room holds semicircular leather booths, barrel-vaulted tile ceilings, and white tablecloths that evoke a retro steakhouse.

Youthful servers are as attractive as they are professional, happily guiding diners through the daily-changing menu. Dishes like smashed fingerlings fried in duck fat appear alongside Moroccan-spiced lamb chops. The clientele is equally varied—neighborhood families next to the young and fashionable, some dressed to the downtown nines and sipping killer signature cocktails, others in jeans and t-shirts selecting from the reasonably priced wine list. With its outdoor biergarden, outfitted with metal furniture and a ping-pong table, The Standard Grill is a welcome breath of easy elegance in the glitzy Meatpacking District.

PLAY

Bar Veloce
Wine Bar

This ultra-modern, European-style "fast bar" was not designed as a place to linger. With its raw wood bar and tables, rows of wine bottles, and a mirror spanning the back wall, Bar Veloce gives off a swanky feel.

176 7th Ave
(btwn 20th & 21st St)
212-629-5300
Mon-Sun 5pm-3am
1 to 18th St
Average Glass $10

But despite the somewhat sterile décor, young urban professionals flock here for a panino and a bottle to split before hitting the town. And what this wine bar lacks in intimacy, it makes up for with a killer wine list, which is extremely approachable and fairly priced. Each wine is listed with a spot-on description, giving you the opportunity to order exactly according to your fancy. They also now offer a small selection of spirits, sake, and beer. And though they don't take reservations, you won't need to wait, for you'll be seated and back on the street before you know it.

The Frying Pan
Outdoor, Live Music, DJs

Sitting pretty on the end of Pier 66 is this exhumed sunken ship and its corresponding barge-turned-bar. In the evening, sit on

Pier 66 (at W 26th St
& West Side Highway)
212-989-6363
Daily 12:30pm-12am
C E to 23rd St
Average Drink $7

deck to enjoy the sunset with a calamari salad and an aperitif, and by nightfall go below decks for some music with a bucket of Coronas and a burger. Although the space is grungy, old, and wet, the hundreds of young professional patrons who frequent tend to dress up for a

Brass Monkey

Beer Bar, Rooftop bar

This lively waterfront alehouse eschews the glitz and pretension of nearby Meatpacking clubs for the simple pleasures of comfort food done right, good beer, and a casual, no-nonsense atmosphere. Tucked away between the High Line park and the West End Highway, Brass Monkey marries old country charm with Manahattanite scale.

55 Little West 12th St
212-675-6686
Daily 11am-4am
A C E L to 8th Ave-14th St
Average Drink $6

There are two stories of bars, ample seating, a large projector screen reserved for notable sporting events, and a rooftop that offers prime views of the Hudson. Despite its size, the bar has a welcoming, homey vibe, with a wood interior bathed in warm light and filled with intimate booths in discreet nooks. Dig into a plate of classic pub grub, like the crispy fish n' chips and bangers n' mash served in a sea of gravy, and order a pint from the respectable selection of 100 draughts and bottles.

night offshore. After dining and drinking, dancers can choose between DJs at the bow of the ship or live bands at the stage deeper down in the hold. Be sure to explore the rusted bowels of the boat in search of dark nooks outfitted with old leather chairs, perfect for impromptu make out sessions, and then take a break in the fresh air for a beautiful view of the harbor.

Magnet Theater

Comedy

Small crowds of twenty-somethings settle into the intimate seating of this black box theater. Shouts of improv and sketch comedians warming up bounce off the

254 W 29th St
(btwn 7th & 8th Ave)
212-671-0044
See magnettheater.com
for schedule
A C E to 34th St-
Penn Station
Average Ticket $5

walls, decorated with the advertisements and posters of past performances. The improvisers, all graduates of the Magnet Theater's comedy classes, perform in troupes with quirky names like "Hello Lazer" and "The Boss."

Expect an eclectic audience—grown women with pigtails, bearded men, and performers' parents cram into chairs that sit on riser-eque platforms. The bar doesn't sell munchies, but you can grab a PBR before the lights dim.

Upright Citizens Brigade

Comedy

Best known for its Sunday night ASSSCAT 3000 shows (featuring special guests from

307 W 26th St (near 8th Ave)
212-366-9119
1 to 28th St, C E to 23rd
Tickets $10 & under

SNL and Conan), this improv and sketch comedy theater showcases the freshest funny faces with affordable shows seven nights a week. Founded by Second City alums like Amy Poehler in 1996, UCB maintains a spirit of community through its many sought after classes, including Sketch Comedy Writing, Improv Basics, and long-form improv study called "Harold." Make sure to reserve space ahead of time and come early—seats are assigned on a first come, first serve basis.

GRAMERCY

Gramercy is one of New York's most upscale and least exciting neighborhoods. Built around a private park of the same name (one of only two such nuisances in the city), it's a neighborhood of multi-million dollar townhouses and towering glass structures housing publishers and ad agencies.

Since the first grandiose rowhouses were constructed around the gated Gramercy Park in the mid-19th century, the district's name has been synonymous with wealth and exclusivity. Turn-of-the-20th-century residents like Theodore Roosevelt and Edith Wharton made it one of the most fashionable addresses in the City. Today it stands as a residence for modern aristocrats.

The boundaries of present-day Gramercy are somewhat ill-defined because it lacks a distinct character to differentiate it from the other upscale, mixed-zoning neighborhoods on the east side. Neighboring enclaves, like Kips Bay, Murray Hill, and the Flatiron District, possess the same easy blend of serenity and privilege.

Still, there is much to be enjoyed in this neighborhood, if only because of the lack of frenetic energy that draws so many to Manhattan. Tree-lined streets offer pristine strolls along architectural masterpieces. The best of these well-groomed streets surround Gramercy Park, one of the largest and most elegant private parks in the country. The picutresque Madison Square Park offers visitors a far more democratic park alternative.

Southwards lies a more diverse community. Curry Hill, on 28th St, has what is perhaps the greatest density of Indian restaurants this side of Mumbai. And the neighborhood's colleges, some NYU-affiliated, some not, breath young life into the otherwise static neighborhood. Though few students can afford to live in the area, their youthful attempts at urban dissipation keep things from getting too stuffy.

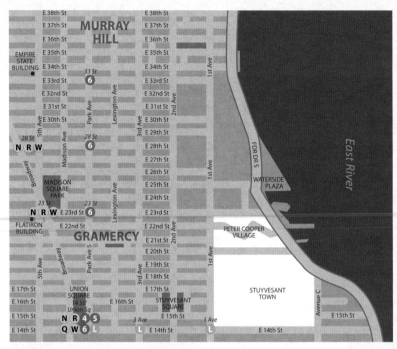

Gotham Comedy Club

Removed from the many stand-up comedy clubs that crowd Chelsea, this Gramercy comedy spot is well-known

208 W 23rd St
(btwn 7th & 8th Ave)
212-367-9000
Shows start 5:30pm-10:45pm
1 C E to 23rd St
Tickets Free-$25

to be one of the best in the city. Featuring performances from newbies and veterans alike—including some acclaimed acts that can be seen on Comedy Central—the club hosts shows nightly. Their premiere program, "Live At Gotham," takes place every week, showcasing new talent and often hosted by famous comedians like D.L. Hughley and Ralphie May. Tickets are never more than $25, but their two-drink minimum is a bit of a pain. They offer pricey stand-up classes for all levels—and Thursday night open mic sessions, open to everyone, for free.

Madison Square Park

A welcome spot of green in the center of the Flatiron District, this park has recently

Btwn 23rd St, 26th St, 5th Ave,
& Madison Ave
6 R W to 23rd St

been transformed into over six acres of prime turf devoted to communal relaxation. Lie on the grass amid modern sculptures and watch the working hordes flock to the area at lunch. The Madison Square Park Conservancy hosts a summer evening concert series and works to maintain the park as a neighborhood gathering spot. Though one frequently finds families attending the many cultural programs, on weekdays the park is mobbed by young professionals, often in line at the ever popular Shake Shack.

Museum of Sex

Unlike the Met or the Guggenheim, this museum has a poster reading, "Please do not touch, lick, stroke, or mount the exhibits" to forewarn you of the impending sexual exhibits you'll witness—but not participate in—at the gallery. The first room welcomes visitors with the mating rituals of animals—the focal point is a statue of two Giant Pandas partaking in the act.

233 5th Ave (at 27th St)
212-689-6337
Adults $15, Students $14
Sun–Fri 11am-6:30pm,
Sat 11am-8pm
ⓇⓌ to 28th St-Broadway,
❻ to 28th St-Park Ave

Video snippets on the pick-up techniques of various birds and mammals play throughout the gallery. As you move into further galleries, the presentations turn their focus to the sex lives of human beings. Various galleries are dedicated to pornographic films, the cultural history of sex, erotic equipment, and rotating exhibits like the Sex Lives of Robots. Bringing friends, a healthy sense of humor, and an open mind is strongly suggested.

The National Arts Club

Located in the historic Tilden Mansion, the exclusive National Arts Club— membership is by invitation only—supports both established and

15 Gramercy Park South
(near Irving Pl)
212-674-8824
Mon-Fri 10am-5pm
ⓇⓌ to 23rd St

emerging artists. The Victorian sandstone facade and stained glass dome ceiling are impressive in their own right, but the interior of the mansion is stunning in style and substance. In parlor rooms high-backed chairs huddled together in nooks and at windows, as if they are exchanging secrets, and ornate chandeliers hang from high ceilings. Count on exhibits here to be well-edited and impressively high quality. The five galleries are open weekdays to the public, but check ahead as events often close the club to visitors. The National Arts Cub also hosts book signings, lectures, and concerts.

SHOP

Reminiscence, Inc.

Stop by this humorous vintage and novelty store to unleash your inner eight-year-old. Shelves house action figures, retro

50 W 23rd St
(btwn 5th & 6th Ave)
212-243-2292
Mon-Sat 11am-7:30pm
Sun 12pm-7pm
ⒻⓋⓇⓌ to 23rd St

lunch boxes, whoopie cushions, and other gag items. Rubber duckies come wearing a variety of ridiculous facial expressions. The back of the store houses a fun selection of vintage clothing,

feather boas, and Hawaiian print shirts. Piece together your Halloween costume or snag all the goods necessary for *Home Alone*-esque shenanigans. They also offer a serious selection of anti-Hallmark birthday cards. Retro-inspired and bound to make you laugh, this shop is a breath of fresh air in often stuffy Gramercy.

Vintage Thrift

Most New York thrift stores offer a monetary compensation for items brought in. Vintage Thrift does

286 3rd Ave (at 23rd St)
Mon-Thurs 10:30am-8pm,
Fri 10:30am-dusk, Sat closed,
Sun 11am-7pm
212-871-0777
❻ to 28th St-Park Ave

things a little differently: in exchange for goods, customers get a tax reduction. Everyone from blue-haired old ladies to frugal college students visit this shop for everything and anything antiquated at a moderate price. Shelves are packed with goodies like costume jewelry, beautiful satin slips, and outrageous 70s print tops. If they don't have what you're looking for, savvy staff can direct you to stores that might. Most people who work there spend their free time scavenging flea-markets and other thrift stores for worthy pieces. The store's always getting new garments, furniture, and knickknacks to sell—so each visit promises new discoveries.

FLATIRON DISTRICT

Though now packed with white collar offices and big-name retail chains, the Flatiron District still preserves the architectural character and dynamic atmosphere that have made it a hub of culture and recreation since the turn of the 20th century. At the heart of this vibrant neighborhood is **Madison Square Park** (*at the intersection of 5th Ave, 23rd St, & Broadway*), an inviting and well-maintained haven of tree-lined pathways and ample bench space. The small, shaded dog run along Madison Avenue makes this park a favorite among canine-lovers. Mid-afternoons find the park populated by patrons of **Shake Shack** (*Madison Ave & 23rd St*), whose devotion to the burger stand compels them to queue up daily around the park's southeast corner. Described by the park conservancy as "a free gallery without walls," the square frequently hosts public art installations, featuring fun and thought-provoking work from contemporary artists throughout the year.

Surrounding the park are fine examples of the architecture that gives the Flatiron District its distinctive style—and its name. **The Flatiron Building**, the celebrated early skyscraper by Chicago architect Daniel Burnham, slices defiantly through the New York grid like the prow of a ship. Completed in 1902, it remains a thrilling expression of Beaux-Arts architecture and has become one of the city's most iconic sights.

Right around the corner from the neighborhood's signature edifice is **Metropolitan Life Tower**, a 50-story variation on the Campanile in Venice that was, until 1913, the world's tallest building. Just to the north is the **New York Life Building** (*26th St at Madison*). With its cathedral-like detailing, perched gargoyles, and unmistakable gold pyramid at the peak, this insurance tower by Cass Gilbert is a Gothic masterpiece.

EAT

A Voce
Italian

41 Madison Ave (at 26th St)
212-545-8555
Brunch Sat-Sun, Lunch Daily
11:30am-3:30pm,
Dinner daily 5:30pm-11:30pm
6 to 28th St
Prix fixe lunch $29
Dinner Appetizers $12-16,
Entrees $19-38

The slick surroundings at this acclaimed Italian location on Madison Square Park prepare the diners for the hearty, refined warmth of the fare to come. Antipasti like the cassoncini, a plate of fried crescenza-filled pastries served with prosciutto di parma and a dish of whipped ricotta, are simply exquisite. Standout pasta dishes include the rich, smoky rabbit pappardelle and nutty ravioli di caprino. Entrees of fish, meat, and chicken, such as the superbly tender grilled lamb chops or the "ippoglosso in acqua pazza," a generous slab of halibut in a broth spiked with Calabrian chili peppers, are equally lovely. Desserts like the panna cotta and semifreddo put elegant, modern twists on Italian classics. A new, David Rockwell-designed location is now open at the Time Warner Center with a similar menu, private dining rooms, and stunning views of Central Park.

Bar Jamón
Spanish

125 E 17th St (near Irving Pl)
212-253-2773
Mon-Fri 5pm-2am,
Sat-Sun 12pm-2am
N O R W 4 5 6 L to
14th St-Union Square,
Small plates $5-15

This Gramercy tapas bar bears striking similarity to a childhood fort—it's dark, you eat tiny foods, and it's packed with friends to the point of bursting. Though some menu items are quite expensive (a small plate of Jamón Iberico Fermin runs $30), many of the most delicious offerings, like duck liver with apricots and the bocadillo de Bar Jamón, are reasonably priced and generous enough in size to push the definition of tapas to its limit. Pair these with a $30 bottle of the delightfully crisp house cava (Spanish sparkling wine), called Cava Mono after Bar Jamón's neighbor restaurant Casa Mono. Sipping cava from slender flutes, a sophisticated young crowd packs tight around the marble bar and two wooden tables—all part of Bar Jamón's casual charm.

Bar Stuzzichini
Italian

Classic Italian cooking, fine wines, and New York style dominate at this Flatiron trattoria. Red banquettes fill the large room, which

cleverly utilized supporting posts divide into pockets of intimacy for vibrant, professional crowds. Knowledgeable servers suggest wine choices and encourage guests to begin their meal with the Stuzzichini Misti, a tasting of Italian-style tapas. Among these, the buttery, tender octopus and the rich, melted mozzarella are the stand-outs. Main courses of traditional Italian preparations are marvelously flavorful, though modestly sized, leaving room for desserts like the orange and olive oil cake or the daily selection of sorbets. Those not convinced by Stuzzichini's penchant for lighter dining can check out the three-course prix fixe lunch for $20, or the $26, four-course Sunday dinner, La Familglia Domencia.

928 Broadway (near 21st St)
212-780-5100
Brunch Sat-Sun 11am-3pm,
Mon-Thurs 11:45am-11pm,
Fri-Sat 11:45am-12am
Sun 11:45am-10pm
F V 6 to 23rd St
Appetizers $4-10,
Entrees $13-24

Chinese Mirch
Indo-Chinese

Unlike other Curry Hill favorites, this Indo-Chinese eatery offers dishes influenced more by the wok than the tandoor. The first NYC restaurant of its kind, Chinese Mirch offers Indian spins on traditional Chinese options like kung pao chicken and chicken Manchurian. As the name implies—'mirch" is Hindi for "pepper"—the dishes here are almost all given a fiery kick, crispy Szechuan-style lamb being an outstanding example. In traditional Indian style, the menu bypasses beef and pork, offering many good vegetarian choices instead. The food is presented as elegantly as the small, minimal space in which it is served, down to desserts like the house-recommended chocolate cake with green tea ice cream, and the refreshing, chilled Bengal lychees, both ideal conclusions to a unique, border-crossing meal.

120 Lexington Ave
(near 29th St)
212-532-3663
Mon-Fri 12pm-2:45pm
& 5:30pm-10pm,
Sat-Sun 12:30pm-3:15pm ,
& 5:30-10pm
6 to 28th St
Appetizers $5-9, Entrees $9-17

Defonte's of Brooklyn
Sandwiches

This Manhattan outpost of the Brooklyn original is a shrine to old-school sandwich making. A family-

261 3rd Ave (at 21st St)
212-614-1500
Mon-Sat 9:30am-8pm,
Sun closed
6 to 28th St, **L** to 3rd Ave
Sandwiches $8-10

run business since its founding in 1922, Defonte's did not branch out to Manhattan until recently. Better late than never. This branch of the famous sandwich shop has maintained the quality (and quantity) of its famously fresh, gargantuan heroes during its move. Beautiful, fresh ingredients constitute basically the only décor at the bright, immaculate shop. Thanks to these ingredients, ordinary sandwiches like a smoked ham and cheese sandwich with roasted red peppers is deeply flavorful and its massive proportions make it hugely filling. Defonte's may be a newcomer to this borough, but its old-fashioned Italian recipes and no-nonsense style have already made it one of the best sandwich spots in town, and arguably the best cheap bite in its neighborhood.

Ravagh
Persian

The sage green walls, dim lighting, and recorded sitar strumming in the background are all par for the course	11 E 30th St (5th Ave) 212-696-0300 Daily 11am-11pm ⑥ to 33rd St, ⓇⓌ to 28th St Appetizers $4-7, Entrees $12-18

at Middle Eastern restaurants—but steaming basmati rice, succulent grilled meats, and flavorful stews handily distinguish Ravagh from the dozens of watered down ethnic joints sprinkled south of 42nd Street. Order the off-menu tadigh as an appetizer—this crunchy rice from the bottom of a pot comes topped with steaming stew made from lamb, tenderly cooked with eggplant and tomato. The chicken barg and sultani kabobs are particularly juicy and well-seasoned entrees, though all meat kabobs are hearty and satisfying. Served with rice and grilled vegetables, entree portions are huge, so split with friends or take leftovers home.

Resto
Belgian

The seasoned waiter dispenses this gem of wisdom between beer expositions: the best dishes require an adventurous spirit. With that in mind, attempt the tete di cochon, a delightfully spicy take on the pulled pork sandwich that is bold, robust, and rustic—ideal beer food. The unparalleled deviled eggs on pork toast are another swine-based triumph and traditional

NATIVE'S PICK

Shake Shack
Burgers & Dogs

In a city of many disparities, Shake Shack is the great culinary equalizer: New Yorkers of all ages and income brackets flock to this squat, steely burger hut in Madison Square Park, and all earn their grub the old-fashioned way—by waiting. The snaking line is a testament to the universal appeal of the ShackBurger,

Madison Ave (near 23rd St)
212-889-6600
Daily Mar-Oct 11am-1?pm, Nov-Feb 11am-7pm
ⒼⓃⓇⓌ to 23rd St
Burgers $4-10, Shakes $5-7

a gloriously messy pile of perfectly proportioned meat, cheese, lettuce, special sauce, and buttery bun. The 'Shroom Burger is the sole vegetarian-friendly option on the menu, though with its irresistible crispy shell of fried mushroom and bubbling muenster and cheddar cheeses, even non-herbivores would do well to order one. Or order the Double Stack or Shack Stack and get a mushroom patty in addition to beef. No meal here is complete without one of their "concrete" thick shakes that give the shack its alliterative name—try the black and white hand-spun shake, just a bit less sweet than the others.

moules and frites, the Belgian dish par excellence, are cooked to perfection. Celebrating Belgium's 500-year-old brewing tradition, this elegant spot offers an exhaustive list of beers, including sought-after trappiste bottles and unique fruit lambics. The knowledgeable staff can help pair one of these brews with your meal for a dining experience without equal—except, of course, in Belgium.

> 111 E 29th St (Park Ave)
> 212-685-5585
> Brunch Sat-Sun 10:30am-3pm,
> Lunch & Dinner Mon-Thurs
> 12pm-11:30 pm, Fri 12pm-
> 1am, Sat 10:30am-1am,
> Sun 10:30am-10:30 pm
> **6** to 28th St
> Appetizers $9-14,
> Entrees $12-27

Rickshaw Dumpling Bar   *Asian*

Chef Anita Lo's dumpling joint is a refreshing break from the national chains supported by lunching Flatiron nine-to-fivers. Lo

> 61 W 23rd St (near Sixth Ave)
> 212-924-9220
> Mon-Sat 11:30am-9:30pm,
> Sun 11:30-8:30
> **6 V R W** to 23rd St
> Dumplings half dozen $5.50,
> Combo meals $9

brings a gourmet sensibility to her healthy, flavorful snacks, serving them up with the polish and efficiency of a big chain—the flavors and ingredients, however, are anything but franchised. Try six Hudson Valley duck dumplings with soup or the Asian salad for a basic meal, or a lighter bento box of four vegan-friendly edamame dumplings, white rice, and fresh steamed greens. Dumpling aficionados argue that the smaller-than-average morsels can't match Chinatown prices or authenticity, but Rickshaw's under $10 price tag and gourmet fillings beg otherwise. When not in the area, look out for the Rickshaw Truck, plying its cheap and tasty wares across town.

Saravanaas   *Indian, Vegetarian*

Sitting pretty among the bevy of Indian restaurants on Curry Hill, this American outpost of a popular Chennai-based Indian chain garners praise

> 81 Lexington Ave (E 26th St)
> 212-679-0204
> Mon-Fri 8:30am-3pm & 5pm-
> 10pm, Sat-Sun 8:30am-4pm
> & 6pm-10pm
> **6** to 28th St
> Small plates $4-6, Dosas $7-
> 11, Combo plates $11-17

from native-born Indians as well as those previously uninitiated into the vibrant world of subcontinental cuisine. Cramped seating, the heavy aroma of curry, and speedy waiters greet diners upon entering Saravanaas, an

appropriate preparation for the classic, all-vegetarian South Indian fare that will follow. Detailed explanations of dishes make unfamiliar foods less daunting, though the safest bet is still one of the expertly prepared dosas. For the indecisive, various thalis, or plates, offer culinary tours of India's tropical southern region, with dishes like idly (steamed rise patties), uttapam (rice and lentil pancakes), and the ubiquitous sambar (a spicy vegetable broth) served in various combinations. Halva or gulab jamun make for a fittingly traditional and delightfully sweet ending to the South Indian feast.

Tiffin Wallah   *Indian, Vegetarian*

It would be easy to overlook this Curry Hill treasure were it not for the line that forms outside around lunchtime. The South Indian food served at the $7.50 buffet is shockingly fresh,

> 127 E 28th St
> (btwn Park & Lexington)
> 212-685-7301
> Mon-Fri 11:30am-3pm & 5pm-
> 10pm, Sat-Sun 12am-10pm
> **6 N R W** to 28th St
> Snacks $3-5, Meals $6-9

entirely delicious, and, as it's all vegetarian, fairly healthy. Pancake-like uttapam are moist, mild, and particularly delicious when dipped into the sambar (the spicy, soup-like South Indian staple) served on traditional metal tiffin trays. Straying from the buffet won't break the bank either, as every dish on the expansive menu costs less than $10. For those unfamiliar with South Indian cuisine, the staff will patiently define samosas, vadas, and idli better than the menu glossary, and they will undoubtedly point you to the restaurant's magnificent $8 Rava Masala Dosa. The traditional paper-thin, crispy semolina pancake stuffed with spiced potatoes might well be Tiffin Wallah's bid for perfection.

'wichcraft   *Café, Sandwiches*

11 E 20th St
(btwn Broadway & Fifth Ave)
212-780-0577
Mon-Fri 8am-10pm,
Sat-Sun 10am-10pm
6 **R** **W** to 23rd St
Sandwich $7-$10

The casual sandwich shop from Craft creator Tom Colicchio has bloomed into trendy, inexpensive dining destination with 12 locations citywide. This Flatiron District location, the flagship, is the only one with a seating area and the first to serve dinner. Beloved by most for lunch and breakfast sandwiches (served all day), 'wichcraft also serves a number of fairly priced wines and beers. Popular favorites include the roasted turkey sandwich with onion relish and the $1 cream'wich cookies. Order your food and head upstairs to sit in the brick-walled, brightly lit dining room or outside in a backyard oasis of potted plants. Three meals a day served in stylish digs with good wine and free WiFi make 'wichcraft a modern sandwich shop with upscale flavor.

PLAY

Beauty Bar   *Club, Theme*

231 E 14th St (near 2nd Ave)
212-539-1389
Mon-Fri 5pm-4am,
Sat-Sun 7pm-4am
N **Q** **R** **W** **4** **5** **6** **L** to
14th St-Union Square,
L to 3rd Ave
Average Drink $5
Happy Hour: Mon-Fri 5pm-9pm, Buds & drafts $3,
Well Drink $4

Get a manicure from a tattooed chick, sip a complimentary dirty martini, and rock out to The Keys and Nirvana at this salon-turned-club. Fill up on gossip with the $10 cocktail-and-mani special and stick around—the place transforms into dance bar by midnight. Predictably, at this salon-turned-club kitsch is the status quo. With pink glitter sprinkled wallpaper, old hair-dryer chairs, black-and-white female silhouette-stenciled walls, and 80s records on blast, Beauty Bar looks and sounds like a girl's ideal place to wreak havoc—with perfect French tips or blood red nails, of course. The bar's status as bachelorette party central draws in dudes that equalize the testosterone-estrogen ratio at what you'd expect to be an overwhelmingly feminine establishment.

Black Bear Lounge
Beer Bar, Dive

274 3rd Ave
(btwn 21st & 22nd St)
212-253-2178
Daily 2pm-4am
6 R W to 23rd St
Happy Hour: Daily 4-8pm

Fake wooden logs bedecked with snowshoes and skis panel the walls at this lodge-themed dive. Set up like an old log cabin, this narrow bar is divided into four rooms for drinking on the cheap. The dim lights and candles on every surface cast long shadows against the walls. Though the TVs and corner arcade games don't jive with the otherwise mountain-man-type décor, after a few $10 buckets of beers, you'll barely notice. Although the small rooms and often raucous weekend crowd mean it can get uncomfortably warm, ample seating makes it the perfect place to hang out with a big group.

Rodeo Bar
Tex-Mex, Live Music

375 3rd Ave (at 27th St)
212-683-6500
Mon-Thurs 11:30am-3am,
Fri-Sat 11:30am-4am,
Sun 11:30am-12am
6 to 28th St
Average Drink $9
Happy Hour: Mon-Sat
4-8pm, Sun 6-9pm,
Margaritas $6, Draft Beer $4

As a one of the bar's performers quipped, "You don't go anywhere else for dinner and see boobs, do you?" Though this is only true during Rodeo Bar's burlesque show on the last Tuesday of every month, near-nudity isn't the only draw of this Western-themed bar: delicious food and strong drinks are nightly staples. Try their signature margaritas in flavors like frozen mango and lemon for tons of tequila in a single glass. Grub consists of lovingly prepared comfort food, like Slow Smoked Texas BBQ and Dakota Bison Burgers. Try to catch one of the bar's shows—authentic Southern bluegrass, comedy shows, and burlesque dancers follow one another, making the evening fly by in a tipsy whirl of songs, jokes, and striptease.

Wined Up
Wine Bar

913 Broadway (at 21st St)
212-673-6333
Mon-Wed 5pm-12am,
Thurs-Sat 5pm-2am
R W to 23rd St
Average Glass $13

After spending an evening with Wined Up's passionate sommelier, Joshua Hakimi, visitors will come away thinking he's obsessed, brilliant, or a bit of both. With his unparalleled respect and ardor for wine, he brings stellar bottles at affordable prices to this second-floor wine lounge. Hakimi and his well-trained staff will guide budding connoisseurs to some truly excellent and rare wines, many for less than $16. But the Wined Up experience goes beyond what's found in its bottles—Chef Matt Corbett runs a small kitchen in the back where his team prepares carefully selected pairings of fine cheeses and meats to accent your selection. These platters, coupled with entrees available from Punch Restaurant's kitchen downstairs, ensure that guests will leave sated, happy, and a bit more appreciative of the subtleties of wine.

GREENWICH VILLAGE

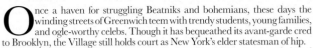

Once a haven for struggling Beatniks and bohemians, these days the winding streets of Greenwich teem with trendy students, young families, and ogle-worthy celebs. Though it has bequeathed its avant-garde cred to Brooklyn, the Village still holds court as New York's elder statesman of hip.

In New York's 19th-century explosion, wealthy residents commissioned famous architects to design their buildings, and Greenwich Village thrived as an upscale suburban area. During Prohibition, seedy speakeasies packed in patrons from all parts of the island. An artistic culture emerged in the late 50s and 60s, as black-turtlenecked crowds gathered in coffeehouses to hear Simon and Garfunkel strum their first chords, while jazz lairs like the Village Vanguard and The Blue Note echoed the early tunes of Charlie Parker and John Coltrane. You can still visit Electric Lady Recording Studio, where Jimi Hendrix recorded his first album, or sip a cappuccino at Caffee Reggio, where Kerouac was rumored to pen his poetry. The neighborhood grew famous for its wild parties, candlelit tearooms, novelty nightclubs, and bizarre boutiques.

The Village also had an instrumental role in the production of independent theatre: the neighborhood is not only home to The Cherry Lane Theater, the city's oldest off-Broadway production house, but also the birthplace of the off-off-Broadway movement that began as a revolt against commercial theatre. In 1969, the Village was the site of a series of riots between Christopher Street's growing gay population and the police. Collectively called the Stonewall Rebellion, these protests are considered by many historians to mark the beginning of the Gay Rights Movement.

No longer the hotbed of activism it once was, the Village is still home to a dynamic scene of comedy clubs, concert halls, and street performances. And on the winding roads west of 7th Ave, every wrong turn leads to another lovely spot, another tucked-away coffee shop, bookstore or tree-lined block so singular and gorgeous, you may never find it again.

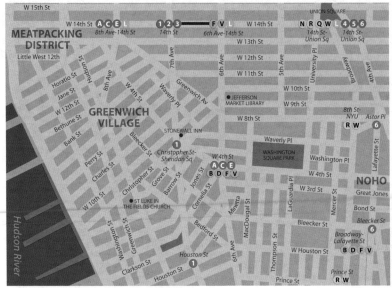

EXPLORE

Angelika Film Center

Soho's veteran movie theater has indie charm and creature comforts to spare. If you visit, chances are

18 W Houston St (at Mercer St)
212-995-2000
F V to Broadway-Lafayette,
R W to Prince St

seeing is a movie isn't all you'll be doing—the Angelika invites you to relax for as long as you please in their large, chandelier-lit lounge and café. Plan to arrive at the theater early to take in the scene with a fresh coffee or gourmet snack. It's an ideal place to kill time before your showing, read the many film reviews on display, admire the vintage posters, or chat up fellow film buffs. Grab a good seat downstairs, where six small screens beam high-brow films—mostly arthouse gems and documentaries—to your chair. The sound and picture are crisp, but the rumbling of the nearby F train can be an annoyance.

Film Forum

If Anthology Film Archives holds a monopoly on New York's hardcore cinephiles, Film Forum is left to cater to the more casual movie fanatic—still the sort that flocks to Truffaut retrospectives and appreciates the crispness of a real print over digital

209 W Houston St
212-727-8110
1 to Houston St,
A C E F V to W 4th St
Cash only at box office

projection. But Film Forum doesn't run rings around its audience with the obscurity of its selections—the theater mixes its repertory series with premieres of new features to hit the New York indie circuit. The lobby is too small for the crowd that lines up before doors open, so grab a baked good or fresh espresso from the concession stand and engage one of the friendly solo film buffs in conversation as you wait on Houston St—these ones don't bite.

The Forbes Galleries

Tucked inside the confines of Forbes Magazines' headquarters, The Forbes Galleries are devoted to showcasing a rare

62 Fifth Ave (at 12th St)
212-206-5548
Tues-Sat, 10am-4pm, Thurs
reserved for group tours
1 2 3 F V to 14th St,
4 5 6 N Q R B W L to
14th St-Union Square

breed of art—toys. Peruse the selection of over 500 toy boats—all manufactured between 1870 and 1950—and the 10,000 miniature soldiers, including GI Joes and figurine versions of Alexander the Great, George Washington, and Buffalo Bill. Perhaps the gem of its permanent exhibit is the Monopoly collection, which includes myriad offshoots of the household staple as well as its prototype version (who knew that Monopoly was originally called "The Landlord's Game"?). Always free and never jammed, Forbes Galleries is renowned for its surprising temporary showcases. Expect anything from Romanov Fabergé eggs to JFK's handwritten inauguration speech to the specs Lincoln wore when he was assassinated. If visiting the gallery now, bypass Sabina Forbes's paintings for the quirky handbag collection and the display of flower-themed jewels by Cartier.

Grey Art Gallery

NYU's fine-arts gallery will entice and engage you with innovative art. Like many museums of the area, it's geared toward a young, hip demographic—the art, while not technically

100 Washington Square East
212-998-6780
Tue & Thurs-Fri 11am-6pm,
Wed 11am-8pm,
Sat 11am-5pm
Ⓐ Ⓒ Ⓔ Ⓕ Ⓥ to W 4th St,
Ⓡ Ⓦ to 8th St

DAY TO DAY

Community Board 2: 3 Washington Square Village, #1A, 212-979-2272.

Dry Cleaner: Brown Bag Laundry, 208 Mercer St, 212-505-2440.

Groceries: Morton Williams, 255 W 14th St, 212-645-7260.

Gym: Crunch, 152 Christopher St, 212-366-3725.

Hospital: Beth Israel Medical Center, 10 E Union Square, 888-762-2167.

Library: Hudson Park Library, 66 Leroy St, 212-243-6876.

Media: *Greenwich Village NYC*, nycgv.com.

Volunteer Opportunities: Greenwich Village Youth Council, 345 E 15th St, 5th Floor, 212-475-7972.

Lomography Gallery Shop

Art & Supplies

41 W 8th St (near 6th Ave)
212-529-4353
Daily 10:30am-9pm,
Sun 11am-10pm
1 to Christopher St, **A C E**
B D F V to W 4th St

The Lomographic Society has marvelously capitalized on, if not orchestrated, the return of the vintage camera. Remaking and marketing classics like the Diana, Lomo, and Holga analogue cameras, it's fostered a one million-strong worldwide social network of experimental, creative, and brand-loyal photographers. The airy gallery-style store hosts regular workshops and exhibits, and features the largest LomoWall in North America—comprised of 35,000 hand-picked and hand-mounted lomographs. Check out the wide range of original and resurrected cameras—Russian, medium format, panoramic, pin-hole—and accessories like underwater shells, extreme fish-eye lens adapters, and color ring-flashes. Photo fiends will appreciate the store's limited edition selections, like the twin-lens USSR-made Lubitel. And anyone can enjoy the beautifully produced photo books sold with cameras.

contemporary, maintains a modern feel, and is displayed in a range of inventive fashions. Beside the cutting-edge new exhibits that rotate every three months, there is a reserve of 6,000 19th and 20th century works, American paintings from the 1940s to the present, and a collection of Asian and Middle Eastern art. Notable highlights include one of Picasso's sculptures and a stained glass window from a Frank Lloyd Wright house. Explore the work of Gottlieb, Matisse, de Kooning and more with a student-guided tour, then rest up from your art fix in the neighboring Washington Square Park.

The Village Vanguard

For over seven decades, patrons have descended an unassuming staircase to this West Village landmark. Originally a performance space for left-leaning poets, the 70-year old Vanguard eventually became the destination for prime gigs from the innovators of jazz. The club consists of a cramped room adorned with photographs of Charles Mingus, Dexter Gordon, and other

legends playing on the very stage in front of you. It may be hard to believe that some of the best live jazz albums were recorded in this triangular basement, but in fact it is the Vanguard's unique shape that is credited

178 7th Ave South
(near Perry St)
212-255-4037
Doors 8pm, Nightly sets 9pm,
11pm, & sometimes additional
Sat 12:30am
1 2 3 F V to 14th St,
A C E L to 8th Ave-14th St
Cover Mon-Thurs $30-35 &
Fri-Sun $35, Drinks $10-$45,
Tickets $20 with $10 drink
minimum per set

for its incredible acoustics. Needless to say, anyone playing at this "Carnegie Hall of Jazz" (so dubbed by one musician) better be killing it.

Washington Square Park

At various times this Village landmark was a marsh, a

W 4th St & MacDougal
A C E B D F V to W 4th St

parade ground, and the site of public executions. Nestled among NYU buildings at the foot of Fifth Ave, it is now a popular congregation spot area locals. Tourists, NYU students, hippies, ex-hippies, artists, writers, and musicians all flock to its well-shaded paths and benches. A majestic marble arch built to commemorate the 100-year anniversary of Washington's inauguration looms near the center, standing 77 feet tall. After passing beneath it, take a rest at the recently-renovated fountain and catch a street performance. If you're a chess whiz, head to the park's southwest corner—a legion of legendary players sit there all day and are always up for a challenge.

SHOP

McNulty's Tea & Coffee Company

The scent of teas and coffees emanates from this quaint store, which is a tad out of place in the neighborhood with its antique teapots and burlap sacks in the window display. Since 1985, McNulty's has been the nation's leading carrier of rare teas and coffees, offering over 100 selections of each, including the aromatic French Roast Java Mountain Supreme coffee and the Golden Money Premium Grade tea. You'll be stunned by the volume of bags and barrels—all filled to the brim with various tea leaves and coffee beans—that make up the bulk of the décor. While no coffee or tea is available to order or taste, the friendly staff will help you make your decision, offering their input and personal favorites.

109 Christopher St (near Bleecker St)
212-242-5351
Mon-Sat 10am-9pm, Sun 10am-7pm
❶ to Christopher St, ❹❸❹ ❸❺❺❹ to W 4th St
Coffes & teas $8-20 per lb

Nepa Bhon'

Stepping through the narrow doorway of this shop, your senses will be overwhelmed by the sweet smell of burning incense. A warm glow is cast about the store, emanating from lamps wrapped in Lokta paper shades. This strong, textured paper, made from a special type of shrub found only in the Himalayan foothills, is the specialty of Nepa Bhon'. The paper comes in an array of beautiful colors—deep blues, pinks, and greens, and with various patterns and weavings. Lokta is used in a wide variety of other items—from stationary and albums to decorative wall hangings, all of which are sold

106 MacDougal St (near Bleecker St)
212-477-8723
❶ to Christopher St, ❹❸❹ ❸❺❺❹ to W 4th St

at Nepa Bhon'. Other handcrafts, including wooden wall decorations, Om carvings, and exotic incense, can also be purchased here.

Partners & Crime Mystery Booksellers

This independent bookstore nods to the deviousness implied by its name with its sub-street-level location. The store houses a wide variety of mystery novels and has a friendly staff that's genre-savvy enough to help you navigate it. It's not strange to find various staff-written book recommendations pinned around the store, nudging deliberating customers in the direction of favorites like *The Accomplice* by Elizabeth Ironside and *A Corpse in the Koryo* by James Church. For those looking for more than just the casual visit, there is a rental system that speed-readers can join for $20, as well as a late-night Saturday radio show that is broadcast from the store.

44 Greenwich Ave (btwn Charles & Perry St)
212-243-0440
Mon-Thurs 12pm-9pm, Fri-Sat 12pm-10pm, Sun 12pm-7pm.
❶❷❸❺❹ to 14th St

Strand Bookstore

They claim to have "18 miles of books"—after one stop at this mammoth independent bookstore, you'll be inclined to agree. Carts of $1 and $2 books line the sidewalk that wraps around the store. Inside, four floors count countless rows of bookcases, their huge wooden shelves sagging under the volumes of human intellect. Jostle around wobbly-kneed tables of books with fellow bibliophiles or stakeout a spot in a vacant corner to read. There are new and used books—many of which are a few dollars cheaper than you'll find at corporate mega-stores—as well as an antiquarian section with rare books and first editions. They even offer an exhaustive selection of books in languages other than English. A hunt for a specific read will have one blissfully lost in the stacks of the colossal—and colossally famous—Book Row relic.

828 Broadway (near 12th St)
212-473-1452
Mon-Sat 9:30am-10:30pm, Sun 11am-10:30pm, Rare Book room closes daily at 6:20pm
❹❺❻❻❹❷❸❹ to 14th St-Union Square

Zachary's Smile

This stellar vintage clothing boutique is ideal for the no-muss, no-fuss shopper. Forget having to dig through rack after rack of haphazardly

arranged skirts, shirts, and dresses. Here every rack full of beautiful timeless items is organized by type and color, putting the dress you've been coveting right in your line of sight. Open-toe, high-heeled, and colorful vintage shoes can be snagged here, as well as various accessories. Splurge on one of ZS's own signature dresses made from recycled vintage fabrics. While the prices for these reconstructed dresses run a bit steep (most costing around $200), each dress is one-of-a-kind and will have you grinning all around town.

9 Greenwich Ave (at Christopher St)
212-924-0604
Mon-Sat 11am-8pm, Sun 12am-7pm
❶ to Christopher St, ❹❻❺
❷❹❻❼ to W 4th St

EAT

Aamchi Pao
Indian

Give the Atkins diet a rest at this bite-sized Bleecker Street Indian joint where Pao—a starchy Mumbai street-food—is the star. At Aamchi Pao the traditional fried patty of spiced mashed potatoes and vegetables on a bun is served with any number of meat, fish, and vegetable additions, all of which are topped with a sweet, aromatic chutney. Be sure to sample the tandoori chicken and pulled goat

194 Bleecker St (near MacDougal St)
212-228-1909
Mon-Sun 12pm-11pm, Fri-Sat 12pm-5am
❹❻❺❷❹❻❼ to W 4th St-Washington Sq
Entrees $6-8, Sides $4

varieties. If you're a vegetarian, the spinach lentil tikki makes a flavorful alternative. These sandwiches are a tad messy to eat on-the-go, but the bright, simply-furnished, 12-seat room is comfortable enough. If you stick around, follow your pao with a dessert brought over directly from Chef Sahni's other gig as pastry chef at the gourmet Indian institution Dévi.

Commerce
New American

Tucked away at the end of the picturesque Cherry Lane (aka Commerce St), this upscale eatery is proof that fine dining doesn't have to be stiff or stuffy. Modern elegance tempers the discrete, old-school New York feel for a relaxed but refined dining experience. Traditional starters like the creamy foie gras and citrus-marinated yellowtail appear alongside the less conventional "ragu of odd things," made with oxtail, trotters, and tripe. Fitting for such a convivial location, the most popular entrees are the four signature plates for sharing: rack of pork, whole chicken, leg of lamb, and a decadently-sized, impeccably tender porterhouse for two—shown whole in the pan before dished out into manageable serving sizes. A soft yellow light bathes the dining room and adjacent bar, decorated with WPA-style murals, an homage to the space's past incarnation as a prohibition-era speakeasy.

50 Commerce St (near Bedford St)
212-524-2301
Mon-Thurs 5:30pm-11pm., Fri-Sat 5:30pm-11:30pm, Sun 1pm-9:30pm
❶ to Christopher St, ❹❻❺
❷❹❻❼ to W 4th St
Appetizers $15-19, Entrees $23-36

Corner Bistro

Burgers

331 W 4th St (near Jane St)
212-242-9502
Mon-Sat 11:30am-4am,
Sun 12am-4am
A C E to 14th St
Burgers & Sandwiches $5-7

It looks like a lackluster neighborhood pub: dark, tiny, and crowded. But laidback locals and informed out-of-towners who brave the long line are quick to discover this West Village mainstay's M.O. Corner Bistro is famous for serving one of New York's very best burgers. Tossed carelessly about the table on a flimsier-than-average paper plate, the Bistro Burger is topped with perfect proportions of bacon, lettuce, cheese, tomato, and raw onion. The meal is complete with a mug of super-cheap McSorley's beer and side of crispy shoestring fries that hold a hint of bacon flavor, assuring diners that Corner Bistro merits the praise it receives tenfold—it's truly transcendent pub grub. Is it really worth the wait? Visit during peaceful, weekday off-hours, and you won't have to ask.

Ditch Plains

American, Seafood

29 Bedford St (at Downing St)
212- 633-0202
Daily 11am-11pm
1 to Houston St
Breakfast & Lunch $10-14,
Dinner Appetizers $8-15,
Entrees $14-25

This low-key bar and eatery in the West Village takes its industrial-cum-nautical inspiration from the seafood classics served up at Montauk, where the real Ditch Plains beach is located. Seafood dishes are the specialty here, from the crispy fried calamari to the grilled fish of the day, but beach-bum foods like the cheese-smothered "ditch dog" are equally delicious. Prices on entrees run high, but breakfast and lunch menus are quite affordable. If you're looking for an evening snack, stop by to munch on some appetizers and browse the surprisingly lengthy and affordable wine list, which, instead of offering wines by the glass, conveniently allows diners to order any bottle by the half.

Fatty Crab

Malaysian

This Malaysian joint has its act down to the T,

NATIVE'S PICK

August

Mediterranean

359 Bleecker St
(near Charles St)
212-929-8727
Mon-Thurs 12-3:30pm 5:30-
11pm, Fri 12-3:30pm 5:30pm-
12am, Sun 11am-3:30pm
& 5:30pm-10pm
1 to Christopher St, **A C E**
B D F V to W 4th St
Appetizers $9-15,
Entrees $24-30

From behind its modest glass storefront, this low-key destination radiates rustic warmth. Scents from the wood-burning oven fill the tiny front room, from its antique floorboards to its barreled cork ceilings. Out back, a glass ceiling encloses a small garden room and opens on warm summer nights. The eclectic menu features traditional yet unusual European fare prepared with fresh local produce. A summer meal might begin with an inspired charred octopus with melon, tomato, olives, and cilantro and continue with bone marrow-crusted cod over pimetons, fingerling potatoes and salsa de tinta. These satisfying dishes are served by a staff that does more than its share to contribute to August's inimitable glow.

serving delicious, elevated street food in a fun and hip way. With a menu conducive to sharing, you're encouraged to order an assortment of duck, pork, and crab dishes that straddle the spicy-sweet dichotomy of chili, mint, and coconut. Servers can pair your meal with a creative cocktail—like the Chupacabra and the Fatty Sling—or with one of many Asian beers (they have an extensive wine list, too). The space celebrates simplicity with its exposed brick walls, green tin ceiling, and worn ceiling fan, but its bathroom suggests a playful ethos with bamboo wall ornaments and newspaper-clipped Asian porn ads. You may have to wait for a table, but the experience at the Fatty Crab is befitting stimulating—and chances are you'll leave with a buzz that's not just from the booze.

643 Hudson St
(btwn Gansevoort St &
Horatio St)
212-352-3592
Mon-Wed 12pm-12am,
Thurs-Fri 12pm-2am, Sat
11am-2am, Sun 11am-12am,
Brunch Sat-Sun 11am-4pm
Ⓐ Ⓒ Ⓔ Ⓛ to 8th Ave,
❶ ❷ ❸ to 14th St
Appetizers $5-9,
Entree $11-17

'ino Café and Bar — *Italian*
Inside this cubbyhole of a restaurant awaits a delightful dining experience, complete with a lengthy wine list, generous panini, and friendly service. No matter the time of day—'ino serves brunch, lunch, and dinner—the eight candlelit wooden tables and general warmth of the décor strike the perfect balance between friendliness and romance. The no-reservation policy means you may not be seated immediately, but ordering wine or beer at the bar passes the time pleasantly, and a surprisingly quick turnaround keeps waits manageable. The menu of classic Italian dishes like the antipasti, rucola salad, and the olive bowl, can woo any diner, vegetarian, carnivore, or otherwise. Sharing an appetizer or an order of bruschetta before indulging in a panini will sate any appetite and please any palate. Surprisingly for a place this tiny, credit cards are welcomed with neither sneer nor jeer, though with such reasonable prices you'll be unlikely to need it.

21 Bedford St (at Downing St)
212-989-5769
Mon-Sun 9am-2am
❶ to Houston St,
❻ to Broadway-Lafayette,
Ⓐ Ⓒ Ⓔ Ⓑ Ⓓ Ⓕ Ⓥ to
W 4th St-Washington Sq,
Appetizer $3-10,
Entree (panino) $11

Lassi — *Indian*
With whitewashed brick walls and no seating besides a few bar stools, Lassi is attractively minimal. Like the décor, the food is simple, but

28 Greenwich Ave # 2
Tues-Sun 12pm-10pm,
Mon closed
212-675-2688
Ⓐ Ⓒ Ⓔ Ⓑ Ⓓ Ⓕ Ⓥ to
W 4th St-Washington Sq,
❶ to 6th Ave
Parathas $4-6, Entrees $6-14

it offers an exciting burst of flavor and spice. For no more than $15, you can easily sample several items, or with a group (ideally a small one to fit in the compact space) order an array of Indian snacks and try them all. The menu is small, focusing on the classic Indian breakfast and snack food called paratha (a pan-fried, stuffed flat bread), some traditional North Indian curries, and the refreshing yogurt drink from which the restaurant takes its name. For a traditional snack, get a gobhi paratha, stuffed with cauliflower, and a mango lassi to eat and drink on the go.

Mamoun's
Middle Eastern

119 MacDougal St
212-674-8685
Daily 11am-5am
ACE BDFV to
W 4th St-Washington Sq
Dishes and Sandwiches: $3-13

The dingy, multi-colored light fixture hanging from the ceiling does little to illuminate the tiny space that houses Mamoun's. Of course, there's very little to look at, anyway. Two weathered booths are crammed in, but with a perpetually long line of hungry NYU students and nostalgic Middle Easterners, sitting down is always more trouble than it's worth. The food, thankfully, is worth waiting for. The falafels—perfectly crisp and without grease—are expertly smashed into a warm pita with sweet, ripe tomatoes and slathered with thick tahini. The lamb shwarma, impossibly moist and fragrantly seasoned with cumin and cinnamon, ranks among the best in the city. End your meal with the buttery, sticky baklava, but move along quickly—the gruff gentleman who mans the cash register has little patience for diners who hold up his line.

The New French
New American

522 Hudson St
(near W 10th St)
212-807-7357
Mon-Fri 11:30am-4pm &
5pm-11pm, Sat 10am-4pm &
5pm-11pm, Sun 10am-4pm &
5pm-10pm
1 to Christopher St-Sheridan Sq
Appetizers $9-11,
Entrees $12-25

The name of this charming West Village bistro is deceiving: it's new all right, but it certainly isn't French. Wood floors, black wooden banquettes, yellow walls covered in childlike sketches, and a chalkboard back wall listing the day's specials set the quirky-romantic tone for the chattering crowd. Welcoming service and reasonable prices make the eclectic, seasonal menu all the more enticing. The chicken liver and date crostini makes a wonderful sweet-savory start. Main dishes like tender roasted chicken with mushrooms are classic bistro fare, while vegetable curry veers toward Thailand, and a beer-braised pulled pork sandwich takes a happy jaunt into Germany. After a bottle from the eclectic (and equally reasonable) wine list you won't be any surer of The New French's geographic pedigree, but with food this tasty at prices this reasonable, it's better not to ask too many questions.

Num Pang Sandwich Shop
Cambodian, Sandwiches

21 E 12th St
(btwn 5th Ave & University Pl)
212-255-3271
Mon-Sat 11am-10pm
456 NQRW L to
14th St-Union Square
Sandwiches $7-9

The tiny first floor of this Village storefront is barely large enough for the cash register, miniscule kitchen, and a cramped ordering area. Choose from one of the rotating sandwiches on offer and either eat it on-the-go or at one of the several bar stools up the metal staircase at the back. Sandwiches at Num Pang are made as often as possible with local, organic ingredients and come on fresh toasted semolina rolls, ensuring that the pickled carrots, sliced cucumber, chili mayo, and fresh cilantro on each sandwich are crisp, fresh, and healthy. The Duroc pulled pork is smoky, rich and meaty, while the hoisin veal meatball sandwich makes a wonderfully messy, sweet and intensely flavored treat. Sip on a delicious blood orange lemonade while you watch the cooks stuff your sandwich before your eyes.

NY Dosa Cart
Indian

Washington Square Park
(W 4th St at Sullivan St)
917-710-2092
Hours vary
ⒶⒸⒺⒷⒹⒻⓋ to West
4th St-Washington Sq
Snacks & Dosas $6 & under
Cash Only

This park-side food cart may be the closest thing to an authentic dosa in Manhattan. Run by a single Sri Lankan Chef, NY Dosa Cart doesn't have much in the way of options: you can get the regular masala dosa with spicy potato stuffing, the pondicherry dosa with curried vegetables, or some fried snack foods. All choices are "purely vegetarian" and purely delicious. The cart draws a diverse crowd of devotees—young mothers and their babies, cash-strapped NYU students, yogaholics, and Indians in search of an authentic bite. Most gather their piping hot dosa and head newly renovated Washington Square Park. Be sure to visit the cart early—with a following this huge, the cart's usually out of food by 2pm.

Peanut Butter & Co.
American

240 Sullivan St (near 3rd St)
212-677-3995
Sun-Thurs 11am-9pm, Fri-Sat
11am-10pm
ⒶⒸⒺⒷⒹⒻⓋ to West
4th St-Washington Sq
Sandwiches $6-8

This shrine to peanut butter is a cross between a fast food joint, a soda shop, and your mom's kitchen. Staffed by a corps of uniformed grannies, PB&Co. serves sandwiches in endless varieties. First choose between white, wheat, and vegan bread, then between potato chips and carrot stick sides. The Elvis sandwich, made with peanut butter, banana, and honey, is the most famous offering, followed by the Seinfeld special, cinnamon raisin peanut butter on a bagel, and the Fluffernutter, a childhood delight of marshmallow and peanut butter. Rather than too sweet peanut butter varieties like the "honeyed bee's knee"s and the "white chocolate wonderful," sate your sweet tooth with a "death by peanut butter" sundae or one of their many shakes. And since offerings have no trans-fats or high fructose corn syrup, peanut buttery gorging comes guilt free.

Risotteria
Italian

270 Bleecker St
212-924-6664
❶ to Christopher St,
ⒶⒸⒺⒷⒹⒻⓋ to West
4th St-Washington Sq
Average Meal $11
Daily 12am-11pm
Appetizers $6-10,
Entrees $10-19

This Greenwich Village risotto specialist runs on the assumption that healthy food can taste good, and that Italian food ought to be accessible to

everyone, no matter their dietary restriction. The starch-heavy menu at this sliver of a restaurant offers a great variety of gluten-free and vegetarian options without compromising the authenticity of the delicious Italian fare on offer. Try the crunchy, garlicky, gluten-free breadsticks, one of the 40 varieties of risotto, or a fresh salad for something lighter. On Tuesday nights, Risotteria serves massive bowls of pasta for sharing at unbeatable prices. Though the wait for one of the few tables can be long, the payoff is health-conscious but hearty Italian food to impress even the most discerning risotto addict.

Sammy's Noodle Shop & Grill *Chinese*

At this West Village Chinese stop, standards like orange chicken come out of the kitchen crispy, spiked with red pepper and topped with a *lot* less sauce—sure signs of

453-461 6th Ave
(btwn 10th & 11th St)
212-924-6688
Sun-Thurs 11:30am-11:30pm,
Fri-Sat 11:30am-12am
①②③ to 14th St,
ⒻⓋⓁ to 8th Ave
Appetizers $2-8,
Entrees $6-16

a step up from your average cheap Chinese joint. Dishes like authentic, Cantonese-

(99 MacDougal) or **Mamoun's** *(119 MacDougal)*, where spicy chicken rolls and delicious falafel sandwiches are all less than $5. If you have a student membership at the **IFC Center** *(323 6th Ave)* dish $3 to catch the latest foreign flick. Kill time at **Fiddlesticks** *(56 Greenwich Ave)*, where happy hour starts at 4pm and drinks start at $3. Then pay the $5 cover to listen to a live band at **Fat Cat** *(75 Christopher St)*. For a different musical ending, catch a jazz show at **Arthur's Tavern** *(57 Grove St)* or **Smalls** *(183 W 10th St)*.

style barbecued meats (pork is the classic) are delicious and otherwise difficult to find outside of Chinatown, but it is the plump, perfectly cooked, filling noodles that brought Sammy's its first taste of fame. Try any of the noodle soups or sample a sizzling platter, in which noodles are topped with items like fresh vegetables and Sa Cha beef. Portions are typically huge, often large enough to split three ways, so plan to share and take home leftovers. Whether you stay to eat in the simple red room (no cheesy décor here) or order delivery, the service is fast and always friendly.

Taïm *Israeli, Vegetarian*

For those of us whose falafel usually comes from a questionable-looking cart, this trendy falafel and smoothie bar is

222 Waverly Place (at 7th Ave.)
212-691-1287
Daily 11am-10pm
①②③ to 14th St
Sandwiches, Salads, &
Spreads $5-8, Platters $10

something completely different. Taïm, Hebrew for "highly pleasant to the taste," focuses on simplicity and freshness. Co-run by an Israeli chef and her French husband, it has the green-walled, blackboard-menued aesthetic of a hip coffee house. Twenty-somethings congregate on the sidewalk and along the bar, the only seating at this diminutive restaurant. The menu is based on three equally delicious kinds of falafel and offers seemingly endless opportunities for variation with toppings. Try a classic falafel sandwich with hummus and tahini, a Falafel platter with salad and tabouli, or a boat of crispy French fries with aioli. As a bonus, most dietary needs are non-issues here: everything served is vegetarian and gluten-free, and products containing dairy or egg are clearly marked.

Wallsé *Austrian*

Located about as far west as the Village goes, Kurt Gutenbrunner's nine-year-old Austrian mainstay remains refreshingly aloof

344 W 11th St
(near Washington St)
212-352-2300
Brunch Sat-Sun 11am-2:15pm,
Daily 5:30-11pm
Ⓛ to Bedford Ave
Appetizers $12-20,
Entrees $27-34

from the trends of downtown dining. Two modest, comfortable dining rooms are dressed with artwork inspired by early 20th-century Austrian minimalism, including paintings by renowned artist (and regular patron) Julian Schnabel. Chef Gutenbrunner crafts exquisitely prepared plates that revel in delicacy instead of comfort food excess or overly inventive spins. A foie gras terrine with sugared plum is a veritable dissertation on balance of texture and flavor; a roasted lamb chop is deep crimson in color, silky in texture, and so subtle in flavor it seems untouched. Charming waiters are on hand to pair your dish with selections from their entirely Austrian wine list. A night out at Wallsé is a refreshing reminder of just how pleasurable classic elegance can be.

PLAY

124 Rabbit Club
Beer Bar

124 MacDougal St
(near Minetta Ln)
212-254-0575
Fri-Sat 6pm-4am,
Sun-Thurs 6pm-2am
🅐🅒🅔🅑🅓🅕🅥 to W
4th St-Washington Sq
Average Drink $10

Down a set of metal steps off crowded MacDougal Street lies a mysterious unmarked black door—a reference to the Rabbit Hole down which Alice so famously fell. The romantically run-down interior inside evokes the whimsy of its namesake. With rough stone walls, pressed-tin ceilings, dilapidated chandeliers, and faded fleur-de-lis wallpaper, 124 Rabbit Club has the feel of a seedy Old World speakeasy—exclusive and secret, even if it is regularly crammed with many of the neighborhood's bright young things. With 70 odd brews from the US, Belgium, Germany, and Britain to choose from (plus a small selection of wines), the bar focuses on far more than cocktails. Still, friendly bartenders are on hand to recommend strong brews certain to make the stumble out of Rabbit Club a bit more difficult than the tumble in.

The 55 Bar
Jazz

55 Christopher St
(near W 4th St)
212-929-9883
Daily 4:30pm-4am
🅐 to Christopher St,
🅐🅒🅔🅑🅓🅕🅥 to West
4th St-Washington Sq
Average Drink $4
Cover Free-$20

A departure from the "boy's club" culture of the legendary New York jazz scene, this venue lets both up-and-comers and hardened veterans of the genre share the floor. Patrons cram in to hear the music, which comes without pretense and extraordinarily cheap, surrounded by vintage posters and Christmas lights. Covers range from free to $20 (for late and bigger-name sets), and the drinks are good and heavy-handed with liquor. 55 Bar makes a point not to cater exclusively to jazz die-hards, unlike other more famous clubs. And to hear young lions and ancient greats grace the stage together feels like history is being made right in front of you.

Art Bar
Art, Lounge

With $8 mini-pitchers of sangria and haphazardly arranged comfy seating in the back room, this popular lounge is the perfect place for laid-back romance. If you're not seeking the privacy of a dark corner, head to the bar and sip on creative drinks like the ginger cucumber cocktail, or satisfy your sweet tooth and relax with a butterscotch or pumpkin pie martini. Check out humorous updates on classic artworks—try identifying the celebrities (including, among others, Marilyn Monroe) who've replaced the biblical figures in the back room's modern version of Da Vinci's Last Supper—scattered throughout the dimly-lit interior. The front lounge offers a more bustling and louder atmosphere—expect plenty of 80s music.

52 8th Ave (near Horatio St)
212-727-0244
Daily 4pm-4am
🅛 to 8th Ave, 🅐🅑🅒
🅐🅒🅔 to 14th St
Average Drink $9
Happy Hour: Daily 4-7pm

Bar 13
Lounge, Nightclub, Rooftop

35 E 13th St (at University Pl)
212-979-6677
Daily 5pm-4am
🅐🅑🅒🅝🅞🅡🅦🅛 to
14th St-Union Square
Average Drink $6
Happy Hour: Mon-Fri
5pm-8pm, 2 for 1 drinks

On a typical weekend, plan on getting friendly with strangers as you undoubtedly brush up against them in the limited, intimate space of this sleek, dark club. The dance floor upstairs is no more spacious, but additional lighting helps lessen the claustrophobic effect. After grooving, head to the third floor—a comfortable rooftop bar where dancers can rest their weary legs and the muted music allows for conversation. Sunday rooftop Brit-pop parties and Monday night poetry readings add unexpected diversity to a venue that does "dance club" so well. So if you're looking to let loose after work, exams, or papers (and can get past the cover charge and mediocre drinks), you'd be hard pressed to find a better playground for grown-ups.

Blind Tiger Ale House
Beer Bar

281 Bleecker St (at Jones St)
212-462-4682
Mon-Sun 11:30am-4am
🅐 to Christopher St
🅐🅒🅔🅑🅓🅕🅥 to West
4th St-Washington Sq
Average Drink $8
Happy Hour: 11:30am-8pm

From balding regulars to the frat-boy frequenters, this revered beer bar quenches one and all with a selection of 28 cask, gravity, vintage, and unusually creative draught beers. With wood from a 19th century farmhouse and stable-style windows, it looks more French village than Greenwich Village.

But the bar bustles with the conversation of friendly patrons who've opted out of the night prowl to enjoy a pint with buddies. Ask the bartenders to help choose your new favorite beer—Jolly Pumpkin Bam Biere Farmhouse and Smuttynose Shoals Pale Ale probably aren't your usual picks. The fare is tasty American tapas cuisine—the beet salads, cheese plates, and sweet Italian sausage sandwiches are notably delicious. They host weekly events on Wednesdays, but drop by anytime for a solid bottle of vintage beer.

Bowlmor Lanes
Bowling

Bolwmor Lanes brings upscale class to the bowling alley. With 40 lanes for a crowd of multi-generational regulars, Bowlmor invites competitors to play back-to-back rounds or unwind with a few drinks on sleek leather couches

110 University Place
(btwn 12th & 13th St)
212-255-8188
Mon & Thurs 4pm-2am,
Tues & Wed 4pm-1am, Fri
4pm-3:30am, Sat 11am-
3:30am, Sun 11am-12am
④⑤⑥ⓃⓆⓇⓌⓁ to
14th St-Union Square
Average Game $11,
Shoe Rental $6.50
Fri & Sat 21+ after 7pm

and private booths. On screens above the lanes, computer-animated pins keep track of scores and bounce rhythmically to recent radio hits. The complex's multiple floors provide additional lounging space just up the stairs at Pressure Nightclub & Billiards. Though prices can put a hole in your wallet, $4 games on Formerly Employed Wednesdays and drink deals on Monday Night Strike—when a live DJ spins all night—bring trendy bowling to the masses.

Fat Cat
Live Music, Jazz

In the heart of the Village music scene, this peeling-paint palace houses jazz, big band acts, and jam sessions seven nights a week. Like the giant basement of an eclectic, pool-playing hermit, Fat Cat combines mismatched chairs and sofas with Tibetan prayer flags, fishing nets, pool tables, and a dog with many names (is it Craig? Big Dog? Pasta?). Good beers on tap, like Magic Hat and Old Speckled Hen, and tasty Ginger Sour

75 Christopher St
(near Seventh Ave)
212-675-6056
Mon-Thurs 2pm-5am,
Fri-Sun 12pm-5am
❶ to Christopher St
Average Drink $6

Le Poisson Rouge
Music Venue, Bar

For a music space that appears intimidatingly hip at first glance—sinister, coffin-like fish tanks dangle ominously over the dark entrance hall—the mood at LPR is refreshingly lively and unpretentious. Take in the contemporary art and sip on drinks by the warmly-lit Gallery Bar before moving upstairs for a show. The main stage morphs with chameleonic ease to accommodate everything from experimental hipster bands to classical quartets, making the versatile venue a new favorite among artists of all musical persuasions. Food offerings are as diverse as the musical line-up, and include sushi, chicken satay, and a $5 comfort food menu to sate your late night cravings of PB&J. Ticket prices for the reliably good shows are more than reasonable, so come back and bring friends.

158 Bleecker St
(near Thompson St)
212-505-3474
Daily 1pm-4am
❶ to Houston St
Ⓐ Ⓒ Ⓔ Ⓑ Ⓓ Ⓕ Ⓥ to West
4th St-Washington Sq
Average Drink $9
Tickets $10-15

cocktails help yuppies, NYUers, and old hippies kick back and enjoy the music, puzzling décor, and shuffleboard games. Fat Catters rent paddles, pool cues, and chess pieces for a couple bucks. Go for the games, tunes, bargain drinks, and try to guess the dog's name while you're at it. He's used to it.

HERE Arts Center
Theater

145 6th Ave
(Entrance on Dominick St,
south of Spring St)
212-647-0202
Hours vary, shows start
btwn 7-11pm
❶ to Houston St,
❸❸ to Spring St,
❸❸ to Prince St
Tickets $15-30

Twenty to thirty visitors keen on the cutting edge congregate in two small theaters to experience a punk rock Kabuki, a puppet Kafka, the sweet musical venom of Taylor Mack, or other hybrid stage-breeds of multidisciplinary performance. Hosting artists-in-residence, visiting artists from across the globe, puppeteers and playwrights, this alternative center supports and curates some of the city's strangest and most entertaining works—sure to wow theater nerds and newbies alike. Stop by the cozy side lounge before shows for beer, wine, and bistro fare. Just be sure to come early for a good seat—you don't want to miss seeing a captain engulfed by a slide projection of Antarctica, or something equally creative.

Lelabar
Wine Bar

422 Hudson St (at Leroy St)
212-206-0594
❶ to Houston St,
Mon-Thurs 5pm-12am,
Fri-Sat 5pm-am,
Sun 5pm-11:30pm
Average Glass $14,
Bottles start at $33

A long oval bar surrounded by commodious stools and friendly chatter fills the small room of this refined neighborhood wine bar. Candlelit by night and bright sun that shines through the glass storefront by day, Lelabar is a romantic and unpretentious spot where wine and conversation flow with equal ease. Situated inside the oval bar are two knowledgeable and friendly sommeliers, who dispense advice and generous pours chosen from a concise, creative, and carefully chosen list of international wines. The staff can also help to pair your wine with cheeses, meats, and small plates from the short food menu, and guide you towards more obscure bottles. Convivial, elegant, and inviting, Lelabar may become your favorite neighborhood watering hole, even if the West Village isn't your neighborhood at all.

Le Royale
*Dance Club, Lounge
Live Music*

21 7th Ave South (at Leroy St)
212-463-0700
Daily 7pm-4am
❶ to Houston St
❸❸❸ ❸❸❸❸❸ to West
4th St-Washington Sq
Average Well Drink $7
Cover $10

Both levels of this mod, 60s style spot transport you back to a time when going to a club meant more than dancing awkwardly with strangers to overplayed club remixes. Classically hip but never intimidating, Le Royale offers an Art Deco-style first floor lounge and an upstairs dance space without any of the would-be velvet rope pretension. The music is a DJ spun blend of new and obscure—but never esoteric—beats, with some Top 40 hits and live performances by up-and-coming bands thrown in to shake things up. Come to dance and break to sip a cocktail in the back while watching a man in red skinny jeans amuse lady friends with God-awful but charming dance moves. Whether lounging downstairs or dancing upstairs, you'll be hard-pressed to escape the thumping baseline.

Little Branch
Cocktail Longe, Jazz

22 7th Ave (at Leroy St)
212-929-4360
Daily 7pm-3am
❶ to Houston St,
❸❸❸ ❸❸❸❸❸ to West
4th St-Washington Sq
Average Drink $13

This low-key, candle-lit spot harkens back to New York City's golden age: the men are dapper, the women are beautiful, and the drinks are strong. Bartenders in pinstripes pour fresh juices for haute cocktails and give change in two-dollar bills. A classic pressed tin roof stretches from the bar back to the few private booths that fill the narrow room. Though some cocktails exceed $20—even the "Depression Specials" are over $10—each is a miniature masterpiece mixed with artful precision. Trust the bartenders and be rewarded with a beverage you've never heard of (Corpse Reviver, anyone?) that's twice as strong and four times more delicious than any drink you'll find elsewhere in the city. True to speakeasy form, Little Branch hosts live jazz weekly.

Marie's Crisis
Piano Bar

In the neighborhood since the 1850s, this cozy hole-in-the-wall welcomes music-lovers, musical theater nerds, and anyone else in the mood to belt out pop ballads and show tunes late into the night. Low ceilings and an underground location enhance its historical feel, as does the amusing

but inexplicable French Revolution mural behind the bar, proudly sporting its motto of "Liberté, Égalité, and Fraternité." Colorful Christmas lights strung along the ceiling give the tiny bar a warm glow. As the night progresses, the boundaries between performers and audience blur, and the standing crowd—don't expect to find a seat—gently sways to the live music. Drinks are basic, and the crowd slightly older, but anyone looking to sing is sure to feel at home.

59 Grove St (near 7th Ave)
212-243-9323
Daily 4pm-4am, Piano bar daily 5:30pm-4am
❶ to Christopher St
Ⓐ❿Ⓔ❽Ⓓ❺Ⓥ to West
4th St-Washington Sq
Average Drink $5
Happy Hour: Daily 4-9pm, Drinks $3-$5

Peculier Pub

Beer Bar

The name has no typo—it comes from an old English ale, appropriate for a pub so passionate about beer. A slightly out-of-place jukebox and tiny TV cast shadows over the main decorations: beer caps. In portrait form, in wayward paths, even jammed into the wood—bottle tops dominate. Although it sits

145 Bleecker St (btwn Thompson & La Guardia)
212-353-1327
Sun 4pm-2am, Mon-Thurs 5pm-2pm, Fri 4pm-4am, Sat 2pm-4am
❶ to Christopher St
Ⓐ❿Ⓔ❽Ⓓ❺Ⓥ to West 4th St-Washington Sq,
❻ to Bleecker St
Average Drink $7

on a street virtually devoted to drinking, this bar stands out with 300 foreign and domestic selections from over 50 countries. The menu is a veritable beer encyclopedia, but don't be intimidated—bartenders will ask what you like and pour accordingly. East Coasters should be sure to try the selections from Colorado's Left Hand Brewery, totally worth their $9 price tag. And after you've imbibed to your fill, the obscure bottle cap chemistry equations on the walls might make sense.

Vol de Nuit

Beer Garden

This sexy Belgian bar with dim red lighting and dark stone walls offers a break from the madness of West 4th St. The beer menu features 40 bottled

148 W 4th St (at 6th Ave)
212-982-3388
Sun-Thurs 4pm-1am, Fri-Sat 4pm-2:30am
Ⓐ❿Ⓔ❽Ⓓ❺Ⓥ to West 4th St-Washington Sq
Average Drink $7

and tap varieties, but don't worry if you're lost—knowledgeable bartenders will serve up your Leffe Brown in the very particular glass it was meant for and pair those moules frites with one of the 11 house-made sauces. Enjoy the delectable evening refreshments on the open-air patio with a crowd of smoking NYU-sters or crash on the back sofas next to after-work beer connoisseurs. Either way, the exceptional selection of Belgian brews is worth the trip.

Against the lush green leaves of the West Village streets, a dozen can-can dancers cut quite a figure. Paris Commune, the legendary downtown bistro, is full of these beautiful creatures, painted into poses against scarlet walls and a tangled wreath of twinkling lights. Add in the city's handsomest waiters, rose petal strewn cocktails and beautifully plated food, and you'll see why Paris Commune has been home to New York's pretty young things (regardless of age) for almost thirty years.

This summer, Paris Commune is in the midst of its own little revolution, having brought in a new executive chef and a few culinary surprises to round out the traditional French bistro fare. An ever-changing Foie Gras de Jour leads the menu of new additions. Inventively seared and paired with Paris Commune's famous gingerbread one day, then served atop a poached egg and English muffin another (a la Eggs Benedict with some serious flair), the delicious amuse-bouche creations are as surprising as satisfying. New seasonal appetizers like the Ahi Tuna Ceviche join old favorites like Steak Tartar (served in the classic style and topped with a quail egg) and French Onion Soup (complete with the crispy, gooey indulgence of a crouton and melted Gruyere top) – and traditional bistro entrees like Coq au Vin, Steak Frites and Lobster Thermador now share equal billing with Ostrich, Pan Roasted Chilean Sea Bass, and Beef Wellington.

Famous throughout the city for its brunch, Paris Commune now offers its unparalleled French Toast and Frittatas seven days a week – along with its lengthy Bloody Mary menu and refreshing champagne cocktails. There's never been a better reason to drink before sundown...

But just in case you do wait until sunset to sip something sultry, the Paris Commune's Rouge Wine Bar has you covered. Recently voted one of the top five wine bars in New York City, Rouge offers an impressive array of French wines – then tops it off with an eye-opening (and taste-bud-tickling) variety of South African, Chilean, and American bottles. With a full cocktail menu, dinner service, and weekly live music acts, Rouge is the best surprise in the West Village. Located underneath the main dining room, the wine bar blooms into view beneath a side staircase, revealing a mirror-ceilinged room with full-wall murals and a bar scene so convivial, even a revolutionary would cozy up for a drink.

Paris Commune is the downtown bistro for the whole city – a destination for anyone in search of a lively environment, an unparalleled meal, a real New York City night, and a dozen can-can girls ready to call this place home.

For reservations, please call 212.929.0509.

★ PARIS COMMUNE ★

99 BANK STREET at GREENWICH STREET, NEW YORK

EAST VILLAGE

The birthplace of punk rock, hip hop, and poetry slam for decades, the East Village has for decades defined counterculture cool. The neighborhood was jump-started by intellectuals, artists, musicians, and writers frustrated with the rising rents that were domesticating the West Village in the late 60s. They set up coffee shops, poetry houses, bookstores, saloons, bars, and jazz clubs, and brought a level of political and artistic radicalism for which its western neighbor was a bit too genteel. The anything-goes mentality of this urban bohemia had its cost, however. The hard drug use of literary luminaries like William S. Burroughs exploded in the economic plunge of the 70s, only to be tamped down with the turning of the century.

In recent years, local landmarks like CBGB closed their doors and up-and-coming artistic crowds packed their bags and jumped the river (see Williamsburg for more details). For nightlife, the East Village remains a dynamic destination, full of happening late-night eateries, colorful bars, and well-worn hookah lounges. Children run amok in Tompkins Square Park while hippies and hipsters match wits in chess, checkers, and dominoes. Lush community gardens have emerged in recent years among the once-dilapidated tenements of Alphabet City. But the neighborhood cleanup comes at a cultural price. The onslaught of shiny steel and Starbucks is redressing the once-grungy streets. Young professionals moving into the area are chipping away at what little is left of the old bohemian guard.

Still, the East Village abounds with bastions of its former culture. Tea retailers, leather tanners, and Wiccan magic suppliers maintain their storefronts. It's been years since squatters rioted against redevelopment, but Cooper Union students still wave signs in protest of gentrification. And underground art spots like Bowery Poetry Club and Sunshine Cinema still draw crowds that line up around the block.

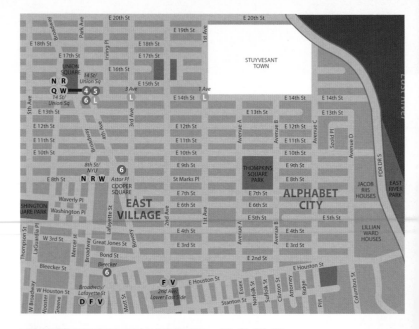

EXPLORE

Bowery Poetry Club

Don't let the smoke from the deep-frier near the door confuse you—the Bowery Poetry Club is not a sooty hangout for chain-smoking beat poets. The poetry

308 Bowery
(btwn Houston & Bleecker St)
212-614-0505
Mon-Fri 4pm-4am,
Sat 12pm-4am, Sun 12pm-12am
6 to Bleecker St, **F V**
to 2nd Ave-Lower East Side,
Cash only

events take place in the back room, which a dividing curtain keeps haze-free from the front bar. On Mondays, local eccentrics Taylor Mead and Bingo Gazingo belt out heartfelt, poetic obscenities. The beats come for Tuesday urban poetry slams, but the Club's brick-walled back stage also attracts high school jazz aficionados for experimental concerts and Queens clubbers for cheap dance parties that rage until 4am. Cheap fare compensates for the fact that most shows have cover charges: $3 PBRs at the bar, $5 burgers in front, and $4 PBRs with a giant hot dog.

The Public Theater

From innovative new works to re-imagined classics, this theater presents some of Off-Broadway's

425 Lafayette St
(btwn 4th St & Astor Pl)
212-539-8500
6 to Astor Pl, **R W** to 8th St

most accessible and exciting works. With five spaces that range from the intimate Shiva to the mainstage Anspacher, The Public houses almost a dozen productions every season. Adjacent to the theaters is Joe's Pub, a well-known venue for emerging voices in live-music and performance. In keeping with their mission to produce new works, the Public holds its annual Under the Radar Festival (January) and the Summer Playwrights Festival (July) to showcase new works at incredibly student-friendly prices—tickets are often $10. And in addition to the groundbreaking works it presents here, The Public is also famous for producing two free, star-studded productions at "Shakespeare In The Park" every summer in Central Park.

St. Mark's Church-In-The-Bowery

This historical church has been an East Village

community haunt since 1799. Today it invites visitors in to expand their cultural horizons and engage in the arts. St. Mark's Church-In-The-Bowery is home to the Poetry Project, a poetry organization that offers weekly readings and writing workshops, as well as the Danspace Project, a dance organization that hosts weekly creative performances. The Ontological-Hysteric Theater even performs multiple eclectic performances each week. Structurally, the church is most noticeable for its tall, thin steeple. The inside décor is minimal— bare white walls, bold lighting, and beautiful stained glass windows. Services are held on Sunday mornings, Wednesday evenings, and Friday afternoons.

131 E 10th St (at 2nd Ave)
212-674-6377
6 to Astor Pl, **R W** to 8th St

The Stone

This non-profit black-box is the last iconic downtown venue for experimental and avante-garde music. When the

16 Avenure C (at 2nd St)
the stonenyc.com
Tues-Sun Shows 8pm & 10pm
J M Z to Essex St-Delancy St
Cover $10 (Unless otherwise
stated), Ages 13-19 Half-off

DAY TO DAY

Community Board 3: 59 E 4th St, 212-533-5300.

Dry Cleaner: Dion Cleaners Corp, 444 E 14th St, 212-420-9114.

Groceries: Trader Joe's, 142 E 14th St, 212-529-4612.

Gym: Gladiator's Gym, 503 E 6th St, 212-674-9803.

Hospital: New York Downtown Hospital, 170 William St, 212-312-5000.

Laundromat: 97 2nd Ave Launderette Inc, 212-674-7151.

Media: eastvillagevisitorscenter.com

Volunteer Opportunities: 4th Street Food Co-op, 58 E 4th St, 212-674-3623, 4thstreetfoodcoop.org, Cardinal Spellman Center, 137 E 2nd St, 212-677-6600.

NATIVE'S PICK

Nuyorican Poets Café

Café, Slam Poetry

236 E 3rd St (btwn Ave B & C)
212-780-9386
Tues-Sat 7pm-1:30am,
Sun 3pm-12am
Events Tues-Sun: Times vary
F V to 2nd Ave-Lower East Side

Musicians, spoken word artists, and those who snap and murmur in appreciation for them gather here on Friday nights for some of the city's best poetry slams. The room is charged, the lights are dim, and the music flows as smoothly as the lyrical lines. A single expectant microphone stands confidently in the spotlight of a makeshift stage. Tables and accompanying chairs crowd the platform, their youthful patrons overflowing onto the floor. Founded in the 1970s, Nuyorican has evolved to become one of the country's most highly respected non-profit arts organizations. Both rising and established performers work here, giving theater, music, hip hop, and comedy shows and collaborating with local youth for teen poetry slams.

UNION SQUARE

Arguably the heart of New York, Union Square sits at the nexus of several neighborhoods and reflects the cultural diversity of the city. Every kind of New Yorker passes through its stone courtyards: street performers, roaming hipsters, suits on their lunch break, artists, tourists, travelers, collegians, and hobos. It's a venue for crafts fairs, public pillow fights, student protests, drum circles, and much more. So named because it sits at the union of Broadway and Fourth Avenue, Union Square possesses a rich tradition of political activism. A patriotic rally after the fall of Fort Sumter in 1861 was held here, as was the nation's first Labor Day celebration in 1881. More recently, there was a massive protest in defiance of Iran's disputed 2009 Presidential elections results. Surrounded by the cultural hubs of Chelsea and the Village, Union Square lies at the center of a profusion of dining, nightlife, and entertainment scenes. Among the myriad events that take place at the park is the **Union Square Greenmarket** (*17th St btwn Broadway & Park Ave*) where, every Monday, Wednesday, Friday, and Saturday, chefs from local restaurants purchase top-quality fresh fruits and vegetables. During November and December, drop by for the spectacular **Union Square Park Holiday Market**, when artisans set up kiosks and sell everything from cheap hand warmers to carefully handcrafted, expensive leather bags. The park's many historical monuments, including statues of George Washington, Abraham Lincoln, and Mahatma Gandhi, are also worth a visit. But this is no place for a leisurely walk or a quiet afternoon—never dormant, never dull, Union Square is where you go to see New York in action.

famed Tonic club failed to survive downtown gentrification, New York Underground legends settled in here. Artistic director John Zorn and their new monthly curator choose to exhibit musicians who make instruments do odd things and turn odd things into instruments. Visitors appreciate the raucous jazz, chamber distortions, and hypnotic, post-minimalist moon lute solo. With performances by the likes Marc Ribot and Lou Reed, crowds pack on the cramped floor space. Check the calendar and show up early— New York's oldest new-age musical relic doesn't do advanced ticket sales.

Tompkins Square Park

Once a haven for heroin junkies, Tompkins Square has become the open air heart of Alphabet

Avenue A to Avenue B,
East 7th to East 10th St
6 to Astor Pl,
F V to 2nd Ave-
Lower East Side,

City. With lawns, playgrounds, footpaths, basketball and handball courts, game tables, mini pool, and dog-run, the park serves as an outdoor home for locals of all ages and walks of life. Annual events hosted by the park include the famous "Wigstock," a Labor Day festival for

drag queens and their entourages, the "Howl Festival," a three-day summer poetry festival in honor of Allen Ginsburg, the "Charlie Parker Jazz Festival," and "Laughter in the Park," a series of outdoor comedy shows. And all events are free—throwing back to a time when Alphabet City housed penniless artists.

SHOP

Academy Records & CDs

The collection of classical and opera recordings here may be the best in the city. Collectors and meticulous searchers are beckoned by walls of discs and vinyls.

12 W 18th St
(btwn 5th & 6th Ave)
212-242-3000
Mon-Sat 11:30am-8pm,
Sun 11am-7pm
F V L to 6th Ave-14th St,
4 5 6 N Q R W L to
14th St-Union Square

But the owner's penchant for classical music is only rivaled by his passion for plastic dinosaurs, evidenced by the dozens of dino toys that line the highest shelves at this small record shop. Peruse the thousands of CDs for a recording of Madame Butterfly, Salome, or Tosca, or round

out your Mahler, Chopin, and Fauré catalogue without emptying your wallet—most LPs are under $10. For the true bargain hunter, check out the $4-and-under classical section. There is a small rock selection, ranging from the boring to the obscure, as well as some DVD steals worth browsing, but the classical collection is this shop's forte.

Archangel Antiques

Two adjacent shops make up this antique trinkets treasure hub, which is famous for its collection of 2.5 million buttons. They range in rarity, from buttons with images of Bettie Page, Frida Kahlo, Elvis, and Kafka costing $2-$4 to the irreplaceable Liberty of London sterling button with enamel trim, which goes for $250. For 15 years, Archangel has provided set and costume designers, jewelry makers, and writers with unique materials and inspiration. Also on display is a regularly-replenished photograph collection, featuring 1950s Marine prom dates

334 E 9th St
(btwn 1st & 2nd Ave)
212-260-9313
Tues-Sun 3pm-7pm or by appointment
6 to Astor Pl, **L** to 1st Ave,
R W to 8th St-NYU

and other images captured from the past. What you see in the store is only a small fraction of what's hidden in the back. Dive in and find the perfect gift among the hundreds of pairs of cufflinks, eye-wear from the 19th century, bead purses, and other oddities—daguerreotype earrings anyone?

Enchantments

Though this witchcraft supply store offers $40 cauldrons, skull candles, books like Modern Magical Keys, and has a token black cat slinking about, this specialty shop is more "new age" than "eye of newt." Look past the pagan kitsch to find candles for tranquility and Enchantments' own brand of incense, "Witch Stick." Browse the impressive "magickal" herb selection for "baths, incense, voodoo, potpourri, spells"—oversized jars house motherwort, eyebright, and even basil. The shelves are lined with starter kits containing candles, oils, and instructions for charms both

424 E 4th St
(btwn 1st Ave & Ave A)
212-228-4394
Mon & Wed-Sun 1pm–9pm,
Tues closed
F V to 2nd Ave-Lower East Side, **L** to 1st Ave

ST. MARKS PLACE

A ten-minute walk from Union Square, the legendary St. Mark's Place takes up three blocks of E 8th Street between 3rd Avenue and Avenue A. It's a tiny pocket of diverse sights, sounds, and smells, and even if you have no set destination, it's a fun place to explore. The street teems with tattooed rockers, gruffy beatniks, glitzy clubbers, badass 13-year-olds, and old street vendors. For upscale entertainment, catch a play at **Pearl Theatre** (*80 St. Mark's Place, near 1st Ave*). Grab some yummy low-key Asian cuisine at **Dumpling Man** (*100 St. Mark's & 1st Ave*), or stop by **Crooked Tree** (*110 St. Marks btwn 1st Ave & Avenue A*) for some of the best crepes in the city. **Tompkins Square Park**, at the eastern end of St. Mark's Place, is one of New York's most bizarre parks, featuring as many families and small children as wacky old-timers and punk rockers. No trip to the area is complete without grabbing a cup of NYC street coffee from the famous, bright orange **MudTruck** (*Cooper Sq & E 8th St*) and spinning the fifteen-foot-cube at Astor Place, known as **The Alamo**.

practical ("Winning at Court") and passionate ("Sexual Attraction"). The knowledgeable staff is willing to answer any and all questions so clients can perfect their 'craft.

Pageant Print Shop

69 E 4th St (near 2nd Ave)
212-674-5296
Tues-Sat 12pm-8pm,
Sun 1pm-7pm
6 to Astor Pl,
R W to 8th St-NYU

Collectors and shoppers come from all over the city to peruse the huge selection of maps and ephemera at this 63-year-old family-owned boutique. The hyper-organized shop arranges its thousands of prints by category and sub-category, making searching for the right item painless. Most of the collection features pieces from the late 1800s and the turn of the century, but there are a handful of "modern" works from the 1930s and 40s. The prints come from all over the world, and range from American political cartoons to 19th-century advertisements to book art to insects, and there is an entire wall devoted to original maps. Though some prints go for hundreds of dollars, patience and persistence can yield a one-of-a-kind find for just a steal.

St. Mark's Bookshop

31 3rd Ave
(btwn 9th St & St. Mark's Pl)
212-260-7853
Mon-Sat 10am-12am, Sun
11am-12am
6 to Astor Pl,
R W to 8th St-NYU

This legendary bookshop is renowned for its attention to cultural theory, poetry, and small press publishing. Aging academics and flannel-clad hipsters dot the winding, metal-framed aisles of the deceptively large space, scanning the shelves for their next read. Whether customers are fishing for a current bestseller or an obscure foreign periodical, St. Mark's has it—along with the complete Casanova series, political comic books, and hand-made greeting cards. There's even a special shelf for self-published authors. With no place to sit, customers hog stepping stools or crouch in the aisles to peruse the extensive titles and genres. Given the shortage of lounging space, the store holds its poetry and fiction readings at Solas Bar around the corner two Thursdays a month (see noslander.com for details).

EAT

Artichoke Pizza

Pizza

328 E 14th St (near 1st Ave)
212-228-2004
Mon-Sun 12pm-late
⑥⑦⑧⑨④⑤⑥ to Union
Square, ① to 1st Ave
Slices $3-5, Pies $12-20

The average passerby may be shocked by the constant lines at this hole-in-the-wall pizzeria, but word is spreading quickly: the slices at Artichoke are well worth the wait. Not the greasy cheese-laden fare served at most pizzerias, each pie at Artichoke is prepared with the utmost precision and care. The signature artichoke slice, served with a thick crust and a wine-and-butter-based cream sauce, not unlike artichoke dip, is the most popular, but crab, margarita, and Sicilian slices are just as delicious. To compensate for the lack of seating inside, Artichoke has two rough benches outside, but wiser diners avoid the scramble for seating altogether and take their slices either to nearby Union or Stuyvesant Square.

Back Forty

American

190 Ave B (E 12th St)
212-388-1990
Brunch Sat 12pm-3pm, Sun
11:30am-3:30pm, Dinner
Mon-Thurs 6pm-11pm, Fri-Sat
6pm-12am, Sun 6pm-10pm
① to 1st Ave
Brunch Appetizers $4-10,
Entrees $9-14,
Dinner Appetizers $4-10,
Entrees $11-20

From the owners of SoHo mainstay Savoy comes your local greasy spoon all grown up—with a liberal arts degree, a local produce fetish, and a stylish address to boot. Using only organically grown, locally sourced, and sustainably produced ingredients, this candlelit gastropub serves classic American cuisine in rustically sophisticated digs. Here, grass-fed beef is sourced from upstate ranches, and fish is caught wild in the Catskills. French fries are made from fingerling potatoes and aren't fried at all: they're roasted and doused in rosemary sea salt. Portions may not be huge, but sides like Tokyo turnips and onion rings with smoked paprika aioli make substantially delicious supplements. The menu of hand selected microbrews and wines, along inventive cocktails, are just a few more pleasantries of refined, grown up life.

Caracas Arepas Bar

Venezuelan

No matter the hour, this Venezuelan gem is always packed. With looming Jesus and Mary statues, tin ceilings, exposed brick walls, and appropriately kitschy plastic tablecloths, Arepas Bar crams a lot of atmosphere in a tight space.

93 1/2 E 7th St (at 1st Ave)
212-529-2314
Daily 12pm-11pm
① to 1st Ave, ②⑦ to 2nd Ave,
⑥ to Astor Pl, ®Ⓦ to 8th St
Plates $11-14, Arepas $5-7,
Sides $5-8

Though the menu runs the gamut from empanadas and salads to mixed plates, the signature arepas (cornbread cakes filled with cheese) should not be missed. Generous side dishes for the table—such as the tajadas and the guasacaca and chips—make perfect accompaniments to just about anything. If the inevitable waits and no-reservations policy are turnoffs, stop by the take-out location next door for arepas to go, or have the Venezuelan national dish delivered to you. However you eat them, Caracas' arepas will blow your mind—without breaking your bank account.

ChikaLicious

Dessert

204 E 10th St (2nd Ave)
212-475-0929
Daily 3pm-10:45pm
⑥ to Astor Pl, ®Ⓦ to 8th St,
① to 1st Ave
Average Meal $11
Dessert Prix Fixe $14

The menu at this minuscule, glass-fronted dessert bar changes seasonally, enticing New Yorkers with new and inventive sweets. Sit at the bar and chat with friendly chefs as they prepare your dishes: the standard three-course prix fixe begins with a light, refreshing amuse—a gelatin-like palate cleanser, then continues with a main dessert of your choice, and ends with dainty petits fours. Mainstays like the warm chocolate tart with peppercorn ice cream are popular, but seasonal desserts offer delightfully fresh flights. A light summery option might be a crisp peach sorbet served with a creamy toasted almond panna cotta and dainty lemon poppy seed puffs. Be warned, though: the portions here are as dainty as the delicately painted china they're served on, so eat before (or after) you come.

Momofuku Bakery & Milk Bar

Dessert

207 2nd Ave
(Entrance on 13th St)
212-254-3500
Mon-Fri 8am-12am, Sat-Sun
9am-12am
① to 1st Ave. ① to 3rd Ave
Desserts $3-6

Walking into the newest addition to the Momofuku family can turn even the most hardened New York gourmand into a giddy, sugar-craving

child. As ovens open and close in the kitchen, the room fills with the sweet smells of baking cakes, built before your eyes by the staff of young chefs. Big, seat-less tables are the perfect place to enjoy Milk Bar's core offerings of cakes, cookies, and pies. Wildly inventive choices like the Arnold Palmer cake (made with lemon mascarpone cream and iced tea jelly) are matched by the glee-inducing simplicity of confections like the aptly named crack pie, made from little more than butter and sugar. Soft serve in flavors like fireball, rosemary, and salty pistachio and a rotating handful of savory items round out the menu, which changes regularly according to pastry chef Christina Tosi's ingeniously sweet whimsy. Head next door to Momofuku Ssäm Bar for Chef David Chang's innovative Korean options, like pig's heard terrine and beef tendon.

Momofuku Noodle Bar
Korean

Customers have been cramming into stools at the slick wooden bar and tables here at celebrated chef David Chang's first restaurant ever since it opened in 2003. Though the menu

171 1st Ave
(btwn 10th & 11th St)
212-777-7773
Lunch Daily 12-4:30pm,
Dinner Sun-Thurs 5:30-11pm,
Fri-Sat 5:30pm-2am
🄵🅅 to 2nd Ave-
Lower East Side
Appetizers $9-11, Entrees $11-18

changes regularly, the best places to start are with old standbys. The house ramen noodles are not those wimpy, dehydrated noodles best known

for their sodium jolt, but instead arrive steaming and fresh in an enormous bowl of flavorful broth, heaped with pork belly, scallions, mushrooms, and poached egg. For a lighter, equally delicious dish, try the ginger scallion noodles. As at any Chang restaurant, the famous pork buns, made with pork belly, hoisin, and cucumber are practically mandatory here for the first time visitor. House-made soft-serve in creative flavors and Momofuku blueberry soda both have surprising and delicious sweet-tart kick. Come early to avoid the lines of avid Chang fans.

Persimmon
Korean

A communal table and twenty backless wooden stools adorn the small, bright room where diners can view Chef Youngsun Lee's precise plating of neo-Korean experiments. This modern kimchi

277 E 10th St
(btwn 1st Ave & Ave A)
212-260-9080
Lunch Wed-Sat 12pm-4pm,
Dinner Mon-Sat 6pm-
11:30pm
🄻 to 1st Ave
Prix Fixe $37
BYOWine

house features a prix fixe menu—an opportunity for aspiring foodies to sample an assortment of playful spins on traditional cuisine. The menu changes biweekly, rotating inventive new dishes with seasonal favorites. The wait staff's close knowledge of the ever-shifting offerings eases navigation of lesser-known plates. On a recent menu, standouts included the smoky grilled octopus salad with crispy, seared water chestnuts and pickled Asian plum, and the beef bi bim bab, a traditional rice dish with freshly steamed vegetables and house-made chili pepper paste. Finish off with the sweet, dense bread pudding with black sesame seed sauce. They don't sell wine, so feel free to bring your own for a small corkage fee or sample some Bek Se Joo sake.

Porchetta — *Italian, Sandwiches*

110 E 7th (near 1st Ave)
212-777-2151
Sun-Thurs 11:30am-10pm,
Fri-Sat 11:30am-11pm
6 to Astor Pl
Sandwich & Plates $7-12,
Snacks $3-6

This meat-lovers' takeout spot is interested in doing only one thing well: pork. The management at Porchetta is single-mindedly focused on the traditional Italian pork preparation, where the hollowed body of a pig is rolled up with layers of fat and herbs and slow-roasted for hours. Seasoned behind the counter just before being served as a sandwich or a platter, the pork takes on a darkly sweet and tender quality reminiscent of duck. The payoff for this obsessive relationship with pork (it's used in nearly everything here, even potatoes and beans) are the huge crowds, exacerbated by a meagre seating capacity of ten. Throughout the day, Porchetta invites regulars along with nostalgic old Italians, and, later at night, drunk 20-somethings to enjoy cheap, filling, and magnificently tasty pork sandwiches.

Prune — *American*

54 E 1st St
(btwn 1st & 2nd Ave)
212-677-6221
Brunch Sat-Sun 10am-3:30pm,
Lunch Mon-Fri 11:30am-
3:30pm, Dinner Mon-Thurs
5:30pm-11pm,
Fri-Sat 5:30pm-12am,
Sun 5:30pm-11pm
6 V to 2nd Ave
Brunch $8-18, Dinner
Appetizers $8-15, Entrees
$21-30, Bar Menu $4-8

This diminutive neighborhood favorite turns out haute-homestyle fare nightly to East Village patrons lucky enough to nab one of its 30-odd seats. Warm lighting, a marble bar, and patinated mirrors lend a bistro-like ease, and in warm weather large French doors open the front of the restaurant to unparalleled people-watching on East 1st Street. A short, careful menu reads like the list of an eccentric foodie's home-cooked meals—roasted marrowbones and octopus, king mackerel and lamb chops. Modest surroundings complement the food well, comfortably transforming

unusual dishes like grilled veal heart into satisfyingly familiar favorites. Tasty desserts (the ricotta ice cream is lovely), classically inventive cocktails, and an inexpensive bar menu round out the evening offerings, while Prune's celebrated Sunday brunch draws crowds from around town for nine variations on the Bloody Mary and more of Chef Gabrielle Hamilton's infectiously joyous cooking.

S'MAC — *Macaroni & Cheese*

345 E 12th St (near 1st Ave)
212-358-7912
Mon-Thurs & Sun 11am-11pm,
Fri-Sat 11am-1am
(kitchen closes at 11pm)
L to 1st Ave
Individual Bowls $5-11

Its walls spattered with golden yellows and orange elbow noodle fixtures, this sunny East Village nook looks very much like the only thing on its menu—macaroni and cheese. A shrine to the perfect comfort food, S'MAC offers far more than your average box of Kraft. Variations like the Garden Lite with cauliflower, broccoli, Portobello mushrooms, parmesan, and white Cheddar appeal to the vegetarian crowd. Other options like the Cheeseburger, with ground beef and American and Cheddar cheeses, will make even the most dedicated carnivores feel right at home. S'MAC also caters to health junkies and those with dietary restrictions, offering multi-grain and gluten-free macaroni. While the "nosh" size proves just right for a snack or lite meal, the "major munch" should sate even the greediest appetites.

The Smith — *American*

55 3rd Ave (btwn 10th & 11th)
212-420-9800
Sun 10am-12am, Mon & Tues
8:30am-12am, Wed & Thurs
8:30am-1am, Fri 8:30am-
2am, Sat 10am-2am
4 5 6 to Astor Pl,
L to 3rd Ave,
R W to 8th St-NYU
Brunch $12-19, Dinner
Appetizers $6-10, Entrees $14-25

A sleek, contemporary diner done in black, white, and gray, this East Village spot is known for its perfectly-prepared American classics, like the mac and cheese, burgers, and stellar brunch dishes, all executed with quality ingredients. At breakfast or brunch, the eggs Benedict and aptly named Croaker—an American take on the croque madame—could hardly be better, making this one of the neighborhood's favorite spots for morning eats. Mac and cheese, a specialty at The Smith, arrives bubbling in a cast iron skillet, and should not be missed. The Smith serves an enormous menu of sundaes, from the "Big Chocolate" to the fun, childish "Birthday Cake" (yellow cake, vanilla ice cream, fudge frosting and a candle), which at only five bucks a piece, are some pretty sweet deals.

Tsampa
Tibetan

Amid droves of loitering youth in St. Mark's Place, Tsampa's cool, candle-lit interior is a haven of quiet sanity. Tasteful Tibetan

212 E 9th St
(btwn 2nd & 3rd Ave)
212-614-3226
Daily 5:30-11pm
6 to Astor Pl,
R W to 8th St
Appetizers $3-5, Entrees $9-13

decorations and rich wooden surfaces create a mood of permanent evening—even at the height of day. Over Tibetan pop music servers deliver specialty dishes like momos, delicate Tibetan dumplings stuffed with your choice of well-spiced meats and vegetables. Use fiery red and green chili sauce to spice up more basic proteins on the menu, or order nopa (a baked noodle dish served with meat or vegetables) instead. The Tsampa dessert is a traditional cake of roasted ground barley with yogurt, honey, and dried cranberries and makes for a sweet and healthy end to your meal. To earn your Himalayan stripes, acquire a taste for Bocha, salty Tibetan butter tea, before returning to the hectic city outside.

Veselka
Ukranian

It might look like any other late night sandwich-and-soup joint, but one bite and you'll understand why this warm and

144 2nd Ave (at E 9th St)
212-228-9682
Daily 24 Hours
6 to Astor Pl, **R W** to 8th St
Appetizers $5-8, Entrees $7-15

welcoming restaurant is a 55-year-old institution. They offer all the standard diner options, but you'd do better to explore the menu's trove of traditional Ukranian dishes. The house borscht is bold and beefy. The meat-stuffed cabbage (very stuffed) and kielbasa sausage, both served with heaping sides and sauce, scrimp on neither size nor taste. Open 24/7 with a to-go counter, Veselka is the ideal place to sit down for a late-night dinner or grab a blintz and homemade challah for the ride home. Try the Ukranian import beer Obolon—a great and surprisingly tasty value at $5.50 for a 21-ounce bottle. Finish a long night of East Village barhopping with their platter of housemade fried pierogis.

PLAY

12th Street Ale House
Beer Bar

It's hard to believe that this humble sports bar used to be Dick's, a beloved gay bar with a somewhat seedy reputation. After adding a couple fresh coats of plum

192 2nd Ave (near 12th St)
212-253-2323
Mon-Sat 5pm-4am, Sun
1pm-4am
N Q R W **4 5 6 L** to
14th St-Union Square,
L to 3rd Ave,
Average Drink $6

paint, the new owners reopened the location in late 2007 with twelve ales on tap and a more

UNDER $20

EAST VILLAGE

Grab fresh coffee for only $1 from the famous, bright orange **MudTruck** (*307 E 9th St*), then head over to the **East Village Visitors Center** (*308 Bowery*) to take a tour of this historic neighborhood for only $15. Pick up lunchtime reading material at **St. Mark's Bookshop** (*31 3rd Ave*) and enjoy it over a $5 plate at **Hummus Place** (*109 St. Marks Pl*), $8 half chicken and rice at the **Puerto**

PG vibe. The roomy interior is speckled with beer signs and plasma flat screens permanently broadcasting sports channels, and the bright red chairs add an unexpected and charming touch. Friendly bartenders, a working jukebox, and large group tables in the back room make for a laid-back neighborhood watering hole. Come for a relaxed night with friends, test your arm at a game of darts, and get to know the locals.

Ace Bar
Dive, Games

For adults who haven't outgrown their hometown mall's local arcade, this expansive bar is an ideal place to get wasted while playing some favorite childhood games. Near the entrance, shelves of retro lunchboxes line the walls and nostalgic customers play pinball. Visitors linger near the bar taking shots, while larger groups drinking $3 PBRs monopolize the coveted diner-style leather booths across the way. Around the back of this dark, noisy space, inebriated 20-somethings stumble around pool tables, complaining about faulty electronic scoring on the skeeball

> 531 E. 5th St (near Ave A)
> 212-979-8476
> Daily 4pm-4am
> ⊕ ⓥ to 2nd Ave-
> Lower East Side,
> ⓛ to First Ave
> Average Drink $6
> Happy Hour: Daily 4-7pm

Rican Casa Adela (*66 Ave C*), or $7 pizza at **Otafuku** (*236 E 9th St*). At night, get spectacularly smashed with $3-5 drinks at neighborhood dives **Mars Bar** (*25 E 1st St*) and **Blarney Cove** (*510 E 14th St*). Drag your staggering friends to late night joints **Pomme Frites** (*123 2nd Ave*) or **Plump Dumpling** (*299 E 11 St*) for drunk munchies before the late train ride home.

machines. This lovable dive stays packed throughout the night with a mixed crowd of hipsters and young businessmen. Beware of the life-size, 3-D werewolf poster across from the bar—it surprises unsuspecting and slightly tipsy bar hoppers.

Aces and Eights
College Bar, DJ

While the nonstop beer pong tournaments might be more frat row than East Village, Aces and Eights offers a grown-up version of the college drinking experience. The bottle service, cozy couches, and DJ on the second floor hardly resemble the typical collegiate atmosphere, and

the dark wood bar and leather booths on the first floor are more conducive to deep conversation than to getting schwasted. Around midnight, the bar floods with patrons in their late twenties and early thirties, making it a lively end-of-the-night spot. The bartenders are friendly, many more-than-willing to have a drink or three and dance on the bar with customers. A jukebox of rock, pop, and hip-hop classics encourages drunken singalongs and video games like Buck Hunter offer casual diversions. Finally, Aces and Eights has what your college frat never had—six beer pong tables and twelve-dollar Michelob pitchers.

> 34 Avenue A
> (between 2nd and 3rd St)
> 212-353-2237
> Mon 12am-4am, 5pm-4am,
> Tue-Sat 5pm-4am, Sun
> 5pm-12am.
> ⊕ ⓥ to 2nd Ave,
> Average Drink $5

Anthology Film Archives
Cinema

The large, brick-slab warehouse may seem like an unlikely setting for a movie theater, with its rumored leaky ceiling, gray walls, and comparably stiff audience seating. But this roughened gem is one of the city's leading houses for underground cinema, encouraging innovative, creative, and unusual programming for 40 years. Trendy artists and film geeks alike flock to Anthology to find the best in avante-garde and independent film. A haven of cinematic history, it offers two motion picture theaters, a reference library, a world-famous film preservation department, and a gallery that boasts obscure classics and unknown new treasures.

> 32 2nd Ave (near 2nd St)
> 212-505-5181
> Open Daily
> ⊕ ⓥ to 2nd Ave-
> Lower East Side
> $9 General Admission,
> $7 Students

Botanica
Dive, Lounge

Built into the same red brick basement that was once the original home of the Knitting Factory club, this 13-year-old, laid-back lounge comes dressed in the dim orange light of candles and old lamps. DJs spin all types of music nightly from the niche by the front window, denizens lounge on the plush leather seating in the small, subterranean back room, and bartenders are fast and friendly with the $5 well pours. A

> 47 E Houston St
> (near Mulberry St)
> 212-343-7251
> Mon-Fri Sun-Tues 5pm-2am,
> Wed-Friday 5pm-4am, Sat
> 6pm-4am
> ⑥ ⓑ ⓓ ⓕ ⓥ to
> Broadway-Lafayette
> Average Drink $5
> Happy Hour: Nightly until 8pm

younger, skinny-jean-clad crowd descends en masse for the bi-monthly clothing swaps, and there's Williamsburg kitsch to be found in the old beer taps in museum casing, but a hipster haven this isn't. Botanica has charm and easygoing cool to spare, with a generous happy hour ($3 beers) and a short list of signature cocktails, like the Dark and Stormy, that are worth the try.

Cheap Shots — *Dive*

U n d e n i a b l y irresistible drink prices fill this dirty, narrow corridor of a bar to capacity every night. In line with their name, they offer five shots for $10—one of many deals that attracts everyone from hipsters to frat boys to middle-aged women. Once a year they re-paint the walls and welcome drunk patrons to scribble love notes and profanities on every surface within reach, including the internet jukebox, the black light table air hockey table, and the picnic tables in the back of the room. Drink for free on your birthday and for half-price on Tuesdays if you can beat the bartender at rock-paper-scissors.

140 1st Ave (near 9th St)
212-254-6631
Daily 12pm-4am
6 to Astor Pl, L to 1st Ave
Average Drink $4

Cozy Café — *Hookah*

Widely considered one of the best cheap hookah bars in the city, this Arabian-themed lounge is the perfect place to relax and take a deep breath with friends. There are 69 flavors of hookah to choose from, including regular favorites like Apple and Rose, as well as exotic blends—Viagra Hookah's fresh fruit and wine base offers a particularly flavorful flight. Regular DJs and an incredibly attentive staff add to the cozy feel, but the bar adopts a sexy atmosphere on Friday and Saturday nights, when belly dancers entertain the smoke-filled room. The outdoor patio, ample drink list, and group discounts make this a great spot for large parties. Be sure to try the new Stella's Special Hookah, with fresh watermelon, champagne, and an ice base.

43 E 1st St
(btwn 1st & 2nd Ave)
212-475-0177
Sun-Thurs 2:30pm-2:30am,
Fri-Sat 3pm-4am
F V to 2nd Ave-
Lower East Side

Crocodile Lounge — *Dive, Games, Pizza*

"Beer = Pizza" proclaims the sign that flanks the stairs to this basement dive. Crocodile Lounge offers made-to-order pizza for free with every drink. Sample specialty draughts like Goose

The Bourgeois Pig
111
EAST 7TH
STREET
New York, NY
10009

The Bourgeois Pig — *Wine Bar, Lounge*

The red damask-printed interior and casually sensual atmosphere welcomes a crowd ready for late night revelry. This French wine and fondue lounge could seduce patrons by looks alone, but the Pig also delivers on flavorful food, as the fit-for-a-pig cheese platters make clear. Come with friends and order one of three extravagantly rich chocolate fondues, all of which come with cakes, brownies, and every kind of fruit imaginable. The beer and specialty cocktail lists are extensive, but the best drinks are those you pour yourself: on Mondays and Tuesdays, bottles of wine are half-off. Whether you go with raucous or romantic intentions, The Bourgeois Pig is designed for debauchery—nothing wholesome can come from all that chocolate and wine.

111 E 7th St
(btwn 1st Ave & Ave A)
212-475-2246
Sun-Wed 5pm-2am,
Thurs-Sat 5pm-4am
L to 1st Ave
Average Drink $10
Happy Hour: Daily 4-8pm

Island Honkers Ale or go for a more traditional brew, then get your personal pan pizza fresh from huge ovens near the tiled bar. The main room is lit with chili pepper lights strung along exposed pipes and littered with mismatched couches where crowds from NYU hover. If new-school arcade games and skee-ball aren't for you, escape to the quieter, more private open-air courtyard. Stop by Wednesday nights for trivia games, where winners claim free shots and bar tabs. Remember to tip well and often—skimping on an extra dollar may cost you your next pizza.

325 E 14th St (at 1st Ave)
212-477-7747
Daily 12pm-4am
🄻 to 1st Ave
Average Beer & Well drink: $6
Happy Hour: 12pm-6pm ($3 Yuengling Drafts & Well drinks)

KGB Bar
Lounge, Lit Club

85 E 4th St (near 2nd Ave), 2nd Floor
212-505-3360
Daily 7pm-4am
🄵🄥 to 2nd Ave-Lower East Side
Average Drink $5
Happy Hour: Daily 4-8pm

Up a steep flight of stairs gather expatriates, eccentrics, and the occasional real ex-KGB to drink Baltika beers at this former local headquarters of the Ukrainian Socialist Party. The red walls are plastered with socialist realist art, authentic propaganda posters, and Soviet souvenirs. Misha the bear, a 1980 Olympics Soviet mascot, watches from the corner while a quiet bartender spins the Pixies and pours 20 different kinds of vodka. This is the only bar in New York that publishes its own literary journal, and several times a week barflies metamorphose into an audience for the innovative, local writers who share their work at events like the monthly "Drunken! Careening! Writers!" reading series. It feels like a friendly, secret club—perfect to hone your craft, feed your head, and nurse an extremely strong drink under a judgmental bust of Lenin.

McSorely's Old Ale House
Beer Bar

Since 1854, this dive bar has served its famed ale to everyone from Abraham Lincoln to John Lennon. Although it was forced to allow women to enter in 1970, McSorley's continues to cater to a crowd composed almost entirely of very masculine men, who

CURRY ROW

Started by competing Bengali proprietors in 1976, this monoculture of nearly-indistinguishable South Asian restaurants stretches along East 6th Street between 1st and 2nd Avenues. Thirty years of rivalry have yielded a reliable standard for good-but-not-great Indian fare at shockingly low prices. If you're in the mood for some satisfying saag paneer, chicken tikka masala, and warm garlic naan, any one of these dozen or so cramped enclaves will do. Armed with Darwinian aggressiveness, waiters stand outside to hype the economy of their respective restaurant's dinner specials to passersby. **Brick Lane Curry** (*306-308 E 6th St*) is modeled after London curry joints and is a tad more upscale than the rest. Everyone has their favorite, but **Banjara** (*97 1st Ave*) is the one that the locals keep talking about. **Panna II** (*93 1st Ave*) stands out for its audacious décor: every single inch of the interior is covered in Christmas lights; naturally, the three neighboring spots followed suit. Visit **Dual Specialty Store** (*91 1st Ave*) for cheap imported beers beforehand—even though some Curry Row restaurants are licensed, they'll often look the other way if you BYO (just remember to ask beforehand).

varies depending on the evening's theme (80s on Friday evenings and Konkrete Jungle on Mondays), but rarely exceeds $10. Patrons don't seem to take the theme nights too seriously—they come to rock out to Blondie and down $4 vodka tonics.

Sultana _Hookah_

128 E 4th St
(btwn 1st Ave & 2nd Ave)
212-228-7678
Mon-Fri 5pm-4am,
Sat-Sun 2pm-4am
F V to 2nd Ave-
Lower East Side
Hookah $15,
Drink Minimum $5

Cozy and perfumed with the scent of tobacco and rose, sheesha aficionados and amateurs alike sink into the snug rows of plush couches here to smoke hookah, expertly packed and well-attended by the omnipresent owner, whose grave expression when handling his precious tobacco softens to a smile if you engage him. Too many Manhattan hookah bars never get past the novelty of smoking fruity tobacco out of gaudy glass towers and settle for transporting tourists to a kitschified vision of the Middle East. Thank goodness, then, for Sultana and its authentic, quality smoke. Most glorious, though, is the lounge's BYOB policy, and the corkage fee that covers the $5 drink minimum. If you're not drinking, satisfy the modest requirement with the refreshing floral mint tea or a slice of red velvet cake from the bakery next door.

cheer loudly when their baseball team scores a run and occasionally burst into impromptu nationalistic chants of "USA! USA!" Busts of John F.

15 E. 7th St (near 3rd Ave)
212-473-9148
Mon-Sat 11am-1am, Sun
1pm-1am
N R W to 8th St-NYU,
6 to Astor Pl
Average Drink $2.25

Kennedy and numerous clovers scattered among the dusty knickknacks remind customers of the joint's humble beginnings as an Irish workingman's bar, as does the simple menu, which offers a cheese and onion plate or a small bowl of soup for only $3.50. And with mugs of the house ale served in pairs for only $4.50, drinks seem priced for a different century too.

Pyramid Club _LGBT_

101 Ave A (near 6th St)
212-228-4888
Mon 11pm-4am, Tues & Sun
8:30pm-1am, Thurs & Sat
9pm-4am, Fri 10pm-4am
F V to 2nd Ave-
Lower East Side
Average Drink $3

A mixed crowd of gay men and the straight girls that follow them packs the darkened halls of this low-key, two-story hangout. Minimal bursts of bold decorations—including a giant set of glittery, red lips behind the bar and colored Christmas lights along the ceiling—add sparkle to what would otherwise resemble a simple dive bar with a dance floor. Madcap performances of the odd, the entertaining, and the oddly entertaining dominate the stage and lithe bodies pack the tiny floor. The cover charge

The Sunburnt Cow _Dive_

137 Ave C
(btwn 8th & 9th St)
212-529-0005
Mon-Fri 4pm-4am,
Sat 11am-4am, Sun 11am-
12am, Kitchen closes: Mon
10pm, Tues-Fri 12am,
Sun 9pm
L to 1st Ave, **F V** to 2nd
Ave-Lower East Side
Average Drink $7

Friendly Aussie service, drunken dance parties, and delicious drinks guarantee a sloshed and happy night at this exceedingly eccentric dive. A confederation of college-age clientele flock to the outback restaurant and bar for a hearty meal of Roo Bangers and Mash or Mutton Stew, Moo Juice (creative and fruity highballs), and a glorious night of debauchery. With a $20 anytime special to drink as much as you can in two hours, the endearingly ugly decor will grow progressively more attractive—as will the person dancing next to you at the bar. Come early for their Australian barbecue dinner and stay for drinks on the strange, paper-machete-cave-looking deck 'til 4am. Then return with cash seven hours later for the $18 Endless Brunch.

"WHAT FREUD DID FOR SEX!"

—*Time Out, London*

photo: ©Junichi

ST⬤MP™

$40
Sundays
@ 7pm

ORPHEUM THEATRE

Tue-Fri @ 8
Sat @ 3&8
Sun @ 3&7

Second Avenue @ 8th Street www.stomponline.com

ticketmaster (800) 982-2787

SOHO & TRIBECA

With its overpriced boutiques and weary bag-laden tourists, Soho ("South of Houston," but don't call it that) is the City's excessively posh outdoor mall. A flagship arts district in the 60s, its avant-garde population was quickly outbid by a well-heeled fashion elite. Galleries dwindled as Diesel and Marc Jacobs laid claim to the cobbled streets, but the south end of the neighborhood still retains much of its character. Boasting the highest concentration of cast-iron buildings anywhere in the world, southern Soho is an open-air museum of elegant, late 19th century architecture, where many of its artsy residents still dwell in their coveted lofts.

Tribeca ("Triangle Below Canal") is one of the smallest and priciest zip codes in the US. Like Soho, its character has changed dramatically in recent decades. Once dominated by warehouses, Tribeca is now littered with boutiques, high-end restaurants, and loft apartments populated by yuppie families looking for a quiet corner of Manhattan. Despite its proximity to Soho, Tribeca is considerably less toured, and you're much more likely to see the streets filled with stroller-pushing nannies than picture-snapping visitors. Though several popular after-work bars dot the area, it's definitely not the place to come for raucous nightlife. Don't be surprised to see a star or two on the street—resident Robert De Niro launched the Tribeca Film Center, and Gisele Bündchen, Jay-Z, and Jon Stewart all call the neighborhood home.

Though neither neighborhood is as cutting edge as it once was, both remain among the most iconic areas in the city, preserving the unique architecture of Manhattan's long-disappeared industrial heritage. For many, they offer some of the most desirable locales to live in. For others, they just reiterate the classic New York story—the chic restaurants and luxury co-ops are in, and the bohemians are out.

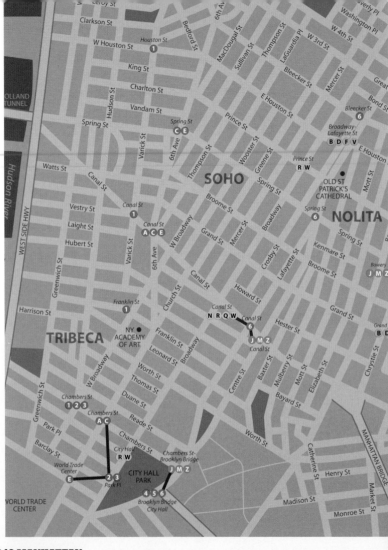

EXPLORE

The Drawing Center

Most art museums and galleries feature a wide range of media on their walls. Not so for the Drawing Center. Founded in 1977 on a side street in Soho, this tiny, unadorned not-for-profit art gallery is known for displaying one thing only—drawings. Ranging from the traditional to the truly bizarre, the pieces are always interesting, and the gallery is small enough that it's easy to view all of them in one go. Don't be put off by the seemingly limited scope. The drawings—often unexpected, unforgettable, and wholly original images—are hardly the dull stuff you might expect.

35 Wooster St (at Grand St)
212-219-2166
1, A C E, 6 J M Z
N Q R W to Canal St

The Flea Theater

An off-off-Broadway theater that sits on a quiet corner, The Flea has achieved great recognition for its theatrical experimentation and willingness to provide up-and-coming artists, actors, musicians, and dancers with opportunities to showcase their work in its cozy maroon-walled black box theater. In addition to more standard productions like *Twelfth Night*, The Flea also hosts a handful of festivals—like Music with a View—throughout the year. This downtown artistic retreat has also established its own set of in-house workshops for both actors and writers, called "The Bats." The Flea takes risks when it comes to choosing the productions they house, which is what gives this downtown theater an edge on the more conventional uptown venues.

41 White St
(btwn Broadway & Church St)
212-226-0051
1 to Franklin St, **A C E**,
6 J M Z N Q R W to
Canal St

Museum of Cartoon and Comic Art

Ka-POW! Bam! Swoosh! Comic book and graphic novel heroes get their glory at this intimate and vivid museum of the cartoon art form. On the blue, yellow, purple, and white walls various

594 Broadway, Suite #401
(btwn Houston & Prince St).
212-254-3511
Daily 12pm-5pm
6 to Bleecker St, **R W** to
Prince St, **B D F V** to
Broadway-Lafayette

DAY TO DAY

Community Board: (SoHo): Community Board 2, 3 Washington Square Village, #1A, 212-979-2272. (**Tribeca**): Community Board 1, 49-51 Chambers St, Room 715, 212-442-5050.

Groceries: Gourmet Garage SoHo, 453 Broome St # A, 212-941-5850, Whole Foods Tribeca, 270 Greenwich St.

Gym: Equinox (SoHo): 568 Broadway, 212-334-4631. (**TriBeCa**): 54 Murray St., 212-566-6555.

Library: NYPL Mulberry St Branch, 10 Jersey Street, 212-966-3424.

Media: *SoHo Weekly News*, www.sohoweeklynews.com. *Tribeca Tribune*, www.tribecatrib.com.

Volunteer Opportunities: Association of Community Employment Programs for the homeless, sohonyc.org.

comic book panels are displayed in simple black frames. Telling just enough of their respective stories to get every visitor to the next page, each exhibit leads you deeper into the mind of the artist. Many frames have sketches and notes of underdeveloped ideas in the margins, explaining the thought process that led to the work. The artwork changes every four months, but one section of the museum is always worth a look—where the staff of the museum (all volunteers) showcases its own comic art. Past exhibits include The Art of Watchmen and Uncanny X-hibit- Comic Book Legends Unite.

Wooster Group

Though it performs across the country, the Wooster Group is an original New York creation. Focusing on the abstract and edgy side of performing arts, the Wooster Group has its home in the The Performing Garage in Soho. The Group has been around for some 30 years, but retains its fresh approach to theatre. Known for meshing together the

33 Wooster St (near Grand St)
212-966-9796
1, A C E, 6 J M Z
N Q R W to Canal St

Housing Works Bookstore Café and Thrift Shop

This bookstore looks like a library tucked away in the corner of an elegant Colonial mansion. Books with warn, intriguing covers line the dark wooden shelves, and murmuring crowds congregate around teeny tables that dot the floorspace. The book haven is an outpost of Housing Works, an organization created to provide homes, medicine, and legal aid to those with AIDS/HIV. A refreshing change from the endless "save the world" campaigns run by corporate giants, not-for-profit Housing Works raises money through its businesses. After purchasing a book, head to the airy thrift store next door, filled with exciting finds like name brand blazers and glazed pottery. Leave feeling guilt-free about purchases—the money goes to a good cause.

126 Crosby St
(btwn E Houston & Prince St)
212-334-3324
Mon-Fri 10am-9pm,
Sat-Sun 12pm-7pm
B D F V to Broadway-Lafayette

---

unexpected—think 17th-century opera mixed with 60s sci-fi movies—the Wooster Group is a unique experience not to be missed. The Group does not limit itself to simple props and traditional scenery. Instead, it uses everything from found materials, films, both modern and classical texts, and dance to bring its vision to the stage. Because the company's schedule rotates regularly, be sure to check the website or call the playhouse before going to see what you're getting into.

SHOP

Evolution

Staffed with science gurus and affiliated with city science, art, retail, and educational councils, this two-level shop is licensed to sell just about everything but human tissue. Dinosaur teeth are scattered near woolly mammoth femurs, taxidermy, and fossils.

120 Spring St (near Greene St)
800-952-3195
Daily 11am-7pm
6 C E to Spring St, R W
to Prince St, B D F V to
Broadway-Lafayette

Necklaces with a 4.5-billion-year-old meteorite pendants, butterfly-wing earrings, and killer bees in a vial are available too. Venture upstairs to see the skeletons of a ten-thousand-year-old cave bear and a human family. The most popular items are healing magnets, alligator heads, small animal skulls, and lollipops filled with edible scorpions and insects. Museums, photographers, and shoppers searching for rare novelties all find what they're searching for here.

In God We Trust

Twenty-somethings looking for wardrobe basics and a hint of whimsy flock to this charming boutique. With wooden shelves along the wall and various antique end tables and mirrors scattered throughout, customers will instantly feel at home browsing through the racks at this tiny clothing store. Find kitschy barrettes topped with plaid bows and card cases featuring engravings like "in it to win it"—perfectly quirky additions to

265 Lafayette St (near Prince St)
212-966-9010
Tues-Sat 12pm-8pm, Sun
12pm-7pm, Mon closed
6 C E to Spring St, R W
to Prince St, B D F V to
Broadway-Lafayette

any outfit. Brightly-colored dresses with large gold buttons hang next to charm necklaces and chunky heels. Men's crisp, button-down shirts are displayed next to a pile of navy tennis shorts. Prices may be high, but items are full of character and timeless enough to be staples of any wardrobe.

MarieBelle

With all the glam and charm of an old Hollywood movie, this café and chocolate shop sells delectable sweets

484 Broome St (near Watts St)
212-925-6999
Mon-Sun 11am-7pm
6 to Spring St,
A C E to Canal St

in dizzying variety. The goods are prepared by MarieBelle, a professionally-trained chef originally from Honduras, who's renowned for infusing traditional dark chocolate with exotic and unusual flavors. The shop is most famous for its Aztec hot chocolate, a rich blend of 60% Colombian chocolate. Also popular are the truffles and dark chocolate squares filled with passion fruit, champagne, cardamom, and other tongue-tingling flavors. The café offers brunch, lunch, signature hot chocolates, and pastries from the shop's bakery. Friendly wait staff delivers dishes to tiny marble and wood tables, each adorned with a single flower.

Posteritati

With 12,000 pieces from over 30 countries,

Posteritati is one of the leading purveyors of movie posters in the world. Here posters are revered as works of art: the

239 Centre St
(btwn Grand & Broome St)
212-226-2207
Tues-Sat 11am-7pm, Sun
12pm-6pm
R W to Prince St

airy space functions as both a store and gallery, with only a few themed pieces on display at any time. The shop also frequently lends pieces to film organizations and festivals throughout the city. As for selling the posters, three user-friendly computers in the store's center grant access to the archives. Use the computer search engines, also available online, to narrow your search by details like film, genre, country of origin, and actor. Posters start $20 and reach the thousand-plus dollar mark—and with a selection as varied as the prices, Posteritati has wall décor for dorm rooms and duplexes alike.

Topshop

This NYC outpost of the British-based clothing chain lives up to its reputation as a destination for cheap, stylish

478 Broadway
(btwn Broome St & Grand St)
212-966-9555
6 to Spring St,
J M Z to Bowery

clothes. The style is a hybrid between H&M and Forever 21, but the glitzy tops, 5-inch heels, and club-like décor make this one stand out. Topshop continues to heighten its fashion world credibility by carrying the Kate Moss line—a

NOLITA

Check out this trendy hotspot (short for "North of Little Italy") for a Soho atmosphere without the crowds. The area was once considered part of Little Italy, but an influx of young professionals transformed the nook between Houston, Broome, Lafayette, and Bowery into a swanky locale to rival its chic neighbor to the west. Mingle with well-heeled New Yorkers shopping for the latest page-turner at **McNally Jackson Booksellers** (*52 Prince St*) and dining at the **Prince St Café** (*26 Prince St*). Watch posh European tourists as they shop for vintage accessories at **I Heart** (*262 Mott St*), and then end an afternoon of window shopping at **Ceci Cela Patisserie** (*55 Spring St*), where the delicately buttery French pastries will make your taste buds thankful that you ventured north of Little Italy.

collection of edgier looks that are more runway than street. Throw in the personal shoppers, a 10% student discount, and a DJ that spins while you shop, and you begin to understand why Topshop's debut was as highly anticipated as the opening of a celebrity club.

Uniqlo

While skinny jeans may once have been exclusively available in Upper East Side boutiques, Uniqlo makes the fashion-musts available to all.

546 Broadway
(btwn Spring Prince St)
917-237-8800
Mon-Sat 10am-9pm, Sun 11am-8pm
R W to Prince St,
6 to Spring St

The pure white interior of the store plays off the colors of the jeans; rotating mannequins model dark washes, light washes, and maroon and purple dyes. The vast store is arranged by color, and the altitudinous shelves, stocked full of jeans, cashmere items, and gritty graphic tees, wrap around the store. After purchasing your new favorite pair of jeans, you can have them tailored on site—for free! Uniqlo's mission statement is to become the world's premier casual clothing company and, given the many celebs who frequent this Soho boutique, it's well on its way.

EAT

Blaue Gans

Austrian

Diners at this casual neighborhood restaurant sit at a central communal table and feast on the contemporary Austrian cuisine of renowned chef and restauranteur

139 Duane St
(near W Broadway)
212-571-8880
Daily 11am-12am, Bar until 2am
1 2 3 to Chambers
A C to Chambers
Brunch $10-20, Lunch Prix Fixe $20, A la carte $8-18, Dinner Appetizers $8-14, Entrees $9-28

Kurt Gutenbrunner. Black leather banquettes nuzzle up against walls plastered with avante garde art. The menu boasts Austrian classics like an assorted wurst platter, fresh herb spätzle, and quark cheese ravioli with mint and brown butter. Rich entrees like East Coast halibut with artichokes and sauce pistou offer excursions into less familiar Austrian fare. Pair your meal with a wine from their massive list or one of the eight Bavarian beers on tap. And in the summer, enjoy the musical stylings of live jazz bands that play across from the lavishly stocked, dark wood bar.

NATIVE'S PICK

Café Habana

Cuban

New York may not wear hot, muggy nights so well, but a trip down to this Nolita Cuban hotspot, where stylish, young locals knock back frozen margaritas, mojitos, and moritas (the mind-blowing hybrid of the first two), can make those semi-tropical evenings not only bearable, but also delicious. With a tin exterior and corner-diner charm, Café Habana has become an institution in a fashionable locale without losing its honest sensibilities and unpretentious attitude. Simply presented, richly flavored plates featuring combinations of beef, chicken, pork, rice, black beans, and plantains are most popular, though fish and vegetarian-friendly cheese and avocado dishes are equally delicious. Café Habana's most celebrated offering is its corn on the cob, decked out with chili powder, cheese, butter, and lime. Attack the corn as vigorously as you like—Café Habana provides plenty of toothpicks for smiling patrons on those humid, Havana-in-New-York nights.

17 Prince St
(btwn Elizabeth & Mott St)
212-625-2001
Daily, 9am-12am
6 to Spring St, **R W** to Prince St, **B D F V** to Broadway-Lafayette
Appetizers $5-8, Entrees $9-15

Bouley Bakery & Market

Café

Chef David Bouley's bakery, market, and café are the reasonably priced alternatives to his celebrated fine-dining restaurant across the street. The interior is a foodie fantasy, with various stations for vegetables, prepared meats like Long Island Duck or the more homey beef chili, and plenty of baked goods. Bread is wonderfully crusty outside and pillowy within. Raisin Anise, fig, and pepper loaves are all fragrant and boldly flavored. Desserts include variations on beloved staples: flourless chocolate cake, pain au chocolat with pears, and French-style macaroons sandwiched with fruit jams or raspberry butter. Order to go or enjoy your food at one of the sidewalk tables. During the day, seating is also available at Bouley's Upstairs—a casual, full-service dinner spot next door.

120 W Broadway (at Duane St)
212-219-1011
Bakery 7:30am-7:30pm,
Market 10am-7pm
1 2 3 to Chambers,
A C to Chambers
Pastries $2-4, Breads $5-8,
Salads & Sandwiches $5-12

Café Colonial

Brazilian

Small tables squeeze into every nook of this breezy Nolita spot, lit by dim, romantic candles that illuminate the South Africa maps that adorn white washed brick walls. Chatter of young neighborhood regulars fills the cozy room and tables spill onto the corner sidewalk on warmer nights. The menu boasts traditional Brazilian fare, from generous, light salads to a fish-heavy list of entrees. In keeping with the regional cuisine, larger plates combine tropical and Portuguese flavors. Moqueca de peixe—a stew of salmon, tilapia, and shrimp with coconut milk, peppers, tomatoes, and cilantro—is a popular dish emblematic of their flavorful specialties. A side of yucca fries or homemade bread makes the perfect vehicle for leftover sauce. Desserts like chocolate bread

276 Elizabeth St
(near E Houston St)
212-274-0044
B D F V to Broadway-Lafayette
Lunch Appetizers $6-13,
Entrees $10-15,
Dinner Appetizers $3-12,
Entrees $15-18

---

pudding and caramel flan provide rich, creamy, and utterly unskippable endings.

Civetta
Italian

98 Kenmare St
(near Cleveland Pl)
212-274-9898
Sun-Wed 12pm-12am,
Thurs-Sat 12pm-12:45am
6 to Spring St, **R W** to
Prince St, **J M Z** to Bowery
Appetizers $8-16,
Entrees $15-35

The uptown Italian gem Sfoglia gets a dose of downtown cool without losing its homey, familial style at this sister restaurant. At Civetta, antipasti come in sharable portions rather than precious bits, so come with friends and an appetite. The spinach and goat cheese sformato—a savory soufflé with a flaky pastry crust—makes a light, flavorful start, while a main course of grilled branzino with marmellata offers a refined balance of sweet, sour, and salty. Save room for exceptional desserts like the espresso semi-freddo or the bomboloni, small sugar donuts filled with a touch of marmalade and drizzled with warm melted chocolate. Dishcloth napkins and worn farmhouse tables keep things humble while the low, arched ceilings and wax-covered candelabras evoke a romantic, loungy vibe. To cap off your meal, head to the downstairs bar to sip a glass of house-made limoncello.

Cubana Café
Cuban

110 Thompson St (btwn
Spring & Prince Sts)
212-966-5366
Sun-Thurs 11:30am-11pm,
Fri-Sat 11:30am-11:30pm
C E to Spring St
Average Meal $10

A flight of stairs leads down to plastic-covered tables and walls livened by pastel renderings of Spanish phrases, a kitschy rendering of Havana at the height of its early 20th-century popularity. With its pressed-tin ceiling and walls lined with Cuban artifacts, Cubana Café feels more like a period film set than an authentic sliver of the island—but its easy, tropical charm and cozy atmosphere win over SoHo crowds. The food falls just short of authentic but rarely fails to satisfy. A stuffed poblano chile is creamy, cheesy, and just spicy enough. The plate of pulled pork combines flavorful meat with a mild, sweet puree of whipped plantains. Hearty dishes like these, served at prices to match the homey basement setting, pair well with strong mojitos and sangria.

Kelley and Ping
Thai

127 Greene St (E Houston St)
212-228-1212
Daily Lunch 11:30am-5pm,
Dinner 5:30pm-11pm
6 to Bleeker St,
R W to Prince St, **B D F V**
to Broadway-Lafayette
Lunch $5-10,
Dinner Appetizers $7-9,
Entrees $11-22

The real "Kelley" and "Ping" families still bustle around this Thai spot, serving noodles and vegetables to shoppers, NYU kids, and lunch break crowds. The cafeteria-style dining room combines the loud hustle of Chinatown with an attractively sparse grocery-inspired aesthetic—the Manhattan incarnation of a Bangkok hole-in-the-wall. Wok dishes like Thai

UNDER $20

SOHO & TRIBECA

Stock up on $3.50 yucca fries at $3.75 fresh watermelon smoothies **Pan Latin** (*400 Chambers St*), then ta your treats to **Nelson A. Rockefelle Park** just across the street. Scoping o art exhibits in this area is a must, so che out the quirky (and free!) installatio at **The Dream House** (*275 Chu St*), **Soho Photo Gallery** (*15 Wh St*), or **The Broken Kilometer** (3 *W Broadway*). Digest the art with a $ fish taco made from line-caught Ma Mahi and organic vegetables at **Pinch**

wide noodles are expertly cooked and seasoned. Lunch boxes stack dumplings, fried brown rice, sprout-heavy pad Thai, and other goodies together in practical metal compartments. You can add chicken or shrimp to most dishes for $1, but even by themselves the vegetables and noodles pack plenty of flavor. The front bar offers Thai iced tea and Vietnamese coffee, both blended with the traditional condensed milk and chicory. Be sure to grab a few of the buttery walnut cookies for a sweet treat on the way out.

La Esquina

Mexican

114 Kenmare St
(near Cleveland Pl)
Reservations 646-613-7100
Delivery 646-613-1333
Taqueria: Breakfast Mon-Fri
8am-11:30am, Daily, 12pm-
2am, Café: Brunch Sat-Sun
11am-4pm, Daily 12pm-12am
6 to Bleeker St
R W to Prince St
Tacos & Tortas $7-12,
Entrees $15-22

A glaring red sign beckons wayward late-night partiers from blocks away to this tiny taqueria, where they spill noisily out onto the sidewalk with a wide variety of tacos, tortas, and Mexican beers in hand. The

aquería *(227 Mott St)*, then head over **Housing Works Bookstore Café**, *26 Crosby St)* for book browsing and free Comedy Night Tuesdays. Music junkies shouldn't miss the **Jazz Gallery** *290 Hudston St)* and **Rockwood Hall f Music** *(196 Allen St)*, where you can njoy free live music with your drink. you think you're good enough to ake your own music, stick around the eighborhood and head to the **Canal oom** *(285 W Broadway)* for $3 Rockstar araoke every Thursday.

bistec tacos and elotes callejeros (grilled corn on the cob) are favorites among regulars at the take-out window, while those preferring comfortable diner-style digs stick to the café section, where they can relax in cozy booths with a pitcher of Sangria and a longer menu of Mexican comfort foods. The Tinga de Pollo, a chicken stew flavored with chipotle and slight hints of cinnamon, complements the young, casual

atmosphere. Insider's tip: behind a nondescript door, there is a bouncer-guarded, exclusive brasserie and tequila bar in the basement. Rumor has it that for those lucky enough to snag a reservation early in the day, a celebrity sighting is all but guaranteed.

L'Ecole

French

462 Broadway (near Grand St)
212-219-3300
Brunch Sat & Sun 11:30am-
2:30pm,
Lunch Mon-Fri 12:30pm-2pm,
Dinner Mon-Sat 5:30pm-7pm
(4-course prix fixe)
8pm-9pm (5-course prix fixe)
N Q R W to Canal St
Brunch $20, Lunch $28,
Dinner $42

A large black-and-white photograph of a chef's hands graces the formal dining room of this restaurant at the French Culinary Institute, a reminder that dining here is as much about the process of cooking as it is about the finished product. Since 1984, L'Ecole has served as the primary training ground for the institute's upper-level cooking students. Using classic techniques, supervised student chefs prepare creative, richly detailed dishes both traditional (roasted duck in cherry sauce) and forward-thinking (watermelon gazpacho with feta). The $42 prix fixe dinner—four courses prepared by the instructors and, later in the evening, five courses by the students—$28 three-course lunch, and $20 brunch make L'Ecole accessible to diners as young as the chefs that cook there.

Lombardi's

Pizza

32 Spring St (near Mott St)
212-941-7994
Sun-Thurs 11:30am-11pm,
Fri-Sat 11:30am-12am
6 to Spring St,
R W to Prince St
14" plain pizza $16,
5 toppings $8
Cash only

Credited with inventing the New York-style pizza, Lombardi's is as much a historic landmark as it is a destination dining spot. Though it moved down the street from its original location (over 100 years after opening), Lombardi's has maintained all its red-and-white-checkered tablecloth glory—and it still makes one of New York's best pizzas. Expertly prepared Neapolitan pies can be ordered with any number of fresh toppings heaped onto Lombardi's famous crust: crisp and crunchy outside, ludicrously soft within. The famed clam pie—a Lombardi's crust piled with freshly shucked Connecticut clams, olive oil, garlic, herbs and Pecorino—is a savory seafood masterpiece. Pizzas can only be

bench and watch shoppers and yuppies walk by. For neighbors whose schedules don't allow lunch breaks, they offers online ordering and delivery. No matter your pace, Olive's serves up laid back classics that have locals and tourists alike coming back for more.

Pinche Taquería
Mexican

227 Mott St (near Spring St)
212-625-0090
Mon-Thurs 11am-11pm, Fri-Sat 11:00-12:00am,
Sun 11am-8pm
6 to Spring St,
R W to Prince St, **B D F V**
to Broadway-Lafayette
Average Taco $3, Salad $7

This lively taquería is the antidote to the overpriced bistros that have taken over SoHo. Bright red walls complete with cacti and a Frida Kahlo portrait rendered on a beaded curtain, and reggae playing in the background, keep Pinche from falling into the standard Taquería mold. Though it takes about three tacos to constitute a meal, prices are wallet-friendly. Pinche burritos come stuffed with enough goods for two. One bite of these fried-to-perfection masterpieces goes a long way to prove that Mexican food in New York isn't as dismal as those pesky LA natives like to claim. At least one typically Soho trend has caught on at Pinche, setting it apart from most other cheap eats destinations: Pinche makes all of its food using fresh, wholly organic ingredients—that means no canned goods, no microwaves

Rice to Riches
Dessert

37 Spring St
(btwn Mott & Mulberry St)
212-274-0008
Sun-Thurs 11am-11pm,
Fri-Sat 11am-1am
6 to Spring St
Individual Serving $5

A space age dessert bar, Rice to Riches does one thing and one thing only: rice pudding. Regularly rotating, cheekily named options can include Sex Drugs and Rocky Road, Rest in Peach, and Fluent in French Toast. Toppings like oven roasted fruit, oatmeal coconut crumble, and caramel vanilla sauce will transform an already decadent treat into an all-but-unjustifiable excess. Set in hyper-designed surroundings, Rice to Riches is as much about décor as it is about its single, delectable dessert offering. All orders are served in vibrantly colored plastic bowls with matching lids and spoons that can be saved and reused later, either as Tupperware or convenient cereal bowls. Right on the border of trendy Soho and trendier

ordered as full pies, so come with a group or plan to take some home, and remember to come with cash. When it comes to payment, Lombardi's remains in the 19th century.

Olive's
Café

120 Prince St (at Wooster)
212-941-0111
Mon-Fri 8am-7pm,
Sat 9am-7pm, Sun 9am-6pm
R W to Prince St,
to Broadway-Lafayette,
6 to Bleeker St
Average Meal $15

This made-to-order take-out spot has become a staple for Soho denizens on the go. Olive's mean sandwiches, soups, salads, and breakfast pastries are as pleasantly homey as its small, attractively worn space. Stop by in the morning for a muffin and coffee, or in the afternoon for a turkey sandwich with avocado mayo, a homemade cookie, and a glass of freshly squeezed lemonade. Run to your next stop or sit outside on the storefront red

Nolita, Rice to Riches brings a glut of style to the gluttonous, rice-pudding downing masses.

Snack
Greek

105 Thompson St
(near Spring St)
212-925-1040
Mon-Wed 12pm-10pm,
ThurS-Sat 12pm-11pm,
Sun 12pm-9pm
C E to Spring St
Lunch Appetizers $6-12,
Entrees $8-13,
Dinner Appetizers $9-11,
Entrees $17-20

This tiny ten-seater, with its graceful décor and Greek cooking, has all the charm of a neighbor's kitchen. Take-out from an abbreviated, bargain-laden lunch menu is popular with the restaurant's many regulars (the lamb sandwich has acquired a cult-like following), but Snack is best enjoyed in the evening, when flickering electric candlelight from tiny Greek Orthodox shrines transforms the cute lunch joint into an intimate dinner destination. Dive into the impressive menu with the meze platter, a refreshing sampler of Greek standards like carp roe and potato-garlic puree. Memorable entrees are unmistakably Greek, but forget the flavors you're used to at the local gyro cart—try the pastitsio, a beef casserole with hints of cinnamon, or the lamb stifado, braised to tender perfection and infused with apricot. Finish with a blissfully nutty baklava and rich Greek coffee.

PLAY

Antarctica
Dive

287 Hudson St (near Spring St)
212-352-1666
Mon-Wed 4:30pm-2am,
Thurs-Fri 4:30pm-4am,
Sat 7pm-4am
C E to Spring St,
1 to Houston St
Average Drink $5

When the bar opened 11 years ago, the owners joked about how far south and isolated it was—inspiring the dive's name. Now, the popular drinking hub happily opens its doors to an after-work crowd that unwinds with $1 pool games and weekend hordes that commandeer the eclectic jukebox. Even when filled with hoarse patrons belting No Doubt classics off-key, there's plenty of room to enjoy a drink comfortably in this spacious, oak-floor dive. The bar prides itself on continent-sized drinks, all served in pint glasses—including the $6 house vodka-soda. Bring a

NATIVE'S PICK

MercBar
Lounge

151 Mercer St
(btwn Prince & Houston St)
212-966-2727
Sun-Wed 5pm-2am, Thurs-Sat 5pm-4am
6 to Spring St, **R W** to Prince St, **B D F V** to Broadway-Lafayette
Average Drink $13
Happy Hour: "Retro Hour"
Daily 5-8pm, $8 Select Cocktails, $6 Beers

Thick wood paneling and large hanging canoes collide with deep red walls and plush seating at this relaxed mountain lodge-themed lounge. Citizen Cope and Sublime echo off the exposed piping and track lighting—industrial touches that urbanize the *Dances with Wolves* aesthetic. Cowhide and plush paisley couches are perfect for cozying up with a date or letting loose with friends, and the large table and bar area allow for pleasant mingling with Euros from the nearby Mercer Hotel and with hip Soho regulars that make up the clientele. Fridays and Saturdays find little room to move, so come early to scope out a space to sip on a spicy Diablo or sparkling Pear Tree before the bar gets busy. If you want your own room in this swanky cabin, rent out the back Red Room.

group of friends, kick back, and chat up the cute bartenders. If you're lucky and your ID matches the evening's Name Night, take advantage of free drinks all night.

Circa Tabac
Smoking Lounge

It's not difficult to imagine Hemingway or Kerouac calling this cigar lounge their haunt of choice. Cosmopolitan types sit with furrowed brows lit by the cherried embers of their cigarettes, and the burgundy trim and velveteen curtains that adorn the walls of the dark space create a unique scene that's romantic, if not downright seductive. While you can buy a pack of foreign cigarettes from their vast selection (The Shepherd's Hotel, from Germany, is spicy and rich), there's appeal for the non-smoker as well. The cocktails, like the elegant Rio, with coconut rum and Chambord, are fantastic. Patrons also benefit from a fantastic ventilation system, which leaves no remnant of smoke except for a faint and altogether pleasant musk.

32 Watts St (near Canal St.)
212-941-1781
Sun-Mon 5pm-2am,
Tues-Sat 5pm-4am
① Ⓐ Ⓒ Ⓔ to Canal St
Average Drink $13
Cigars $15-30

S.O.B.'s
Live Music, DJs

At this renowned venue for world music—with a special focus on Brazilian and Caribbean vibes—the young and old mingle together to show of their dance moves, imbibe cool caipirinhas, and revel in live beats. The minimally adorned, swanky space offers nightly events inspired by everything from Afro-Brazilian to salsa grooves. Catch your breath from dancing on their expansive and often packed floor to lounge at a small tables along the wall or near the back bar. The menu features generous portions of Latin and Brazilian specialties, like grilled snapper and feijoada, and the bar serves everything from domestic Bud to Cuban mojitos. Whether stopping by for a drink after work, shaking it at a late night samba session, or going for a private party, Sounds Of Brazil's promises to deliver a top notch multi-sensory experience.

204 Varick St (at Houston St)
212-243-4940
Sun-Thurs 7pm-2am, Fri
5pm-5am, Sat 7pm-5am
① to Houston St
Average Drink $8
Tickets $10-$35

CHINATOWN

Over 130 years ago, the first Chinese immigrants began moving eastward to escape discrimination in the western states. Today, what was once a tiny community of 200 Cantonese has become one of the largest Chinese communities in the western hemisphere, with almost 300,000 people representing every region of China.

Vivid yellow and red banners spell out Chinese advertisements for dim sum palaces and Fujianese bakeries. Hawkers stand on corners ready to lead tourists to rooms full of knock-off Coach purses and counterfeit perfumes, and honking cars drown out the Mandarin tones of casual conversations. Produce vendors' stalls overflow with ripe lychee and durian, and fishmongers pitch seafood so fresh, it's swimming till it's sold. Prepared food is similarly unbeatable—this isn't your hometown General Tso's Chicken. Here restaurant owners prepare the best dishes of their home provinces. Menus tend to be written in regional dialects, so you might have to resort to the language of pointing and signing, but the fantastically cheap prices and authentic fare make it worth the effort. Recently, Canal Street's packed sidewalks swarm with ambitious out-of-towners armed with steely resolutions to haggle, but Mott and Bowery Streets provide the real Chinatown experience. The stalls on these side streets are filled with shining fish eyes, porcelain tea kettles, wizened ginseng roots, and tiger-penis aphrodisiacs—a bizarre bazaar, indeed.

Chinatown seems caught in perpetual chaos, with too many people doing too much in too small a space—and indeed, the neighborhood is bursting out of its seams. Rapidly rising rents have slowed Chinatown's expansion and threaten to send it the way of its neighbors. Having successfully reduced Little Italy to a single-street, Disneyland-like simulacrum of its former self, Chinatown is now gunning for the Lower East Side and even SoHo.

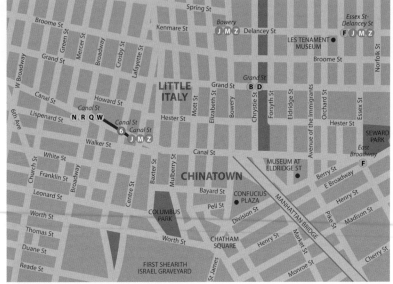

EXPLORE

Asian American Arts Center

Founded in 1974 as the Asian American Dance Theatre, this museum and cultural center is devoted to fostering the

26 Bowery (at Bayard St)
212-233-2154
Mon-Wed & Fri 12:30-6:30pm, Thurs 12:30-7:30pm
B D to Grand St, **6**
N Q R W J M Z to Canal St

growth of Asian American artistic and creative expression. It accomplishes this through a vast network of programs and resources, which include performance presentations, folk arts research and documentation, exhibitions, catalogue publication, and public education. The permanent collection contains hundreds of art pieces, ranging from traditional folk art to postmodern sculpture, and the Center also stores one of the largest historical archives of Asian American artists, with records dating back to 1945. Don't miss the annual Lunar New Year Folk Arts Festival, where you can participate in hands-on arts and crafts demonstrations from experienced artisans.

Columbus Park

In the middle of the glorious chaos that is Chinatown lies a small center of tranquility at Columbus Park.

67 Mulberry St (near Bayard St)
Daily 8am-9pm
6 N Q R W J M Z
to Canal St

Formally known as The Five Points, the stomping ground of local Irish gangs in the 19th Century, the park is now a favorite spot for the locals who come out in rain or shine for their daily games of Mahjong and Chinese Checkers. There are few better places in the city to people-watch on a nice day. The recent renovations, including a new field perfect for lounging in and a restoration of the park's ornamented pavilion, make Columbus Park a great place to pass the hours. For those looking for more vigorous activity, there are basketball courts and playgrounds, where a much younger set of locals can be found.

Mahayana Buddhist Temple

Feeling meditative? There couldn't be a better place to forget the aggressive crowds of Chinatown than

133 Canal St
(at Manhattan Bridge Plz)
212-925-8787
Daily 8am-6pm
B D to Grand St
Free

the Mahayana Buddhist Temple, just a few blocks east of Canal Street's most hectic stretch. The dissonant echo of singing voices ushers you into the vestibule, where you can light an incense stick or leave an offering of fruit at the impressive shrine that greets you just inside the doors. A little further on you'll encounter the most dramatic space in the building: the main temple, where the spiritual proceedings are watched over by a giant gold Buddha—said to be the biggest in New York—lit by a distinctly urban halo of blue neon. Upstairs is a sleek, well-lit gift shop stocking everything from ying-yang tank tops to intricate ivory sculptures. Before leaving, take a rolled-up fortune—a $1 donation to the temple gets you a slip of paper with five nuggets of prophetic wisdom (cookie not included).

Museum of Chinese in the Americas

Situated before a former industrial repair shop, this museum brings the history of Chinatown to life with its bevy of cultural artifacts. Its collections, which are constantly

	211 Centre St (btwn Howard & Grand St)
	212-619-4785
	Mon 11am-5pm, Thurs 11am-9pm, Fri 11am-5pm, Sat-Sun 10am-5pm
	⑥ⓃⓄⓇⓌⒿⓂⓏ to Canal St
	$7, Free Thurs

developing, have been showcased in exhibits such as the Chinese Musical and Theatrical Association (CMTA) Collection—which featured 108 articles, including approximately 26 intricate opera costumes and 24 rare instruments—and Fly to Freedom, a collection of 123 paper sculptures of passengers who immigrated to America on the Golden Venture. It also hosts a great deal of offbeat cultural events like the Asian American ComiCon and the Asian American International Film Festival. A new location will soon house a permanent collection of old street signs and traditional lion headpieces.

SHOP

Aji Ichiban

Satisfy your sweet tooth— and whichever tooth is responsible for dried seafood cravings—at this popular Hong Kong-based confectionery. Inside the tidy, wood-paneled store you'll find a

DAY TO DAY

Community Board 3: 59 East 4th St, 212-553-5300.

Dry Cleaner/Tailor: 54 Cleaner, 48 Mulberry St # 2, 212-964-5566.

Groceries: Dynasty Supermarket, 68 Elizabeth St, 212-966-4943.

Hospital: Saint Vincent's Hospital Chinatown Clinic, 25 Elizabeth St, 212-431-5501. New York Downtown Hospital, 170 William St, 212-312-5000.

Media: *Downtown Express,* downtownexpress.com.

veritable emporium of East Asian treats. Browse their back wall for dried fruits, roots, and other delicacies, like plum,

	37 Mott St (at Pell St)
	212-233-7650
	Daily 10am-8pm
	⑥ⓃⓄⓇⓌ, ⒿⓂⓏ to Canal St

guava, peach, and ginger. If you're feeling more adventurous, try the dried squid, grouper, and satay fish. But the real treasures sit in the center of the store, where you can fill up on bags of imported Asian sweets like tea candy, pineapple rice cakes, and Thai coconut candy. More exotic offerings aren't exactly cheap (dried fruit and packaged candy will typically run you upwards of $10/lb, and some seafood and salted meats costs twice as much) but free samples are plentiful and well worth the visit.

Asia Market

Finding a food market in Chinatown is easy. Finding one that stocks everything you're looking for takes a

	71½ Mulberry St (Bayard St)
	212-962-2020
	Daily 8am-7pm
	⑥ⓃⓄⓇⓌ, ⒿⓂⓏ to Canal St

little more work: Enter Asia Market. Behind its unassuming storefront vegetable stand lies an extensive grocery selection that covers your needs without hurting your wallet. Imported tempura batter mix, rice crackers

with seaweed, and canned bamboo shoot tips are just a few of the bargains packed on their shelves. Large refrigerators stock desserts, frozen seafood, and Thai tea drinks. But half of the fun here comes from wandering through the unlabeled aisles and stumbling upon unexpected ingredients (the market specializes in Filipino, Thai, and Malaysian goods). For familiar fare, visit the epic wall of Ramen: a magnificent shrine to dorm room cuisine. Just $2 buys five packs of noodles in flavors far more exciting than the standard chicken broth.

Tai-Pan Bakery

At this Hong Kong- and Taiwanese-style bakery, visitors ogle freshly-baked items and speak in the language of pointing. Walk in and head

194 Canal St
(btwn Mott & Mulberry)
212-732-2222
Daily 7:30am-8pm
Ⓑ Ⓓ to Grand St, Ⓖ
Ⓝ Ⓠ Ⓡ Ⓦ Ⓙ Ⓜ Ⓩ to Canal St

to the back of the room for a stand of buns in a variety of flavors. The pineapple bun and pork bun are more authentic options, but the sugar doughnut and hot-dog bun are equally excellent. Once you've made your choice, move to the counter, where you can search through rows of smaller items—everything from pork pastries to fruit tarts—and also order your

drinks. Take your food with you or enjoy it on one of the few store benches outside. Just make sure you don't leave Tai-Pan without tasting an egg tart—this flaky puff-pastry is delicately crispy outside and custardy sweet within.

Yunhong Chopsticks

The Yunhong Chopstick brand is well-known in China, but as the staff at this sleek, tidy shop will proudly

50 Mott St (near Bayard St)
212-566-8828
Daily 10:30am-8:30pm
Ⓖ Ⓝ Ⓠ Ⓡ Ⓦ
Ⓙ Ⓜ Ⓩ to Canal St

tell you, this location is the company's first in the States. Dark shelves line the small boutique's walls, the perfect contrast to eye-catching displays of colorful chopstick sets. A quick glance reveals that these utensils have personality, but a closer inspection finds beautiful chopsticks crafted out of wood and crystal. Some pairs feature official characters from the Beijing Olympics—there's even a set engraved with "Chairman Mao's Favorite Phrases." Pick up a pack of neat, unadorned plastic sticks for just a few bucks, or go all out for a $590 mahogany set. The chopsticks here make distinctive Chinatown souvenirs, and the attractive space is a pleasure to browse—even for die-hard devotees of the fork.

LITTLE ITALY

Now consigned to a mere four blocks of Mulberry Street, Little Italy once sprawled out as far as Canal and Houston. Transformed by a rapid influx of Italian immigrants in the early 20th century, this Manhattan neighborhood has seen its original population trickle away to establish Little Italies in the Bronx, Queens, Brooklyn, and Staten Island. Impacted by the continuing expansion of Chinatown to the south and east and encroaching Nolita boutiques to the north, what remains of the Manhattan original is now a bustling tourist destination. Native New Yorkers usually avoid the neighborhood's cookie cutter checkered-tablecloth cafés and go elsewhere for authentic Italian fare, but local attractions make Little Italy worth a visit. The **Old St. Patrick's Cathedral** (*260-264 Mulberry St*), constructed in the 1810s, served as the shooting location for several scenes from the *Godfather* Trilogy. **DiPalo's Fine Foods** (*200 Grand St*) is one of several Italian groceries in the area, offering the best in imported ingredients to fine restaurants and consumers alike. And at the **San Gennaro Festival** in September, the streets teem with live music, parades, and activities. Keep an eye out for the **Feast of San Gennaro**, where visitors can gorge on gluttonous treats.

EAT

Banh Mi Saigon Bakery — *Vietnamese*

138 Mott St (near Grand St)
212-941-1541
Tues-Sun 10am-7pm, Mon closed
Ⓑ Ⓓ to Grand St, Ⓕ
Ⓝ Ⓞ Ⓡ Ⓦ Ⓙ Ⓜ Ⓩ to Canal St
Entrees $4-6
Cash Only

Despite being tucked inconspicuously behind a jewelry store counter, this Vietnamese sandwich shop's endless train of customers ensures that it's difficult to miss. Even with the glut of banh mi shops opening all over town, patient locals wait it out to grab a sandwich from this tiny Chinatown spot. Prices start as low as $3.75 for the traditional pork banh mi and peak at a whopping $5.50 for vegetable spring rolls. The traditional and much-loved Vietnamese sandwich comes with your choice of pork or chicken, packed between slices of slightly sweet, baguette-like bread. Sandwiches are also garnished with a spicy sauce and stuffed with carrots, cucumbers, peppers, and plenty of cilantro—as wonderfully salty, sweet, and fresh as a good banh mi ought to be. Portions are large enough to share, but with prices this low, why bother?

Big Wong King — *Chinese*

67 Mott St (near Canal St)
212 964 0540
Ⓖ Ⓝ Ⓞ Ⓡ Ⓦ Ⓙ Ⓜ Ⓩ to Canal St
Appetizers $4-6,
Entrees $8-15, Congee $3-5

It may look like every other restaurant in the neighborhood, but Big Wong King boasts some of the most flavorful Cantonese dishes at cheap prices, drawing crowds of Chinese foodies for over 30 years. Don't expect outlandish spices and egregious amounts of fat. The portions are decent, the plates are consistently well-prepared, and the flavors are subtle yet satisfying. The typical Chinese dish—beef and broccoli—is cooked with meat so tender and light it's almost soothing on the tongue. The broccoli actually retains the taste of a vegetable—unusual for a cheap Chinese joint in the city. The roast duck is hearty and fresh, and the congee (rice porridge) is filling yet light. Dishes here are far from greasy and over-spiced—no wonder it's a favorite among Chinese expats.

Chinatown Ice Cream Factory — *Dessert*

65 Bayard St (near Mott St)
212-608-4170
Sun-Sat 11am-10pm or 11pm ("depending on weather")
Ⓑ Ⓓ to Grand St, Ⓕ
Ⓝ Ⓞ Ⓡ Ⓦ Ⓙ Ⓜ Ⓩ to Canal St
$3.75 per scoop

Tiny though it may be, Chinatown Ice Cream Factory is easily identified by the massive hanging flag of a chubby green dragon holding a tub of ice cream—its insignia, all but plastered on every wall of this joint. Underneath the dragon, a sidewalk-stretching line of devotees wait to order some of the best (and strangest) ice cream in New York. The menu often surprises new customers: vanilla is termed exotic, whereas pandan, red bean, and zen butter—which tastes of rich caramel and cream—are all listed as standard. For an unusual textural experience, try the cupcake ice cream—it's chock full of teeny bits of cupcake icing. And be on the lookout flavor oddities like wasabi and avocado that occasionally appear amongst tamer options. Whether drawn here by curiosity or an unexpected craving for black sesame ice cream, most people find a reason to return.

Doyers Vietnamese Restaurant
Vietnamese

11 Doyers Street (near Bowery)
212-513-1527
Sun-Thurs 11-10, Fri-Sat 11-11
Ⓕ to East Broadway
Appetizers $3-6, Entrees $7-11

In the heart of Chinatown, tucked into a basement on the forbidding, somewhat dilapidated Doyers Street is some of the most authentic Vietnamese food in New York. With nearly 300 items listed, the menu at Doyers Vietnamese Restaurant can be a bit overwhelming. Thankfully for the first-timer and regular alike, both Vietnamese classics and the more unusual dishes are prepared with equal skill, showcasing the sweet, complex flavors of Vietnamese cuisine. Old favorites like grilled lemongrass chicken, satay beef, and pho (traditional soup noodles) are a good starting place before venturing into less familiar territory like frog legs and eel. And with prices this low you should feel free to bring the whole gang—it's literally a bargain basement.

Food Sing 88 Corp
Noodles

2 East Broadway
(near Catherine St)
212-219-8223
Daily 9:30am-10pm
Ⓕ to East Broadway
Noodles $4-7
Cash Only

The noodle soups at the strangely named Food Sing 88 Corp are cheap, fast, and absolutely delicious. Wedged into a corner of Chinatown between the Manhattan and Brooklyn Bridge overpasses, Food Sing 88 Corp is immediately recognizable by the window into its tiny kitchen where cooks pull noodles by hand. The meats on offer along with these house-made noodles range from familiar standards like pork rib and beef steak to less common choices like stomach and

NATIVE'S PICK

Congee Village — *Chinese*

Tucked away from the droves of tourists on Canal Street, Congee Village keeps its credibility as a haven for authentic Cantonese cuisine with its mostly-Chinese clientele and a huge menu that will be largely unfamiliar to most American diners. Named after a popular Chinese rice porridge, Congee Village offers 30 different varieties of the the dish, in addition to a massive menu of atypical meats, fish, and vegetables. More familiar dishes such as juicy pork buns and Singapore noodles are equally delicious favorites and ideal for sharing. Go with a group and focus on the company and the food rather than the hilariously over-the-top décor, complete with floor to ceiling wood panelling and fake trees. Enormous, shareable portions, cheap drinks, and an atmosphere that takes kitsch to new heights ensure that an evening spent at Congee Village is as affordable as it is fun.

100 Allen St (near Delancy St)
212-941-1818
Daily 10:30am-12:30am
F J M Z to Essex St-
Delancy St, B D to Grand St
Entree $9-21,
Dim Sum $1-4

tail. For under $10, a bowl of the savory house special, which includes all of the aforementioned meats, will happily feed two people. The plain, cramped dining room and hasty wait staff won't encourage you to linger, but in warm weather the benches in Chatham Square just outside make a pleasant spot for some al fresco noodle slurping.

Nice Green Bo — *Shanghainese*

Don't judge a restuarant's food by its décor. The newspaper-plastered front window of this Chinatown staple isn't particularly inviting, but at one of their seven dinner tables you'll eat some of the best—and cheapest—Shanghainese specialties in the city. Steamed pork and crab tiny buns are tender and juicy, and the scallion pancake promises a crispy golden crust and soft, onion-studded insides. Appetizers are supplemented by a substantial range of classic seafood and

66 Bayard St
(btwn Mott & Elizabeth St)
212-625-2359
Mon-Sun 11am-11pm
6 N O R W,
J M Z to Canal St
Appetizers $2-7, Entrees $7-13
Cash Only

meat entrees, like the beef with mushrooms and bamboo shoots, and the inimitable lo mein, mei fun, rice cakes, and pan fried noodles. Bring friends to share the generous servings and prepare to sit next to strangers in whatever seating available.

Prosperity Dumpling — *Chinese*

The single element of décor that stands out at this humble Chinese dumpling shop is its English awning—the only one on its block. Otherwise Prosperity Dumpling is grubby Chinatown all the way. It is the work that goes on in the shabby cooking space that gives this spot an edge. With the kitchen in full view, half the fun of a visit to Prosperity Dumpling is watching the cooks churn out these plump, stuffed wonders with astonishing speed. The limited seating (there are only six barstools in the whole "restaurant")

46 Eldridge St #1 (near Hester St)
212-343-0683
Daily 7:30am-9pm
B D to Grand St,
F to East Broadway
Dumplings $1-2,
Noodles & Buns $1-3
Cash Only

make take-out the best option. Both pork and mixed vegetable dumplings are available at the almost-unbelievable price of 5 for $1. For those seeking more than a dumpling fix, Prosperity offers huge quantities of steaming hot soups, as well as various noodle and pancake dishes to supplement a plate of the namesake snack.

PLAY

Lolita
Lounge

The exposed brick, low lighting, comfortable leather couches, and short wooden stools encourage conversation with youthful strangers and familiars alike at this low-key lounge. Stand at the bar, kick back in the main lounge area, marvel at the (purchasable) local wall art, or head downstairs for a private party—Lolita

266 Broome St (near Allen St)
212-966-7223
Daily 5pm-4am
B D to Grand St,
F J M Z to Essex-Delancey St Average Drink $6
Happy Hour: Daily 5-8pm

guarantees a fun, laidback experience with a bit of class and no pretense. A well-stocked bar holds your favorite standards of bottles, tap, and spirits listed at reasonable prices, so pass through for a drink or camp out here for the night. Regardless, the recognizable tunes spinning in the front room and prompt service from the bartenders guarantee fun.

Santos Party House
Dance Club, Live Music, DJs

Beneath the swirling haze of green, purple, and red lights hangs a neon sign that reads: "Party is our middle name." Both levels of this music venue and dance club are packed before midnight with a crowd of quirkily dressed partiers, ranging in age from 18 to 50. It's no place to play the shy kid—waste more than a moment catching your breath and a

96 Lafayette St
(near Canal St)
212-584-5492
Hours vary by event,
Doors btwn 7pm &11pm
6 N Q R W,
J M Z to Canal St
Average Drink $8
Cover up to $15

NATIVE'S PICK

The East Side Company

East Side Company Bar
Cocktail Lounge

Bar czar Sasha Petraske, of Milk & Honey fame, brings freshly squeezed juice cocktails to the unpretentious twenty-somethings that come to this unmarked cocktail lounge. Tucked inconspicuously next to a pickle store, East Side Company Bar sets itself apart with exquisitely crafted drinks, mixed and poured with elegant precision. A classic pressed tin wall curves into the ceiling, dimly lit by a long row of wall candles that cast a warm, intimate glow from the front bar to the back booths. Thursday Reggae nights and a DJ booth, often occupied by two of the bar's owners, rejuvenate the classic speakeasy for a younger crowd. Though the most popular drinks are the Old Cuban and the champagne-sweet Love Affair, try one made with egg whites for something more adventurous—or stop by on slower Tuesdays, when the bartenders mess around with new concoctions.

49 Essex St (near Grand St)
212-614-7508
Mon-Sat 7pm-4am
F J M Z to Essex-Delancey St, **B D** to Grand St
Average Cocktail $12
Happy Hour: Mon-Sat 7-10pm Cocktails $7, $2 off all other drinks

metamorphose to the rock, hip hop, and house played by regular DJs and live music.

LOWER EAST SIDE

Once boasting a population as densely packed as present day Bombay, the Lower East Side has been home to immigrants as long as the city's had them. Irish and German families crammed into its dilapidated tenements in the mid-1800s, Poles and Ukrainians later peddled housewares and established tiny clothing stores on Orchard Street, and Yiddish theaters hosted the first gigs of George Gershwin and the Marx Brothers around the turn of the century

The newest transplants are not poor, huddled masses but yuppie creative types looking for converted loft space. They've abandoned uptown hangouts and emigrated in droves to open up bars, bistros, and clubs, prompting New York publications to unanimously declare the Lower East Side "up-and-coming." Galleries that moved there in the 80s are burgeoning with a success that rivals the Chelsea scene. A tolerance for high-minded experimentation has also drawn some of the city's best chefs to Clinton and Allen Streets. And the nightlife crowd is a who's who of trendsetters, from Salvation Army hipsters across the river to gauche young professionals with company AmExes.

Today the neighborhood is a cultural mosaic of old and new. Upscale boutiques and pricey restaurants stand next to family-run tailors and pickle stores. One of the city's most historic museums lies blocks from one of its newest and most avant-garde. The sign on Orchard Street that reads "Bargain District" may now be more ironic than historic, but past and present have made peace living side by side. Coalitions like the Lower East Side Conservancy work to maintain the delicate balance and prevent rapid gentrification.

If the Lower East Side's history is a saga of immigration trends, then it's fitting that Chinatown is leaking in from the west. The continuing influx of mainland Chinese means the neighborhood's present, as well as its future, once again bears the stamp of another country. More practically, it means dumpling houses and delis on Grand St. America's melting pot is a delectable thing.

EXPLORE

ABC No Rio

Across from an ordinary bodega on an ordinary street lies this decidedly extraordinary old building, covered in colorful graffiti from the ground up. Though it began as a gallery for the community, ABC No Rio now also houses a screenprinting studio, a darkroom, a radical 'zine library, and a computer lab. Use of their resources can be had for a moderate fee, usually on the honor system. They also host weekly poetry readings and experimental performances that reflect the gallery's diversity. Visitors are of all ages, genders, and races, and are—like the art featured—very politically minded. It's the ultimate counter-culture resource center for the starving artists of the Lower East Side.

156 Rivington St
(btwn Clinton & Suffolk)
212-254-3697
Hours Vary
F **J** **M** **Z** to Essex St-
Delancey St
Admission varies by event

Bowery Ballroom

The Bowery Ballroom is regarded as one of the best intimate venues in the country—everyone's favorite band eventually stops in for a fun, well-delivered show. The tri-level Ballroom hosts mostly 18+ events, showcasing everything from hot new international weirdos to established locals and even the occasional icon. Past performers include Coco Rosie, the Yeah Yeah Yeahs, and Monotonix. The lower level is a dark, booth-lined, red-lit swanky lounge with a well-stocked bar. Stairs lead up to the performance hall, which has renowned acoustics and sight lines, a wide stage, a bar, and a spacious, semi-crowded standing area for 550 music fans. Expect to mingle and dance with plenty of other fans—and even the musicians.

6 Delancey St
(btwn Bowery & Chrystie St)
212-533-2111
Most shows start 7pm-9pm
6 to Spring St,
B **D** to Grand St, **F** **V** to
2nd Ave-Lower East Side,
J **M** **Z** to Bowery
Tickets $10-$25
Tickets sold online,
Cash only at the door,
Most shows 18+

East River Park

Designed about 80 years ago as a companion to FDR Drive, East River Park spans almost 60 acres. Boasting some of the best views of the East River, the park offers great recreational facilities for basketball, tennis, handball, softball, football, baseball, and track. Other visitors can fish, picnic, or bike alongside the river promenade. The recently restored 1,000-seat East River amphitheater, which overlooks the waterfront, is the site of a regular concert series and plays host to various performances throughout the year. Footbridges over the expressway offer easy access at 10th and Delancey Streets.

East River (btwn Montgomery St & E 12th St)
Daily 6am-1am
🄵🄹🄼🅉 to Essex St-Delancey St, 🄻 to 1st Ave

New Museum

Seven silvery stories stack oh-so-precariously on top of each other, varying in size and presiding over the run-down wholesalers that line Bowery. Let the Met have its volute columns, the Guggenheim its inconvenient spiral—the New

DAY TO DAY

Community Board 3: 59 E 4th St, 212-533-5300

Dry Cleaning: Special Touch Valet Cleaner, 559 Grand St, 212-677-5810.

Grocery: Whole Foods, 95 E Houston St, 212-420-1320.

Gym: Ludlow Fitness, 100 Delancey St, 212-260-9222.

Hospital: Gouverneur Hospital, 227 Madison, 212-238-7000.

Laundromat: Lau's Wash and Dry, 123 Rivington St, 212-777-8541.

Library: Chatham Square Branch of NYPL, 33 E Broadway.

Media: savethelowereastside.blogspot.com.

Volunteer Opportunities: Lower East Side Tenement Museum, tenement.org/jobs.html.

Tenement Museum   *Museum*

This tours-only museum is a darling of city history buffs—and interactive enough for fanny-packed families and elementary school groups to enjoy. Explore the city's rich immigrant history by taking one of five themed tours, capped at 15 people. Tour guides begin by asking the visitors' immigrant histories and encourage group discussion—which is informative and surprisingly engaging—throughout the tour. Groups cram into the tiny foyer of the restored tenement building and wind their way through a few of the six total restored apartments, where layers of wallpaper and linoleum tell tales from before the Panic of 1873 to after the Great Depression. Museum-sponsored Tenement Talks and Kitchen Conversation events are sure to satiate the curious mind—and check out the gift shop for, among other things, a book of paper Obama dolls.

> 108 Orchard St (near Canal St)
> 212-982-8420
> Daily 10am-6pm
> **B D** to Grand St, **F J M Z**
> to Essex St-Delancey St
> Adults $20, Students $15

Museum shatters artistic convention almost as much as the art it houses. Made of materials stripped, exposed, and raw, the building is a nod to neighborhood grit. Subtly angled walls give way to skinny skylights, so a new day brings new light to the avant-garde art. Each floor is a gallery, and none are home to a permanent collection. The ground floor is also a loading dock and café, free to the public and built of glass walls, as if to punctuate that fact. Past exhibits include "Younger than Jesus," featuring artists born after 1976, and "Rigo 23," installation art inspired by political prisoners.

> 235 Bowery St (at Prince St)
> 212-219-1222
> Wed, Sat & Sun 12pm-6pm,
> Thurs-Fri 12pm-9pm,
> Mon-Tues closed
> **B D F V** to Broadway-
> Lafayette St, **J M Z** to
> Bowery, **R W** to Prince St,
> **6** to Spring St
> Adults $12, Students $8,
> 18 and Under Free

Sarah D. Roosevelt Park

Artists, gym bodies, elderly immigrants, and young families all gather under the shade of this narrow, multi-facility park in the heart of the Lower East Side. Trees tower over worn chalk on the park's three playgrounds. Benches look onto a new synthetic turf soccer field, often home to shirts-versus-skins matches. Wide steps at the park's Houston entrance act as spillover seating for Whole Foods folk who meander over and stay to watch a heated basketball game on the full sized courts at the north end of the park. The park's volunteer-maintained M'Finda Kalunga Garden is an adorably unkempt natural space, complete with toddler benches and vine covered archways. A roller-skating rink, senior center, and some checkerboard tables round out the park as a community space for locals young and old.

> Chrystie St & Forsythe St
> (btwn E Houston St & Canal St)
> **B D** to Grand St, **F J M Z**
> to Essex St-Delancey St

SHOP

Babycakes NYC

This corner bakery is a different breed from many of its compatriots, as its mission is to serve sweets to New Yorkers no matter their dietary restrictions. Much of the delicious, colorful delectables are vegan-friendly, gluten-free, sugar-free, egg-free, and kosher. This coffee shop uses Agave nectar to sweeten its treats, and each cupcake comes in two varieties: baked

248 Broome St
(btwn Orchard St & Ludlow St)
212-677-5047
Two-for-One Mon 10am-8pm,
Tues-Thurs 10am-10pm,
Fri-Sat 10am-11pm,
Sun 10am-8pm
F J M Z to Essex St-
Delancey St

with spelt flour or with gluten-free garbanzo/fava bean flour. Besides coffee and the huge variety of cupcakes, the bakery offers loaves, brownies, cookie sandwiches, cinnamon buns, pies, and a host of other pastries. If you dare, try the store's unique speciality: the frosting shots. Everyone knows that frosting is the best part of the cupcake—and this frosting is rich and frothy going down, without being heart-clogging.

Bluestockings

At first glance the paper lanterns, plastic patio furniture, and vegan cookies distinguish this bookstore-café from

172 Allen St
(btwn Stanton & Rivington St)
212-777-6028
Daily 11am-11pm
F V to 2nd Ave-Lower
East Side

its counterparts—but the real division lies in Bluestockings' self-proclaimed status as a "radical bookstore, fair trade café, and activist center."

The name pays homage to the Blue Stockings Society, a female literary society in the 1700s, and only hints at what books stock the shelves. The literature focuses on topics such as anarchism, feminism, class, and labor. Bluestockings hosts community events nearly every night of the week, including open-mic nights and readings—and the store regularly supports movements that challenge oppression and hierarchy.

Green Depot

Whether you're light green curious or dark green committed, this one-of-a-kind eco-friendly home improvement store offers enough effective b i o d e g r a d a b l e alternatives to make

222 Bowery (near Prince St)
212-226-0444
Mon-Thurs 10am-7pm, Fri-Sat
10am-8pm, Sun 11am-6pm
6 to Spring St,
F to 2nd Ave, **B D F V**
to Broadway-Lafayette St,
J M Z to Bowery,
R W to Prince St,

Al Gore squeal with glee. Built on the site of the original YMCA, this shop carries hypo-allergenic paints and cleaners, biodegradable kitchen bags, and recycled glasses. Their Natural Solutions Cleaning Kit makes a great gift for green newbies at $34.50, but the best deals are on "oops paints" (color gaffes), retailing for 50% off. Bring in your own container and fill up on cleaning fluids for 12 cents/ounce from the five different beer tap-

like spouts. Giant signs of "How We See Green" and framed facts about green living hang on the walls, demystifying the eco-friendly lifestyle and making the shopping experience as educational as it is enjoyable.

Reed Space

This is a mecca of locally-made, high-quality street and skate wear. From the graphic tees to the windbreakers and hats, the focus here is both the design and the designer. Except for those insiders familiar with names like Penfield, most labels will be unknown, but Reed Space doesn't simply sell the brands they carry—it aims to support and promote the up-and-coming companies as well. Descriptions of each brand's history hang above the racks and tables of graphic tees, hats, and colorful windbreakers. Hanging from a wall is an impressive and artistic display of magazines stacked onto small, white chairs hung from the wall. Neighboring them is a collection of CDs, Lomography cameras, and hard-to-find watches that will satisfy any remaining desire for street-wise merchandise.

151 Orchard St
(btwn Stanton St & Rivington St)
212-253-0588
Mon-Fri 1-7pm,
Sat-Sun 12-7pm
🄕🅥 to 2nd Ave, 🄕🄙🄜🅩
to Essex St-Delancey St

Some Odd Rubies

Dare to imagine it—a vintage store without shoulder pads! The owners of this boutique scour estate sales for vintage dresses languishing on lost racks and revive them with updated fittings and designs. Most of the fabrics are synthetic or silk, and the expert transformations create beautiful new looks. Light and fluttering summer dresses in bright floral patterns and sophisticated black pieces are the main offerings. Because each dress is made from a unique piece of vintage clothing, you can rest assured that every item in the store is unlike anything on the shelves of the mega-chains. Prices reflect the rarity of the garments, but these gems are worth it. They also sell ornate, dangling earrings, over-sized golden bracelets, and shirts in standout patterns with daring necklines. You'll be treasure hunting here all afternoon.

151 Ludlow St
(btwn Stanton & Rivington St)
212-353-1736
Mon-Fri 1-8pm,
Sat-Sun 12-8pm
🄕🅥 to 2nd Ave-Lower
East Side

The Sound Library

Walk down the gritty stairwell to a stark, white room with hardwood floors, precisely organized vinyls, and little else. The focus here is the music, evidenced by the three neat rows of records that decorate the walls and the white cubbyholes of plastic-sleeved albums. Collectors, tourists, and music aficionados come to buy, sell, and swap LPs. The Sound Library features an expansive

165 Orchard St
(near Stanton St)
212-460-4800
Mon-Sun 12pm-8pm
🄕🅥 to 2nd Ave-
Lower East Side

UNDER $20

LOWER EAST SIDE

Get your caffeine fix with a side of vegan pastries at **Teany** (*90 Rivington St*), the delightfully progressive little café by musician Moby. If bagels are more your speed, head to **Russ & Daughters** (*179 E Houston St*) for the best smoked salmon south of 14th St. Then browse the different merchants that set up at the indoor **Essex St Market** (*120 Essex St*) for a free dose of culture or a cheap bag of fresh fruit. Go across the street to visit **The Pickle Guys** (*49 Essex St*) for a 75-cent treat of the green and sour variety and munch on your snack as you walk.

selection of the essential, the obscure, and the old school in rap, hip-hop, R&B, soul, and disco. They also have a respectable selection of jazz, Latin, and Brazilian records. De La Soul, Marly Marl, and everything in between goes for $5 and up—and when the albums are signed, way up. But browse the boxes of "Budget Disco," "Budget Hip Hop," and "Budget Soul" and you can still snag Biggie's Notorious single for $3.

EAT

Allen & Delancey — *New American*

Buffed mahogany and rich black leather cover every inch of this cozy, discrete Lower East Side notable. The space is lit almost exclusively by wall candles, casting shadows over

115 Allen St (at Delancey St)
212-253-5400
Dinner Mon-Sat 6pm-10pm,
Sun 6pm-10pm,
Bar & Lounge Sun, Mon, Wed,
& Thurs 5:45pm-11pm, Tue,
Fri, & Sat 5:45pm-2am
🄵🄹🄼🅉 to Essex St-
Delancy St, 🄱🄳 to Grand St
Average Meal $40

books, pictures, and knick-knacks that suggest a colonial-era library or the boudoir of an English intellectual. An "Arctic char tartar" is as much fun to eat as it is to say, with pungent yuzu jelly cutting through the rich fish. The summer sea bass is layered with preserved tomatoes and crisp phyllo-dough, the flavors and textures perfectly suited to the delicate fillet. The comfortable bar up front serves inventive and potent cocktails as subtly elegant as the back dining room. The crowd, chic as the space, maintains a kind of secretive calm amid the candlelight, making Allen & Delancey feel like a marvelous secret— one you'll be hard-pressed to keep.

Café Katja — *German*

It gets loud and crowded in this cozy, rustic Austrian spot where the taps pour steins of imported brews and the kitchen turns out rich, meaty dishes for discerning

79 Orchard St (near Broome St)
212-219-9545
Sun-Thurs 5pm-11pm,
Fri-Sat 5pm-12am
🄵🄹🄼🅉 to Essex-Delancey St,
🄱🄳 to Grand St
Salads & Snacks $4-12,
Mains $6-16

carnivores. Try the creamy liverwurst, topped with sweet red onion jam and served with freshly toasted bread to start. The sausage sampler entree, perfect for splitting between two or more, is a staggering smattering of juicy pork belly, moist bratwurst, crispy links, tangy sauerkraut, and hearty dumplings. The extraordinarily tender Austrian meatballs come topped with crisp pieces of fried onions and served on a bed of mashed potatoes, gravy, and roasted carrots. Though beer is the beverage for such hearty fare, Katja supplements its selection of brews with a wine list drawn primarily from Central Europe, as well as a large selection of schnapps.

Clinton Street Baking Company — *Brunch*

Diners patient enough to snag tables at this beloved breakfast and brunch spot are rewarded with buttery banana-topped French toast, sugar-cured bacon, and fruity grits. Peer

4 Clinton St
(btwn Houson & Stanton St)
646-602-6263
Mon-Fri 8am-4pm & 6pm-
11pm, Sat 10am-4pm & 6pm-
11pm, Sun 10am-4pm
🄵🅅 to 2nd Ave-
Lower East Side
Brunch $9-15, Baked Goods
$2-3, Lunch & Dinner $10-17
Cash Only

into the busy kitchen until you can grab a breakfast plate, a savory counterpart to the giant scones and biscuits offered in the bakery. The unpretentious simple wood paneling and old photos keep the focus on the food, and über-comfortable booths and chairs support the ballooning weight of sated patrons. Lunch and dinner menus offer continent-sized Po' Boy sandwiches and Buttermilk Fried Chicken, as well as breakfast favorites like the Wild Main Blueberry Pancakes. Etta James croons over the speakers, while the customers rightly ignore their guilt and line up to order extra muffins.

through **Sara D. Roosevelt Park** (*Forsyth & Chrystie btwn Houston St & Canal St*)—check out the community garden if it's open, or just snag a bench and watch a soccer or basketball game. Hit up **Falai Panetteria** (*79 Clinton St*) for popular $10 plates of pasta and panini, but be sure to save room for dessert: the dizzyingly well-stocked **Economy Candy** (*108 Rivington*) sells sugar highs at sweet prices. End (or start) your night by dancing at **Bob Bar** (*235 Eldridge*)—it's packed, more fun than an annoyingly posh club, and free before 10pm.

Freemans

New American

End of Freemans Alley
(off Rivington St btwn Bowery
& Chrystie St)
212-420-0012
Brunch Sat-Sun, 10am-4pm,
Lunch Mon-Fri, 11am-4pm,
Dinner Daily 6pm-11:30pm
Ⓕ Ⓥ to 2nd Ave-Lower East
Side, Ⓙ Ⓜ Ⓩ to Bowery
Appetizers $6-15,
Entrees $13-26

The recent expansion of the Lower East Side's best-loved, back-alley haunt has cut down on waits, but not on the feel of cozy exclusivity diners enjoy in its dimly-lit dining room. Taxidermy-lined walls and a gold ceiling evoke an early-American hunting lodge, the perfect place to sip a Freeman's Cocktail (a sweet, complex concoction of rye, lemon juice, and pomegranate molasses) and feast on rustic American delicacies. Old-school hospitality from the attentive, young staff will help you through a menu including a lush artichoke and spinach dip and the Devils on Horseback (cheese-stuffed prunes wrapped in house-cured bacon that simultaneously melt, sizzle, and burst in your mouth). Follow with the impressive pork chops and down another signature cocktail or two. Stumbling from Freemans Alley back to the modern world, you will continue to bask in the old world glow of this clandestine gem.

Il Laboratorio Del Gelato

Dessert

95 Orchard St
(near Broome St)
212-343-9922
Mon-Sun 10am-7pm
Ⓑ Ⓓ to Grand St, Ⓕ Ⓙ Ⓜ Ⓩ
to Essex St-Delancy St,
Small Cup or Cone $3.25

The storefront is the store at this gelato and sorbet spot, started a few years ago by Ciao Bella founder Jon Snyder. With small batches, fresh local fruit, and an operation run entirely under one roof, Laboratorio scoops some of best flavors in the city. Peer through the open front window to watch someone peeling fresh mangos for tomorrow's gelato or packing pints to be shipped off to a restaurant in Queens. They have 200 flavors to their name and rotate the store's 20 daily offerings every couple hours—though

Bereket Turkish Kebab House

Turkish

187 E Houston St
(at Orchard St)
212-475-7700
Daily 24 Hours
Ⓕ Ⓥ to 2nd Ave-
Lower East Side
Appetizers $3-5,
Entrees $6-15

This neighborhood staple is packed from 7pm until early morning with herds of post-pub rovers looking to satiate late night cravings. Night-owls and food cart connoisseurs the world over clamor for Turkish doner kebab—the beloved street food of juicy, aromatic, spit-roasted lamb or beef that Bereket does to perfection. Order it in a pita sandwich with white and red sauce if you're planning to walk and eat. Or stick around the fast food-style digs and order the platter: a build-it-yourself joy served with rice pilaf, pita, a cucumber and tomato salad, and a heaping mound of meat. An order of flaky, pistachio baklava makes a perfect, not-too-sweet ending to your savory, late night indulgence.

there are always at least two types of chocolate available. Take advantage of samples to narrow down the mind-boggling array of options, which include flavors like Honey Lavender, Basil, and Rose Petal. Pair your frozen treat with one of three homemade toppings, or get the iced coffee—it comes chilled by coffee iced cubes.

Kampuchea
Cambodian

78 Rivington St (at Allen St)
212-529-3901
Lunch Fri-Sun 12pm-4pm,
Tues-Thurs 5:30pm-11:00pm,
Sat & Sun 5:30pm-12:00am,
Sun 5:30pm-10:30 pm
Ⓝ Ⓠ Ⓡ Ⓦ to 2nd Ave
Small plates $8-14,
Entrees $10-17

This laid-back spot, whose name means Cambodia in the Khmer language, brings the dynamic flavors of another Southeast Asian cuisine to the LES. The high-stooled noodle bar is lit by rustic chandeliers and natural light that floods through wall-to-wall windows, creating a stylish, no-fuss atmosphere. Among the many small plates on offer, the grilled sweet corn, dribbled with house-made chili mayo, chili powder, and coconut flakes, comes highly recommended by the exceptionally attentive staff. For main courses, both noodle soups and num pang (Cambodian sandwiches) are on offer. The subtler soups are loaded with vegetables, meats, and seafoods, and spiced with curry, jasmine, or basil. The num pang pack a more flavorful punch, combining various meats with pickled carrots, cucumber, cilantro, and chili mayo. With such rich offerings, Kampuchea makes a welcome culinary ambassador from its namesake nation.

Kuma Inn
Filipino, Thai

113 Ludlow St, 2nd fl
(near Delancey St)
212-353-8866
Sun & Tue-Thu 6pm-11pm, Fri-
Sat 6pm-12am, Mon closed
Ⓕ Ⓙ Ⓜ Ⓩ to Essex St-
Delancy St
Small Plates $7-13
BYOB

Up a set of unadorned and slightly grimy stairs, this LES Filipino favorite has the feel of an off-the-beaten-path find, the kind of anti-tourist place that New Yorkers relish so dearly. Chef King Phojanakong's Thai-Filipino heritage is on display both in the elegantly austere interior of light wood and streamlined angles, as well as in food that is both highly refined and wildly exciting to eat. Blissfully crisp sweet-and-salty Chinese sausage is cut with the pungency of a green chili-lime sauce. A dish of fried rice

crepes is sauced with the rich, savory, cryptically titled "Kuma bolognese." Be forewarned—the menu of small plates prompts continuous ordering that adds up to a check more than you may have expected, but the restaurant's BYOB policy, and the quality of the food will leave you sated and eager to return.

Russ & Daughters
Deli

179 Houston St
(btwn 2nd Ave & Chrystie St)
212-475-4880
Mon-Fri 8am-8pm, Sat 9am-
7pm, Sun 8am-5:30pm
Ⓕ Ⓥ to 2nd Ave-
Lower East Side, Ⓕ Ⓙ Ⓜ Ⓩ
to Essex St-Delancy St
Sandwiches $2-16,
Other goods vary by lb.

This is the type of place that makes you long for Old New York, a City you've heard of but have never seen. Well, take a look at the tin facade of Russ & Daughters; it's about as close as you can get these days. Inside this 90-year-old institution, the gorgeously lopsided handmade bagels come in every imaginable grain and flavor, and serve as vehicle for the deli's star: its fish. They offer herring, caviar, and seven different kinds of smoked salmon, fresh enough that availability rides on the season. Thankfully, Russ & Daughters is a place where you can afford to loosen both your wallet and your epicurean inhibitions. You can't go wrong here with the classic bialy and lox, but you could also branch out and try the "Super Heeb," a thickly layered concoction of whitefish, baked salmon salad, and wasabi-infused tobiko.

Shopsin's General Store · *American*

No parties larger than four, no to-go orders, and everyone seated must have a meal. This itsy-bitsy general store in Essex Market may look like an

Stall #16, Essex St Market
120 Essex St
(No Number)
Tues-Fri 9am-3pm,
Sat 9am-2pm
F J M Z to Essex-Delancey St
B D to Grand St
Brunch & Lunch $7-20

oversized family pantry—cheerful blue shelves carry miniature condiment bottles for customers and industrial-sized tubs for cooking—but it sure has a lot of rules. Rest assured, it's a friendly place where the waiters and short order cooks joke around and chat about the Mets between serving customers breakfast and lunch. The immensely varied menu features everything from an Asian Waldorf salad to Blisters on my Sisters (eggs, cheddar cheese, rice, and beans on corn tortillas). For lunch have a generously sized, creatively executed sandwich with a mound of skinny, crispy, and delightfully greasy fries. Trendy suits, old bikers, and even the odd lady-who-lunches all come for great plates and a helping of kitschy store humor.

Spitzer's Corner · *American*

Neighborhood hipsters and prepsters coexist peacefully at this gastropub, united by a shared preference for no-fuss fare and truly potent potables. Spitzer's is as casual as they

101 Rivington St
(near Ludlow St)
212-228-0027
Mon-Tue 12pm-3am, Wed-Fri
12pm-4am, Sat 10am-4am,
Sun 10am-3am
F J M Z to Essex St-
Delancy St
Snacks & Starters $4-11,
Entrees $9-19

come—every piece of the place, from the floor to the communal tables, was built from reclaimed wood. Gus' Pickles provide their signature tart, crisp complement to any of 40 available drafts, which include impressive (and unpronounceable) German and Belgian options. Main dishes are comfort foods reinvented, like truffle mac and cheese, and can

NATIVE'S PICK

The Slipper Room — *Burlesque*

167 Orchard St (at Stanton St)
212-253-7426
Tues-Sat 8pm-4am
F V to 2nd Ave-Lower East Side,
J M Z to Essex-Delancy St

Dedicated to offering some of life's simplest pleasures—alcohol, bawdy humor, and scantily clad dancing women—this burlesque and comedy bar has shows that run on most nights of the week. A crowd of young, hip, Lower East Side men and women show up regularly for the dancers' moves and the host's sharp wit. The show, though based on women dancing around in thongs and pasties, deliberately ends up being more amusing than arousing. It's clear that the performers have adjusted their acts specifically for the amusement of the audience, which contains a surprisingly even mix of guys and girls of all orientations, making their show a fun and funny tribute to the old art of burlesque.

sure satisfy even the hungriest of patrons. Enjoy a stuffed omelet and organic Bloody Mary at the weekend brunch—the perfect antidote to the hangover that, in all likelihood, could have started right here the night before.

Sugar Sweet Sunshine Bakery *Bakery*

126 Rivington St (btwn Essex & Norfolk)
212-995-1960
Mon-Thurs 8am-10pm, Fri 8am-11pm, Sat 10am-11pm, Sun 10am-7pm
F J M Z to Essex-Delancey St
Cupcakes $1.50 each, $18 per dozen

Between the orange walls adorned with images of flowers, hearts, sunshine, rainbows, and homely furnishings—duct taped plush chairs and footstools seemingly salvaged from a LES street sale—this homestyle bakery is as sweet as the delightful confections it sells. Moist chocolate, coconut, yellow, pumpkin and pistachio cakes fresh from the oven come topped with creamy mocha, lemon, and vanilla buttercream icings. The menu boasts eleven signature cupcakes, with catchy names like the "Ooey Gooey" and the "Lemon Yummy." Get

your Red Velvet served "Sassy" (with chocolate almond buttercream) or "Sexy" (with satin buttercream). If cupcakes don't satisfy your sweet tooth, there's a smattering of bundts, cookies, sweetbreads, shortcakes, brownies, butterscotch bars, and chilled banana and chocolate puddings. It's not the largest space—you may have to take your sweets to go—but this cozy nook feels worlds away from the gritty city.

PLAY

The Living Room *Live Music*

154 Ludlow St (near Stanton St)
212-533-7237
Sun-Thus 6pm-1am, Fri-Sat 6pm-4am
F V to 2nd Ave-Lower East Side
Average Drink $6

This acoustic rock music venue—best known as the place where Nora Jones got her start—attracts an easygoing crowd of all ages with its casual, welcoming vibe. Despite soaring ceilings, the vintage-inspired décor and plush red couches near the entrance

enliven the space with a homey feel. The Living Room showcases performers with varying styles—the only universal requirement is that the music be heartfelt and sincere. The front bar has space for patrons to hang out and chat, but most visitors opt to listen silently and attentively behind the velvet curtains that separate the two stages from the rest of the space. Upstairs is the smaller, more intimate Googie's Lounge, and past the bar lies the larger main stage. With up to ten sets per night, everyone is sure to find a show to enjoy at this cozy bar.

Max Fish
Lounge

One of Ludlow Street's oldest, largest, and brightest bars, Max Fish is a great place to kick off your night with $3 PBRs and some pool or pinball. Watch the

178 Ludlow St
(btwn Houston St &
Stanton St)
212-529-3959
Daily 5:30pm-4am
F V to 2nd Ave,
J M Z to Essex-Delancey St
Average Drink $4

skate videos or Kung Fu movies projected on the walls above local art. On a slow night, a drunk bartender might give you a free beer for guessing his favorite Lee Hazelwood song.

On a crowded night—and there are many during the summer—just getting to the counter can be a challenge as large groups of locals in various degrees of hipsterdom laze about in loud comaraderie. But on the best kind of night, you'll see Taylor Mead, the adorable 85-year-old Warhol superstar, get treated to a beer in the corner before going off on his nightly walk around the Lower East Side to feed stray cats.

Motor City Bar
Dive, DJs

Decorated like a tribute to the American car industry, Motor City Bar welcomes the weary with cheap drinks and hot-rod spirit. Despite what the name suggests, the crowd of this Lower

127 Ludlow Street
(btwn Rivington & Delancey)
212-358-1595
Daily 4pm-4am
F to Delancy,
J M Z to Essex St
Average Well Drink $5
Happy Hour Mon-Fri 4-7pm
Two-for-one drinks

East Side dive is a mix of plain-clothed hipsters and seasoned bar hoppers rather than hardcore motorists. Groove with a gyrating grindhouse go-go dancer moving to DJ-spun Nuggets Era garage rock spiked with the Cramps, Huey Smith & the Clowns, and lounge covers of Nirvana

underneath the disco ball. Or just enjoy a Stella on the car seat couch. It can get mellow on early or rainy nights—a perfect time to play Space Invaders or pinball below the neon Ford signage.

Parkside Lounge

Comedy, Music

A refuge from the nearby Ludlow party scene, this neo-gritty dive welcomes Lower East Side ramblers with a front bar and back room of nightly entertainment. The

317 East Houston
(between Avenue B and C)
212-673-6270
Daily 1pm-4am
F V to 2nd Ave,
J M Z to Essex St
Average Drink $6
Happy Hour 2-8pm

drink specials attract a mix of neighborhood mainstays and newcomers who enjoy the never-ending variety of live acts, including music, comedy, and burlesque. Not in the mood for a show? Chat up the friendly bartenders, try your hand at foosball, play a game of pool, or just enjoy the jukebox's steady stream of classic rock tunes. Though there's no food, "Parksizing" your favorite beer from sixteen to twenty-two ounces for $1 will leave you sated. This spot is roomier than most in the area, so it's perfect for groups of thirsty friends. Check the calendar for $4 liquid brunch mimosas, salsa dancing, Potluck Sundays, and other ecclectic events.

Sapphire Lounge

Dance Club

Despite its name, there's little lounging at this small club. While there are a few sparse tables lining one wall, nearly everyone is on the dance floor. A young

249 Eldridge St
(btwn Houston & Stanton St)
212-777-5153
Mon-Sat 7pm-4am,
Sun 8pm-4am
F V to 2nd Ave
Average Drink $5
Cover $5

crowd packs the space on busier weekends, making conversation near impossible and leaving no choice but to boogie. There's not much in the way of décor, unless a white wreath-like object behind the bar counts, but once you're dancing to pop ballads from the likes of Duran Duran and Beyoncé, it's difficult to notice anything beyond rhythm and sweat. Plus, most of your energy will probably go into avoiding collisions with the gyrating bodies near you, since quarters are especially close. There's no entrance fee before 10pm, but the late night $5 cover charge is well worth dancing 'til 4am.

FINANCIAL
DISTRICT

No New York neighborhood captures the historic evolution of the city better than the Financial District. On the labyrinthine, cobblestoned streets that wind through Manhattan's southern tip, cold gleaming glass-and-steel cathedrals of commerce stand alongside some of the oldest buildings in the country.

Devoured daily by commuters traveling by ferry, train, and tinted-glass Lincolns, the Financial District is, first and foremost, the center of global capitalism. The white-collared army that floods the narrow streets from nine to five bumps elbows with gaggles of wandering tourists hoping to snap a picture of America's past. Among the neighborhood's treasures is Bowling Green Park, New York City's oldest designated park. The Neo-Gothic Trinity Church, constructed in 1846, still stands at the foot of Wall Street, and its adjoining graveyard houses tombs dating back to the Revolution. The historic South Street Seaport in the east lies mere blocks from the brand new luxury high rises and modernist parks of Battery Park City.

The received wisdom is that the neighborhood south of Chambers Street rouses and retires with the opening and closing bells, after which the frenetic bustle of traders gives way to a ghost town. Not so.

Since 9/11 Lower Manhattan has been the focus of numerous revival projects and development incentives. Arts initiatives like the annual River to River Festival bring free concerts and events to the piers and parks of the Battery. The nightlife scene booms at the trendy restaurants of South Street Seaport and along the strip of taverns that dot the Stone Street promenade. The downtown population has doubled since 2001, as more and more young professionals and families settle down in the birthplace of American capitalism, bringing with them a cavalcade of baby strollers to join the daily frenzy.

EXPLORE

Battery Park

The southern tip of Manhattan is a modest escape from the raucous Financial District, and its rich history continues to bring throngs of tourists to its greens. The park holds historic sites like the Castle Clinton National Monument, which was built to defend the city during the War of 1812. The site was named West Battery during the war, but in 1824 was turned into Castle Garden, an entertainment site for New Yorkers. It was then converted into the official port for new

Battery Pl, State St, & Whitehall St
4 5 to Bowling Green

immigrants, and later was briefly the site of New York Aquarium. Today it is a national monument and a venue for summer concerts and scattered works of modern art. The park also holds The Sphere, a sculpture which was originally a symbol of peace situated between the Twin Towers at the World Trade Center. After 9/11 the damaged piece was relocated to the park, where it now stands over an eternal flame as a temporary memorial to those lost in the attacks.

Bowling Green

Established on March 12, 1733, New York City's first public park is the proverbial elephant in the skyscraper-populated

Broadway & Whitehall St
4 5 to Bowling Green
R W to Whitehall St

room, its wedge shape enclosing a fountain and flanked by historical architecture. After visiting Ellis Island and the Statue of Liberty, an extensive spectrum of tourists stop to rest here, sharing the bench-lined walkways and fenced in grass with locals on lunch breaks. Bowling Green is known as the alleged location of Dutch settler Peter Minuit's purchase of the island of Manhattan, bought from Native Americans for sixty Dutch guilders worth of goods. Modern-day businessmen can handle office-related matters here as well, as this historical park offers WiFi. Just outside the Green is Wall Street's ever-charging symbol of optimism—the Bowling Green Bull, sculpted by Arturo Di Modica—which was installed in 1989.

City Hall

Completed in 1816, this French Renaissance-inspired building is the oldest city hall in the nation to still serve its original governmental function. The marble Georgian interior is home to the mayor's office and the chambers of the New York City Council. The front entrance often

260 Broadway (at Chambers St)
212-788-3000
Mon-Fri 9am-4pm
®Ⓦ to City Hall
Free Tours

DAY TO DAY

Community Board 1: 49-51 Chambers St, Room 715, 212-442-5050.

Dry Cleaners: Alpine Cleaners, 25 Saint James Pl, 212-349-1899.

Groceries: Zeytuna, 59 Maiden Ln, 212-742-2436.

Gyms: Crunch, 25 Broadway, 212-269-1067.

Hospitals: New York Downtown Hospital, 170 William St, 212-312-5000.

Libraries: New York Public Library: New Amsterdam Branch, 9 Murray St, 212-732-8186.

Media: *Wall Street Journal*, wsj.com. *Dealbreaker*, dealbreaker.com.

Volunteer Opportunities: Wall Street Rising, 55 Exchange Pl, Suite 401, 212-509-0300. Wall Street Catholic Young Adults, Our Lady of Victory Church, 60 William St, 212-517-1722, Wscab@aol.com.

hosts live press conferences. Over the years, it has seen its share of historic events—its landmark rotunda housed the coffins of Ulysses Grant and Abraham Lincoln—and accumulated historical artifacts like Washington's desk in the Governor's room. Free building tours are offered on weekdays with an online reservation, but you can always enjoy the park outside without previous arrangement. Furnished with 19th-century gas lamps and a central fountain, City Hall's park provides quiet refuge from the bureaucratic bustle of the surrounding buildings.

Federal Hall National Memorial

Before DC and Philadelphia there was Federal Hall, the first capitol building of the United States. A bronze statue of George Washington stands on the front steps, marking the original site of his inauguration in 1789. In September 2002, approximately 300 members of Congress convened in Federal Hall to show support for New York City, the first time Congress had met in the city since 1790.

26 Wall St (at Broad St)
212-825-6888
Mon-Fri 9am-5pm
1 **R** **W** to Rector,
4 **5** to Wall St,
J **M** **Z** to Broad St

Although the original structure was razed in 1812, the current building, erected in 1842 as the country's first Customs House, is one of the best examples of Greek revival architecture in New York. The rotunda houses exhibits on the site's history, including Washington's inauguration (the Bible on which he took his oath is on display) and New York's ratification of the Bill of Rights. Visit Federal Hall on April 30th for the annual reenactment of Washington's inauguration, courtesy of the New York Freemasons.

Federal Reserve Bank

In 1928, this branch of the Federal Reserve built the world's largest gold storage vault eighty feet under the streets of lower Manhattan. Today this vault holds over 25% of the world's monetary gold supply. With few concerns for security, the Fed allows visitors the opportunity to ogle its clients' massive stock of gold in person—just be sure to reserve several weeks in advance, and to bring identification. If

33 Liberty St
(btwn Nassau & William St)
212-720-6130
Tours Mon-Fri (except Bank holidays) 9:30am, 10:30am, 11:30am, 1:30pm, 2:30pm & 3:30pm
2 **3** **J** **M** **Z** to Fulton St

NATIVE'S PICK

Skyscraper Museum

Not all New York museums are flooded with tourists and overstocked with oil paintings. The Skyscraper museum is a monument to urban design that captivates but doesn't drain, and can be appreciated in less than two hours. Manhattan's towering skyline may well be New York's greatest icon, and this museum is devoted to the innovation, creativity, and artistry required over the years to make its man-made structures. Complete with hand-carved, scale models of midtown and lower Manhattan, as well as construction photographs of the city's most iconic skyscrapers, the permanent collection seeks to illuminate the history of this spectacular cityscape. Don't miss the exhibit on the World Trade Center and development at Ground Zero.

39 Battery Pl (near 1st Pl)
212-968-1961
Wed-Sun 12pm-6pm
1 to Rector St,
4 **5** to Bowling Green,
R **W** to Rector St
Adults $5,
Students & Seniors $2.50

you haven't got a reservation, skip the tour and take an hour to admire its gallery on the history of money, which rivals the British Museum's. The American Numismatic Society's coins include those that George Washington removed from circulation, calling the use of his portrait "tyrannical," and the last 1933 Double Eagle—the world's most valuable coin.

Fraunces Tavern Museum

Perched on Pearl Street, this small tavern opens its doors to anyone with a hunger for history. Samuel Fraunces,	54 Pearl St (at Broad St) 212-968-1776 Mon-Sat 12pm-5pm **❹❺** to Bowling Green, **Ⓡ Ⓦ** to Whitehall St Adults $10, Seniors & Under 18 $5

founder, first owner, and tavern keeper, was a Revolutionary spy and friend of George Washington, who delivered his farewell address to the officers of the Continental Army at the tavern in 1755. Now a museum, its rooms—still furnished with the original rugs, oil paintings, and furniture of the 1700s—tell stories of New York's Revolutionary past with original documents, prints, weapons, and relics, including Washington's false teeth and a lock of his hair. Additional traveling exhibits bring in treasures like the Magna Carta. A historical relic itself, the tavern housed offices of the Departments of Treasury, War (now the Defense Department), and Foreign Affairs (our State Department) when New York was the nation's capital. The museum is on the second floor above the tavern, now a restaurant offering deluxe pub fare and hosting colonial-style weddings.

Museum of the American Indian

Housed in the Alexander Hamilton U.S. Custom House, the Smithsonian Institution's 15th	1 Bowling Green (at State Pl) 212-514-3700 Daily 10am-5pm, Thurs 10am-8pm **❹❺** to Bowling Green, **Ⓡ Ⓦ** to Whitehall St

museum showcases the history and culture of the Native Americans from as early as the ancient Paleo-Indian. The separate galleries of media, paper, object, and photo archives are interwoven to tell the complete story of the first Americans. Two levels of exhibits host extensive archives with over

FOLEY SQUARE

Once part of the infamous Five Points district, this patch of green is surrounded by several administrative buildings, making it the nexus of NYC government. The **New York County Supreme Court**, the **Thurgood Marshall Federal Courthouse**, and the **United States Courthouse**, all impressive edifices built in the neo-classical style, tower over the square. To the east is the looming **New York County Municipal Building** which is topped by **Civic Fame**, a golden statue of a Greek woman holding a crown with five turrets that symbolize the five boroughs of the city. The **African Burial Ground Site** is marked by a monument at the center of the square. Here the remains of 400 Africans were unearthed for the park's construction. **Tweed Courthouse**, the construction of which was indeed funded by Boss Tweed, lies just around the corner, and offers free tours on Fridays at 2pm. The **Foley Square Greenmarket** operates year-round on Fridays on the corner of Centre Street between Worth and Pearl Streets. It's difficult to imagine that this flourishing area was once a rancid pond that supplied NYC inhabitants with water—and typhus and cholera.

WORLD TRADE CENTER SITE

The **World Trade Center Site** (*btwn Liberty & Vesey Streets at Church St*) is finally under development. The construction of five of the six new towers is underway, one of them being the 1,776-foot-tall Freedom Tower, as well as the first steel beams of the Reflecting Absence memorial. Also under construction is the World Trade Center Transportation Hub, designed by Santiago Calatrava to resemble a bird being released from a child's hand.

The greatest memorials to the catastrophe of 9/11 are more ephemeral than these, however—the **Tribute WTC Visitor Center** at (*12 Liberty St*) offers walking tours ($10) guided by those who lived and worked in Lower Manhattan on the day of the attacks. Proceeds from admission fees go to the September 11th Family Association. Lucky passersby may also meet Harry Roland, an amateur urban historian who quit his job as a security guard a block away in order to tell his firsthand stories of 9/11 for free.

The best view of the Twin Towers' site is from the **Winter Garden** (*2 World Financial Center*), from which the Survivor's Stairway is still visible by Vesey St. Another poignant memorial is the World Trade Center Cross, which was formed by two fallen beams and has been moved to **St. Peter's Church** (*22 Barclay St*). And every New Yorker has seen the Tribute in Light, two parallel beams that will pierce the sky every year on September 11th until the completed Freedom Tower shoots its single beam upwards.

324,000 photographs dating back to the 1860s, 12,000 media items, and more. Dance and music performances, film and video screenings, workshops, and symposia are also presented by the museum. Exhibits change frequently, so be sure to check back throughout the year.

South Street Seaport

Picture your favorite suburban shopping mall, and then imagine it transported into 18th- and 19th-century buildings along the scenic lower Manhattan waterfront. This collection of shops and eateries are chock full of tourists, but even locals drop by to enjoy cheap food and postcard views of the Brooklyn and Manhattan bridges. The cobblestone block of Fulton Street is home to more upscale shops and restaurants, but the old wooden pier is where you'll find food stands, clothing kiosks, and more random sellables like balloon animal crafts. More shopping can be found inside the Pier 17 building—and the third floor houses amazing views of the Brooklyn waterfront and an impressive food court of

Fulton & South Streets, Pier 17
212-SEA-PORT
Mall Mon-Sat 10am-9pm,
Sun 11am-8pm
❷❸❹❻❼ to Fulton St
Food Court $6-$8

seafood, margarita bars, and even a Nathan's Hot Dogs. Whether you tour a tall ship in the harbor or sit on the deck in the mall—the Seaport provides a relaxing waterfront escape from the forest of skyscrapers downtown.

SHOP

The Mysterious Bookshop

Take out your magnifying glass and trench coat—there is sleuthing to be done at this specialty bookstore. Literature here is not for the faint of heart (get lost, Nancy Drew and Hardy Boys fans), as it stocks everything from noir, pulp, and murder mystery to detective, supernatural, and suspense. Wheeled ladders rest against looming 12-foot shelves, where rare books and autographed first editions stand like suspects in a line up. The shop specializes in rare books and first editions signed by authors, and also circulates a

58 Warren St
(btwn Broadway & Church St)
212-587-1011
Daily 11am-7pm
❶❷❸ to Chambers St-W
Broadway, ❷❼ to City Hall-
Broadway, ❶❷❸❹❻ to
Chambers St-Park

monthly pamphlet that untangles the minds of prominent authors. Stop in for a special event, as The Mysterious Bookshop hosts parties for Thrillerfest and regularly invites authors in to discuss their works with fans.

simple cut of meat lasagna basking in creamy sauce, round out the selection. Order from a variety of competent antipasti and salads to start, and top off your trip with a funky choice of cocktails for $11 each, like the house specialty, Nutella 'Tini.

EAT

Adrienne's
Italian, Pizzabar

A picturesque reprive from the frenetic downtown rush, Adrienne's is humble pizzeria by day and swanky hangout by night. Co-owners are pizza legends Nick Angelis, Harry Poulakakos, and Peter Poulakakos, who serve up slices of their "old-fashioned pizza"—a square, thin-crusted variant on the usual New York pie—to Wall Street suits during the lunch rush. But by late afternoon the spot settles into a quieter, candlelit feel, eschewing the grab-and-go slice in favor whole ten-inch pies. Other dishes, like a

54 Stone St (near Hanover Sq)
212-248-3838
Mon-Sat 11am-12pm,
Sun 11am-10pm
②③④⑤ⓇⓌto Wall St,
ⒿⓂⓏ to Broad St
10-inch Pies $10-17,
Appetizers $6-12, Entrees $10-15

Alfanoose
Middle Eastern

Another contender for the best falafel joint in the city, Alfanoose enjoys a loyal following among Financial District locals and

8 Maiden Ln (near Broadway)
212-528-4669
Mon-Sat 11am-9pm
②③④⑤ⒶⒸⒿⓂⓏto
Fulton St-Broadway Nassau
Small Plates $3-5, Mains $8-14

falafel fiends for its flavorful, grease-free rendition of the Eastern Mediterranean standard. Exotic dishes like foul and kibbeh are offered here alongside more familiar favorites like baba ghanoush and schwarma. All dishes are made to order with extraordinary care, fresh ingredients, and rich, bold flavors. The food may cost a bit more than your average street-corner halal cart, but once you've tasted Middle Eastern food the way it's meant to be, you'll never go back to an oily falafel cart again.

Beckett's Bar and Grill   *Pub, Outdoor*

The rowdy after-work Wall St crowd descends nightly upon this large and convivial bar, where at least two games are always playing on TV and the music's on full-blast. Patrons talk shop or cheer their team over pints, sliders, and platters of blue corn nachos. In addition to drawing a devoted nightlife crowd, Beckett's is open for lunch daily and brunch on weekends, serving up pub fare and all-American standbys. Pull up a chair at the long bar downstairs or take a seat at one of the outdoor tables out back on Stone St. The first paved street in New York City, this charming and boisterous one-block cobblestone promenade is open seasonally and houses outdoor communal seating for Beckett's and the handful of neighboring taverns and grub hubs, including The Dubliner, Beckett's new sister pub.

81 Pearl St (btwn Coenties Alley & Hanover Sq)
212-269-1001
Daily 11am-2am
❷❸ to Wall St, Ⓡ Ⓦ to Whitehall St-South Ferry
Average Drink $7
Happy Hour: Mon-Fri 5pm-7:30pm

Patriot Saloon   *Dive*

This gloriously skeezy bar revels in its trashiness: the mascot is an enormous s u r f b o a r d i n g alligator hanging from the ceiling with multicolored bras dangling off of it. In addition to this spectacular centerpiece, the bar has all the hallmarks of a good southern dive. The beer is dirt cheap (and well drinks are served with disdain), the loud country music's pumped out of two jukeboxes, and the hot bartenders dressed in conveniently low-cut tank tops could probably kick your ass. Two levels house arcade games and a pool table—welcome distractions to rampant pitcher guzzling. The Patriot is the perfect place to start a night, as long as you're not looking for too much intellectual stimulation.

110 Chambers St (near Church St)
212-748-1162
Mon-Sat 11:30am-4am, Sun 12pm-4am
❶❷❸ⒶⒸ to Chambers St
Average Beer $4

BROOKLYN

GREENPOINT

Before hipsters there was industry and before industry there was farmland, but throughout its history, the Greenpoint peninsula has been characterized by both its geographic and cultural isolation from the rest of Manhattan. Before the construction of the infamous G train—the only subway line that does not enter Manhattan—the best way to get to and from Greenpoint was by boat. In those days, the locale was all farmland owned by a few families whose presence lives on in the names of Greenpoint's streets.

In the early 18th century, as the development of Manhattan made the island less practical for shipping, Greenpoint's long coastline became a trade hub, marking the beginning of its history as a commercial center. Originally named Green Hoek by early Dutch settlers for its grassy lowlands, Greenpoint's landscape today is marked by the extensive industrialization and immigration it experienced during the 19th and 20th century. Industrial decline threatened to drive the neighborhood into poverty and obscurity, but the perseverance of the residents preserved and transformed the neighborhood into the community it has become.

Today, old smokestacks are interspersed with the steeples of churches, many of which cater to the neighborhood's large Polish population. Indeed, in recent years, Greenpoint has been dubbed "Little Poland"—nearly half of Greenpoint residents claim Polish ancestry, constituting the largest Polish population in any New York City neighborhood.

In Greenpoint today, the old and new cultures mingle daily on the main drag, Manhattan Avenue. Alongside multi-generational Polish families are also growing numbers of Brooklyners that have moved north to escape the rising rents of an overflowing Williamsburg. This has contributed to a curious dynamic between the native non-English-speakers and the incoming hipsters—on one street, you'll find specialty Polish fur shops and the best cups of organic coffee in Brooklyn. And, along the waterfront, amid the relics of old industry, you can catch some of the most stunning views of Manhattan.

Map labels (top to bottom, left to right): Eagle St, Freeman St, George Apen St, Huron St, India St, Java St, Kent St, Greenpoint Ave, Milton St, Noble St, Oak St, Calyer St, Meserole Ave, Quay St, N 15th St, N 14th St, Norman Ave, Lorimer St, Manhattan Ave, Nassau Ave, Franklin St, West St, East River, GREENPOINT, McGuinness Blvd, Provost St, Greenpoint Ave, Leonard St, Eckford St, Newell St, Diamond St, Jewel St, N Henry St, Russell St, Monitor St, Norman Ave, Humboldt St, Grandparents Ave, Kingsland Ave, Sutton St, Morgan Ave

EXPLORE

Greenpoint Waterfront

For a picture-perfect view of the Manhattan skyline,

> Java St or Huron St, off West St
> Ⓖ to Greenpoint Ave

visit this eerie and neglected industrial locale—complete with abandoned meat trucks and a graffiti-ed surveillance sign. Walk down Java or Huron to the shore of the East River and you'll find a parking lot frequented by lovers, fishermen who speak broken English, and hippies filming the newest clip for their YouTube video blog. Be sure to bring a camera: with a panorama that spans the Williamsburg Bridge and downtown Manhattan skyscrapers, including the iconic Empire State Building, it's no wonder that the Greenpoint and Williamsburg waterfronts have been called the "gold coast of Brooklyn."

Historic District

Located in the heart of Greenpoint, the Historic District—as

> Roughly bounded by Kent,
> Calyer, Noble, & Franklin St,
> Clifford Pl & Manhattan Ave
> Ⓖ to Greenpoint Ave

designated by the City of New York in 1982—offers a glimpse of the neighborhood's past as a center for shipbuilding and waterborne commerce. Tree-lined streets leading down to the waterfront are home to landmark 19th-century rowhouses, built to house industrialization-era merchants and workers. Constructed of red brick and white limestone trim, the Roman Catholic Church of Saint Anthony stands tall as the skyscraper of Greenpoint on the corner of Milton Street and Manhattan Avenue. It's one of five churches within the boundaries of this peaceful area that contributes to Brooklyn's reputation as "the city of homes and churches."

Monsignor McGolrick Park

Greenpoint newcomers seeking the more popular McCarren Park

> Between Driggs Ave, Russell
> St, Nassau Ave & Moniton St.
> Ⓖ to Nassau Ave

will probably be redirected by savvy locals to this lush, quiet alternative. Originally named Winthrop Park for assemblyman and lifelong Greenpoint resident Winthrop Jones, McGolrick Park is perfect for peaceful people watching. Watch Polish families congregate on the shaded benches, toddlers escape their strollers to play on multicolored jungle gyms, or local vegans puzzle over the morning crossword while Ray Banners bike over to a favorite coffee shop for their daily fix. The most striking feature of the park is a World War I memorial statue of a victorious Argonne, which stands in the middle of a pavilion reminiscent of Versailles. The HBO Series *Flight of the Conchords* picked up on the French vibe here: look out for McGolrick Park in their music video "Foux Da Fa Fa."

SHOP

B's Bike Shop

If you're looking for bikes, parts, repairs, or just a community of cyclists, B's Bikes is your place.

262 Driggs Ave
(btwn Eckford & Leonard St)
718-349-1212
Daily 12-8pm
Ⓖ to Nassau Ave

It's small, and made even more so by bikes encroaching on all sides and wheels hanging from ceiling hooks—a testament to their extensive selection. Every species of bike exists here, from street to mountain, as well as a myriad of baskets, pedals, horns, and other cycling accessories. The knowledgeable staff is a mix of artists and musicians who come together over their mutual love for the engine-less two-wheeler, and are willing to assist all mechanically-challenged customers. They

DAY TO DAY

Brooklyn Community Board 1: 435 Graham Ave, 718-389-0009.

Groceries: Met Food, 131 Driggs Ave, 718-389-6429. The Garden, 921 Manhattan Ave 718-389-6448.

Gym: Maxim Health and Fitness, 193 N 9th St, 718-486-0630.

Hospital: Woodhull Medical and Mental Health Center, 760 Broadway (at Marcus Garvey Blvd), 718-246-8170.

Laundromat: Greenpoint Laundromat, 132 Franklin St.

Library: Brooklyn Public Library: Greenpoint Branch, 107 Norman Ave, 718-349-8504.

Media: *Greenpunkt*, greenpunkt.com.

Volunteer Opportunities: Greenpoint Soup Kitchen, 138 Milton St.

also offer custom builds for used bikes that need a good revamping. And a bike pump is always kept outside for itinerant cyclists who need a quick fill up.

GREENPOINT

The first and only store of this online shopping site carries all the clothing and desirable unnecessaries a quirky girl could want: ice cream cone lamps stand tall near Edgar Allen Poe action figures. Brightly colored dresses, skirts, and accessories hang behind over-sized sunglasses and other fun goodies. Most items run in the $10-$20 range, though larger ones can go for upwards of $100 (turntables, anyone?). You'll be drawn in by the chipper schoolgirl atmosphere and good humor of it all, and leave with your roommate's belated birthday present in hand.

Kill Devil Hill

Exploring Kill Devil Hill is like rummaging through a well-stocked garage sale in the heart of

170 Franklin St (near Java St)
347-534-3888
Daily 12pm-9pm, Wed closed
Ⓖ to Greenpoint Ave

New Mexico: delicately painted tea sets stand stacked next to beaver skulls and woven Navajo tapestries, earthy beaded necklaces sit in a bowl by snapping turtle shells, and thick-rimmed frames are propped up near illustrated greeting cards from the 50s. The shelves of this small two-room shop overflow with antiques the owners have collected through their numerous road trips. You may not need $150 portraits of Hank Williams Sr., vintage Life magazines featuring Steve McQueen, or miniature scythes selling for $5 apiece, but browsing the collecting is a charming way to spend an afternoon. Take a tip from the neighborhood kids and drop a dime in a jar for some candy on your way out.

Word

Cheery yellow walls and an "Eat Sleep Read" poster make you wax nostalgic for your third grade

126 Franklin St.
718-383-0096
Mon-Thurs 11am-8pm, Fri-Sat
11am-9pm, Sun 12-8pm
Ⓖ to Greenpoint Ave

classroom at this community boookstore—but its shelves are stocked with far more than *Little House on the Prairie*. Word carries a wide selection of new literature, including fiction, non-fiction, and gift books. They also offer a sizable selection of children's books, puzzles, and stationary that makes for excellent browsing or buying. True to its community roots, it hosts a monthly book club for neighborhood bibliophiles and throws launch parties for local authors. Pop

Eat Records

Relax and kick back with a cup of coffee—this record store and café redefines the term "cozy." Locals

124 Meserole Ave
718-389-8083
Mon-Sat 9am-7pm,
Sun 9am-7pm
Ⓖ to Greenpoint Ave

in worn jeans gather around small tables, with mugs and Macbooks. Running the length of a bright yellow wall opposite the tables, is a varied selection of old vinyls. Stored in large cork board boxes, the records are divided by genre on the right and range in price from $5 to $10. Shuffle through the less clearly designated boxes on the left for new arrivals. In their varied and well-edited selection you can find Johnny Cash for your uncle and Pink Floyd for your brother, then grab a warm cup of coffee for yourself—and do it all without spending an entire paycheck.

Fred Flare

The inside of this shop looks like a tidy closet of an impossibly cute 16-year-old girl.

131 Meserole Ave
718-349-1257
Wed-Sat 12pm-7pm,
Sun 12pm-5pm
Ⓖ to Greenpoint Ave or
Nassau Ave

into a not-so-young-adult book discussion or an author reading on a free afternoon. While away hours at this literary getaway—just make sure you bring bookmarks.

Settle in with your Negro Modelo among the sombreros and fake roses that decorate the walls and tabletops. If there for breakfast, try their Crunch French Toast—an unexpected favorite made with challah and corn flakes.

EAT

Acapulco Deli & Restaurant *Mexican*

This local favorite has everything a great Mexican place should—huge portions, low prices, and blaring Latin radio—plus the unexpected addition of a full deli. You won't hear much English at this corner restaurant, situated on a seemingly abandoned stretch of Manhattan Ave, but the authentic Mexican more than makes up for it. Though they also serve diner and deli fare, their tacos and burritos (few of which exceed $7) come staff-recommended and easily compensate for the potential language barrier and the nine-block walk from the G train.

1116 Manhattan Ave (at Clay St)
718-349-8429
Mon-Fri 7am-10pm,
Sat-Sun 9am-10pm
Ⓖ to Greenpoint Ave
Breakfast $4-6,
Appetizers $3-10,
Entrees $5-14

Anella *Italian*

This must be one of the only restaurants in New York that can claim to literally put down roots in its neighborhood: Anelia's quaint but impressive garden out back provides many of the kitchen's herbs, fruits, and vegetables. The emphasis on freshness extends to the whole menu, which includes meats, pastas, salads, and gourmet pizzas. Start with the perfectly crisp piccolo fritto misto, a lightly fried vegetable and calamari appetizer. Among entrees, the seared wild salmon with pepper relish is a standout. For the complete relaxed, backyard experience, choose garden seating— the outdoor décor is an eclectic mix of found

222 Franklin St (near Green St)
718-389-8100
Tue-Thurs 5:30pm-10pm,
Fri-Sat 5:30pm-11pm,
Sun 11am-4pm & 5pm-10pm
Ⓖ to Greenpoint Ave
Appetizers $6-12,
Entrees $12-20
Cash only

NATIVE'S PICK

Lomzynianka *Polish*

A garland-draped deer head presides over the hipsters and Poles gorging themselves at this tiny Polish hovel—where the quick kitchen and pretty waitress serve up crispy pierogies, juicy kielbasa sausage, and other meat-heavy entrees. Staticky pop radio (some fresh Kelly Clarkson on your goulash?) and "red brick" wallpaper are only off-putting before your first bite of borscht, which comes neon red with dumplings or oily white with boiled eggs and kielbasa. Entrees like stuffed cabbage, packed with chicken and rice, and the placki wegierskie (goulash with a fried potato pancake) round out the menu of traditional Polish foods. The farmers' blintzes, filled with sweet cheese and berries and served with tart yogurt, make for a satisfying dessert.

646 Manhattan Ave
718-389-9439
Mon-Sun 12pm-9pm
Ⓖ to Nassau Ave
Entrees $3-3.50

objects that contributes handily to Anelia's urbane rusticity. If you ask nicely, a friendly server may even strum a few notes on the old piano skeleton hanging by the back door.

Five Leaves

New American

Tucked away in a dusty, unkempt section of Greenpoint, this warm, lively Australian-American eatery is something of a diamond in the rough. The nautically-themed interior is cozy and welcoming—wooden planks cover the floor and ceiling, maritime maps cover the bit of wall space between the old-fashioned bar and the large, scratched-up mirror. The menu is creative (if a little scattered), and the eager, friendly wait staff can help even a more nervous diner navigate what might otherwise be intimidating culinary waters. Sweet pineapple, fried egg, and beets top one of their signature hamburgers. Amid more whimsical dishes, traditional choices like

18 Bedford Ave
(at Nassau Ave)
718-383-5345
Daily 8am-12am
Ⓖ to Nassau Ave
Entrees $13-22,
Appetizers $7-15

fried oysters are prepared with due aplomb. Five Leaves is also a kind of memorial to the late Heath Ledger, who helped establish the restaurant, and it was completed with money left in his will.

Thai Café

Thai

A old favorite for locals, this no-frills eatery has kept a loyal following by serving authentic food at unbeatable prices. Unlike the typical corner Thai joint where the "extra spicy" is watered down to suit American palates, Thai Café injects its dishes with a generous helping of heat. Spicy noodles with seafood, vegetarian mock-duck, and basil chicken are popular favorites, but an extensive menu and bargain-basement prices compel most diners to order much more. Though Thai Café has a reasonably attractive dining room and a fair amount of seating, service is speedy, so you probably won't get too comfortable. The emphasis on

925 Manhattan Ave
(at Kent St)
718-383-3562
Daily 11:30am-11pm
Ⓖ to Greenpoint Ave
Average Appetizer $4,
Average Entree $7.50

NATIVE'S PICK

Black Rabbit

Pub, Absinth Den

This low-key Irish pub's dark wood counters, faded family portraits, and private booths will instantly remind you of your favorite European bar (if you have one, that is). However, there's more to Black Rabbit than its classic European ambiance. Owner and bartender Kent Lanier, well-loved by all the regulars, offers an original cocktail menu that's put together each night based on "what's on the shelves." If cocktails aren't your cup of booze, there's a wide selection of wine and beers (running as cheap as $3), as well as four traditional servings of absinthe. Kent's wife runs the kitchen, turning out everything from burgers to beer fondue. Their oak-laden den is warmly inviting, and on Tuesday nights—local comedy shows host trivia nights, awarding free absinthe shots to winners.

91 Greenpoint Ave
(near Franklin St)
718-349-1595
Mon-Wed 4pm-2am,
Thu-Fri 4pm-4am, Sat 1pm-4am, Sun 1pm-2am
Ⓖ to Greenpoint Ave
Average Beer $5, Mix drinks $9
Happy Hour: Mon-Sat 4pm-8pm, Sun 4pm-7pm

efficiency here means you could probably come in, eat, and get out within a matter of minutes. Still, a slightly rushed atmosphere and a cash only policy can't detract from this kind of deal.

PLAY

CoCo66
Live Music, Lounge

66 Greenpoint Ave (at Franklin St)
718-389-7392
Daily 4pm-4am
Ⓖ to Greenpoint Ave
Average Drink $6

Located in the heart of the Greenpoint bar crawl, this multi-roomed bar and live music venue keeps its cred as a local hangout by not pandering to transplanted hipsters and yuppies. With three posh rooms, CoCo66 has enough cleverly designed space to suit all your nightlife needs. The décor draws heavily from the space's past life as a wood shop. Visit the dimly lit first room for a piping hot grilled cheese sandwich and an after-work beer by the metal bar. Eventually head to the second room, heated by a fake fireplace, to enjoy DJ-spun tracks and play a game of pool or foosball. The third room—a combination performance space and extended game room—offers cozy sofa lounging underneath a massive circular sky light.

Van Gogh's Radio Lounge
Open Mic, Live Music, Dive

147 Franklin Ave (btwn Java & India Sts)
718-701-4004
Daily 4pm-4am
Ⓖ to Greenpoint Ave
Average Drink $5

When owner Tony Petillo accepted that his band Van Gogh's Radio wasn't going to make it big, he decided to keep the band's namesake alive by opening this joint in his home neighborhood of Greenpoint. A haven for those searching for a beatnik Eden, the requisite exposed brick walls and sunflower decorations of Van Gogh's Radio Lounge lend rundown charm free of Bedford Ave pretention. Sports games play on a projector and locals throw darts in the back, but newcomers pack in nightly for the drink deals—Mondays girls drink free and Sundays offer $6 make-your-own-Bloody Mary. Relax on the plush crimson couches, guzzle PBR, and admire the wall art—a 21st century response to 1800s post-impressionism by an artist identified only as "Jared."

WILLIAMSBURG

Though Williamsburg was purchased in 1792 with the intention of creating a suburban escape for New Yorkers, over the next two centuries it developed into a highly industrial neighborhood. Factory jobs attracted large numbers of Jewish, Italian, Polish, and Hispanic immigrants who populated the neighborhood until the late 20th century, when factories underwent rampant closures. As expansive, unused workhouses were converted to low-cost lofts in the 1990s, New York's artistic crowd, pushed out of Manhattan by rising housing costs in the Lower East Side and Soho, conquered Williamsburg and transformed it into the young, artsy neighborhood it is today.

Low buildings, tree-lined streets, mom and pop cafés, and plenty of outdoor patio space make Williamsburg feel more like a quaint little town of its own rather than the first stop off the L train from Manhattan. A mecca for indie music and fashion, the modern 'burg is a virtual sea of iPod earbuds snaking out of unkempt hair. Young artists and musicians toting moleskin journals and instruments overrun Bedford Avenue. Beautiful people in impossibly tight jeans float from one hot bar to another, discussing bands still scuttling under the radar of mass taste.

Unfortunately, the last few years have seen a drastic increase in neighborhood housing prices. Locals complain that the streets have lost their authenticity and become too much of a faux-hipster haven. But the thousands of twenty-something residents that can still afford to live here find a community of like-minded peers. Although its vintage stores and vegan eateries may seem to adopt an affected hipster mentality, the neighborhood's numerous galleries and art projects legitimize its claim as the new home for New York City's avante-garde scene.

EXPLORE

3rd Ward

Founders of this trendy design center converted an old warehouse into a venue for

195 Morgan Ave (at Stagg St)
718-715-4961
Mon-Fri 8am-12am,
Sat-Sun 9am-12am
🅻 to Bedford Ave

photography, fashion, digital media, film, and fine arts. The naturally lit photography studio, full-fledged wood and metal shop, dynamic media lab, and open office space for freelancers are all available to members for a small monthly fee, enabling many to explore the creativity otherwise cramped by their small studios. Classes are available in everything from textile hand printing to silversmithing to "making crappy stuff awesome." Keep tabs on their eclectic event schedule, and you may soon find yourself in a room with instrument inventors exploring the DIY music scene, eating pizza, and watching movie shorts by local filmmakers, or drinking ward-provided beer (PBR, of course) while sketching a live model.

Brooklyn Bowl

Undoubtedly the greenest bowling venue in the city, Brooklyn Bowl will win you over with its 600-person capacity and 16 lanes. Built in a former iron foundry of 23,000

61 Wyeth Av
(btwn 11th & 12th S
718-963-336
Mon-Thurs 6pm-2am
Fri 6pm-4am, Sat 11am-4am
Sun 11am-2ar
🅻 to Bedford Av
$40 per hour per lane
$30 during happy hou

square feet, the interior marries Coney Island esque nostalgia (one of the bars is a converte shooting gallery) with state-of-the-art amenitie (like eight enormous high definition TVs but it's the alley's environmental streak tha sets it apart. The place is completely wind powered, and much of the furnishings ar constructed from reclaimed materials, like th 100%-recycled truck tire floor of the stag There's also gourmet food from Blue Ribbo and a selection of 10 draught beers, all brewe in Brooklyn. Bring some friends and come fc reduced prices during happy hour (6-8 pm o weekdays) to ease the impact on your wallet.

Brooklyn Brewery

Created in 1987 by partners Steve Hindy and Tom Potter, this classic American institution has been brewing, bottling,

79 N 11th St (at Wythe Ave)
718-486-7422
Sat-Sun 12pm-6pm
🚇 to Bedford Ave
Happy Hour Friday, 6-11pm
Beers $4, Six for $20

and distributing its own right here in Brooklyn. Stop by for Friday Night Happy Hour (6-11pm) and enjoy live music while lingering over your brew. Every Saturday and Sunday, the building opens its door for guided brewery tours—patrons are invited to sample some house-made lager and specialty ales while learning a little bit about the fermentation process. The lively warehouse is an ideal place to gather with friends around long tables and sample from the brewery menu's fifteen selections while noshing on a pie from one of the local pizza joints.

East River State Park

Steps away from Williamsburg dining and shopping scene, East River State Park offers a calm

90 Kent Ave
(btwn N 10th & N 7th St
10am-Dusk
🚇 to Bedford Ave

alternative to bustling Bedford Avenue. With its broad lawn, ample picnic tables, and unbeatable panoramic view of the Manhattan skyline, this park is a prime destination for families and

DAY TO DAY

Brooklyn Community Board 1: 435 Graham Ave, 718-389-0009.

Dry Cleaner/Tailor: Top Hat Tailors & Cleaners, 592 Lorimer St, 718-782-7779.

Groceries: Matamoros Puebla Grocery, 3193 Bedford Ave, 718-782-5044.

Gym: Maxim Health and Fitness, 500 Driggs Ave, 718-486-0630.

Hospital: The Brooklyn Hospital Center, 121 DeKalb Avenue, 718-250-8000.

Library: Brooklyn Public Library: Williamsburg Branch, 240 Division Ave (at Marcy Ave), 718-302-3485.

Media: *Free Williamsburg*, freewilliamsburg.com.

Volunteer Opportunities: Partnership for the Homeless, partnershipforthehomeless.com.

tourists alike. It's bordered by Williamsburg warehouses and sports a cobblestone trail dating back to the 19th century. The park sometimes doubles as concert venue in the summer,

summoning skinny jean crowds and outbound Manhattanites to hear Grizzly Bear croon under the stars.

Mast Brothers Chocolate

Owned by a pair of brothers who deem themselves "Leaders of the Chocolate Revolution," Mast Brothers Chocolate is the only bean-to-bar chocolate factory in New York City—here the employees delicately handcraft all chocolate on site. Processing cocoa beans plucked everywhere from Madagascar to Venezuela, the brothers creatively season their chocolate with salt and pepper, yielding unusual and unfailingly delicious flavors. Prettily packaged in wallpaper designs, the delectable chocolate is shipped to independent stores throughout Brooklyn and the other boroughs. Don't plan on a weekday visit though—the factory store is only open on weekends.

105A N 3rd St
(btwn Whythe Ave & Barry St)
718-388-2625
Sat-Sun 2pm-8pm
Ⓛ to Bedford Ave

Williamsburg Art & Historical Center

Housed in a landmark 19th-century building, the Williamsburg Art and Historical Center is a bedrock of the neighborhood's cultural scene. The not-for-profit organization displays significant historical artifacts, features art exhibits, and hosts concerts, poetry readings, and film screenings. Most contributors are local Brooklyn artists, and the series held here often examine Brooklyn's cultural roots—a recent exhibit highlighted Williamsburg's Latino population with public art installations and spoken word performances. Stop by and you might catch a panel discussion on the role of the female artist in major collections or find yourself listening to harp and classical guitar by intimate candlelight.

135 Broadway
718-486-7372
Sat-Sun 12pm-6pm
Ⓛ to Bedford Ave

SHOP

Beacon's Closet

This neighborhood favorite is a must-stop on the Brooklyn thrift-shopping tour. Don't be fooled by its name—the "closet" is a gargantuan 5,500 square feet, and

88 N11th St
(btwn Berry & Wythe)
718-486-0816
Mon-Fri 12pm-9pm
Sat-Sun 11am-8pm
Ⓛ to Bedford Ave

NATIVE'S PICK

Spoonbill & Sugartown Booksellers

Bookstore

Nestle up on antique rugs with the house cat and read from the extensive selection of rare art books at this cozy spot. Spoonbill and Sugartown specializes in new and used books on art, architecture, and design, but they also carry carefully selected works of literature and non-fiction, as well as a large number of unusual magazines.

218 Bedford Ave
(near N 5th St)
718-387-7322
Mon-Sun 10am-10pm
Ⓛ to Bedford Ave

You're sure to find something to spark your interest in this atypical collection, with books ranging from photo volumes of Finnish summer houses to high-tech paper airplane crafting guides. The store also sells rare children's books and a few quirky home items, such as an inflatable moose head to stick above your fireplace.

crammed with hip vintage clothing, shoes, sunglasses, and accessories from different decades and many designers. Be prepared to hunt, as sizes are jumbled together on the tightly-packed racks, and prices are just as haphazardly organized. But their sound system makes for a fun shopping experience—head bopping tunes and epic soundtracks interrupted with Star Wars dialogue play on loop. Beacon's Closet also buys clothing for cash (35%) or store credit (55%). The practical, wearable selection and reasonable prices—especially compared the dozens of overpriced vintage stores in Williamsburg—are sure to satisfy vintage cravings.

Bedford Cheese Shop

This homey, old-fashioned shop sells everything from rich, aromatic St. Marcellin to creamy Fourme d'Ambert blue. Wheels, blocks, and jars of cow, goat, and sheep cheeses—from farms local and foreign—are stacked high on shelves and behind the glass counter. The scrupulously-trained staff is more than eager to help customers find the perfect selection. But gourmet cheese isn't Bedford's only specialty—it also offers a variety of meats and antipasti, as well as a decadent collection of chocolate and tubs of Nutella. The manager oversees this dairy shrine to guarantee an exquisitely pungent social and dining experience.

229 Bedford Ave
(btwn 4th & 5th St)
718-599-7588
Mon-Sat 11am-9pm,
Sun 10am-8pm
🜚 to Bedford Ave

Earwax Records

Supplying its Ray-Ban and faded tee clad customers with an all-inclusive collection, this corner music store carries all materials needed for the resurrection of the record player. Rock and indie CDs and sidle up next to jazz, reggae, and alternative records in large floor bins and on colorful shelves. The incredibly knowledgeable staff is happy to help you find your next favorite album—be it space age pop or country—or guide you towards up-and-coming bands and their genre predecessors. Earwax also carries a few working record players, priced fairly and perfect for playing old school tracks. With a huge

218 Bedford Ave (at N 5th St)
718-486-3771
12pm-8pm
🜚 to Bedford Ave

ear hanging bizarrely from the old-fashioned tin ceiling, the store's name isn't just an affectation—Earwax is the real deal.

Mini Minimarket

Catering to the color-loving and vintage-obsessed, this boutique—one of the oldest in the neighborhood—is girlie heaven. The independent store offers clothing and accessories from stand-out designers and craft lines. Subway map umbrellas lean against racks of strappy sandals and colorful peep toe heels on the red and white checkerboard floor. Flowery bubble dresses, bottles of scents, and shelves of necklaces fill the rest of the shop. Browse their nifty sales rack, try on a pair of retro sunglasses, and pick up your Brooklyn pride essentials: "Someone loves me in Brooklyn" t-shirts and double-finger "Brooklyn" rings. The prices may not be cheap, but you're bound to dig up something you won't find on anyone else.

218 Bedford Ave
(btwn 4th & 5th St)
718-302-9337
Mon-Sat 11am-8pm,
Sun 11am-6pm
🜚 to Bedford Ave

Shoe Market

The makers of Mini Mini Mart bring you this new, adorable little shoe shop. Bright green walls and playful window displays make for a jovial atmosphere. It stocks both men's and women's casual and formal styles with brands like Dolce Vita, Vivienne Westwood for Melissa, and Sam Edelman. Shoe Market even has its own brand of shoe—only sold here. Items from their vibrant collection of scarves, sunglasses, and socks—even knee-highs— are sure to sate shopaholics and casual browsers alike.

160 N 6th St
(btwn Bedford Ave & Berry St)
718-388-8495
🄻 to Bedford Ave
Mon-Wed & Sun 12pm-8pm,
Thurs-Sat 12pm-9pm

EAT

Bridget — *Small Plates, Wine Bar*

The urban tasting room for Long Island's Bridge Vineyards, this brightly elegant blue and white space has the relaxed atmosphere of a friend's apartment with an extensive cellar of New York state wines served with imaginative small plates. No detail has been overlooked at this Williamsburg winery—the endive salad is served in vegetable "boats," the managers personally visit the farms upstate where they get their products, and every brick was individually hand-painted a slightly different shade of white to create the desired airy effect. As a true nieghborhood gathering place, Bridget also hosts weekly movie screenings and monthly events for local artists. Most visitors come for the wines and stay for the chef's creative combinations—wine-poached figs on raw turnip with chèvre, anyone?

20 Broadway (near Kent Ave)
718-384-2800
Mon-Fri 7am-12am,
Sat-Sun 8am-12am
🄻 to Bedford Ave,
🄹🄼 to Marcy Ave
Wine $5-10, Food $5-12

Egg — *Brunch, New American*

This beloved breakfast spot has a simple design of white walls, wooden chairs, and lilac-filled white vases that reflect the menu's home-style simplicity. Known for using their own free-

135 North 5th St
(at Bedford Ave)
718-302-5151
Mon-Tues 7am-3pm,
Wed-Fri 7am-10pm,
Sat-Sun 9am-10pm
🄻 to Bedford Ave
Average Meal $11

range eggs and local ingredients whenever possible, the food at Egg is famously fresh and well-prepared. Their most popular dish is the Eggs Rothko, an easy-cooked egg in a slice of brioche with melted Grafton cheddar—though any are highly recommended. The sustainably grown coffee is made to order in a French press that comes in sizes suitable for one, two, or four guests. Tea comes in a personal teapot, steeping as guests laugh their lazy mornings away

over candied bacon and homemade sorghum granola. Saturday often sees lines stretching around the corner as crowds come for brunch or, at the very least, a side-order of Egg.

La Superior — *Mexican*

From outside, this popular Williamsburg Mexican spot blends into the bricks, but one encounter with the $2.50 taco and

295 Berry St (near 2nd Ave)
718-388-5988
Mon-Sat 12pm-2am,
Sun 12pm-12am
🄻 to Bedford Ave
Quesedillas $3.50,
Tacos $2.50, Entrees $7-13

even skeptics become regulars. A casual space booming with house music, La Superior serves generous portions of fresh, filling Mexican favorites. Tilapia-filled tacos (never fried) with tomatoes, onions, and piquant spices provide a light and fresh alternative to the heavier dishes typical of Mexican fare. If you prefer your Mexican food with some heft, try one of the "street-style" quesadillas, priced at $3.50. The Papa Con Queso Quesadilla is a thick

duds at **Bird** (*203 Grand St*) and pricey retro furniture and kicknacks at **Future Perfect** (*115 N 6th St*). Of course, a trip to Williamsburg isn't complete until you've made the vintage rounds, so rummage through the racks at **Buffalo Exchange** (*504 Driggs Ave*), **Salvation Army** (*180 Bedford Ave*), and **Beacon's Closet** (*88 N 11th St*). Then drop your bags and unwind at **Harefield Road** (*769 Metropolitan Ave*), where Brooklyn brews go for $3 during happy hour. And grab late night munchies at **Foodswings** (*295 Grand St*), a vegan snack bar, before heading home.

crust of dough stuffed with potato, deep-fried, smothered with ricotta-like cheese, and served with a side of tomatillo salsa. With virtually everything under $10, the menu at La Superior offers many more substantially satisfying deals for vegetarians and carnivores alike.

Mesa Coyoacan *Mexican*
Though wooden tables and exposed light bulbs suggest a sophisticated and urbane experience, eating here is like dining at Chef Ivan Garcia's family table. Start with the tamales (the smoky chicken mole is a standout), tacos, or ceviches, but be sure to save room for the entrees—undeniably the forte of the kitchen. Garcia elegantly plates his grandmother's recipes, mixing standbys like the light and citrusy enchiladas verdes with specialties from Coyoacán, the Mexican region his family hails from. Try the Coyoacán mixiotes: a dish of succulent lamb spiced with ancho and guajillo chillies and steamed with banana leaves. Served with a peppery cactus salad, minced habaneros, and hot tortillas, the dish is a steal at $14. For a sublime postscript to your meal, smear some dangerously addictive churros with generous dabs of goat's milk caramel.

372 Graham Ave
(near Conselyea St)
718-782-8171
Daily 5 pm-12am
to Graham St
Appetizers $7-10, Entrees
$10-15, Dessert $4.50

Oasis *Middle Eastern*
All of New York is nursing a crush on its Middle Eastern food, and the young denizens of Williamsburg are no exception. This simple hummus-and-pita joint right in front of the Bedford Avenue subway stop serves traditional, and occasionally inspired, Middle Eastern cuisine. Familiar staple sandwiches, like pita and greasy falafel, come stuffed with extras that are sure to satisfy. Lending a bit of crunch and an enticingly piquant sweet-and-sour flavor, the pickled red cabbage is the standout amongst the toppings—but do yourself a favor and order your sandwich with everything. A heavy dose of tahini on the slightly rubbery shawarma leaves the pita a bit too sloppy, that is if you object to wearing some of your lunch. Opt for the mint-laden, fragrant taboule over the too-sweet baba ganoush as a side dish.

161 N 7th St (near Bedford Ave)
718-218-7607
Daily 11am-3am
to Bedford Ave
Sandwiches $3-5, Plates $5-9

Peter Luger *Steakhouse*
Leave your diet in Manhattan, bring cash, and come hungry for steak. With its Tudor-style interior, New York's perennial favorite steakhouse seems virtually untouched since its 1887 founding. Even with a reservation, you

178 Broadway (at Driggs Ave)
718-387-7400
Mon-Thurs 11:45am-9:45pm,
Fri-Sat 11:45am-10:45pm,
Sun 12:45-9:45pm
to Marcy Ave
Steak for one $32, Sides $7-12

WILLIAMSBURG

Fette Sau

American, BBQ

This barbeque shrine treats whiskey, meat, smoke, and time with due reverence. Tender beef brisket benefits from hours spent in the smoker, and crispy, robust pork belly puts on no airs of daintiness, reveling in its rich, fatty splendor. Thankfully, Fette Sau steers clear of sweet meats, abstaining from typically overwhelming brown-sugar glazes in favor of musky dry rubs. Any sweetness withheld from the meat can be found in the otherworldly baked beans, which are nearly rich enough to constitute a dessert. After placing an order at the counter, grab a mason jar of the Black Hole Stout from the local Chelsea Brewing Co., or choose from an impressive list of bourbons, then head for one of the communal picnic tables and wait for your order. The flames playing on the TV screen in the fireplace don't throw any warmth, but Fette Sau heats up its Williamsburg cool with a healthy dose of good ole Southern comfort.

354 Metropolitan Ave
(near Havemeyer St)
718-963-3404
Sun-Thurs 5pm-2am,
Fri-Sat 5pm-4am
Ⓛ to Bedford Ave
$15-20 per lb of meat,
$5 per side

---

may wait a minute or ten to be seated, and once at your table, the brusque server will order you with just-enough politeness not to touch this or move that—he'll do it all for you with the no-nonsense finesse of a New Jersey gas-station attendant. Before long, an enormous aged porterhouse from Luger's own butcher-shop will arrive, cooked to medium-rare perfection, in succulent strata from the crisp exterior to tender red center: just the way steak should be. Tangy house steak sauce comes in a gravy dish and begs to be poured liberally. Hearty sides make great leftovers—if you don't lick your plate clean, that is. Ignore the seafood. Get the beef.

Roebling Tea Room   *American, Café*

A typically hip Williamsburg café in a converted warehouse space, this popular location goes from a luncheon-and-laptop spot by day to a late-night hangout for pretty plaid-clad hipsters enjoying old-school comfort foods like burgers and wursts. An organic, free range burger is a magnificent, cheese-dripping mess, and creamy

mac and cheese comes with optional bacon on top (you'd be crazy to skip it). As per its name, Roebling Tea Room features an extensive list of teas from across the globe, many of them served in pretty woven tea bags. Should you find yourself wandering hungrily through Williamsburg, Roebling is an ideal spot to stop for a casual, reasonably priced snack or meal at just about any time of day or night.

143 Roebling St
(at Metropolitan Ave)
718-963-0760
Mon-Thurs 9am-1am,
Fri 9am-2am, Sat 10am-2am,
Sun 10am-1am
Ⓛ Ⓖ to Metropolitan Ave-
Lorimer St
Brunch & Lunch $7-15,
Dinner $10-25

Silent H   *Sandwiches, Vietnamese*

A sleek yet unpretentious purveyor of self-described "street food" by day and an inventive, upscale eatery by night,

79 Berry St (near N 9th St)
Tues-Sun Lunch 12pm-4pm,
Dinner 6pm-11pm
718-218-7063
Ⓛ to Bedford Ave
Lunch $6-7, Dinner Small
Plates $6-7, Entrees $14-18

Silent H offers Williamsburg an exciting range of fine Vietnamese cuisine. The Street Shop menu, available Tuesday through Sunday for lunch, offers exotic fruit shakes, summer rolls, and Silent H's specialty: banh mi. With your choice of meat (or a vegan option) topped in traditional style with carrots, cilantro, jalepeño, and aioli on a fresh baguette, these sandwiches are rich, sizable, and reasonably priced. Try the classic pork banh mi for $6 with a jackfruit shake for $4 and you are likely to join the ranks of regulars who linger at the long counters or pick up their orders to go. From 6pm-11pm, Silent H switches to "Viet Tapas," salads and entrees that highlight the French influence on Vietnamese cooking, with crepes, curries, and summer rolls all on offer.

Vinnie's Pizzeria

Pizza

148 Bedford Ave
(btwn 8th & 9th St)
718-782-7078
Mon-Fri 11am-12am,
Sat-Sun 11am-3am
🅛 to Bedford Ave
Large Pie $15-24

Loaded with unexpected toppings, the unusual pizzas steal the spotlight at this quirky and creative four-booth hovel—but a framed, dangling sign over the counter reads, "I assure you, we have plain slices." Vinnie's is best known for dishing out vegan pizzas and other imaginative specialties, like the Black Bean Avocado Pizza and the "T. Hanks" with BBQ chicken, bacon, mozzarella, and cheddar. Friendly staff play a fun blend of new-school funk and old-school classics over the speakers, and an offbeat sense of humor pervades every detail of the tiny shop. As you depart, a note scrawled on the bottom of a nearby mirror proclaims, "You are hot," a good-humored sign-off from the staff, fortifying customers against the humbling gaggle of stylish hipsters outside. A must-visit for vegans, Vinnie's also makes a perfect pit stop for any Williamsburg wanderer jonesing for a slice.

PLAY

Barcade

Arcade Games, Beer Bar

388 Union Ave
(btwn Ainslie & Powers St)
718-302-6464
Mon-Fri 5pm-4am,
Sat-Sun 2pm-4am
🅖🅛 to Lorimer
Average Beer $6
Happy Hour: Daily 4-8pm

This converted warehouse is a haven for gamers and beer enthusiasts alike. Don't expect a Super Smash Brothers battle—at a mere quarter a turn,

the games are flat-out old school, including vintage arcade classics like Donkey Kong, Joust, and lesser-known treasures for die-hard fans, like 1943: The Battle of Midway and Ladybug (Ms. Pac-Man, but meaner). Luckily for the inexperienced arcader, Barcade also specializes in microbrews, serving twenty-four taps of rotating specialty beers from the Northeast. After a round of Tetris or kickass IPA, take a seat in one of the wooden stalls, have a smoke on the spacious patio, or just laze on the barrel kegs stacked in the corners. That is, if you can find space amid the brew fans who fill the floor on weekends.

Bembe
Bar, Live Music

81st S. 6th St (at Berry St)
718-387-5389
Mon-Thurs 7:30pm-4am,
Fri-Sun 7pm-4am.
Shows Mon-Thurs 10pm-4am, Sun 9pm
Ⓛ to Bedford Ave,
ⒿⓂⓏ to Marcy Ave
Average Drink $9

Behind its plain wooden doors and heavy velvet drapes lies a warmly lit interior brought to life with global music, fresh fruit concoctions, and monthly art exhibits as multicultural as the clientele. Recycled objects found throughout New York City decorate the exposed brick walls of this cinnamon-scented two story lounge, creating an offbeat urban getaway near the Williamsburg bridge. Be sure to carry a few bucks for the cash-only bar—the mango-guava margarita and rum punch are too tempting to miss. Whether coming to hear the DJ or live drums, Bembe feels like a trip to the dark, exotic regions of South America.

HiChristina!
Dance Club, Open Mic, Performance Space

632 Grand Street
(at Leonard St)
347-495-5868
Hours Vary By Event,
Check http://hichristina.com
ⒼⓁ to Lorimer
Cover $5

Artists, performers, and wannabes are all welcome at HiChristina!, where losing one's inhibitions is not only acceptable —it's thoroughly encouraged. Owned by eccentric couple Christina Ewald and Fritz Donnelly, this interactive performance space hosts about five nightly activities a week, ranging from sock puppet construction to punk rock pilates. Bring in your writing pieces, original artwork, or photography to share—there is little room for humiliation here. Even nudity makes an occasional appearance. On Thursdays, the venue hosts an offbeat open mic, which thankfully attracts more than the standard folk guitar fare. The warm and accepting atmosphere invites friends and strangers to get closer—and don't be surprised if any impromptu dance parties happen.

Kings County
Dive

286 Seigel St, Bushwick
(btwn White and Bogart St)
718-418-8823
Sun-Wed noon-2am,
Thurs-Sat 1pm-3am.
🄻 to Morgan Ave,
Average Drink $4
Happy Hour: Daily 4-8pm

Despite the intimidating wrought-iron door and cramped, grungy interior, neighborly regulars add an inviting ambiance to this former welding workshop. The exposed brick walls are dimly lit and display a rotating gallery of neighborhood artists' work. The metal bar furniture, made by one of the owners, and heavy metal music of bands like Metallica create a gruff attitude that attracts the few remaining bohemians of deep Bushwick. Smokers trickle into the quieter alley and patio area, where strangers make conversation in an intimate atmosphere. Not to be missed is Wednesday Gay Night, where a DJ spins cuts while simultaneously serving mac 'n' cheese to the mainly heterosexual crowd.

Mugs Alehouse
Beer Garden

This old school tavern distinguishes itself from the somewhat yuppified Bedford Street crawl with its old-school vibe and no-frills charm. Mugs comes complete with over 30 domestics and imports on tap, dark wooden countertops, big tatted guys, antique décor, and all the familiar pleasures of an all-American bar. Plasma TVs still blast the big game, back booths pack burly jocks, and power ballads play on loop from the jukebox.

125 Bedford Ave
(near 10th St)
718-486-8232
Mon-Fri 2pm-4am,
Sat 11am-4am
🄻 to Bedford
Average Drink $5

Friendly waitresses are on hand to navigate the beer list—which is lengthy enough to rival any enoteca's flashy wine repertoire. The menu includes pasta and salad options for the picky, but the standard bar grub—burgers, fries, and nachos—is good, greasy, and satisfying.

Pete's Candy Store
Bar, Live Music

709 Lorimer St
(near Richardson)
718-308-3770
Sun-Wed 5pm-2am,
Thurs-Sat 5pm-4am
🄻 to Bedford, 🄶 to Nassau
Average Drink $5

Once a candy shop, now a bar, restaurant, and stage hall, this intimate space hosts nightly music, poetry readings, quizzes, and spelling bees. Often the hall is packed to its 150-person capacity for singer-songwriters, ska trios, indie bands, South American groups, and rockabilly ensembles serenading the crowds at no charge. Antique lamps hang above the checkered floors, 1940s wooden stools sit by the bar, and the theatrical lighting casts subtle swaths of red and gold

Spike Hill
Live Music, Whiskey Bar

The intricate dark mahogany molding, over 80 quality whiskeys, and a wide selection of Belgian beers draw a crowd of devoted regulars to Spike Hill, which welcomes newcomers with none of the would-be-expected snobbery. Scotch neophytes need not fear—friendly, knowledgeable barkeeps will steer you to the glass of your dreams, down to the appropriate number of ice cubes. Seasoned expert? Featured flights of single malt or blended whiskeys should please the educated palate. Stick around for the late night snack menu, offering pub food with a Williamsburg twist (e.g. fish 'n' chips with panko bread crumbs). Or check out the funkier adjacent barroom and performance space where local bands play seven nights a week.

184 & 186 Bedford Avenue
(near N 7th St)
718-218-9737
Daily 12pm-4am
Ⓛ to Bedford Ave
Average Whiskey $13,
Average Beer $6

---

down the narrow space (the owner is, after all, a stage designer). Unexpected artistic discoveries are frequent—Pete's boasts one of the best open mics in the city. And their signature drink menu offers sweet spins on classic cocktails, like the Ginger Whiskey Sour.

Public Assembly
DJ, Live Music, Performance Space

Due to the convenient two-room setup, soft alternative rock and experimental electro-pop can occur simultaneously within the stark, shadowed stone walls of this former mayonnaise factory. The clientele, however, remains almost the same throughout—an artsy group that drinks PBR and Colt .45 while enjoying the acoustics of solid, often local bands. These folks aren't half as crunchy as the tattooed female bartenders who pour them cheap malt liquor, but even they look forgiving behind the dark hued, ever-damp bar. The expansive space is

70 N 6th St
(btwn Kent & Wythe)
718-384-4586
Hours vary by event, visit
publicassemblynyc.com
Ⓛ to Bedford Ave
Cover $10, Beers $2-4
Happy Hour: Daily 4-8pm

ideal for big crowds, though the cryptically titled "back room" is great for meeting and mingling with moody locals. Or hang out near the front room's converted stage if you want to be closer to the soft guitar wailing from the vocalizer.

Spuyten Duyvil
Beer Bar

The mind-numbing variety of beers, ales, meads, and wines at this heralded Belgian bar draws enthusiasts from all over the tri-state area. But with red punched tin ceilings, cream wood panelling, Belgian kitchenware, and assorted 1950s curios, the bar is more local sock-hop soda shop than beer Mecca. The entire selection is cataloged on chalkboards by their country of origin, from Sweden to Japan, and the six domestic beers on tap rotate frequently to keep the selection fresh. One whole board is devoted to Belgian imports and subdivided by Lambic,

359 Metropolitan Ave
(at Havemeyer St)
718-963-4140
Mon-Thurs 5pm-11:30pm,
Fri 5pm-12:30am,
Sat-Sun 1pm-12:30am,
Garden open 5pm-11:30pm
Ⓛ to Lorimer
Average Drink $8
Happy Hour: Daily 4-8pm

Sugarland

DJ, LGBT, Live Music

This former dive is home to some of the most lovable hipster homosexuals in Brooklyn. On the outside, a graffiti-splattered garage door bears the nightspot's name in rough stencil,

221 N 9th St (near Roebling)
718-599 4044
Mon-Fri 8pm-4am,
Sat & Sun 4pm-4am
🄻 to Bedford Ave
Average Drink $4
Happy Hour: Sat 4pm-9pm,
Sun 4pm-7pm, 2 for 1
domestic beer & well drinks

but inside stained glass panels glow with fairy lights, illuminating the clean, open space—which includes a modest dance floor and a hideout for smokers out back. There's cozy seating in the early evening by the split-level gallery, but around midnight Sugarland becomes a hot-spot for music and dancing. Live drag performers belt summer anthems and the DJ plays uptempo remixes of kitschy 60s pop. Bring a gaggle of friends, chat up your fellow glam-dancers, and take advantage of cheap drinks at the long wooden bar.

BROOKLYN HEIGHTS & DUMBO

What was once a blighted landscape of abandoned factories and parking lots is now home to upscale apartment buildings and trendy studios of up-and-coming artists. DUMBO, short for Down Under the Manhattan Bridge Overpass, saw an influx of artists and craftspeople that transformed the industrial district into a new center of culture in the 1970s. Home to innovative art venues and the annual Art Under the Bridge Festival, modern DUMBO is a hotbed of cutting-edge visual and performance art. Boutiques and artisan workshops make the neighborhood a popular daytime destination, while its posh clubs and avant-garde theater seduce Manhattanites to visit at night.

DUMBO's narrow cobblestone streets lead to an entirely different scene only blocks away. Brooklyn Heights is a largely residential neighborhood with beautiful architecture and significant history. The original "Town of Brooklyn," Brooklyn Heights was one of the first suburbs that housed the Wall Street crowd in the early 1800s. In 1814, Robert Fulton created the Fulton Ferry, providing quick, convenient means of transportation for the daily commute between Lower Manhattan and Brooklyn Heights.

Today it is home to picturesque brownstones, friendly eateries, Borough Hall (New York City's original City Hall), and the Promenade, a clean and open public space lined with gardens and scenic views of Lower Manhattan. Families walk along the path, bicyclists peddle over from Manhattan, and young couples eat picnics on benches overlooking the water. Taking a page from Union Square's events calendar, Borough Hall hosts a Farmer's Market at Cadman Plaza, where locals flock for fresh, locally-grown treats.

Walk along the Promenade back into DUMBO and head to Brooklyn Bridge Park for iconic views of the skyline. In the summer, you may even catch a free outdoor movie or join crowds and walk across the historic Brooklyn Bridge.

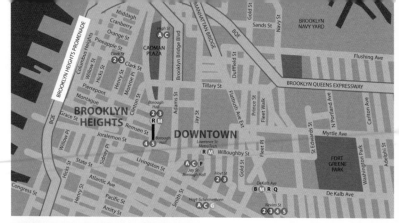

EXPLORE

Bargemusic

Enchanting melodies play at this spot underneath the Brooklyn Bridge, where musicians perform on an

Fulton Ferry landing
(near the Brooklyn Bridge)
718-624-2083
2 3 to Clark St
A C to High St, **F** to York St,
See events at bargemusic.org

unassuming, renovated coffee barge. The ship was built in 1899 and stayed in use until its renovation by Olga Bloom. Since 1977, instrumentalists have held concerts within the warm, dark wood hull of the barge. Behind the stage, a large window reveals the towering behemoth structures of Lower Manhattan, the shimmering lights of South Street Seaport, and the glassy surface of the East River. This floating concert hall holds chamber music performances up to four times a week, as well as a monthly free concert. Past performances include A Tribute to George Gershwin and Celebration of American Composer Charles T. Griffes, 1882–1920.

Brooklyn Borough Hall

New York City's original City Hall is also Brooklyn's oldest public building. The large Greek revival structure has long

209 Joralemon St (at Court St)
2 3 4 5 to Borough Hall,
A C E to Jay, **R** to Court

white steps that lead to six elegantly fluted Ionic columns and a cupola topped with a golden figure of Lady Justice. Visit during the lunch hour and you'll see suited downtown crowds eating Chipotle near the fountain and spacious courtyard in the front. Between 8am and 6pm on Tuesdays, Thursdays, and Saturdays, the courtyard hosts the Borough Hall Greenmarket, a local farmer's market that sells flowers, produce, baked goods, and seafood.

Brooklyn Heights Promenade

This promenade stretches eight blocks on the coast of downtown Brooklyn—and

Columbia Heights
(at Middagh St)
2 3 4 5 to Borough Hall,
A C to High St, **R** to Court

offers simply stunning views. It overlooks downtown Manhattan, the Brooklyn Bridge, South Street Seaport, Ellis Island, New Jersey, and the Statue of Liberty. While the pathway is thin and crowded with bikers, skaters, and strollers, there are plenty of benches to sit on and admire the view. Take some friends and split a pie from Grimaldi's during the day or stroll along the boardwalk with a date at night, and catch the sunset over Manhattan.

Brooklyn Bridge Park (Empire-Fulton Ferry State Park)

With its stunning views and idyllic expanses of lush green grass, there are few better place to play Frisbee, kick off your shoes, or have a picnic after a ride across the Brooklyn Bridge. Until recently, the park was in total disarray—and was comprised of abandoned piers, parking lots, and storage sheds. Thanks to the efforts of the Brooklyn Bridge Park Conservancy, the park has been revitalized into the perfect destination for the warmer months. Attend the annual free weekly film series, "Movies With A View," held here during the summer under the bright lights of Manhattan.

1 Main St (near Water St)
8am-Dusk
(plus seasonal/summer hours)
2 3 to Clark St
A C to High St, **F** to York St,

Dumbo Arts Center (DAC)

Once a cardboard box factory, today this gallery space seems more likely to house a cardboard installation. For the last 13 years, Dumbo Arts Center has pioneered Dumbo's art scene, showcasing the work of new and original artists, who create installation art that makes maximum use of the gallery's 3,000-square-foot

DAY TO DAY

Brooklyn Community Board 2: 350 Jay St, 8th Fl, 718-596-5410.

Groceries: Perelandra Natural Food Center, 175 Remsen St, 718-855-6068.

Gym: Gleason Gym, 75 Front St, 718-797-1050.

Hospital: New York Methodist Hospital, 210 Flatbrush Ave, 718-783-0070.

Library: Brooklyn Public Library: Brooklyn Heights Branch, 280 Cadman Plaza West (at Tillary St), 718-623-7100.

Media: *Downtown Brooklyn Star*, downtownbrooklynstar.com.

rustic wooden space. Visitors ranging from young teens to art world professionals explore the exhibits, pondering the

30 Washington St
(near Plymouth St)
718-694-0831
Wed-Sun 12pm-6pm
$2 Suggested Donation
A C to High St, **F** to York St,

materials used and the ideas that birthed the pieces. After a visit, make sure you mark your calendar to check out the annual D.U.M.B.O. Art Under the Bridge Festival, where the community comes together at the East River waterfront to enjoy a variety of outdoor installations in the last days of summer.

White Wave Dance Studio

Founded by the Young Soon Kim Dance Company in 1988, this innovative studio has since become a perfect venue for dancers to showcase original choreography, as well as a place for interdisciplinary performance projects. Audiences range from friends of the performers to dance professionals, and corporate leaders seeking off-the-beaten-path performances. In recent years, this large, laidback studio also began producing festivals that promote the work of emerging and established artists. Come see all different types of dance at the DUMBO Dance Festival, Wave Rising Series, Cool New York Festival, and the International DUMBO Dance Festival.

25 Jay St, Suite 100
(btwn 1st & 2nd Ave)
718-855-8822
Ⓕ to York St
Hours & admission prices
vary by event

SHOP

Neighborhoodies

A bright orange and yellow scissor decal slices its way across the front window, a symbol of the design-it-yourself possibilities that distinguish this apparel store from similar t-shirt contenders. Inside, rows of shirts wait for creative minds underneath a sign reading "Your design here." Siting in neat piles are garments with names like the Gambler, a super comfy unisex long-sleeved tee, and the Pleasuredome, an American Apparel thermal long-sleeve. Hoodies, sports jerseys, undergarments, pants, and dresses are also available for printing cryptic inside jokes or personal opinions on—and shirts come in a wide variety of cuts and colors. Neighborhoodies is the only store in the city to do on-the-spot stitching in any color to augment your design. Visit to excercise your creativity and personalize your clothing.

26 Jay St (at John St)
718-243-2265
Mon-Fri 1pm-6pm
Sat 11am-5pm
Ⓕ to York St

Zakka

The shop's name translates to "many things," and that's just what you'll find

155 Plymouth St (near Jay St)
718-801-8037
Mon-Sun 12pm-7pm
Ⓕ to York St

here—the best of Japanese fun imported to Brooklyn. An excellent selection of Japanese books and magazines lines the shelves. They cover a wide scope of genres like fashion, illustration, graphics and art, architecture, and design—anything necessary to inspire the artistic mind. The "Creator's Market" showcases and sells artists' works at in-store events. And since it has a branch office in Japan keeping tabs on the art scene, the store often carries hard-to-find items, not to mention Tokyo trends before they hit the States. Displays of plush anime characters, squeeky, thumb-sized Godzillas from a gachpon (a Japanese toy vending machine), and t-shirts with colorful graphics break up the bookshelves. Even the strangest Japanese kitsch has a home at Zakka.

EAT

Alma
Mexican

This chic rooftop eatery treats its guests to high-end Mexican cuisine and jaw-dropping Manhattan views. The reasonably priced menu includes simple dishes like homemade guacamole, braised chicken with ground fruit and chile sauce, fish tacos, stews, and stuffed peppers. Brunch deals and entrees top out at $19 and draw an eclectic mix of locals and travelers seeking homey Mexican fare in refined environs. You may spot a family of four sharing plates next to a young collegiate couple sampling from Alma's tequila list. Attentive, alert, and personable staff weave through the maze of tables to ensure that the atmosphere remains lively and comfortable, if a bit close. Come to gorge on guac while watching the sun set behind Manhattan's skyline.

187 Columbia St (at Degraw St)
718-643-5400
Brunch Sat-Sun 10am-2:30pm,
Dinner Sat-Thurs 5:30pm-
10pm, Fri-Sat 5:30-11pm
Rooftop closed Mon-Wed
December 1-March 2
F G to Carol St
Appetizers $8-10,
Entrees $16-18

DUMBO General Store
American, Café, Sandwiches,

A regular haunt for DUMBO's art crowd, this cheery neighborhood café is the perfect spot to lounge on a lazy afternoon. Worn wooden tables, a large

Persian rug, and vintage Victorian seats warm up the airy room and invite diners to get cozy. Various caffeinated beverages and baked goods are available at the bar, but linger for a full-fledged lunch if you can. The self-proclaimed "famous panini" deserve the title: the delicious roast chicken panino, featuring perfectly toasted, crunchy bread generously stuffed with smokey, seasoned chicken, is a particularly popular choice. For a lighter meal, opt for the goat cheese salad, a house favorite with sugared walnuts, red onion, oregano, and lemon vinaigrette. If the décor and unfussy food don't make you feel at home, the amiable, relaxed staff certainly will.

111 Front St (near Adams St)
718-855-5288
Mon-Sat 12pm-4pm & 6pm-12am, Sun 9am-5pm
Ⓐ Ⓒ to High St, **Ⓕ** to York St
Breakfast $6-11, Lunch $8-10
Cash Only

Grimaldi's *Pizzeria*
Head-shots of Rudy Giuliani, Elijah Wood, and Grimaldi's regular Frank Sinatra are nestled among those of other famous patrons at this legendary brick-oven pizzeria in the shadow of the Brooklyn Bridge. Even after a long wait, one bite of their thin-crust pizza will make you understand why Grimaldi's is the perennial favorite of natives, tourists, and celebrities alike. It boasts vibrantly fresh tomato sauce and mozzarella, though the best trait is the crust: infused with that intoxicating, smoky, brick-oven flavor, its texture a perfect balance of crispy and chewy. The secret ingredient is rumored to be Brooklyn water, but don't worry yourself over the salutary implications. Instead of water, order a Manhattan Special soda. It's not on the menu, but this sweet, coffee-flavored drink is a favorite of Italian-American New Yorkers and a wonderfully refreshing secret sip.

19 Old Fulton St
(btwn Front & Water St)
718-858-4300
Mon-Fri 11:30 am-11pm, Sat 12pm-12am, Sun 12pm-11pm
Ⓐ Ⓒ to High St, **② ③** to Clark St, **Ⓕ** to York St
Large Pizza $14, Toppings $2

Le Petit Marche *Bistro, French*
One of several French bistros in DUMBO,

without the haute attitude. Though the menu veers into fairly creative territory with dishes like a fried soft shell crab over a bed of colorful tomatoes, onions, and herbed goat cheese, Le Petit Marche is at its best in more traditional territory. Truffle mac and cheese, served in a cavernous casserole dish beneath a thin crust of breadcrumbs, is a hearty, luxurious preface to any entree. Follow with the hanger steak, bursting with flavor and served alongside a heaping pile of well-seasoned French fries. A flourless chocolate soufflé with homemade organic pistachio ice cream brings the meal to a simple, refined finale. This dessert is emblematic of Le Petit Marche at its classic, unaffected best.

Appetizers $6-13,
Entrees $15-27

❷❸ to Clark St

work in multimedia performance and puppetry, this converted warehouse is well-known for programming that defies the boundaries of genre classification. Its high walls and bare cement floors create the perfect space for the half-dozen shows it hosts every year. Past programming has featured puppetry, rock'n'roll, Shakespeare, Isben, Lou Reed's "Berlin," and even Julian Schnabel's musical "Saw." The concession stand, catered by Rice Bar, also offers exceedingly above-average theater grub in the way of clever drinks and snacks. Most performances begin at 8pm, leaving you plenty of post-show time to explore other neighborhood nightlife. And after a few drinks, you might actually start to understand what you've just seen.

Hours & cost depend on
show/event
🄵 to York St, ❷❸ to Clark
St, 🄰🄲 to High St

BROOKLYN HTS & DUMBO

Galapagos Art Space   *Cabaret, Theater, Bar, Burlesque*

While the term "performance art" may conjure unappealing images of people slapping their faces with raw meat on stage, the shows at this large cement-and-brick space are a slightly less alienating form of avant-garde. In addition to coming for the American Apparel-clad emcees who dance and perform occasionally disturbing prop comedy, visit this red-lit bar and theater for expectedly bizarre movie reenactments, circus performers, vaudeville acts, and tamer quiz nights and job fairs. Enjoy the surprisingly good music (the DJ's name is Hello Booty) and be sure to grab one of their large, strong, and wonderfully creative drinks—the Long-Stem Lemonade comes highly recommended.

16 Main St (near Water St)
718-222-8500
6pm-2am (event times vary)
🄵 to York St, 🄰 🄲 to High St,
2 3 to Clark St
Average drink: $9,
Average show $10-15

FORT GREENE

Literary luminary and social progressive Walt Whitman once called this area home, and his legacy lives on in the neighborhood to this day. Once an energetic community activist who had the first African American school in New York built on his property, Whitman was instrumental in the creation of Fort Greene Park, and after his death the neighborhood continued to blossom as a cultural destination.

During the early to mid-19th century the neighborhood was popular with wealthy professionals tired of overcrowded Manhattan who were attracted by the short commute. Many mansions over a century-and-a-half old still stand on Clinton Avenue, including those of Charles Pratt, the founder of the prominent art and design school that bears his name. Today, the twenty-five acre campus of the Pratt Institute remains a center of activity in nearby Clinton Hill, serving as a magnet for bohemian culture and artistic talent.

As more young professionals move in from Prospect Heights and Park Slope (where rents continue to rise), gentrification becomes a greater concern to the area's poorer residents, many of whom live in the industrialized area near the 19th-century Navy Shipyard. Whitman's ghost seems to speak from the very streets, though, as his old romping grounds are well known for their unusually amicable economic and racial integration.

Today, the neighborhood is widely known as the home of the Brooklyn Academy of Music and the rich cultural district that has blossomed around it. Although Clinton Hill continues to evolve, the neighborhood is said to lack some of the amenities that are enjoyed by residents of nearby, more affluent neighborhoods (reliable train service, for one thing). Everything in life is a trade-off, though: it is these very annoyances that keep the area affordable.

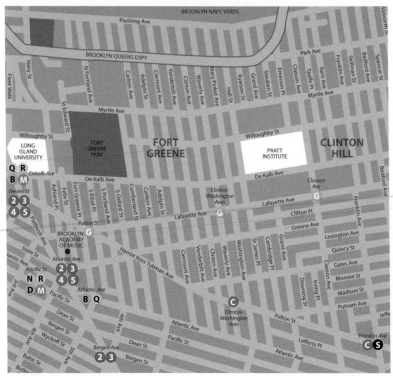

EXPLORE

Brooklyn Masonic Temple

On the corner of Clermont and Lafayette, amid peaceful residential streets, lies one of Brooklyn's hippest concert halls. Even if you are in no mood for music, it's worth exploring this architectural wonder of richly colored tiles and classical columns. But with everything from jazz to indie rock, this large yet intimate venue has nearly all music tastes covered. A small curtained stage is lit by a multicolored glass chandelier as the crowd sips fairly-priced drinks in the spacious viewing area. The space only houses a couple of shows each month—it's just a mystery what happens here the rest of the

> 317 Clermont Ave #4
> (at Lafayette Ave)
> 718-638-1256 Ⓖ to Clinton-
> Washington Ave
> Hours & prices vary

time—but they are definitely worth checking out. Recent performers have included indie powerhouses José González and TV on the Radio. Check online for schedules and tickets at www.masonicboom.com.

Fort Greene Park

Established as the first park in Brooklyn in 1850 and named after General Nathaniel Greene, Fort Greene Park was designed by the architects that did Central and Prospect Parks. Its vast, sloping landscape and shady trees offer ideal spaces to relax, read a book, or people-watch. For those who want to exercise, there are also multiple pathways for strolling, jogging, or bike riding, as well as six tennis

> Btwn DeKalb Ave, Myrtle Ave,
> Washington Park,
> & Saint Edward St
> 718-222-1461
> Ⓑ Ⓜ Ⓠ Ⓡ to DeKalb Ave,
> ② ③ ④ ⑤ to Nevins St,
> Ⓖ to Fulton St

courts, a basketball court, two playgrounds, and large grass-covered and stone swaths of land. The most elevated part of the park is home to the Prison Ship Martyrs Monument, a massive column that commemorates those who died in captivity aboard British ships after the Battle of Long Island in 1776. Near the monument, you can just see the peaks of the Manhattan skyline in the distance.

Irondale Theater

One of the BAM Cultural District's performance venues, this former church was renovated last year and now hosts the Irondale Ensemble. The theater's high ceilings and age-textured walls still bear a few fading religious ornaments overlooking the 200-seat theater. And the troupe's focus on social themes fits well with the church's activist past. The troupe of full-time actors puts on original, experimental plays emphasizing cultural issues and the daily life of ordinary local citizens as well as adaptations of classic Brecht and Shakespeare works re-tooled to deal with contemporary America. Aside from theatrical works, the massive performance space hosts guest shows, educational and community programs, family and kid-friendly weekend performances, and teen improv workshops.

85 S Oxford St
(at Lafayette Ave)
718-488-9233
②③④⑤⑧⑩⓿⓪⓷
to Atlantic Ave/Pacific St
ⓒ to Lafayette Ave,
ⓖ to Fulton St,
Box office opens 1 hour
before show
Tickets online or by phone

Museum of Contemporary African Diaspora Arts

MoCADA's mission is to explore the frequently marginalized history of the African Diaspora through its contributions to art, culture, and society in general. Located on the ground floor of the beautiful redbrick James E. Davis 80 Arts Building, in the heart of the BAM Cultural District, the museum houses constantly rotating creative multimedia exhibitions (past highlights include "The Postmillennial Black Madonna" and "The Middle Passage: White Ships, Black

80 Hanson Pl
(at S Portland Ave)
718-230-0492
Wed-Sun 11am-6pm
②③④⑤⑧⑩⓿⓪⓷
to Atlantic Ave/Pacific St
ⓒ to Lafayette Ave,
ⓖ to Fulton St,
Suggested donation: $4

DAY TO DAY

Brooklyn Community Board 2: 350 Jay St, 8th Floor, 718-596-5410.

Dry Cleaner: Yes Cleaners, 668 Fulton St, 718-858-0388

Groceries: Greene Grape Provisions, 753 Fulton St, 718-233-2700

Gym: Forte Greene Sports Club, 691 Fulton St, 718-797-9464.

Hospital: Brooklyn Hospital Center, 121 DeKalb Ave, 718-250-8080.

Laundromat: Alpine Laundromat, 182 DeKalb Ave.

Library: Brooklyn Public Library: Pacific Branch, 25 4th Ave (at Pacific St), 718-638-1531.

Media: *Fort Greene Brooklyn*, fortgreenebrooklyn.com. *Fort Greene Association*, historicfortgreene.org.

Volunteer Opportunities: Fort Greene Park Conservancy, fortgreenepark.org.

Cargo"). Come for a look into a culture whose rich past often escapes the artistic and historical foci of Americans, and whose continuing influences shape not only Fort Greene and Brooklyn, but the city as a whole.

Urban Glass

Tucked away in what appears to be a deserted side street is the first, and now largest, artist-access glass center in the United States. Urban

647 Fulton St #1 (at Fulton St)
718-625-3685
Closed Mon, Tues-Thurs 10-9pm, Fri-Sun 10-5pm.
② ③ ④ ⑤ to Nevins St, ⑥ to Fulton, ⑥ to Lafayette, ⑧ ⑩ ⑥ ⑥ to DeKalb

Glass provides everything necessary for making a wide variety of glass art, such as furnaces, a mold works, and even a shop for making neon signs. Also offered are various workshops— everything from glassblowing to bead-making lessons. If you're more interested in observing than participating, you can visit the gallery where artist and student works are presented, take a demonstration tour around the studio, or purchase some of the artists' pieces at the store. A large front window allows passersby to glance into the studio, and get a free, up-close glimpse of both masters and novices at work.

Barking Brown

Trendy and relatively inexpensive, this clothing store embodies the essence of the neighborhood. There's no

468 Myrtle Ave
(near Washington Ave)
718-638-3757
Mon-Fri 10am-9pm, Sat 10am-10pm, Sun 10am-8pm
⑥ to Clinton-Washington Ave

Manhattan snobbery here—the atmosphere's just as warm and welcoming as the staff. Choose from demure, airy pieces to skintight, brightly-colored mini dresses, the majority of which come from U.S. designers, including a few Brooklynites. Though the average piece of clothing is $90, jewelry and other accessories are priced between $15 and 50, making it easy for anyone to leave with a new, trendy addition to their wardrobe. Merchandise also rotates frequently, so it's nearly impossible to catch a fashion twin gawking at you from across the street.

Brooklyn Flea

Every Saturday young Brooklynites flock to the white tents on Bishop Loughlin High School's basketball court for Brownstoner's weekly flea

357 Clermont Ave
(near Greene Ave)
Sat 10am-5pm
④ ⑥ to Lafayette Ave,
⑥ to Clinton/Washington Ave,
② ③ ④ ⑤ ⑧ ⑩ ⑩ ⑥ ⑥
& ⑩ to Atlantic Ave/Pacific St

market. Over 150 venders from across New York City sell their vintage and kitschy best, a DJ spin tracks, and hungry shoppers munch on fantastically greasy quesadillas and hot dogs during the seven hours. Rain or shine, this market has enough unique finds to put Urban Outfitter knock offs to shame. With as little as $5, you can find everything from eco-friendly furniture to cotton sarongs.

Dope Jams

Behind the chipped paint and tattered doorway screen lies a music store experience unlike most other in the city.

580 Myrtle Ave
(near Classon Ave)
718-622-7977
Mon-Sat 12pm-9pm,
Sun 12pm-7pm
⑥ to Classon Ave

Browsing the selection will reward you with CDs and vinyls of old school salsa, R&B, hip-hop, and fresh remixes from popular DJs. The selection is so good that local turntablists craft whole playlists out the finds here. There's plenty to choose from when it comes to genres, but their forte is clearly dance music—techno, house, and whatever else gets you moving. Peruse albums of artists like Supercat and Karizma and take in the drifting aroma of burning incense. The store also carries oils, artwork, clothing, books on witchcraft, turntables, and sound equipment for aspiring DJs. Makes you wonder if the store's initials hold more meaning than coincidence.

EAT

67 Burger

Burgers, American

67 Lafayette (at Fulton St)
718-797-7150
Sun-Thurs 11:30am-10pm
Fri-Sat 11:30am-11pm
Ⓖ to Fulton, Ⓒ to Lafayette,
②③④⑤ⒷⒹⓂⓃⓄⓇ
to Atlantic/Pacific
Burgers $6-10, Sides $3-5,
Fries $3-4

With its metal chairs and tables, 67 Burger resembles nothing more than a truly authentic American cafeteria where medium means medium, rare means still bleeding, and the scent of grilling meat wafts out the door. Hamburgers, turkey burgers, veggie burgers, and grilled chicken sandwiches are all prepared using fresh ingredients and customizable with 'extras' of your choice. But they save you the trouble of creating with pitch perfect combinations like "The Parisian," a burger with white wine sautéed onions, mushrooms, and Dijon mustard. The menu is rounded out with above-average fries (on par with the burgers), and a variety of good salads—but, really, why bother? They offer a considerable selections of mostly-local beers, the perfect way to chase down your burger.

Bati

Ethiopian

747 Fulton St
(near S Portland Ave)
718-797-9696
Mon-Fri 5pm-11pm,
Sat-Sun 1pm-11pm
Ⓖ to Fulton, Ⓒ to Lafayette,
②③④⑤ⒷⒹⓂⓃⓄⓇ
to Atlantic/Pacific
Appetizers $5-6,
Entrees $12-15

Large windows up front, rough-hewn wooden tables, and dim lighting make for a warm, sophisticated atmosphere at this trendy, market table style restaurant. Bati's friendly, engaging wait staff will graciously offer in-depth explanations and descriptions of each dish on the menu. The strong, bold flavors of Ethiopian cuisine make a good show here, most notably in mouthwatering sauces and seasonings. Connoisseurs of the cuisine choose kitfo, the Ethiopian answer to beef tartare, or the tikil gomen, green cabbage with garlic and ginger—one of many intensely flavored vegan/vegetarian dishes offered. All mains are served with injera, the spongy, flavorful flatbread that doubles as the only utensil in Ethiopian cuisine. Generous portions make sharing easy, though leaving room for desserts—like the delicious, honey-dressed baklava—proves more difficult.

Black Iris

Middle Eastern

228 DeKalb Ave
(at Clermont Ave)
718-852-9800
12pm-12am
Ⓖ to Clinton-Washington Ave
Appetizers $4-9, Entrees $5-17

Despite its run-of-the-mill Middle Eastern restaurant furnishings, Black Iris is hardly your standard falafel shop. Food at Black Iris, like the décor, doesn't exactly throw diners familiar with the cuisine any curve balls, but does prepare Middle Eastern standards with honest, home-style generosity. Richly seasoned appetizers like baba ghanoush and foul (a traditional fava bean puree) are served with fresh-baked pita bread, and the kebabs are tender, juicy, and flavorful. Slightly less traditional

options like the "special" chicken ouzi—a pastry stuffed with chicken, vegetables, basmati rice, almonds, and raisins—are welcome surprises on the menu of otherwise familiar flavors, and speciality "pitzas" are crispy, light, and delicious. If the huge portions (easily big enough to share) and fresh ingredients don't leave you feeling at home, then the kindly, attentive wait staff will.

Madiba
South African

For ten years, this lively and intimate neighborhood staple has been serving South African food with style to adventurous eaters and local regulars alike. The cozy front lounge features plush seating, large-screen projectors, as well as occasional live music and DJs. Modeled after South African shebeens (outdoor barbecue-speakeasies), the more spacious dining area is decked out with traditional art and modern imports from the continent. The menu offers a wide selection of both the familiar and exotic (including an ostrich carpaccio appetizer), reflecting English,

195 DeKalb Ave
(near Carlton Ave)
718-855-9190
Mon-Thu 4-11pm,
Fri-Sat 4-12am
B M R to DeKalb,
G to Clinton-Washington Ave
Appetizers $8-18,
Entrees $14-24

Indian, and native influences. Carnivores will be particularly pleased—thick tenderloins, rich stews, ribs, and burgers enlivened by generous use of spice make for a hearty meal. Stick around after you're sated to listen to the awesome playlist, try the Malva pudding for dessert, or enjoy one of the bar's twelve specialty cocktails

Tillie's of Brooklyn
Café, Sandwiches

This café may not dazzle with innovation, but its attention to detail—from the outstanding coffee to the carefully selected art on the walls— keeps neighborhood regulars coming back. Used as a gallery for local artists, Tillie's rotates wall art every few weeks and regularly hosts opening events. In other services to locals, Friday nights brings live music at a reasonable price ($3 entry charge for students), Thursdays boast a packed open-mic night, and Tuesdays hold poetry readings. Fresh, homemade pastries and snacks are available to pair with coffee, tea, italian sodas, organic fruit juices,

248 Dekalb Ave
(at Vanderbilt Ave)
718-783-8691
Mon-Fri 7:30am-10pm,
Sat-Sun 8am-10pm
G to Clinton-Washington
Aves, **C** to Lafayette Ave
Average drink $2-4.50
Average Snack $1-8
Pastries $2-5, Sandwiches &
Salads $5-8

BAM CULTURAL DISTRICT

Founded in 1861, Brooklyn Academy of Music (BAM) is the oldest continually-operating performing arts center in America. Though it began as a small concert hall for the Philharmonic Society of Brooklyn, BAM now stands amid a wealth of performance and artistic spaces that it helped to create, known collectively as the BAM Cultural District. Designed by the architectural firm Herts & Tallant, the **Howard Gilman Opera House** (*30 Lafayette Ave*) seats over 2,000 and has staged legendary performances by Enrico Caruso, John Cage, Vanessa Redgrave, and Isadora Duncan. Local cinephiles flock to **BAM Rose Cinemas** (*30 Lafayette Ave*), which screens cinematic classics and first-run independent films alike. Pratt students gather at **BAMcafé** (*30 Lafayette Ave*) for free music performances on weekend nights. And theatre aficionados head to the traditional playhouse **BAM Harvey Theater** (*651 Fulton St*) for Shakespearean revivals, vaudeville reviews, and musicals. The volume of events at BAM is simply staggering—community initiatives, festivals like DanceAfrica and BAMcinemaFEST, ongoing art exhibitions, educational programs, and more. Check out the calendar at bam.org to see what's coming next.

and even old-fashioned Egg Creams for the nostalgic. Plenty of seating and free WiFi for customers are other luxuries afforded by this quintessential neighborhood shop.

PLAY

BAMcafé

Café, Live Music

30 Lafayette Ave
(near Ashland Pl)
718-623-7811
Thurs-Sun 5pm-Showtime
during Summer
② ③ ④ ⑤ ⑧ ⓓ ⓝ ⓠ ⓡ
& ⓜ to Atlantic Ave/Pacific St
Food & Drink Minimum $10
No Cover

BAMcafé feels like a composite of all things "Brooklyn cool"—it's an art space, a bar, a music venue, and a café. Tiny lights glow from inside wire roses and twinkle behind the silver lattice in the middle of each red, high-beamed arch. The huge windows each have circles of lights moving in swirling patterns, reminiscent of stars, clocks, or bull's-eyes. It's a popular place to take a date, grab a relaxed bite before a film at BAM Rose Cinemas, or snag a drink during a BAMcafé live performance. The menu is American with a French twist, featuring an assortment of highbrow bar food like wasabi crusted shrimp with a soy ginger reduction. Every Friday and Saturday night, BAMcafé features free shows from local and emerging jazz, Afro-pop, and spoken word artists.

Frank's Cocktail Lounge

DJ, Live Music, Lounge

660 Fulton St
(near South Elliott Pl)
718-302-6464
Mon 2pm-2am, Tue-Thurs
3pm-2am, Fri-Sat 3pm-4am,
Sun 4pm-1am
ⓒ to Lafayette Ave,
ⓖ to Fulton St, **② ③**
④ ⑤ ⑧ ⓓ ⓜ ⓝ ⓠ ⓡ to
Atlantic Ave
Average Drink $6

The street outside may be packed with loud, young bar-hoppers, but the red awning over this funk and soul lounge draws a more relaxed crowd. This classy neighborhood spot, adorned with strung lights and wooden panels, lends itself to both good conversation and dancing. For those just looking to drink a cold beer at the long bar, snack on salty cocktail nuts, and soak up the throwback vibe, the lounge hosts saxophone players on quiet weeknights. On weekends DJs take over the back room to spin hip hop, R&B, and reggae beats for an energized, sweaty crowd on the dance floor. Stop by on Sunday night for three straight hours of jazz, come by Tuesday or Thursday for a live show, or croon out yourself on Karaoke Wednesdays.

GREATER CARROLL GARDENS

Alternatively known as South Brooklyn, the Greater Carroll Gardens area was unincorporated farmland until the mid-1800s, after which it became home to diverse groups of newcomers to the city. The region consists of Boerum Hill, Cobble Hill, Carroll Gardens (known collectively as "BoCoCa," but don't get caught saying that), Gowanus, and Red Hook, each a distinct neighborhood with its own vibe.

A working-class, predominantly Italian neighborhood, Carroll Gardens takes its name from Revolutionary War leader Charles Carroll, who led an attack on the British in nearby Gowanus. The area's narrow, one-lane roads and decorative streetlights maintain the historic feel, while recently opened restaurants and small businesses add a more modern flair, as young professionals move into the neighborhood in increasing numbers. Young families are especially prevalent in Cobble Hill, a quiet neighborhood of three- and four-story brownstones and brick rowhouses. The area includes more service-oriented businesses, such as dry cleaners and nail salons, as opposed to the more entertainment- and dining-oriented establishments on Carroll Gardens' trendy Smith Street.

Gowanus, location of the 1776 Battle of Brooklyn, is an industrial area whose major landmarks are the Gowanus Expressway and the Gowanus Canal, the subject of much environmental justice activism. The Gowanus Houses, where Spike Lee filmed his adaptation of Richard Price's novel *Clockers*, are actually not located in Gowanus but in nearby Boerum Hill, an equally gritty neighborhood that is home to the Brooklyn House of Detention. Preservationists have restored some of Boerum Hill's historic buildings, improving the area's real estate values.

Similarly, Red Hook, dominated by housing projects and defunct warehouses, is beginning to capitalize on its waterfront location. The area, which Life magazine once labeled "the crack capital of America," is undergoing a renaissance as artists and businesses settle into the neighborhood.

EXPLORE

Brooklyn Waterfront Artists Coalition

In line with the recent trend to revitalize Red Hook, Brooklyn Waterfront Artists Coalition capitalizes

499 Van Brunt St
(near Reed St)
718-596-2506
Sat & Sun 1pm-6pm
Ⓖ to Smith-9th St

on the neighborhoods's empty piers and prime waterfront views to house free exhibitions inside an enchanting brick warehouse. This nonprofit features the work of local artists with a new show every month between May and October. Inside, you'll find over 800 works of art, including black and white photographs, oil paintings, and sculptures. Check the website for opening receptions—you can meet the artists themselves and enjoy the musical stylings of underground Brooklyn talent.

Cobble Hill Park

Slate sidewalks lead to benches made for taking in the gorgeous landscaping at this

At Clinton & Congress St
Dawn-Dusk
ⒻⒼ to Bergen St

patch of green. Shady trees surround a circular pathway with a central garden, and blue and pink flowers dot the park. This neighborhood spot is a great place to rest and read—there are no recreation areas and it's rarely loud, except for Thursday summer nights, when the park offers free concerts mainly geared towards the young neighborhood families. Leave the park to stroll along a nearby street of brownstones, or pop into one of the local cafés for a refreshing post-park snack.

Micro Museum

Home to exhibitions, meetings, classes, and workshops attended by more than 600 art aficionados, the Micro Museum is one of Brooklyn's best resources for

123 Smith St
(btwn Dean & Pacific St)
718-797-3116
Exhibits Sat 12pm-7pm,
Bookings & appointments
Sun-Fri 9am-9pm
ⒻⒼ to Bergen St, ⒶⒸⒼ
to Hoyt-Schermerhorn St
Prices vary

contemporary visual and performing art. The list of contributors includes writers, directors, clowns, painters, belly dancers, and other performers. From themes like surrealist animal kingdom invasions to charcoal activism, the exhibitions range widely and change every two months. Billing itself as a "living arts center," the Micro Museum offers space for artists to create new works and a focal point for a wonderful arts community.

New York Transit Museum

Trudge down stairs leading to an old subway station, purchase tickets at a wooden kiosk, and push through heavy turnstiles to reach this converted museum. Built into the now defunct Brooklyn Court Street Station,

Boerum Place & Schermerhorn St
718-694-1600
Tues-Fri 10pm-4pm,
Sat & Sun 12pm-5pm
②③④⑤ to
Borough Hall, ④⑤⑤ to
Jay St-Borough Hall, ⑩⑪ to
Court St., ④⑤⑥ to Hoyt-
Schermerhorn St
Adults $5, Children $3,
Seniors $3, Free Wed

New York Transit Museum offers displays, historic photographs, artifacts, and numerous hands-on activities about the transformation of public transportation in the greater New York City region. Without a doubt, the museum's 20 vintage train cars are the highlight of the visit. Walk through cars with checkered floors, neon green ceilings, and striped yellow seats. All of them have the original floorplans, color schemes, and advertisements intact—and some even have tables. Visitors can also stop by the museum's gift shop for a t-shirt boasting their favorite line.

Shop Art

In keeping with their belief that "art should not be exclusively reserved for the elite initiate," this eccentric gallery offers paintings,

51 Bergen St (near Smith St)
718-858-4535
Wed-Sat 11am-7pm,
Sun 12-5pm
②③④⑤ to Borough Hall,
⑤⑥ to Bergen St,
⑥ to Court St

drawings, sculptures, and other aesthetic objects for as little as $8. Exhibitions showcase work from both emerging and established artists, with a focus on those from Brooklyn. Bare lightbulbs suspended from exposed rafters illuminate the pieces—the space was converted from a factory building—and create a calming, casual atmosphere far less intimidating than those of more conventional galleries. If you're a beginning collector or a home decorator looking for modern, inexpensive artwork, this is the place to visit.

The Waterfront Museum and Showboat Barge

The Waterfront Museum is a veritable piece of "living history"—or at least it's housed in one. Now docked in Red Hook's

290 Conover St (at Pier 44)
718-624-4719
Thurs 4-8pm, Sat 1-5pm
②③④⑤ to Borough Hall,
④⑤⑥ to Jay St-Borough
Hall, ⑩⑪ to Court St,
⑤⑥ to Smith-9th St
Group tours $7 per person

tranquil Erie Basin, 95-year-old Lehigh Valley Railroad Barge #79 is the last floating cargo lighter in New York Harbor. Since 1986, the resurrected barge has served as not only a relic of New York's rich maritime heritage, but also a classroom, art exhibition space, and a summer showboat—complete with musical and circus performances. Hop aboard for a one-hour tour, where you'll learn about the rise and fall of trade barges, explore the captain's cabin, and wade through an ocean of nautical artifacts without getting the slightest bit seasick.

SHOP

Artez'n

The name of this small, white-walled "gifts and gallery" boutique is as funky and unconventional (the 'e' is actually upside down) as its merchandise. Almost all of the artwork,

444 Atlantic Ave
(btwn Nevins & Bond St)
718-596-2649
Wed-Sat 11am-7pm,
Sun 11am-6pm
Ⓐ Ⓒ Ⓖ to Hoyt-
Schermerhorn St, ❷ ❸ ❹ ❺
to Nevins St, Ⓓ Ⓜ Ⓝ Ⓡ to
Atlantic Ave-Pacific St

jewelry, ceramics, clothing, accessories, and glassware are handcrafted by local residents. It comes as no surprise, then, that Artez'n is especially renowned for its idiosyncratic Brooklyn-themed items: t-shirts emblazoned with Coney Island mermaids, pint glasses imprinted with images of the Bridge and Grand Army Plaza, and hip flasks branded with "Brooklyn Love." Other whimsically witty trinkets include cast iron NYC manhole cover coasters, razor blade necklaces, Unsolicited Comment Cards, and lullaby renditions of AC/DC. Drop by on Wednesday and Saturday nights for silk-screen printing or jewelry-making classes. If there ever was a hipster haven within hipster heaven, this is it.

Brooklyn Collective

Hidden away at the back of an antique store, this boutique showcases original clothing and goods from local designers and artists. Women's

198 Columbia St
(near Sackett St)
718-596-6231
Wed-Thurs 12pm-6pm,
Fri-Sun 12pm-8pm,
closed Mon-Tues
Ⓕ Ⓖ to Bergen St

clothing and jewelry, delicate lingerie, and colorful pottery sit next to vivid artwork, understated prints, and hand-painted cards. And since the designers share the rent and split 100% of the profits, they bypass the stressful demands of mass-market retail, allowing them to create pieces that transcend predictable chain store trends. Prices are reasonable, especially considering the unique finds, but are not always cheap—dresses that grant the wearer a daring silhouette sell for around $120. With rotating exhibits by different artists, the store also mixes fashion and artwork.

Community Bookstore

Shelves buckle under the weight of hefty books, and precariously teetering stacks loom over customers whose noses are buried in their finds.

212 Court St (at Warren St)
718-834-9494
Mon-Sun 3pm-11pm
Ⓕ Ⓖ to Bergen St

Handwritten signs direct you through the labyrinthine shelving, but it may be more fun to get lost in the great selection. This 25-year-old bookstore is stocked with old and used volumes, but also has a section of newer arrivals. Offering more than your corporate chain-store titans, Community Bookstore hosts author readings

UNDER $20

Take in culture at a gallery near the waterfront, like **Gestarc Gallery** (*390 Van Brunt St*) or the nearby **Kentler International Drawing Space** (*353 Van Brunt St*). Then grab a used novel from the dollar shelves of **Community Bookstore** (*212 Court St*), and continue down Court St to **Carroll Park** (*at President St*), where you can sit on a bench and begin your new read—or just people-watch. For sit-down Italian grub on the cheap, walk another block down Court Street and pop into **Fragole** (*394 Court St*) or **Frankie's 457 Spuntino** (*457 Court*

and book-club nights, throws parties, and keeps locals up-to-date on local happenings by posting events. So perch yourself on a pile of books and enjoy all that this bookstore has to offer.

One Girl Cookies

Described by the owner as "the universal symbol of comfort and happiness," the

68 Dean St (near Smith St)
212-675-4996
Mon-Thurs 8am-8pm, Sat-
Sun 11am-9pm
Ⓕ to Bergen St

cookies at this gourmet shop charm visitors with vivid flavors and personal flair. There's a wide variety of unique selections: oat spiced with crystallized Thai ginger, orange butter with shredded coconut, and hazelnut smeared with cinnamon chocolate ganache stock their classic collection. Indulge in a couple on the spot or take them home—the bakery offers pre-prepared assortments in nostalgic packaging with sepia-toned family photographs on the top. Not in the mood for cookies? Shop for cakes, whoopie pies,

St). Sweat off your meal at **Red Hook Park** (*Bay St at Clinton St*), where you can join in on a soccer game or bring a handball and play at the courts. On Saturdays and Sundays, a mouth-watering array of food carts line up between Clinton and Court St to sell enormous cups of ceviche, glasses of coconut juice, corn on the cob covered in cheese and spices, and other Latin American specialties. If you're heading back to Manhattan, take a B77 bus to the **IKEA water ferry** (*1 Beard St*) for spectacularly free city views—it leaves every 20 minutes for Wall St.

cupcakes, coffees, and teas. See if they're offering one of their monthly baking classes while you're in the area, and soon you might be whipping up these heavenly confections.

Sahadi's Fine Foods

From the freshest feta and ripest Mediterranean olives to myriad spices and fragrant ground coffees, this Middle Eastern grocery store has provided locals with deliciously cheap specialty foods and a memorable shopping experience for over 60 years. Choose from an assortment of dried fruits, nuts, and snacks—and watch the grocer scoop, measure, and weigh your treats, and send the bag flying through the air and into your basket in record time. Yes, your personal shopper tosses your order at you, but always with a smile. The tzatziki here is made just right, the falafel is perfectly moist, and the hummus is to die for. Take advantage of the prices at this specialty store and buy in bulk—it all goes fast.

187 Atlantic Ave
(btwn Court & Clinton)
718-624-4550
M-Sat 9am-7pm
②③④⑤ⓂⓇⓌ to
Court St-Borough Hall, **ⒻⒼ**
to Bergen St, **ⒶⒸⒻ** to Jay St

Union Max

A jewelry maker's heaven, this tiny shop overflows with an extraordinary selection of reasonably-priced vintage beads and baubles. Assorted rare beads and buttons pack tightly into jars marked for $3-5, enticing visitors to create their own accessories. Trimmings like 50s faux cocktail rings and retro plastic necklaces dangle from the walls. An ever-rotating selection of women's vintage clothing holds many hidden treasures, as does their section of antique housewares. Browse through the racks and discover skirts selling for $10 and find fabulous dresses for around $25, or pick up a brightly-colored antique lamp to spruce up your living space. With a wide selection and low prices, every customer can afford to let out her inner Zsa Zsa Gabor.

110 Union St (at Columbus St)
718-222-1785
Fri-Sun 1pm-7pm
ⒻⒼ to Bergen St

Vintage Signage

Antique French and American signs and posters, as well as various knickknacks and collectibles, are packed away in this colorful treasure chest. The walls are covered with bright signs that urge you to "buvez un Pepsi" or hype a Parisian art exhibit that took place in 1972. You'll find a delightful and surprising mix of finds here, including a large collection of ancient celebrity photographs, signed boxing gloves, and a large antique picnic basket with the plates, napkins, and silverware still neatly packed inside. Rarities may be

334 Atlantic Ave
(btwn Hoyt St & Smith St)
718-834-9268
Daily 12pm-7pm
ⒻⒼ to Bergen St, **ⒶⒸⒼ**
to Hoyt-Schermerhorn St

pricey, so be prepared to spend some cash, but if you do enough browsing it should be easy to stumble upon some good steals.

EAT

Café LULUc
Bistro, French

The adorable red awning lures locals in daily for brunch, lunch, and dinner at this Carroll Gardens favorite. A cozy cross between a French bistro and an upscale American diner, Café LULUc serves everything from fluffy pancakes to juicy gourmet burgers, all at reasonable prices. With its classic bistro menu, Café LULUc may not surprise its patrons, but it easily satisfies their hunger with generous portions of well-prepared standbys. Conversation flows as easily as the wines on the decent wine list, filling the room of

214 Smith St
(btwn Baltic & Butler St)
718-625-3815
F G to Bergen St
Daily 8am-12am
Brunch $6-10, Appetizers
$6-12, Entrees $9-18

red leather and candlelit booths and beckoning passersby on warm nights when the front opens onto the street. On such nights, the canopy in the beautiful courtyard provides a more peaceful setting. Day or night, LULUc is crammed, so grab a table early and settle in to enjoy an evening of solid, comforting bistro fare.

Frankie's Spuntino 457
Italian

This intimate and hip Italian hotspot draws attractive Brooklyn locals with its laid-back elegance and chic vibe. The menu of light Italian fare incorporates local, and often housemade, products ensuring that your meal is fresh, flavorful, and seasonal. In the summer, the friendly staff will serve up salads like fennel with pecorino and pastas like handmade linguine with garlic and house-made olive oil, along with gourmet sandwiches,

457 Court St
(btwn Luquer St & 4th Pl)
718-403-0033
Sun-Thurs 11am-11pm,
Fri-Sat 11am-12am
F G to Carroll St
Appetizers $6-9,
Entrees $9-18
Cash only

NATIVE'S PICK

Ted and Honey
Café

With its welcoming red storefront, warm indoor seating, and intimate outdoor tables, Ted and Honey is a delightfully homey place to grab a coffee or a bite to eat. Located on the quaintest street in Cobble Hill, this one-year-old café and market offers organic food with a no-fuss ethos. If you can't find a table to enjoy your breakfast sandwich—served all day—head across Verandah Place to their extended dining room in Cobble Hill Park. The menu options satisfy most cravings, from the perfect veggie burger with homemade aioli to breakfast crostini with figs, ricotta, and honey on a soft baguette. Fresh ingredients sourced from local and organic farmers also come well-proportioned. Grab and go, sit for hours mooching the free WiFi, or come to attend a cooking class at this neighborhood spot.

264 Clinton St, Cobble Hill
(btw Baltic St & Congress St)
718-852-2212
Tues-Fri 7:30am-7pm,
Sat-Sun 8am-6pm
E G to Bergen St,
2 3 4 5 M R W to
Court St-Borough Hall
Average meal $6-11

dinner drink at the bar across the street—by the end of your meal, you'll be happy you decided to hang around.

Ghang Thai Kitchen — *Thai*

This long, narrow restaurant, with its chic design, speedy service, and menu of expertly prepared Thai food puts the many other neighborhood Thai eateries to shame. Noodles and curries are always a good choice (pad see ew and massaman curry being particularly delicious), as are Thai standbys like the outstanding duck basil, and if the immense menu is too overwhelming, the friendly staff will happily recommend local favorites. As if there weren't enough choices already, all dishes are served with your choice of chicken, pork, beef, squid, shrimp, vegetarian duck, or vegetables and tofu. Low prices combined with a BYOB policy and no corkage fee make Ghang Thai Kitchen not just the best Thai restaurant in the area, but also one of the best values.

204 Smith St (at Baltic St.)
718-222-5598
Sun-Thurs 12pm-11pm,
Fri-Sat 12pm-11:30pm
🄕🄖 to Bergen
Appetizers $4-7, Entrees $9-15
BYOB

Hana Café — *Japanese*

A plain statement for a plain place: Hana Café is simply adorned, fairly priced, and supremely delicious. In the small, wooden room, intimacy and comfort abound.

235 Smith St
(btwn Butler & Douglass St)
718-643-1963
Mon–Thurs 12pm–11pm,
Fri-Sat 12pm-11:30pm,
Sun 1pm–11pm
🄕🄖 to Bergen St
Rolls $3-13, Appetizers $2-10,
Entrees & Boxes $9-19

The attentive, efficient staff serves the food as soon as it's ready, be it hot and sauced, or cold and rolled. The menu is large and diverse, listing a wide variety of appetizers, entrees, and sushi all prepared with fresh ingredients and brown rice when requested. A long list of special rolls offers creative combinations of spring tempura, eel, spicy tuna, cucumber, and avocado, with original (read: silly) names like the White Dragon,

PLAY

Bar Great Harry — *Beer Bar, Trivia Night*

Past the massive French doors lies this laid back beer bar, which features 12 rotating draughts and a notably well-stocked spirit shelf. Grab a board game and sit at the front tables for a low-key night, or come on Monday Trivia Nights for more organized fun. There's a built-in wooden counter and stools in the quieter back room, where on an average night you might hear woefully inadequate explanations of quantum physics from a boozy 20-year-old who watched *Nova* once. The regulars, primarily neighborhood 20- and 30-somethings, bring their human and non-human friends—dogs are welcome. Put up your feet, down a pint, and make the bar your home for the evening.

280 Smith Street
718-222-1103
Daily 2pm-4am
🄕🄖 to Carroll St
Average Drink $6

Clover Club — *Brunch, Cocktails, Lounge*

If you're looking for a vodka tonic you'll be disappointed: Clover Club only serves liquors widely available in the pre-prohibition era. Named after the group of Philadelphia journalists who met weekly at the turn of the century, this throwback lounge makes classic cocktails and small plates for munching. The cozy, living room aesthetic—complete with exposed brick and hanging antique lamps—is perfect for a relaxing evening with a small group. Sit back in the plush leather seats, chat, and leisurely sip a Calamity Jane (Silver Tequila, Cynar, Lemon, sugar, Prosecco), Little Bird (Gin, muddled kiwi, Aperol, Lime and Bordeaux Blanc), or Champagne Punch, designed for three or four fellow lushes. Clover Club also offers a "liquid brunch" for those in the habit of taking hotcakes with your highball.

210 Smith St (near Baltic)
718-855-7939
Mon-Thu 5pm-2am, Fri
5pm-4am,
Sat 2:30pm-4am,
Sun 2:30pm-12am
🄕🄖 to Bergen St
Average Drink $11

PARK SLOPE

Since its completion in the late 1870s, Park Slope, like many neighborhoods in New York City, has struggled to balance its working class, down-to-earth charm with increasing gentrification and development. Named for its location on the western slope of Prospect Park, the area bloomed in the late 19th century, with an influx of elite New Yorkers. As the twentieth century approached, the "Gold Coast" mansions, a series of Victorian mansions on Prospect Park West, were erected . A decade later the Brooklyn Dodgers were created in Park Slope. By the mid-twentieth century, the neighborhood had become a serene hotspot for middle-class New Yorkers.

In the 1950s, however, the neighborhood fell into decline. The wealthy and middle-class began to abandon New York City for the suburbs. During the urban renewal of the 1960s the city used Park Slope as its poster boy—inviting middle-class families to move back into the elegant brownstones that formerly characterized the area. But the economic blight of the 1970s continued to wreak havoc until the early 90s. Manhattan's inflated rents caused individuals to relocate to affordable areas in the outer boroughs. This made for a very diverse mix in Park Slope, with stockbrokers, working class families, and artists all living as neighbors.

Today, Park Slope attracts many with its lively nightlife scene along 5th Avenue, beautiful park, and diverse cultural offerings. The area has become a haven for families and hipsters alike (those who have outgrown Williamsburg, that is). The diverse blend of residents creates an aura of boutique bohemianism, with a mix of high-end, trendy stores, unique music venues, coffee shops, and farmers' markets. Consistently named one of the top neighborhoods in the US, Park Slope is a hip, wholesome haven from the hectic city.

Brooklyn Botanic Garden

These masterfully-crafted, award-winning gardens are designed to dazzle guests with new blooms throughout the spring and summer months. April brings the cherry tree: delicately arranged in expansive orchards and lining winding walkways, its blossoms draw huge crowds. May sees the Spanish Bluebells' spectacular flowering, turning a plain walkway into a sea on land. June is Rose Month, as the English garden explodes with All-American selections. The gardens also include the Alice Recknagel Ireys Fragrance Garden, creating aromatic and tangible pleasures for the visually impaired, and the intricately crafted Japanese Hill and Pond Garden, which delights visitors with its wooden Shinto arch, cranes, and a pond shaped like the Japanese character for Heart.

1000 Washington Ave (near Crown St)
718-623-7200
Tues-Fri 8am-6pm, Sat-Sun Holidays 10am-6pm, Closed Mon except holidays
❷❹❺ to Prospect Park, ❷❸ to Eastern Parkway-Brooklyn Museum

Brooklyn Conservatory of Music

Designed by German immigrants to be a traditional European conservatory, the Brooklyn Conservatory has evolved into a center for musical growth in the Brooklyn arts community. Their mission is to make music accessible to anyone who wants to learn. The large conservatory hosts over 4,000 students and offers classes in various genres of music, including African drumming, opera, rock, and jazz. Classes meet weekday evenings and weekend afternoons and are priced rather reasonably. In keeping with their promise to bring music to the masses, they offer financial aid to those who need it, as well as ensemble and individual instruction for all ages. The conservatory also holds a wide variety of musical concerts and events, showcasing the talents of their students and faculty and importing world-renowned musicians for performances.

58 7th Ave (near Lincoln Pl)
718-622-3300
❷❹ to 7th Ave, ❷❸ to Grand Army Plaza
Hours and events vary

Brooklyn Lyceum

Once an old gymnasium, this music venue currently hosts cultural events as eclectic as the Brooklyn arts scene itself. The Lyceum offers a large variety of entertainment, including film, live theatre, music, comedy, and dance—guests can even catch an indie film festival and a stand-up show on the same night. The venue is also a popular spot for parties, balls, and galas. But the Lyceum still retains vestiges of its humble heritage—there are daily aerobics classes as well as batting cages and a basketball court in the back. And the original high arched ceilings make for great acoustics. Don't miss the café tucked away in a loft—a great place to sit, have a cup of coffee, and use their Wi-Fi.

227 4th Ave (near President St)
718-857-4816
❼❽ to Union Street, ❻❼ to 7th Ave
Hours and price varies

Brooklyn Museum

Smaller and less frequented than popular Manhattan museums, the Brooklyn Museum of Art showcases a breathtaking permanent collection with the intimacy of a private gallery. The beautiful building that houses the second-largest collection of art in New York City was built by the lauded architecture firm McKim, Mead, and White, and architecture nerds might find the prime example of Beaux-arts

DAY TO DAY

Brooklyn Community Board 6: 250 Baltic St, 718-643-3027.

Dry Cleaner/Tailor: Yes Cleaners, 219 5th Ave (at Union St), 718-857-6668.

Groceries: Park Slope Food Co-Op, 782 Union St, 718-622-0560. Back to the Lands Natural Food, 142 7th Ave.

Gym: Prospect Park YMCA, 357 9th Street, 718-768-7100. New York Sports Club, 324 9th St, 718-768-0880.ve, 718-768-5654.

Hospital: New York Methodist Hospital, 506 Sixth St, 718-780-5500.

Library: Brooklyn Public Library: Park Slope Branch, 431 6th Ave (at 9th St), 718-832-1853.

Media: *On Park Slope*, onparkslope.com. *Park Slope Reader*, psreader.com

Volunteer Opportunities: Brooklyn Green Team, brooklyngreenteam.blogspot.com.

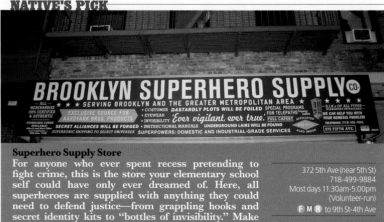

Superhero Supply Store

For anyone who ever spent recess pretending to fight crime, this is the store your elementary school self could have only ever dreamed of. Here, all superheroes are supplied with anything they could need to defend justice—from grappling hooks and secret identity kits to "bottles of invisibility." Make sure to visit the Capery, where you can get a cape fitted and tested at the in-store wind tunnel. The store itself does its part to fight for a better tomorrow by hosting the New York branch of the 826 National foundation, which offers classes and tutoring in creative and expository writing for children aged 6-18. Run by over 1,000 volunteers, the classes encourage students to write stories and essays, which are printed by the in-house publisher. The store sells samples of the students' literature, and all profits go to support 826 NYC.

372 5th Ave (near 5th St)
718-499-9884
Most days 11:30am-5:00pm
(Volunteer-run)
F M R to 9th St-4th Ave

---

construction worth the visit in itself. Inside, you'll find everything from ancient Egyptian necklaces to Flemish paintings to feminist photography (there's an entire permanent section dedicated to

200 Eastern Parkway
(near Washington Ave)
718-638-5000
Wed-Fri 10am–5pm,
Sat-Sun 11am-6pm
2 3 to Eastern Parkway-Brooklyn Museum
Suggested Contribution $10,
Students (with ID) $6,
Seniors $6, Members &
Children under 12 Free

feminist art on the fourth floor). Come on the first Saturday of the month, when the museum offers a variety of free programming, like spoken word open mics, live music, dance troupe performances, and printmaking sessions.

Prospect Park

Covering almost two thirds the size of Central Park, Prospect Park beautifully showcases architects Frederick Law Olmstead and Calvert Vaux's landscaping artistry. On a nice day, you can catch Brooklynites paddling their way through the Prospect Park Lake, Brooklyn's only lake, or tanning themselves on Long Meadow, the largest meadow in any US park. Twilight boat tours—complete with wine and cheese served at the park's famous Boathouse—are

Flatbush Ave
(near Grand Army Plaza)
718-965-8951
5am-1am
2 3 to Grand Army Plaza
B Q S to Prospect Park,
Q to Parkside Ave, to 15th
St-Prospect Park

also available along the lake, through the park's iconic Lullwater. The popular Picnic House accommodates up to 175 visitors and can be rented for special events. Animal lovers can seek refuge in the Wildlife Conservatory's Prospect Park Zoo, which houses over 630 animals. In the winter, the 26,000-square-foot Wollman Rink is open to ice skaters. Embracing the modern age, the park also offers free Wi-Fi at both the Boathouse and Picnic House.

Prospect Park Bandshell

Built during the pre-World War II revitalization of Prospect Park, this unique and mammoth venue for outdoor entertainment hosts events year round. It's best known for Celebrate

Brooklyn!, an annual summer festival showcasing both big names and emerging artists in theatre, film, music, and dance. Most events are free, but the $3

Enter the park at Prospect Park West & 9th St
Gates open one hour prior to performances, otherwise open during park hours
Ⓕ to 7th Ave,
Ⓕ to 15th St-Prospect Park,
❷❸ to Grand Army Plaza

donation isn't too much to dish out, whether you're listening to indie sweethearts MGMT and Animal Collective from the three-story acoustic shell, watching vintage sci-fi movies on the 1,000 square-foot projection screen, or admiring whirling Egyptian traditional dancers on the elevated stage. Get there early if you want to snag one of the 2,000 seats in the circular plaza, or come at your leisure and pull up some grass—the lawn has a 5,000 capacity.

SHOP

The Artful Place

Colorful ceramic tiles on the floor spell "Inspire" and "Play," welcoming creativity from the first steps into this cubbyhole of

171 5th Ave
(btwn Lincoln Pl & Berkley Pl)
718-399-8199
Tues, Wed, & Sun 11am-6pm,
Thurs & Fri 11am-7pm,
Sat 10am-7pm
Ⓜ Ⓡ to Union St

a family-run store. The front of the shop features stone pendants, colorful earrings, and necklaces handmade by the mother and daughter. On the wall? The son's artwork. Stocking far more than Crayola markers, this artistic alcove offers a wide selection of stamps, paints, tiles, brushes, and other tools for artistry. Quirkier favorites include finger paints, glass etching kits, and fabric paints. Learn to wield your finds with precision at one of their classes in drawing, beadwork, mosaics, or painting—they're offered for aspiring artists of all ages.

Monkey Whistles & Motor Bikes

This vintage shop is so packed with merchandise that nearly a fourth of the goods are displayed on the front sidewalk. Clothing, accessories,

176 5th Ave
(btwn Sackett & Degraw St)
212-966-9010
Daily 12pm-7pm
(sometimes extended hours)
❷❸ to Bergen St, Ⓑ Ⓠ to
7th Ave, Ⓜ Ⓡ to Union St

vinyls, luggage, and housewares from the 1920s to the 1980s all cram into this tiny boutique. The main clerk's pet-of-choice, a large white rat, hangs out in a glass tank at the front of the store, and antique housewares are piled at the opposite end—many priced as low as $1. The store's haphazard organization will have you digging for that perfect knickknack, undoubtedly discovering at least five curious items along the way. Whether it's a wildly-colored 1960s tank dress or a small metal Eiffel Tower that keeps you browsing late, clerks will gladly keep the store open past closing time. And vintage fashions are priced at $15-$35.

Odd Twin Trading Company

This brand new vintage shop achieves a comfortable, lived-in atmosphere with full racks, scuffed wood flooring, and convivial staff. Antique photos perch on racks stocked full of 50s bathing suits and spiffy dresses. In the center of the room, wooden tables show off colorful belts, leather wallets, and fedoras. Lining the walls are button-down checkerboard shirts, floral print dresses, and leather jackets—a veritable history through clothing from bygone decades. Teens in cut-off jorts and trendy Park Slope moms scour racks to revamp their style with classic looks. All merchandise is hand-picked and nothing exceeds double digits, making the Odd Twin everyone's favorite shop.

164 5th Ave (at Degraw St)
718-ODD-TWIN
Daily 12pm-8pm
Ⓜ Ⓡ to Union St

Red White and Bubbly

Wine enthusiasts and amateurs alike should indulge in a visit to this impressively well-stocked shop. Hundreds of bottles of wine and champagne cluster on the shelves, prices varying from $9.95 to $1,000. Those who want to train their palate

211-213 5th Ave
(near Union St)
718-636-9463
Mon-Sat 10am-10pm,
Sun 12pm-8pm,
Wine Tasting Fri 5pm-8pm,
Sat-Sun 2pm-6pm
Ⓜ Ⓡ to Union St,
❷ ❸ to Grand Army Plaza

without lightening their wallets too much can enjoy wine tastings held Friday through Sunday. And for the uneducated, the owner displays four handpicked wines every month to ease the selection process. But if you're still unsure, then the warm and knowledgeable staff will come to your aid. If neither red, white, nor bubbly is your beverage of choice, the store is also stocked with a straightforward selection of hard liquors.

Soula

Don't be fooled by the sparse window display or diminutive size of this boutique-like shoe store—it has more than enough to offer. Above the lightly-colored hardwood floors, the shelves are jammed with hot-off-the-runway trends. The store owner worked as a buyer for Barney's, and has used his knowledge of the business to sell shoes that are a fusion of comfort and fashion. Women's color-block sneakers, gladiator sandals, Hunter galoshes, flats, and heels line several racks in the store. Men's and children's sneakers, loafers, and dress shoes fill the remaining shelves. There's nearly too much merchandise, but as it's all so compactly organized, it shouldn't be too hard to find your perfect pair. The original Soula location is located in Boerum Hill at 185 Smith St.

184 5th Ave (at Sackett St)
718-230-0038
Tues-Sun 11am-7pm
Ⓜ Ⓡ to Union St

EAT

Bierkraft

Café, Sandwiches

191 5th Ave
(at Sakett St & Berkeley Pl)
(718) 230-7600
Mon-Thurs 11:30am-8:30pm,
Fri 11:30am-9pm,
Sat 11am-9pm, Sun 11am-8pm
Ⓜ Ⓡ to Union St
Sandwiches $9

Until recently, Bierkraft's primary claim to fame was its immense stock of beers—upwards of 1000, to be exact. But now the converted shop also serves light lunches to diners seated on new, handmade picnic tables. The U-shaped store is divided roughly in half, with long fridges cooling brews on one side, and the dining room and cash register on the other. In the back, a counter with a giant tap of rotating beers connects the two halves. There you can purchase tap beers by the gallon or order a sizable gourmet sandwich, made with homemade mayo and horseradish, as well organic meats, cheeses, and breads whenever possible. They also sell delicious homemade cookies, brownies, and a careful selection of chocolates—including several beer-flavored varieties crafted specifically for Bierkraft—that make for a sweet ending.

The Chocolate Room

Dessert

86 Fifth Ave (near Warren St)
718-783-2900
Sun-Thurs 12-11pm,
Fri-Sat 12pm-12am
❷❸ to Bergen St
Desserts $5-14

With everything made from scratch on site, this ten-table store is a neighborhood favorite for couples and kids alike. From the "Got Chocolate?" shirts worn by the staff to the caramel and chocolate colored walls, this intimate dessert place celebrates all things cocoa. Tiled floors, an exposed brick wall, and a coffered mint ceiling create a humble soda shop vibe. Try the Chocolate Layer Cake with homemade Mint Ice Cream or five-layer Brownie Sundae. No ordinary sweet shop, servers are on hand to suggest a wine pairing for whatever you choose. Visit with a friend, a date, or by yourself—there's a bar in the back for lone chocoholics. And for the sweet tooth on the go, they sell chocolate products in the front. Desserts start at $5, so you won't even feel like you're indulging.

Convivium Osteria

Italian

68 5th Ave (at St Marks Pl)
718-857-1833
Mon-Thurs 6pm-11pm,
Fri-Sat 5:30pm-11:30pm,
Sun 5pm-10pm
❷❸ to Bergen St
Appetizers $8-17,
Entrees $15-25

This romantically rustic eatery has butcher blocks for tables, pots and pans for wall décor, and service as warm and friendly as the food is delicious. Each dish comes prepared with a refined, soulful flair, influenced by Italian, Spanish, and Portuguese cuisine. To start, try the carciofo alla romana, an artichoke braised in olive oil, mint, and

PARK SLOPE

Al Di La

Italian

Every element of this unassuming trattoria strikes an effortless balance between neighborly ease and absolute refinement. Shelves of antiques and knickknacks line red and yellow walls, brightened by light streaming in through the two walls of windows. A murano chandelier hangs from a pressed-tin ceiling, and revelatory dishes arrive without pomp on mismatched antique plates. Using seasonal and often local ingredients, chef Anna Klinger cooks with impeccable clarity of flavor, vision, and execution. Like the rest of Al Di La, the food is unpretentiously prepared with love, care, and consummate skill. And the relaxed buzz of laughter and conversation that fills the restaurant is infectious. Constant lines notwithstanding—even on weeknights it fills to capacity—Al Di La remains a pitch-perfect neighborhood Italian trattoria serving food that transcends boroughs as handily as it does expectations.

248 5th Ave (at Carroll St)
718-783-4565
Mon, Wed & Thu 6-10:30pm,
Fri 6-11pm, Sat 5:30-
10:30pm, Sun 5-10pm
F to 15th St-prospect Park,
M R to Union St
Appetizers $9-13,
Pastas $12-18, Entrees $17-24

garlic. A main of braised rabbit is old-school Mediterranean comfort food, and the startlingly sweet green apple and cinnamon ravioli, tempered dramatically with savory duck ragù, is a creative spin on the Italian dish. For dessert, the fried, ricotta-filled ravioli, bathed of honey and orange zest, is an obvious standout. To complete your meal, choose from an impressive selection of wines—stored in a stunning wine cellar that can be rented out for parties.

Hanco's

Vietnamese

It may look like another humble take-out joint, but this sandwich and bubble tea shop serves up kick-ass

350 7th Ave (at 10th St)
718-499-8081
Mon-Sat 12-9pm, Sun 12-7pm
G to 7th Ave
Sandwiches $6.50, Salads $5,
Drinks $4

banh mi: hot French baguettes, sweet roasted ground pork, pickled carrots and daikon, cilantro, mayo, and butter all in one bite make for a satisfied palette and a full belly. If you're still hungry, or just curious, choose between the green salad or the rice vermicelli salad, or try the summer or garden rolls—they come with perfectly peanutty Hoisin dipping sauce. The menu options may be limited, but the beverage selection more than compensates. They offer taro bubble tea, passion fruit tea, Vietnamese coffee, and even egg yolk soda. The service is quick, if a little curt.

Stone Park Café

New American

Founded five years ago by neighborhood locals, Stone Park is a cheerful and sunny café by day and a dimly-lit date spot by night. An international wine list of some 130 bottles complements a menu offering traditional New England dishes with some flavorful foreign twists—and the emphasis on fresh, seasonal ingredients makes

324 5th Ave (near 3rd St)
718-369-0082
Dinner Sun-Thurs 5:30pm-
10pm, Fri-Sat 5:30pm-11pm;
Brunch Sat-Sun 10am-3:30pm,
Lunch Tues-Fri 11:30am-
2:30pm
M R to Union St
Brunch $12-16, Lunch
$10-15, Dinner Appetizers
$12-15, Entrees $14-28

for a regularly changing menu. A summer menu features spring pea soup with wasabi crème fraiche and tempura lobster knuckles with lemon chipotle dressing to start. Meat and fish entrees are just as imaginatively prepared: striped bass wrapped in pancetta, beef tenderloin served with sautéed escarole and fresh blue cheese gnocchi made in-house. Though Stone Park Cafe is decidedly upscale in style and substance, the $30 three-course Daily Market Menu ensures that it remains the accessible neighborhood restaurant of its founders dreams.

tomatoes, and onions on the Murray. If the weather permits, enjoy an al fresco dawg under the yellow and orange umbrellas in their pleasantly shady backyard. Even without the cheese fries (try the onion rings instead), you'll certainly need napkins for your finger-licking hot dog feast. Dine in, take out, or have your meal delivered directly to your couch, but be prepared to pay in cash only.

PLAY

Tea Lounge *Café*

Sofas, comfy chairs, and coffee tables fill the big room and lend a casual, lived in air to this popular café. A billboard near the entrance is plastered with

837 Union St (near 7th Ave)
718-789-2762
Mon-Fri 7am-9pm,
Sat-Sun 8am-10pm
Ⓜ Ⓡ to Union St,
❷❸ to Grand Army Plaza.
Salads, Sandwiches,
& Snacks $3-7

flyers, and surrounded by bikes and strollers. Denizens here for the free WiFi sit in front of open MacBooks and sip from big cups of coffee (or tea), chosen from an appropriately long list. Group meetings can be held at the large tables in the back, while tinier seating arrangements are conducive to smaller parties and solo work. A surprisingly large menu of snack foods, sandwiches, and salads means you can easily pass a day at Tea Lounge without leaving. Be sure to try the Rugelah—its homey sweetness is the perfect pick me up to countless hours spent staring at a computer screen.

Willie's Dawgs *Hot Dogs*

Offering inventive spins on a New York favorite, this clean yet appropriately kitschy space—think hot dog-painted walls—is perfect for indulging in an afternoon snack or

351 5th Ave (btw 4th & 5th St)
718-832-2941
Mon closed, Tues-Wed
11:30am-9pm, Thus-Fri
11:30am-10pm, Sat 11:30-
12am, Sun 11:30am-9pm
Ⓕ Ⓜ Ⓡ to 9th St- 4th Ave
Hot dogs $3-5, Sides $2-5
Cash Only

a late night craving. Meat-eaters can choose from a selection of all-natural grass-fed beef, or chicken, while vegetarians can opt for tofu, or carrot dogs. Next, pick a challah, rye, or multi-grain roll, then add one of the complementary topping combinations: cheddar and bacon on the Willie; avocado, beans, mayo, jalapeños,

Barbès *Bar, Live Music*

Take the interior of a casual French café, pour alcohol instead of espresso, and host small acoustic bands from South America to Eastern Europe

376 9th St (corner of 6th Ave)
347-422-0248
Mon-Thurs 5pm - 2am,
Fri-Sat 12pm- 4am,
Sun 12pm-2am
Ⓖ to 7th Ave
Average Drink $5

in a back room—that is, essentially, Barbès. Tiny red candles sit atop small wooden tables, lending an intimate coffee shop vibe. The crowd of new and local twenty-somethings chatter in groups, dimly lit through lampshades made of Japanese parasols and old records. Travel to the back room for live tunes from a variety of Latin, jazz, blues, and even Celtic bands. There's not much dancing or crowd surfing here, so pull up a chair and talk to friends—the music's soft enough for you to hear them.

Bar Reis *Lounge, DJs*

Intimate and easygoing, this neighborhood favorite conceals a wealth of charm and space behind its unadorned facade. A

375 Fifth Ave (near 9th St.)
718-832-5716
Sun-Thurs 5pm-2am, Fri-Sat
5pm-4am
Ⓜ Ⓡ Ⓕ to 4th Ave-9th St
Average Drink $6
Happy Hour: Daily 5-8pm

cozy mezzanine at the end of a spiral staircase overlooks the front room, where local artwork hangs from the tin ceiling and decorates the darkened walls. The bar, dressed in shifting neon lights, comes stocked with all the usuals plus a handful of harder-to-find wines and brews. Past a narrow corridor and small flight of stairs, you'll find a funky den with booths, plush chairs, a large projector screen, a pool table, and DJs spinning classic rock and mellow tunes. Outside lies the spacious garden, where you can relax on two tiers of picnic benches and order drinks from the inside bar or get one of the 100 inexpensive gourmet sandwiches (until 2am) from Bar Reis's just-opened shop next door.

The Gate
Beer Bar

This local favorite stands out with its long list of craft brews and spacious outdoor seating area, complete with picnic tables, leashed dogs, flower boxes, and Christmas lights.

321 Fifth Ave (near 3rd St)
718-768-4329
Mon-Fri 3pm-1am, Sat-Sun 1pm-1am (Deck until 2am)
M R to Union St, **M R F** to 4th Ave-9th St
Average Drink $6
Happy Hour: Daily Opening-7pm, $1 off

During colder months cozy up in a low-lit booth with classic rock blasting from the jukebox and the game on TV. Though the collection of 23 domestic and imported beers on tap might seem intimidating, helpful bartenders freely offer tastes from the draughts until you find the perfect match. If hard liquor's more your speed, order from their extensive whiskey menu. And plan on a return visit the following Wednesday for something new—the selection rotates following their weekly ale events, all of which are posted on their blog.

Ocean's 8
Sports Bar

This sports bar is so committed to maintaining old neighborhood character that it kept the pool tables and the name locals use—Brownstone Billiards. The front

308 Flatbush Ave (near 7th Ave.)
718-857-5555
Mon-Wed 11am-2am, Thurs-Fri 11am-4am, Sat 10am-4am, Sun 10am-2am
2 3 to Grand Army Plaza, **B Q** to 7th Ave
Average Drink $5

half of the bar has modern, sexy blue lighting and leather booths, but downstairs sports fans and gamers gather at thirty large screens, thirty pool tables, six ping pong tables, and two bowling alleys. The bar sells 24 draft beers and upscale—but surprisingly affordable—bar bites, like kobe beef sliders on brioche and healthy, grilled chicken sandwiches. Ocean's 8 welcomes locals of all ages to come for

pool lessons and classes, video games, or air hockey, but Thursday nights are reserved for older crowds. Happy hour deals like half-price pitchers and $3 margaritas draw an early evening crowd of regulars, there to break a couple racks over Motown classics.

Soda Bar

DJ, Lounge

629 Vanderbilt Ave
(near St. Marks Ave)
718-230-8393
Sun-Thurs 12pm-2am,
Fri-Sat 12pm-4am
❷❸ to Grand Army Plaza,
❸❹ to 7th Ave
Average Drink $6

If a DJ took over your living room and invited the whole neighborhood for drinks and hip-swaying, then it might look something like this casual one-time soda bar. The bar is unadorned, the outdoor garden mostly concrete, but the seating is comfortable and the antique tables lend the location charm. They serve strictly standard well drinks (so don't plan on sipping Mojitos), and they also offer a snack menu that ranges from pierogies to onion rings. Various DJs (and a lack of seating space) bring drinkers to their feet every Friday and Saturday, playing remixes that make head-bopping irresistible.

Don't feel the need to dress too glitzy—regulars often sit on the red patent leather bar stools in jeans and flip flops.

Two Boots Brooklyn

Bar & Restaurant, Live Music

514 2nd St (btwn 7th & 8th Ave)
718-499-3253
Brunch Sat-Sun 10am-3:30pm,
Lunch Tues-Fri 11:30am-5pm,
Dinner Sun-Thurs 5pm-
10:30pm, Fri-Sat 5pm-12am
❶❺ to 7th Ave
Average Drink $8

Bustling with the laughter of friends and families enjoying Cajun comfort food or after-work cocktails, this Mardi-Gras themed restaurant and bar offers the flavor and laid-back atmosphere of the Bayou. Vibrant colors, funky trinkets, and twinkle lights transform the space at night when the joint rocks to bluegrass blues and hoppin' oldies—Jimmy Cliff's "You Can Get It If You Really Want" is a favorite. The food ranges from jambalaya and Po-Boy sandwiches to their famous thin crusted pizza, and the extensive drink menu includes New Orleans cocktails and seven types of frozen margaritas. Come on the weekend for live music, which draws a regular crowd eager to hear authentic, neighborhood jams.

BRIGHTON BEACH
& CONEY ISLAND

First developed to be an ocean getaway for New Yorkers in the 1870s, Brighton Beach is a now primarily a neighborhood of immigrants. Jewish immigrants moved there in the 1950s, and displaced Russians followed two decades later. Relaxed Soviet polices resulted in a huge influx of immigrants in the 1970s and 80s, and the neighborhood came to be known as "Little Odessa" after the city in the Ukraine.

Today the landscape is dotted with Cyrillic letters and diminutive expatriate septuagenarians in fur coats, inching down Brighton Beach Avenue and shouting over the noise of overhead trains. Golden antique samovars, Soviet-era cassettes, monstrous containers of dried fruit and pickled foods, and long cases of Russian pastries all can be found in the tiny shops and eateries of Brighton Beach. During warmer months bathing suit bodies escape to the shores, and the neighborhood seems to return to its former incarnation as an beach getaway.

So named after by Dutch settlers in the early 17th century for its large rabbit population (Conyne Eylandt is Old Dutch for "Rabbit Island"), Coney Island has been New York City's playground since the post-Civil War era. While it may not have changed as dynamically as Brighton Beach, this popular getaway has been subject to recent gentrification debates. Developers looking to build luxury waterfront condos clash with locals seeking to preserve the area's time-honored attractions.

Although not quite restored to its former grandeur, present day Coney Island is a refreshing departure from uniformly colorless theme park giants. Relics like the Wonder Wheel are just as enjoyable as the day they opened, and relatively new additions like the minor league baseball stadium Keyspan Park enliven the neighborhood. The future of Coney Island is, as always, uncertain, but one thing is for sure: this is the city's great equalizer – a place that brings all types together over funnel cakes, chili dogs, and cheap thrills.

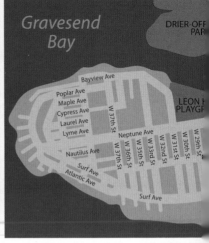

EXPLORE

Burlesque at the Beach

The Sideshows by the Seashore building commands attention at first glance—vividly painted posters of fire breathers, contortionists, and a sword-swallower are splashed across its faded stone facade. These showstoppers may entertain by day, but at night the girls come out to play. The Great Fredini and Bambi the Mermaid lure guests into their intimately small garden of lust, where scantily-clad women perform vaudeville and old-time burlesque shows with salacious names like Lucky Daredevil's Feast of Flesh. The spells of jazzy tunes and a shower of bubbles will seduce you into a wild night of old-fashioned revelry. If you feel inspired, you can even take a burlesque master class with Jo Boobs, who was voted "Best Bump N Grinder" at the New York Burlesque Festival.

1208 Surf Ave (at W 12th St)
718-372-5159
Shows Thurs 9pm &
Fri 10pm All Summer
Tickets $10-15
ⒹⒻⓃⓆ to Coney Island-
Stillwell Ave

Coney Island Museum

To reach the interior of this Coney Island historical gem, you'll have to ascend an ancient staircase. Besides serving as a museum, this spot is also a tourist center, and hosts lectures, walking tours, and films chosen by the Coney Island Film Society. The museum—which only charges a glorious 99 cents for entry—showcases everything Coney Island, including original rides, carousel horses from the 1930s to 1960s, and antique souvenirs. Stop in on a Sunday afternoon to catch lectures like Michael Schwartz's Ghosts on Fire: An Afternoon of Sex, Mrs Stahl's Knishes, and the Cyclone and the Sea. The museum has also served as a filming location for directors like Spike Lee.

1208 Surf Ave (at W 12th St)
718-372-5159
Sat-Sun 12pm-5pm
ⒹⒻⓃⓆ to Coney Island-
Stillwell St

Deno's Wonder Wheel Amusement Park

The only amusement park still fully operating on Coney Island, its bright colors and carny music continue to draw children and light-hearted adults. There are dozens of rides, two arcades, and food vendors. One of the main attractions is the bright teal Wonder Wheel, weighing 400,000 pounds and standing at 150-feet tall. The park is also home to the Cyclone, one of the oldest roller coasters in America, and regarded by many

3059 W 12th St (near Bowery St)
718-372-2592
Summer: Daily 11am-12am,
April, May, Sept, & Oct:
Sat-Sun 12pm-9pm
ⒹⒻⓃⓆ to Coney Island-
Stillwell Ave
Rides $5-$6, Kiddie Ride $2.50

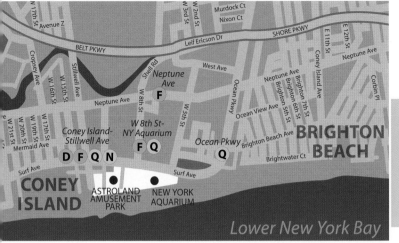

enthusiasts as one of the best in the world—though made entirely of suspiciously wobbly wood. The ride's apex affords prime views of Coney Island and the Atlantic Ocean, and for less adventurous customers, there are also stationary cars, and. At the height of summer, seasonally operating parks spread out on the park grounds around Deno's, but the Wonder Wheel stands as a monument to the carnival spirit year-round.

Keyspan Park

Entirely at home in Coney Island, this minor-league stadium is built like a baseball

1904 Surf Ave (at W 19th St)
718-449-8497
D F N Q to Coney Island-Stillwell Ave

version of the Wonder Wheel Park. A bright blue marquee emblazoned with its name welcomes fans, and glowing hoops of various neon colors circle the light towers. A boardwalk links the right field bleachers to the Grand Concourse, which is lit with hanging neon lights. Even the amusement park rides can be seen from the stands. Though Keyspan was built in 2001, it's saturated in neighborhood history, with statues of Jackie Robinson, Pee Wee Reese, the retired numbers of Gil Hodges, and other Dodgers legends. Now home to the championship-winning Brooklyn Cyclones, this Coney Island monument is a great place to watch a game or concert—even artists like Bjork and Daft Punk have performed here.

New York Aquarium

When it was founded in 1896, the New York Aquarium held only 150 sea creatures. Since then, that number has exploded to 8,000 of the most exotic, adorable, and bizarre

602 Surf Ave (at W 8 St)
718-265-FISH
Mon-Fri 10am-5pm,
Sat-Sun 10am-5:30pm
Summer: Mon-Fri 10am-6pm,
Sat-Sun 10am-7pm
F Q to West 8th St, N Q to Coney Island-Stillwell Ave
Admission $13

water dwellers in the world. Examine exhibits on everything from jellyfish to loggerhead sea turtles and sand tiger sharks. Be sure to stop by the waddling walrus and splashing sea otter tanks, which are surrounded by dozens of ooh-ing and ahh-ing children and their parents all day. Then head to the Aquatheater, where the sea lions' stunts often elicit standing ovations. You can even surf the coast with bottlenose dolphins in their interactive 3D movie exhibit.

Riegelmann Boardwalk

A mainstay for anyone who calls this little stretch of beach home, the Riegelmann Boardwalk is the backbone of Coney

Southern shore of Brooklyn
(from Corbin Pl to W 37th St)
B Q to Brighton Beach,
Q to Ocean Parkway,
D F N Q to Coney Island-Stillwell Ave

Island's commerce and the site of its many

attractions, dining, and nightlife. Strolling or biking this more than two-and-a-half mile long boardwalk is a relaxing way to spend any day or balmy summer night, a reprieve from the bustling spectacle that is Coney Island. Restaurants, bars, and attractions open directly onto the wooden slats of the boardwalk—Cha Cha's Bar and Café, the New York Aquarium, Beer Island, and the famous Cyclone roller coaster are just a few of them. On the other side of the boards, the southern shore of the Atlantic Ocean beckons.

SHOP

Bloom Boutique

This white-walled boutique spotlights funky, trendy, beach-inspired clothing. Bloom styles itself as a contemporary women's clothing

3088 Brighton 6th St
(at Brighton Beach Ave)
718-934-8077
Mon-Sat 9am-6pm
Ⓑ Ⓠ to Brighton Beach
Prices at $50 for clearance,
Up to $1000

store that favors new and rapidly up-and-coming designers, one of whom the store showcases each month. A well-edited selection of dresses and other garments are arranged throughout the store. The warm and knowledgeable owner will gladly enlighten you on any article of interest and its designer—engage her and recieve the proper boutique experience.

Eric's Health Food Shoppe

On the busiest street in Brighton Beach, a humble store with a green marquee houses a superior selection of organic

508 Brighton Beach Ave
(at Brighton 5th St)
718-615-4040
Mon-Fri 8am-8pm,
Sat 9am-7pm, Sun 9am-6pm
Ⓑ Ⓠ to Brighton Beach

and natural health foods. Tiny wild bird eggs, salmon, whole ducks, and rabbits keep cool in an impressive refrigerated storage section. Shelves hold large containers of vitamins and supplements, lined up beside dozens of organic grains and other healthy snacks. An organic juice bar offers different varieties of fresh squeezed juices, smoothies, and unexpectedly flavorful hot and cold coffees and teas. Eager staff is on hand to help with any questions you might have, offer free samples, and dole out health advice to aid your purchasing decisions. Eric's Health Food Shoppe is not like its multiple neighboring markets—it's an all natural breed of its own.

Trump Village Furniture

Though some may consider the past already lived, it's very much alive in the merchandise at Trump. Multi-colored retro lamps, sofas with intermingling

2857 W 8th St
(near Neptune Ave)
718-265-2882
Mon-Sat 10am-7pm,
Sun 10am-6pm
Ⓓ Ⓕ to W 8th St-NY Aquarium

stripes and swirls, shag-pile rugs, and distressed

90s-style chairs are all proudly on display at this furniture shop. The kaleidoscope of colors creates a dizzyingly hip environment with enough familiar goods to be oddly comforting, too. The storeroom makes a great community hangout—cozy carpets perfect for sinking into, and plushy carpets welcome the laid back crowd that makes up the neighborhood. For those who prefer to do their lounging in the comfort of their own home without spending a fortune, the prices in this furniture store can always be haggled—the owner will work with any customer to strike a bargain.

breads, rugelash, and rum balls. They also sell cake—by the pound. With so many pastries packed into such a small space, La Brioche can feel a tad overwhelming, but never fear—the owners will gladly guide you through the sweet sea of choices. Even a mix-up will yield a delicious mistake, so try a little of everything.

EAT

La Brioche Café
Bakery

On Brighton Beach Avenue, the most Russian street in America, this bakery stands out for its Gallic flair. Catering to the local Russian and Jewish customers, the pastry emporium offers a bounty of fresh challahs, virtushkas, and dozens of popular strudels. Cheese danishes, bagels, tarts, and any number of other delectable baked goods are also available, including signature regional items like chocolate babka

1073 Brighton Beach Ave
(near Brighton 12th St)
718-934-0731
Daily 9am-8pm
Ⓑ Ⓠ to Brighton Beach
Pastries 50¢-$3
Cash Only

Tatiana
Russian

With a fish tank beneath the clear floor and murals of ethereal maidens covering the ceilings, this glamorous ballroom-styled restaurant and nightclub draws crowds of high-heeled Russian patrons. The vodka selection is as extensive and varied as the menu, with bottles available for purchase. Start with a steaming bowl of potatoes and shitake mushrooms, move on to the tender lamb chop "karski" or the spicy steak, and finish with warm apple strudel. For a laid-back dining experience, opt to sit in the outdoor area overlooking the boardwalk. Or come on the weekend to enjoy a live performance and dance party, starring a cast of performers in fantastic costumes suspended from the ceiling while singing Beatles lyrics set to Russian pop music.

3152 Brighton 6th St
(at Brightwater Ct)
718-646-7630
Mon-Sun 12pm-12am
Average Entree $22-30,
Ⓑ Ⓠ to Brighton Beach
Banquet Lunch $45-65,
Dinner $55-165,
(prices vary according to day)

QUEENS

LONG ISLAND CITY

In 1970, an 80-year-old public school was reinvented as P.S.1, the second largest contemporary art center in the United States. Thus began the cultural renaissance that has since swept Long Island City, transforming a once-neglected industrial area into one of the premier centers for the arts in the outer boroughs. The neighborhood is a haven for a broad variety of art forms, from high profile art exhibitions rotating through P.S.1 to the ever-evolving street art of 5 Pointz. Avant-garde aesthetes tired of the rarefied glories on Museum Mile come to Long Island City to feast on some of the most cutting-edge and varied art in all of New York.

Long Island City came into existence as a quiet outpost for Manhattan's elite in the early 19th century, but quickly became a hub for industry, commerce, and trade with the rise of the Industrial Revolution. By 1861, an important terminal for the Long Island Railroad had been established at Hunter's Point, and by the early 20th century two major bridges—The Hellgate Bridge, and the Queensboro Bridge—had brought Long Island City within easy access of the rest of New York, only increasing its importance as an industrial center. With the American industrial decline of the 1970s, Long Island City began to shed its former character. Its warehouses and commercial bakeries converted one by one into museums, arts centers, and condos boasting some of the best Manhattan views anywhere in New York.

Today, alighting from the 7 train at its first stop outside Manhattan will leave you among some of the City's most interesting museums, and also at the borough's hub for business and film production. Spend a day museum hopping, or enjoy the greatest work of art New York has to offer—its skyline—for free at the newly developed East River waterfront.

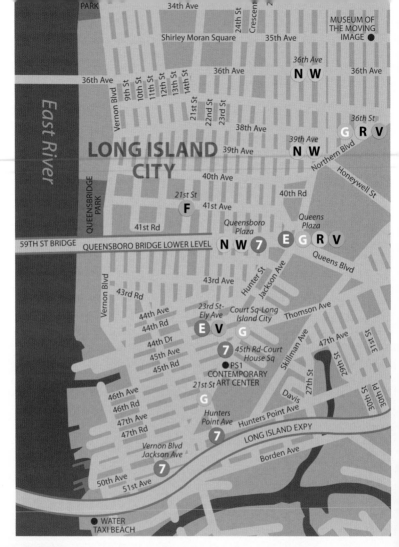

The Chocolate Factory

A recent arrival to the Off-Broadway world, the Chocolate Factory has quickly distinguished itself and already won an Obie for its work. This 5,000-square-foot compound provides rehearsal room and equipment free of charge to support developing artists, and also houses a group of residential artists who build performances from the ground up on contemporary issues. The theater hosts various events and festivals, from traditional music, dance, theater, and visual arts to more bizarre and experimental features—think clowns acting Brecht. The theater itself is an impressive, brick industrial building with a long narrow hallway that opens up into a single, enormous room. When the art becomes too much to process, enjoy one of the theater's biggest perks: $3 wine and $2 beers.

> 5-49 49th Ave (near 25th St)
> 718-482-7069
> **7** to Vernon Blvd-Jackson Ave,
> **G** to 21st St
> Hours vary by show,
> Usually starts at 8pm
> Admission varies, Average $15

Deitch Gallery

Offering more daring fare than many of its neighbors, Deitch Gallery epitomizes Long Island City's contemporary art scene. The term "gallery," which often conjures images of intimate, white-walled rooms, misrepresents this cavernous space. The art is often painted or built directly onto the walls, enticing visitors to walk in and around the elaborately constructed installations. The large scale of the space invites collaboration between artists and their audience—expect to see at least one group show a year and a medley of events ranging from video premieres, music release parties, and live

> 4-40 44th Dr (on waterfront)
> 212-343-7300
> Thurs-Sun 2-8pm
> **E** **V** train to 23rd St-Ely Ave

DAY TO DAY

Queens Community Board 1: 36-01 35th Avenue, 718-786-3335.

Groceries: AA Food Market. 62 Richmond Ter, 718-816-6733.

Gym: YMCA, 651 Broadway, 718-981-4933.

Hospital: Elmhurst Hospital Center. 79-01 Broadway, 718-334-4000.

Laundromat: Grand Avenue Laundromat. 3415 30th Ave. 718-274-5640.

Library: Queens Library: Ravenswood Branch, 35-32 21st St, 718-784-2112.

Media: Local718 Queens Blog, local718. wordpress.com. *Queens Chronicle*, queenschronicle.com.

LONG ISLAND CITY

5 Pointz

This unique venue, dubbed "graffiti Mecca," stands at the crossroads of high concept and street art. The outer walls of this 200,000-square-foot warehouse complex are entirely covered with brightly-colored, spray-painted images, making 5 Pointz one of the leading showcases for graffiti art in the world. The vibrantly styled and massive display is constantly changing, and a weekend visit usually means a chance to see young men with spray cans cover one piece of art with a new one. The graffiti murals are displayed for varying lengths of time depending on the popularity of the piece, but everything eventually is covered over to make room for more images of New York landmarks, animated spray cans, winged elephants, and the like.

45-46 Davis St (near Crane St)
317-219-2685
G to 21st St or Court Sq-Long Island City, **7** to 45th Road-Court House Sq, **E V** to 23rd St-Ely Ave
Free

performances to sewing classes with visiting artists. You'll also notice that Deitch forgoes any kind of explanatory labeling. Though disorienting at first, this ultimately allows the art to speak for itself, while making it accessible to all viewers.

M55 Art

This gallery feels like a friendlier version of its Manhattan counterparts, for its artists have full control of the work displayed. As a result, each show transforms the space in an entirely novel way. The atmosphere remains quiet and low-key—partly a result of low visitor traffic, but also due to the helpful gallery attendant who will happily explain the exhibit or leave you to your own devices. This is a good first stop if you're visiting several galleries during the day, as the smaller rooms will get you warmed up for more extensive shows. With exhibits rotating on a more-or-less monthly basis, and casual openings and closings bookending them, M55

44-02 23rd St
(btwn 44th Rd & 44th Ave)
718-729-2988
Wed-Sun 12-6pm,
& by appointment
E V to 23rd St-Ely Ave

rewards regulars with a new collection of art for thought.

The Noguchi Museum

A pointed, triangular building with an open courtyard, semi-outdoor galleries, and an indoor display space is an odd yet fitting venue for the works of renowned contemporary artist Isamu Noguchi. The outdoor galleries exhibit person-sized, abstract stone sculptures—wavy and smooth with some sharp edges, they explore changes in shape and texture. Inside, the abstractions transform into more recognizable shapes. Harsh rock is fashioned into long, almost playful, serpentine statues and enormous stone rings. Though devoted to a single artist, the Noguchi Museum's collection of work is eclectic enough to warrant a visit and seems entirely complete on its own.

32-37 Vernon Blvd
(btwn 10th St & 33rd Rd)
718-204-7088
Wed-Fri 10am-5pm,
Sat-Sun 11am-6pm
Admission $10,
Students (with ID) $5
N W to Broadway

P.S.1

Once a schoolhouse and now an outpost of MoMA, P.S.1 is one of the major centers of contemporary art in New York and the oldest and largest non-profit institution of its kind in the country. With rotating exhibits, no permanent collection, and extremely diverse featured works, the creative body of the museum is unified by its powerful themes and groundbreaking explorations of media. Among the eclectic displays featured are the inside of an illusionary swimming pool, a traditional photography gallery, and a room entirely covered in red leather. The daring and often strange subject matter draws in unavoidable gaggles of art snobs, but tuning them out provides a rare opportunity to view huge amounts of spectacular contemporary art.

22-25 Jackson Ave
(near 46th Ave)
718-784-2084
G to 21st St-Van Alst,
7 to 45th Rd-Court House Sq,
E G to 23 St-Ely Ave
Thurs-Mon 12pm-6pm
Suggested donation $5,
Students & Seniors $2,
Free for MoMA members
ticket holders within
30 days of purchase

Socrates Sculpture Center

This beautiful park on the East River distinguishes itself among dozens of others in Long Island City with its massive sculptures, which seem to sprout from the grass and blend in with the trees. Created to showcase works too large to be effectively displayed in museums, the Center is home to many child-friendly and interactive pieces, such as a New York-themed obstacle course and a large metalwork house. The park also hosts free fitness classes, Shakespeare performances, and community fairs. Both museum and picnic spot, the Center offers nature and art in equal doses, evoking a special sensation that's well worth the long walk from the nearest subway.

32-01 Vernon Blvd
(near Broadway)
718-956-1819
Daily 10am-Sunset
N W to Broadway
Free

EAT

Arharn Thai
Thai

This small neighborhood spot won't win any prizes for its furnishing, but it will certainly satisfy your craving for Thai. A dazzlingly efficient solo waiter scurries from table to table collecting orders, while the two cooks in the kitchen pump out vividly flavored food. Offering over 100 dishes, the menu lists recommendations for each of its sections to make the selection easier. But

32-05 36th Ave (near 33rd St)
718-728-5563
Sun-Thurs 11am-10:30pm,
Fri-Sat 11am-12am
N W to 36th Ave,
G R V to 36th St
Appetizers $3-8, Entrees $8-16

don't allow yourself to be restrained by restaurant recommendations—with food this good it's hard to go wrong. Crispy fried duck with red curry is spicy and rich without being greasy, the perfect match for sweet, refreshing Thai iced tea. Your best bet is to branch out and, if you're brave, perhaps even choose at random. Don't worry too much—the waiter will quickly let you know if you've ordered something you won't like.

Café Triskell
Bistro, French

This unassuming nook welcomes young families with toddlers in tow and elderly couples on dates with no-fuss, Gallic charm. The bright family-run bistro is

33-04 36th Ave (at 33rd St)
718-472-0612
Wed-Sun 10am-10pm,
later on weekends
N W to 36th Ave,
R V to 36th St
Appetizers $6-10,
Entrees $16-20

so small that a little intimacy is unavoidable— you're bound to make a new friend or two. The owner and chef, Philippe, cooks in the back and his mother-in-law brings plates out and chats with the clientele. Café Triskell has a good handle on the basics: French onion soup with nicely browned gruyère, rich croque madame, savory crepes, and a heaping portion of delectable mussels and fries. Already had dinner? Stop by for one of their signature late night desserts, like the apple cider with sweet crepes—trust the cook

and order a combination from the menu, or get creative and create your own.

Sage General Store
American, Organic

Smack in the heart of Long Island City and just across from the 7 line's first stop in Queens, Sage General Store could convince you that you never left Manhattan. With mismatched

24-20 Jackson Ave
(near 45th Rd)
718-361-0707
Mon-Fri 7:30am-6pm,
Sat 11am-8pm, Sun 11am-6pm
E R W to Queens Plaza,
G to Court Square-
Long Island City
Breakfast & Brunch $3-12,
Lunch $8-13

chairs and tables, Americana ironwork pieces on the walls, and an emphasis on local, free range, and organic food, this lunch spot has the feel of a country store that moved to Queens via the East Village. The restaurant regulars are young professionals and families hip enough to appreciate the simple, fresh ingredients and top-notch comfort foods. The lunch menu offers a large, motley collections of salads and sandwiches, like the Texas Cowboy Steak with chipotle mayo. And the dinner menu's daily blue plate specials come large enough to share.

PLAY

The Creek
Bar, Comedy

A recent favorite among the New York comedy crowd, this restaurant and performance space is located just off the Queensboro Bridge. With free shows seven nights a week and two-for-one margaritas during

10-93 Jackson Ave
718-706-8783
Mon-Thurs 11am-2am,
Fri 11am-4am,
Sat 3pm-4am, Sun 3pm-2am
(Bar opens at 3pm)
7 to Vernon-Jackson
Average Drink $6
Happy Hour: 3pm-7pm
weekdays: $2 off everything,
2-for-1 margaritas

happy hour, The Creek is the perfect place to find a laugh and a buzz outside the Manhattan stand-up scene. In the bar's above-ground room patrons can satisfy their hunger with a sparse selection of Mexican food, while the downstairs lounge features a warm, welcoming mix of mellow lighting, cushy love seats, and a retro Galaga machine. In the performance space, the twenty-something audience is more forgiving than the usual Manhattanites, encouraging brave, young comedians to test new material. Space in the black box theater is often crowded to capacity, so get there early to grab a coveted seat.

Studio Square

Beer Garden

Fortress and funhouse, this converted factory has enough space and generator power to serve cold brews and burgers to a small army during a blackout. The stark steel-and-brick décor nods to the space's industrial past, but the über sleek Studio Square also boasts a state-of-the-art, Versailles-esque hall for special events, complete with a private balcony and posh lounge. And the centerpiece of it all is the open-air beer garden fit for Beowulf himself: 18,000 square feet of communal tables, complete with an open fire and live music

35-33 36th St
(btwn 35th & 36th Ave)
718-383-1001
Mon-Thurs 4pm-4am,
Fri-Sun 12pm-4am
N **W** to 36th Ave,
R **V** to Steinway St
Half Liter Beer $7, Liter $13,
Pitcher $18

on the weekends. Thousands of revelers descend nightly for the ample seating and rich selection of taps that, while standard for hardened beer enthusiasts, definitely lean toward the classy. There's a smattering of sushi and barbecue comfort foods, and an awesome house-made Sangria that, in a nationwide first, is available on tap.

LONG ISLAND CITY

ASTORIA

Originally known as "Hallet's Cove," Astoria was later renamed after multi-millionaire John Jacob Astor, who never once walked through the grounds of the neighborhood that now bears his name. The purpose of the christening was to convince Astor to invest $2,000 in the development of the neighborhood. He only forked over $500, but Astoria took the sum, ran with it, and developed into a bustling neighborhood.

Astoria is largely known for its booming Greek population of 30,000, which is reflected in its numerous Greek restaurants and cafés. This small neighborhood is also home to large numbers of Chinese, Arabic, Italian, Hispanic and South Asian residents, making it the perfect neighborhood to visit for dining, as the various ethnicities produce a wide variety of delicious cuisine options.

Largely residential, Astoria is a quiet neighborhood of old brick houses and lush trees. In some areas the housing is only broken up by necessities like laundromats, small shopping stores, and bodegas. Residents stroll through the streets or sit on front stoops and shoot the breeze with neighbors and family members. Life seems to move at a more leisurely pace, but the looming Hell Gate and Robert F. Kennedy Memorial Bridges are omnipresent reminders of the nearby chaos of Manhattan.

Astoria may not have a pace to match the frenetic energy of the City, but celebrities are not foreign commodities. Legendary Broadway singer Ethel Merman and actor/director David Schwimmer called Astoria home, and the Kaufman-Astoria Studios, where the production of shows like *Sesame Street* takes place, are located here. Additionally, the neighborhood has been used for New York settings in many sitcoms, including *The Cosby Show*.

With so many cultural influences, Astoria is a hodgepodge of tastes and lifestyles. Nonetheless, the serenity brought on by comfortably settled families ensures that Astoria remains a stable neighborhood even as gentrification slips in with its up-and-coming boutiques and more chic scene.

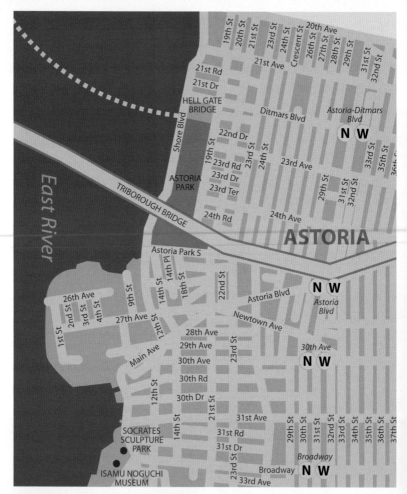

EXPLORE

Astoria Park

Nestled between the Hell Gate and Triborough Bridges, this park along the East River connects visitors to Manhattan and also offers a beautiful

Entrances along 19th St
Pool 11am-7am, late June
through Labor Day
to Astoria-Ditmars BLV,
Q19A to Hoyt Ave

escape from the City. Astoria Park offers plenty to keep visitors occupied—bocce ball courts, playgrounds, and several tennis courts for Astorians to practice their serve and backhand. When the asphalt's too hot to run on in the summer months, make use of their Olympic-sized swimming pool—the oldest and largest in the city. Join runners with iPods and smiling couples pushing strollers along the various paths, or relax on a lawn near picnicking groups. Even on a rainy day, the park is frequented by locals searching for a place to stretch their legs.

SHOP

Alfrha

Astoria's "Little Egypt," a strip of Steinway Street below Astoria Boulevard, is legendary for its authentic Middle Eastern food and cheap, bustling hookah cafés. Those looking to taste some sweet tobacco head to this diminutive, Arabic-covered store. Colorful glass pipes go for a range of prices, and Egyptian sheesha comes in countless varieties like molasses, apricot, and apple. Crates of sticky candied dates and roasted nuts reach the ceiling, and though the joint resembles a typical convenience store, there's nary a Slurpee in sight. The shop owners will provide advice on any unfamiliar hookah wares, and the biggest blessing is the prices, which undercut any Manhattan smoke shop by a wide swath.

25-32 Steinway St
(near 23rd Ave)
718-626-3233
Ⓝ Ⓦ to Astoria Boulevard

DAY TO DAY

Queens Community Board 1: 36-01 35th Avenue, 718-786-3335.

Dry Cleaner: Packard Square Cleaners, 41-32 Crescent St, 718-433-0400.

Groceries: Mayflower Grocery, 2509 30th Ave, 718-545-6894.

Gym: Club Fitness & Spa New York, 31-09 Broadway, 347-523-5818.

Hospital: Mount Sinai Hospital of Queens, 2510 30th Ave, 718-932-1000.

Laundromat: Old Neighbors Laundry, 3417 Broadway, 718-247-8907.

Library: Queens Library Astoria Branch, 1401 Astoria Blvd, 718-278-2220.

Media: *MyAstoria*, myastoria.com. *Joey in Astoria*, astorianyc.blogspot.com. Local718. wordpress.com. Astorians.com.

Volunteer Opportunities: Salvation Army, 4518 Broadway, 718-721-9046, salvationarmyusa.org. Goodwill, 4511 31st Ave, 718-777-9202, goodwill.org.

ASTORIA

NATIVE'S PICK

The Museum of the Moving Image

Museum

Home to over 130,000 digital recording gizmos and gadgets, this interactive museum is a mecca for any media maven. Visitors can learn about the development of film by playing with some of the first flipbooks and arcade games (Pong, anyone?) and explore the detailed steps of filmmaking by listening to the experts' advice on directing. The special effects of movies like *The Exorcist* and *A Nightmare on Elm Street 4: The Dream Master* are presented with movie footage and authentic props and equipment—they're even creepier off screen. Make your own stop-motion animation or star in a video flip book—available for purchase at the front desk for $7.00—or catch a film in the King Tut movie theater.

35th Ave (at 37th St)
718-784-0077
Tues-Fri 10am-3pm
Ⓡ Ⓥ to Steinway, N W to 36th Ave
Suggested donation $7
Under Renovation Until
Summer 2010,
Temporary Entrance on 37th St

priced, mostly used books in various literature genres—a deterrent only to those without the time to treasure hunt. Rows of shelving house prose, poetry, plays, classic texts, and even a wide substantial of textbooks. English-to-Italian dictionaries stack high alongside cook books—the overflow's piled between the photography books and the children's section. They also offer special sections of Greek and African American literature. If you're lucky, while scrounging through the labyrinthine basement you may stumble across something as odd as a French copy of Robinson Crusoe from 1952.

<table>
<tr><td>33-18 Broadway (btwn 33rd & 34th St)</td></tr>
<tr><td>718-267-7929</td></tr>
<tr><td>Mon-Sat 10am-8pm, Sun 11am-6pm</td></tr>
<tr><td>Ⓝ Ⓦ to Broadway, Ⓡ Ⓥ to Steinway</td></tr>
</table>

Site

This high-end home design and furniture store is a favorite among locals. The items range from adorable owl-shaped lamps and grizzly bear salt-and-pepper shakers to sepia-toned photographs of Queens. Vintage maps and posters line the walls, woven pot holders hang from silver hooks, and other unexpected goods lie wherever they fit in this intimate space. Much of the merchandise is made by locals, and every second Saturday of the month Site holds a special event to feature them. On these days artists can set up in the shop on the sidewalk to showcase their jewelry, decorative objects, fine art, and anything else they have to offer. Prices are fair for a boutique, and the warm staff will gladly help you find an item to suit your needs.

35-11 34th Ave (near 35th St)
718-626-6030
Tues-Sun 12pm-8pm, Mon closed
Ⓖ Ⓡ Ⓥ to Steinway St

Candy Plum

This petite boutique carries hand-made jewelry must-haves. Over-sized beaded necklaces, colorful hand-painted stone pendants, and other baubles with slightly vintage twists rest on the shelves. Feathery headbands lay scattered among flashy earrings. Brightly-colored maxi dresses, 50s inspired bathing suits, and "I heart Astoria" shirts hang from racks and pile up on tables. The garments and accessories are made by local designers—the owner creates most of the jewelry herself. Teaming up with various boutiques in the area, Candy Plum hosts trunk sales, fashion shows, and other various events in order to promote local designers.

30-98 36th St (near 31st Ave)
718-721-2299
Wed-Fri 12pm-7pm, Sat 12pm-5pm, Sun 12pm-5pm, Mon-Tues Closed
Ⓝ Ⓦ to Broadway, Ⓡ Ⓥ to Steinway

Seaburn Books & Publishing

If The Strand had a baby and raised it in Queens, it would be Seaburn Books & Publishing. The store is an almost-organized splay of well-

---

EAT

718 Restaurant

Bistro, French, Latin

Like its specialty BBQ-infused olive oil, this bistro offers deliciously u n p r e d i c t a b l e contrasts. Comfortably chic décor and Latin-inflected French cuisine bring trendy Soho dining to

3501 Ditmars Blvd (at 35th St)
718-204-5553
Lunch Daily 12pm-5pm, Dinner Mon-Fri 5:30pm-10:30pm, Sat-Sun 5:30pm-11pm, Tapas Daily until 2am
Ⓝ Ⓦ to Ditmars Blvd
Appetizers $8-15, Entrees $12-25

Queens. A ginger-spiced apple slaw beneath salmon cakes and roast duck breast with passion coriander sauce leave powerful impressions of bold and unexpected flavor combinations. Savory tarts showcase pastry chef and owner Ralphaël Sutter's prodigious skills, honed at renowned Manhattan kitchens before he opened a restaurant in his own neighborhood. Prix fixe brunch and lunch menus are the best bargain, but a buy-one-get-one-half-off happy hour deal draws an after-work crowd of regulars. Late at night the kitchen switches to tapas-only service and on weekends the restaurant transforms into a posh lounge—complete with DJ-spun South American tracks.

Balkh Shish Kabab House
Middle Eastern

23-10 31st St (near 23rd Ave)
718-721-5020
Daily 11am-12am
Ⓝ Ⓦ to Astoria-Ditmars Blvd
Appetizers $-6, Entrees $9-15

The humble red awning does little justice to this charming Afghani eatery. Inside, walls decorated with Afghani posters and housewares set the tone, while regional music provides the atmospheric soundtrack. On a typical evening, Balkh Shish Kabab House fills with Afghani-American families pouring over their delicious native cuisine, which remains inexplicably unfamiliar to the American palate. Kababs, the house specialty, are succulent and subtly seasoned, served over enormous beds of pillowy rice. Though Balkh Shish Kabab House is a strictly dry establishment, a warm pot of cardamom-infused Afghani tea is ideal for washing down the considerable quantities of meat and rice. Alternatively, order the tea at the end of the meal as you may find any plans for immediate movement pleasantly thwarted by the hearty, gut-warming dishes.

Fatty's Cafe
Nuevo Latino

25-01 Ditmars Blvd (at 25th St)
718-267-7071
Mon-Thurs 2pm-11pm,
Fri 2pm-12am, Sat 5pm-12am,
Sun 5pm-10pm,
Brunch Sat-Sun 11am-4pm
❼ to Astoria-Ditmars Blvd
Appetizers $5-8,
Entrees $7-15

The bamboo screens, big umbrellas, small votives, and smooth reggae tunes of Fatty's summertime garden transport guests to the Caribbean. Choose from familiar Latin and American cuisine, rendered extraordinary with creative sauces and toppings. The Yard Burger, made with jerk-marinated beef, features a marvelous añejo rum ketchup. Avocado, sprouts, and garlic aioli top their beloved Charity Burger—and $2 from each one goes to

local charity. Though substitutions are usually discouraged, swap plantains for potatoes when ordering Steak Frites—the garlic drizzle on the tostones perfectly contrasts the rich, meaty Black Angus hanger steak. However relaxed and sated you may be, don't forget to shake hands on the way out. You'll be back soon.

Il Bambino — *Italian*

34-08 31 Ave
(btwn 34th & 35th St)
718-626-0087
Mon-Fri 10:30am-10:30pm, Sat 9am-10:30pm, Sun 9am-9pm
N W to Broadway,
R V to Steinway
Small Plates $4-10,
Panini $7-9

Arrows on the wall of this rustic Italian spot point to sections of a giant pink porker, letting diners know exactly where their prosciutto and soppresata comes from (the thigh and rump, if you're curious). It's nice to know as you're digging into menu favorites like panini, crostinis, cheese plates, antipastos, and tapas. The crunchy, fresh Italian bread of the prosciutto, gorgonzola, dolce and fig spread panini gives way to a masterful blend of sweet and salty inside. Dark wood furniture and a wine bar in the back add elements of understated elegance. For something that's "got a real kick," the smiling, fedora-wearing waiter recommends the chicken cutlet, mozzarella, and arugula panino with spicy mayo. Enjoy a glass of wine or order a fresh-baked cupcake for a warm conclusion to this simple, homey meal.

La Espiguita — *Mexican*

32-44 31st Ave
(btwn 32nd & 33rd St)
718-777-5648
Mon-Sun 9am-11pm
N W to Broadway
Tacos $2, Tortas $5-9,
Platters $5-9

The sizzling sounds of the open kitchen and blaring chatter of Telemundo welcome you to this tiny dive, where not even the unadorned walls and fading laminate detract from the authentic Mexican in heaping proportion. Come for massive steak burritos, spicy chicken enchiladas topped with heaping mounds of rice, lettuce, and corn, and carnitas huarache on a corn tortilla so huge it fills two plates. They offer plenty of other taqueria favorites, but their most memorable dishes are ones you won't find at your typical Tex-Mex. Try the tortas, or Mexican sandwiches, stuffed with avocados, jalapeños, and fresh tomatoes. Wash it all down with their authentic pineapple or tamarind fruit soda.

Vesta — *Italian*

However unlikely it may be, the word "indie" seems to apply to this homey Italian restaurant and wine bar. Dinner is accompanied by Fleet Foxes instead of Dean Martin and local art adorns the worn wood and brick walls. The

seasonal menu neatly juxtaposes the classic and the trendy—pizzas with toppings like potato, pancetta, caramelized onion, apple, and goat cheese are available with whole wheat crust. Even the plating is creative—the pastas are served in the brightly colored pans they were cooked in. The wine selection is primarily Italian, with changing monthly specials on select bottles that are described both on the menu and by the knowledgeable staff. Shot-sized portions are available for those whose palettes bore easily. Don't leave without trying dessert—the winning dish is the "Baby Jesus" cake, a delightful date cake bathed in toffee syrup.

21-02 30th Ave
718-545-5550
Brunch Sat-Sun 11am-3:30pm,
Lunch Mon-Fri 12-4,
Dinner Sun-Mon 5pm-10pm,
Tues-Thurs 5pm-11pm,
Fri-Sat 5pm-12pm
N W to 30th Ave
Appetizers: $3-$12,
Entrees: $10-$22

PLAY

Bohemian Hall & Beer Garden

Beer Garden

2919 24th Ave (29th St)
718-274-4925
Sun-Wed 12pm-2am,
Thurs-Sat 12pm-3am
N W to Astoria Blvd
Average Drink $5

Opened in the early 1900s by Czech immigrants looking to bring their traditions stateside, this Eastern European outpost is the city's last original beer garden. Old world coats of arms and photos of neighborhood World War II soldiers meet MTV generation video games and pop-rock hits playing in the background—the few modernities that update this landmark. Patrons ranging from Czech and Slovak regulars to young denizens gather at the behemoth outdoor garden and indoor booths to share $15 pitchers, $6 bratwurst, and relaxed conversation. Drop by on Thursdays and Sundays for weekly jazz and blues performances. With its extensive selection of inexpensive European beers, welcoming atmosphere, and ample seating, the Beer Garden is still a neighborhood institution.

Hell Gate Social

Lounge

12-21 Astoria Blvd N
(btwn 12th and 14th St)
718-204-8313
N W to Astoria Blvd
Average Drink $7
Happy Hour: Daily 4-8pm

Named after a particularly turbulent stretch of the East River near Astoria Park, this offbeat bar holds unexpected charm. Big, red lit doors open up to a welcoming crowd of neighborhood locals talking over sounds of blues, rock, and R&B from the 50s and 60s. Drop by after midnight for a laid back round with the late-20-something regulars, or come for weekly events—they host Rock Band competitions every Wednesday, and a rockabilly band and burlesque show on the first Friday of each month. If it's barbecue you're craving, visit the beautiful stone patio on Sundays from 4-8, and stay for the sci-fi or B-movie flick that begins at 9.

JACKSON HEIGHTS

Stepping onto the streets of Jackson Heights is like walking into the waiting area of an international airport. European, Jewish, Muslim, Latin American, and Asian communities—the neighborhood has them all. In fact, it is home to more than 100 cultural groups, 150 languages, and an endless array of ethnic restaurants and glittery stores, all of which bring this neighborhood to dynamic life.

Before the start of the 20th century, Jackson Heights had little more than barns, dirt roads, and carriage houses. After the Queensboro Bridge was constructed, however, the city government bought the area and modernized it with pavements and apartment buildings. Inspired by the movement of progressive urban planning in Europe, developer Edward MacDougall sought to make Jackson Heights the first garden city in the United States. The newer streets of Jackson Heights are crowded and colorful, but the Historic District retains the quiet, mellow feel of its original garden apartments.

Jackson Heights was originally created to be a home for upper-middle-class families. Until the mid-90s, its population mainly consisted of two groups: Caucasian and Hispanic. In 1995, however, waves of immigrants from all different backgrounds began to arrive to the area. The famed Little India formed along the man drag, Roosevelt Avenue, and is still comprised of stores that sell sparkly bracelets, inexpensive gold, and Bollywood films from factories far away. Peruvian cafés sell platanos, while older women set up shop on the street and sell delicious frozen ices on hot days and nutmeg-flavored hot chocolate on cold ones.

The neighborhood also includes one of the city's largest gay communities outside of Manhattan. It's striking to see the streets covered with fliers for events ranging from "Gay Disco Night" to "Bible Study," but somehow the collective worlds of the diverse Jackson Heights manage to maintain an unexpected harmony.

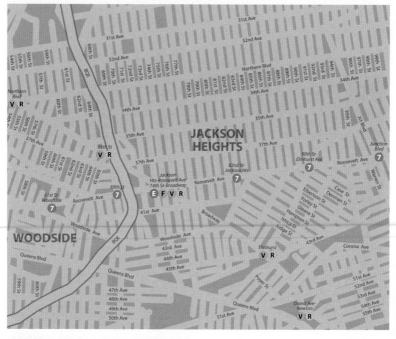

EXPLORE

Garden City Trail

The Garden City movement began in Great Britain with the goal of creating well-balanced living communities infused

> 61st to 91st St
> (btwn Northern Blvd &
> Roosevelt Ave)
> 646-285-8947
> 🄴🄵 to Roosevelt Ave

with greenery. Jackson Heights was the first garden city in America and retains its original charm and mystery today. Along the trail, you'll find a number of exquisitely structured buildings with an old-world feel—unexpected in a city so often dubbed the "concrete jungle." Be sure to stop by the Community Church on 35th Ave and 81st St—enclosed by a small lawn, hewn from rough stone, and topped with a bell tower, it seems to come straight out of a Hans Christian Andersen tale. And take in the historic Garden Homes, old-fashioned buildings screened by rows of lush trees.

Jackson Heights Historic District

The Indian, Peruvian, Russian, and Ecuadorian residents of Jackson

> Btwn Northern Blvd &
> Roosevelt Ave
> 🄴🄵 to Roosevelt Ave

Heights value the structure and upkeep of their homes—ideals exemplified by the Historic District. Its buildings are designed to let in generous amounts of sunlight, and the front yards leave plenty of room for landscaping. During summer months, you might run into women laying out cards for fold-out table solitaire or sewing on squeaky chairs in front of their homes. The streets, lined with magnificent trees, colorful flowers, and decorative hedges, are so well-organized that the District could serve as the study model for good city planning. Don't hesitate to bring along a good book for a restful read on one of the tucked away lawns.

Travers Park

Jackson Heights is known for having a park on practically every corner, but Travers Park is one of the few that's open to the public. This democratic green offers basketball and handball courts, a playground, a roller hockey court, and a scenic family escape. During the summer, concerts and theatrical performances are held on Saturdays, such as shows by Latin jazz musician Chris Washburn and his band. On Sundays vendors flood the park to sell fresh produce from the Jackson Heights Farmers Market. A central location for the community, the park is usually filled with young tots and adults enjoying a leisurely afternoon.

34th Ave (near 77th St)
Open during daylight hours
E F to Roosevelt Ave

SHOP

India Sari Palace

Walk under the royal blue awning into this brightly-lit sari-stocked heaven. The shop is bathed in golden, pink, blue, and red hues from the beautifully embroidered garments that fill the entire store. As the only location in the neighborhood dedicated to saris, I.S.P. lives up to its title with an incredibly vast stock. Glittering gold bangles, earrings, and necklaces are displayed at the front of the store alongside more playful costume jewelry. There is also a section dedicated exclusively to men's formal wear. Fabrics for making these ornate saris and suits can be purchased here as well, so for a regal look—and a custom tailoring job to fit your sari perfectly—head to the Palace.

37-07 74th Street (at 37th Ave)
718-426-2700
Daily 10:30am-7:30pm
7 E F V G R to 74th St-
Roosevelt Ave

Today's Music

This shop is stocked full of bumping Bhangra beats and Bollywood films. Check out the latest hits from film soundtracks by A.R. Rehman or jam to the mixed tapes and remixes of groups like Strictly Punjabi. The store also has a great selection of Bollywood films on DVD, so you can get your Shah Rukh Khan fix easily. Favorites like Jodha Akbar range in price from $15-$20, but rentals are only $3.

73-09 37th Rd (near 79th)
718-429-7179
Daily 11am-9pm
7 to 74th St.-Broadway,
E F V G R to Jackson
Heights-Roosevelt Ave

DAY TO DAY

Queens Community Board 3: 82-11 37th Ave, 718-458-2707.

Dry Cleaner/Tailor: Phoenix French Cleaners, 7603 37th Ave (btwn 76th St and 77th St).

Groceries: Met Food Market, 81-02 Northern Blvd, 718-458-9827.

Hospital: Elmhurst Hospital Center, 79-01 Broadway, 718-334-4000.

Library: Queens Library: Woodside Branch, 5422 Skillman Ave, 718-429-4700.

Media: *Jackson Heights Life*, jacksonheightslife.com/community. *Queens Chronicle West*, queenschronicle.com/history/west.html.

JACKSON HEIGHTS

each table proves it is possible to improve on an already damned good thing. You might also give your arteries a break and try one of Ihawan's inventively fruity drinks or desserts—avocado with milk and crushed ice, is a popular choice. With very little priced above $7, you can easily fill up for under the $20 credit card minimum, which makes Ihawan the perfect place to impress a jaded foodie friend who thinks he's tasted it all.

Stock up on the goods and dance out of it with your friends.

EAT

Ihawan
Filipino

This small, sparsely decorated restaurant serves a loyal crowd of local Filipino families. They plate some of the odder dishes of Philippine cuisine, from pork ears and

40-06 70th St
(at Roosevelt Ave)
718-205-1480
Mon, Tues, Thurs 11am-8pm,
Fri-Sat 8am-8pm,
Sun 8am-7:30pm
7 to 69the St, **E F V R G**
to Roosevelt Ave
Mains $5-11

liver to stewed ox-tail in peanut butter sauce, along with an ample selection of somewhat less startling skewers and filets. All dishes are simply prepared—blessed little is done to cover the pure, smoky flavor of the meat, although a dash of the mysterious brown sauce found on

Jackson Diner
Indian

Ignore the name—this isn't your typical diner. Staying true to the neighborhood's i m m i g r a n t population, Jackson Diner serves traditional, authentic

3747 74th St (37th Rd)
718-672-1232
Sun-Thurs 11:30am-10pm,
Fri-Sat 11:30am-10:30pm
7 E F V G R to 74th St-
Roosevelt Ave
Appetizers $4-$9,
Entrees $10-$22

Indian dishes at wholly inexpensive prices. The Papri Chat transports you to the streets of Delhi—sour with the flavor of yogurt, sweet with tamarind, and enticingly spicy, a delicate textural balance of crunchy and smooth. The samosas are made with just the right amount of oil, leaving them robust and flavorful without being heavy or greasy. Tender Tandoori Chicken and Lamb Roganjosh are favorites among the hearty entrees. The menu is expansive, so prepare tuck in for a savory, whirlwind journey.

Pio Pio
Peruvian

Of Jackson Heights' many Latin American eateries, this Peruvian chicken joint (with additional branches in Manhattan and the Bronx) is probably the most famous. Pio Pio

84-13 Northern Blvd
(btwn 84th St & 85th St)
718-426-1010
Daily 11am-11pm
7 E F V G R to Jackson
Hts-Roosevelt Ave
Appetizers $4-16,
Entrees $4-20

specializes in pollo a la brasa (rotisserie chicken), and there is little reason to order anything else. A perfect blend of spices and plenty of time on the rotisserie leave the meat juicy and gleaming with a golden brown shine. Newcomers may try struggling with utensils, but regulars know to just dive in with their hands and suck the meat right off the bones. A number of sides complement the main event: yucca fries, avocado salad, rice and beans, and plantains, which come either as salty maduros, or as sweet, twice-fried tostones. Three to four friends will be able to share the Matador combo, which includes a whole rotisserie chicken, avocado salad, and four sides for only $30.

Rajbhog Sweets
Dessert, Indian

This Jackson Heights sweets shop is a little bit of heaven on Earth—or at least a little bit of India in New York. A display case that monopolizes an entire wall contains every imaginable kind of Indian sweet. The helpful staff can guide newcomers through the mind-boggling selection, which presents enough options to satisfy even the most ravenous sweet tooth. Those unfamiliar with Indian sweets will have a comprehensive introduction to the diverse world of milk- and nut-based treats ubiquitous on the Subcontinent, while those long fond of their gulab jamun and laddu are bound to find something new. With sweets maxing out at $6 a pound (for the premium, marzipan-like Burfi), visitors can walk away from Rajbhog with

72-27 37th Ave
(btwn 72nd & 73rd St)
718-458-8512
Mon-Fri 10am-2am,
Sat-Sun 10am-2am
E F V R G to Roosevelt
Ave-74th St
Sweets $3 per lb, Meals $5-7

enough candy to last a week, all for the price of a single restaurant dessert.

Rincon Criollo
Cuban

For authentic Cuban eats, look no further than this tasty light at the end of the 7 train. Set in Corona, on the fringes of Jackson Heights, Rincon Criollo sits well towards the edge of most city maps, but this doesn't deter Manhattanites in search of no-nonsense cooking. Locals in the largely-Latino neighborhood flock to this humble eatery, which serves nearly every staple of Central American food with native excellence. Common dishes like ropa vieja are especially juicy and tender here, while specialties like Caldo Gallego, a traditional soup of beans, bacon, and chorizo, are prepared with equal skill. For less than $20, diners can easily fill up on hearty Caribbean fare and have enough left over for lunch the next day.

4009 Junction Blvd
(at Roosevelt Ave)
718-639-8158
Daily 12pm-11pm
7 to Junction Blvd
Appetizers $3-8,
Entrees $10-17

Sammy's Halal

Middle Eastern

73rd St (at Broadway)
917-446-9948
Daily 10am-6pm
7 E F V R G to
Roosevelt Ave-74th St
Meals $5-7

You can tell Sammy's Halal food cart is exceptional as soon as you see it: on a street corner shared by two other food carts, it's the one with a line that could encircle the other two. The menu is no loftier than that of the average food cart—in fact, it's smaller than most—selling a handful of combinations of chicken, gyros, and rice. What distinguishes this particular award-winning cart is the food. Simple and unadorned, it manages to be the best of its kind. The chicken is more tender, the savory gyro more overflowing, and the rice more intensely spiced than anywhere else in the neighborhood. Best of all, even though the food tastes gourmet, an entire meal won't cost you more than six bucks.

Spicy Mina

Bangladeshi

64-23 Broadway (at 64th St.)
718-205-2340
Daily 11am-11pm
G R V to 65th S
Appetizers $3-6, Entrees $9-17
BYOB

Since 2003, dedicated foodies have followed Mina Begum, the motherly Bangladeshi proprietress and chef of Spicy Mina, from Sunnyside to Manhattan and now to Woodside, where she has set up shop at this no-frills eatery.

Though neither Ms. Begum nor her staff has much facility with English, they are unfailingly attentive, serving a basket of steaming hot papadums before diners even sit down and directing them to marvelously fresh dishes like the saag paneer, a classic preparation of spinach and Indian cheese. Your best bet is probably to order the special of the day. Unlike much of the South Asian food in New York, Ms. Begum's creations have a dash of homemade mystery about them, rendering even something as predictable as chicken tikka masala extraordinary—a buttery miracle at once familiar and unlike anything you've tasted before.

SriPraPhai

Thai

64-13 39th Ave
(btwn 64th & 65th St)
718-899-9599
Daily 11:30am-9:30pm,
Wed closed
L to 61st-Woodside
Appetizers $4-9, Entrees $8-14

For New Yorkers with big appetites and an affinity for spice, this celebrated Woodside eatery is the destination for authentic Thai cooking. With over ten pages of menu options, SriPraPhai (pronounced see-PRA-pie) offers an overwhelming abundance of choices for the adventurous eater. Friendly wait staff and smiley-face stickers on the menu marking "popular favorites" help navigate the options. Try the crispy watercress and fried soft shell crab served

with a fresh mango salad to start, and share the main courses for variety. Cooling bubble teas will curb the kick of famously spicy fare. While you might be tempted to fill up on savory entrees like the crispy catfish, be sure to save room for dessert. Among the mind-boggling array of sweets, the pumpkin custard, banana sticky rice with mango, and coconut ice cream are stand-outs.

Taqueria Coatzingo — *Mexican*

Neon signs scream "tacos" and "Mexican" from the outside of this unprepossessing Elmhurst Taqueria, where backlit photographs of food

> 76-05 Roosevelt Avenue
> (at 76th St)
> 718-424-1977
> Sun-Thurs 8am-2am,
> Fri-Sat 8am-4am
> **E F V R** to Jackson Hts-
> Roosevelt Ave
> Tacos $2, Mains $5-10

and a shabbily tiled counter may have some heading out the door before even ordering. But stick around—patrons from Queens to Manhattan agree that Taqueria Coatzingo offers some of the most authentic and delicious Mexican food in all five boroughs. Better still, tacos run a mere $2 each, including toppings like guacamole. Another local favorite is the cemita de queso, a Mexican sandwich prepared with avocado, slabs of swiss and Mexican quesillo cheese, chipotle peppers, and papalo, an herb that imparts a fresh, citrusy, cilantro flavor. Make sure you complement whichever dish you choose with a cup of cool, refreshing horchata, or rice-milk, which helps temper some of that traditional Mexican spice.

PLAY

Friend's Tavern — *LGBT*

As the oldest gay bar in Queens, this dimly-lit, late night hangout has no shortage of old-school personality, complete with a smoke-engulfed dance floor, strobe lights, and a disco ball in the back.

> 78-11 Roosevelt Ave
> (at 78 St)
> 718-397-7256
> Daily 4pm-4am
> **E F V G R** to Jackson
> Heights-Roosevelt Ave,
> **7** to 74 St-Broadway
> Average Drink $6
> Happy Hour 4pm-9pm

Ceilings covered with mirrors, white Christmas lights, and red tinsel meet small South American and rainbow-colored flags on the walls. Bartenders in tight black tank tops are welcoming and attentive, and the majority of the crowd is ready to mingle. Newcomers and locals gyrate to loud Latin pop blasting from speakers and Ricky Martin music videos playing on TV screens behind the bar. The happy hour special of half-price well drinks and domestic beers also make this eclectic neighborhood staple a perfect place to stop for after-work drinks with a group of friends.

FLUSHING

The Dutch that originally founded this neighborhood almost 350 years ago named it after their native city of Vlissingen. English translation: Flushing. In 1657 the first American declaration of religious freedom, the Flushing Remonstrance, was issued here upon the mass immigration of the Quaker population. The legacy of positive social action prevailed for centuries, exemplified by Flushing's multiple stops on the Underground Railroad and by Flushing High School, the oldest public high school in New York City.

The newest wave of immigration thrives in the hub of East Asian culture on Main Street. After emerging from the 7 train, visitors and even seasoned New Yorkers may feel like foreigners here—the largest Chinatown in New York City. Speckled with small businesses, noodle shops, and outdoor grocery stands, Main Street is the place to get filling portions at cheap prices. Of late, Flushing's signature East Asian cuisine—Eastern Chinese and Korean—has been augmented by authentic flavors from central and western China as well, for those daring to experiment.

A haven of music culture, Flushing was home to jazz legend Louis Armstrong, infamous Broadway composer Marvin Hamlisch as well as KISS's Paul Stanley. In fact, KISS first played at the Coventry club on Queens Boulevard and are said to have been named for Kissena—one of Flushing's main drives.

Flushing seems like the undiscovered treasure of the city—and not just because of the good eats. Flushing Meadows Corona Park draws picnickers to its myriad lawns and fields and skateboarders to the makeshift skate park at the iconic Unisphere. And on rainy or winter days, visitors can roam the Queens Museum of Art and the New York Hall of Science.

Flushing's pockets of cultural nuances render the neighborhood the ideal day trip destination. Though it can be a long trek, the views from the elevated subway ride reveal beautiful skylines, making the outbound trip itself a worthwhile experience.

EXPLORE

Louis Armstrong House

The last home of the jazz legend, this unassuming Flushing residence was kept fully furnished and decorated, just as the musician's wife

34-56 107th St
(btwn 34th & 37th Ave)
718-478-8274
Tues-Fri 10am-5pm,
Sat-Sun 12pm-5pm,
Last tour at 4pm
⑦ to 103 St

Lucile left it before passing. Hourly guided individual and group tours show visitors the original décor, memorabilia, and mementos. But the most fascinating part of the visit is hearing authentic sound bites of private moments fed through speakers in every room of the house. Originally used to broadcast a perpetual stream of background music, the speakers now serve as a gateway to Louis' band rehearsals, dinner conversations, and daily musings that he recorded and archived himself. A Visitor's Center opening in 2010 will offer a smorgasbord of concerts, film screenings, lectures, workshops, exhibits, and other public programs.

Flushing Meadows Corona Park

This 1,225-acre park is home to museums, stadiums, athletic fields, mini-golf courses, fountains, reflecting pools, and

Entrances at Perimeter Rd &
111th St
718-760-6565
⑦ to Mets-Willets Point Blvd
⑦ to 111th St

even a zoo. Visitors can roam the grounds and admire the scattered sculptures, or laze about in a meadow. Walk through the Queens Zoo, the undersized and less expensive version of its Bronx cousin, to witness a feeding, shear the sheep, hop on the carousel, or just watch the animals. If sports are your thing, stop in for a New York Mets game at the newly built Citi Field, join in a pickup soccer game, or test your skills in the makeshift skate park at the world-famous Unisphere. Built entirely of steel, the 900,000 pound emblem of Queens and the U.S. Open is the largest globe in the world.

New York Hall of Science

More like a playground than a classroom, the New York Hall of Science invites adults and children of all ages to probe scientific and mathematical questions through interactive exhibits and experiments. Equipped with an Astro Observatory and spaceships dedicated to the search for life beyond earth, the Hall of Science travels the universe in one building. Boggle your mind with optical illusions and eye-crossing equations. Flex your muscles in the Sports Challenge, which tests your perception of speed, balance, force, and work through activities like pitching, surfing, and arm-wrestling. This popular venue for kids' birthday parties is complete with both a Preschool Place and a science technology library—a family-friendly attraction that is both educational and fun.

47-01 111th St (at 47th Ave)
718-699-0005
Schedule varies seasonally,
Always Tues-Sun 10am-2pm
❼ to 111th St
Adults $11, Students (with ID) $8,
Science Playground add
$4 per person, $3 for groups
Check for free admission times

Lewis H. Latimer House

Nestled behind a white picket fence and delicate landscaping, this small, traditional Queen-Anne style house was once home to Lewis H. Latimer, the African American inventor that created the carbon filament in electric light bulbs—still used today. The red and yellow house is now a museum that recreates Latimer's functional in-house laboratory for experimentation. Group and self-guided tours present a comprehensive history of Latimer's life and accomplishments. Latimer House also hosts a number of special events, from Tai Chi workshops to poetry readings, and the house is available to rent for private occasions like baby showers and weddings.

34-41 137th St (at Leavitt St)
718-961-8585
Tues-Thurs & Sat 11am-4pm
❼ to Main St
Donations accepted

Queens Library

A microcosm of the borough itself, this library encapsulates the cultural mix of Queens and greater New York City under one roof. In addition to its vast collection of literature and

89-11 Merrick Boulevard
(at 89th Ave)
718-990-0700
Mon-Fri 10am-9pm,
Sat 10am-5:30pm,
Sun 12pm-5pm
❼ to 169th St

DAY TO DAY

Community Board 7: 133-32 41st Road, Suite 3B, 718-359-2800.

Dry Cleaner: Cherie Cleaners, 4365 Kissena Blvd, 718-353-4818.

Groceries: Trader Joes, 9030 Metropolitan Ave, 718-275-1791.

Gym: Pure Powerhouse Gym, 3511 Prince St, 718-939-7382.

Hospital: Flushing Hospital Medical Center. 146-01 45 Ave, 718-670-5000.

Library: Queens Borough Public Library: 41-17 Main St, 718-661-1200.

Volunteer: Flushing Volunteer Ambulance Corps, 4316 162nd St, 718-353-4965

multimedia materials, the library's distinctive International Resource Center caters to readers with a deep interest in global studies, sponsoring excellent free weekly events such as lectures, seminars, and theatrical presentations. The library also offers computer classes for non-English speakers and workshops in resume writing and interviewing, as well as reactional activities, weekly meditation, summer karaoke, book discussion groups, and craft workshops. Music lovers can come for the frequent free concerts—ranging from instrumental and Broadway to doo-wop and Irish folk tunes.

Queens Museum of Art

Only here can you see the entire city of New York in one room. The one-of-a-kind hand-crafted "Panorama of the City of New York" now resides in the Queens Museum of Art, but back in 1964, visitors came from far and wide to see the 9,335-square-foot model premier at the World Fair in Flushing. Located in Corona Park, the Queens Museum of Art also features rotating exhibits and selections of artwork by Tiffany Glass. The museum hosts additional

New York City Building,
Flushing Meadows, Corona
Park (near Ave of the States)
718-592-9700
Wed-Fri 10am-5pm, Sat-Sun
12pm-5pm, closed Mon-Tues
❼ to Mets-Willets Point
Suggested donation Adults $5,
Seniors & Children $2.50,
Members & Children
under 5 Free

FLUSHING

Golden Shopping Mall

Chinese Food Court

41-28 Main St
7 to Flushing Main St
Most open before 12pm
& Close 8-10 pm
Prices Vary, most under $10

Walk down a flight of steps to enter another world: the dense cluster of tiny underground eateries that comprise the Golden Shopping Mall Food Court. On a Saturday afternoon the shops are full of local customers sampling regional specialties from all over China, from tripe to trotters. Lan Zhou Handmade Noodles serves bowls of long, supple noodles in rich, meaty broth. Xi'an Famous Foods dishes Liangpi Cold Noodles—flat cilantro-flavored noodles with chunks of spongy, dense bread and peanuts in a sour and spicy seagrass sauce. The next shop over sells steamed buns, outer layers of pillowy dough harboring mixtures of aromatic ginger, scallions, and pork as tender as braised meat. Since nothing costs more than $6, this food court also happens to offer one of the best food bargains in Queens.

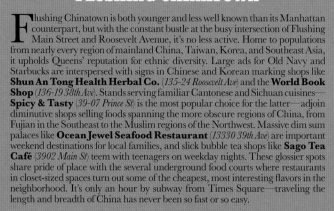

FLUSHING CHINATOWN

Flushing Chinatown is both younger and less well known than its Manhattan counterpart, but with the constant bustle at the busy intersection of Flushing Main Street and Roosevelt Avenue, it's no less active. Home to populations from nearly every region of mainland China, Taiwan, Korea, and Southeast Asia, it upholds Queens' reputation for ethnic diversity. Large ads for Old Navy and Starbucks are interspersed with signs in Chinese and Korean marking shops like **Shun An Tong Health Herbal Co.** (*135-24 Roosevelt Ave*) and the **World Book Shop** (*136-19 38th Ave*). Stands serving familiar Cantonese and Sichuan cuisines—**Spicy & Tasty** (*39-07 Prince St*) is the most popular choice for the latter—adjoin diminutive shops selling foods spanning the more obscure regions of China, from Fujian in the Southeast to the Muslim regions of the Northwest. Massive dim sum palaces like **Ocean Jewel Seafood Restaurant** (*13330 39th Ave*) are important weekend destinations for local families, and slick bubble tea shops like **Sago Tea Café** (*3902 Main St*) teem with teenagers on weekday nights. These glossier spots share pride of place with the several underground food courts where restaurants in closet-sized spaces turn out some of the cheapest, most interesting flavors in the neighborhood. It's only an hour by subway from Times Square—traveling the length and breadth of China has never been so fast or so easy.

drop-in art workshops, and their Art Access program welcomes families for a whole day of free art workshops, tours, activities and prizes. Petite and personalized, the museum proposes a less intimidating alternative to the cavernous spaces and winding halls of Manhattan's art museums.

USTA Billie Jean King National Tennis Center

With three stadiums in addition to nine indoor and fourteen outdoor courts, this massive compound is the largest public tennis facility in the world and the annual host of the US Open. For a couple weeks every August, the center comes alive with music from live bands and wafting smells of fresh waffle fries from the food court. Obsessed fans brave the sweltering heat to watch competitive matches and stalk tennis stars. Bags are not permitted inside during the Open, so be sure to lather up in sunscreen before coming and bring plenty of money for water. When not drawing tremendous crowds during the two weeks of U.S. Open mania, the Center is open daily for public use by tennis lovers of all levels, no pro status required.

Flushing Meadows-Corona Park
718-760-6200
❼ to Mets-Willets Point
Mon-Sat 6am-12am,
Sun 6am-11pm
Court Rental $20-$60 per hour

SHOP

Chinese Harp Music Center

The lilting twang of the guzheng harp—a traditional Chinese musical instrument—mixes harmoniously with the anxious murmurs of onlooking parents at this music center tucked away in the labyrinthine Flushing Mall. Three different rooms house ornately designed instruments and eager students with an ear for intonation. Young tykes and older aspiring musicians alike pluck away at the strings of their zheng instruments, a beautifully bizarre crossbreed of piano, guitar, and harp. Keep an eye out for summer freebie lessons and concerts in the Flushing Mall.

Flushing Mall, 133-31 39th Ave
(near 63rd St)
718-207-0224
Mon-Fri 11-8pm,
Sat-Sun 9:30am-9:30pm
❼ to Flushing-Main St
Instruments $500-$1,000,
Group Lessons $20

Yappi

This charming boutique carries the hottest Korean fashions. Perfectly-cut boyfriend blazers, achieving the tenuous equilibrium between formal and feminine grace, hang near cute graphic t-shirts. These will catch your eye, but the shop's employees—a gaggle of girls who chatter in Korean while straightening their hair—are quick to tell you that Yappi's forte is dresses. Prom queens and wedding invitees flock here for colorful numbers with unique cuts and shapes—it's guaranteed that no dopplegangers will crop up at any event. Most of the dresses go for $100-$180 and require a willingness to show some serious leg, but you'll never stop turning heads.

36-36 Union St
(at Northern Blvd)
718-762-3730
Mon-Sat 12pm-8pm,
Sun 12pm-7pm
🚇 to Flushing-Main St

EAT

Corner 28 — *Chinese*

40-28 Main St (near 41st Ave)
718-886-6628
Daily 6am-2am
🚇 to Flushing-Main St
Takeout window
sandwiches 75¢ each,
Restaurant mains $5-16

Where else in New York can you buy your lunch with quarters? Roasted ducks are strung up in rows at this popular curbside takeout window, where the specialty is Peking duck. A slab of hot, fatty poultry stuffed in a fresh steamed bun and coated with tangy plum sauce costs a mere 75 cents. One Peking duck sandwich is a perfect snack, though two or three might be in order for a full meal. If you have a few more minutes to spare, step into the frenetic main restaurant. The locals crowded around the extensive buffet speak mostly in Mandarin, and menus (also in Mandarin) are of little help, but the point-and-nod method works just fine. Take your food to the cafe-style back area or the unexpectedly peaceful dining room upstairs. And be sure to flash your student ID for a ten percent discount.

Dosa Hutt — *South Indian, Vegetarian*

43-63 Bowne St (at Holly Ave)
718-961-6228
Daily 9am-9pm,
Tues 12pm-9pm
🚇 to Flushing-Main St
Snacks & Dosas $2-6

No tablecloths, no silverware, and no frills: just cheap, fast, and good South Indian food at this humble joint. Dosa Hutt's traditional, all-vegetarian snacks pack a tremendously spicy, flavorful punch for under $5. Their featured item is the oven-crisped, potato-and-vegetable stuffed, paper-thin rice and lentil crêpe that makes up the "dosa." These Titan-sized centerpieces arrive piping hot on flimsy Styrofoam plates. All dosas come with a side of delicate coconut chutney and a cup of sambar, an ochre-hewed vegetable soup. Get the Pondicherry for a nice, rich burn that will settle in your throat, and chase it down with a bite of dripping cheese filling as a creamy salve. Not a dosa fan? Their savory flatbread, uttapam, and steamed rice patties, idli, make for satisfying alternatives. Just come prepared to scout for seating on weekends.

Joe's Bestburger — *Burgers*

While the institutional lighting and red paint common to most burger chains makes an

appearance at this Flushing burger joint, the unfortunately uninspired décor can't detract from the ridiculously cheap and delicious food. Where most fast food places cook their burgers into rubbery oblivion, here the beef remains juicy and tender, topped with

39-11 Main St
718-445-8065
Mon-Fri 10am-12am,
Sun 10am-10pm
🚇 to Flushing Main St
Burgers $2-5, Fries $2-3

a tangy and creamy "special sauce" that actually lives up to its name. Good as the burgers are, the fries—thick and crisp with bits of potato skin on either end—are the highlight of a meal at Joe's. Try them with the mango chutney (which is more like a sweet, fruity mayonnaise) or the spicy chipotle sauce on the side, and be prepared to rejoice when you get your receipt.

Little Lamb *Mongolian*

A Mongolian culinary tradition finds a stateside home at Flushing's Little Lamb. Waiters set spicy, mild, or half-and-half broth on a hot plate sunken in the middle of the table into which diners

pong pros for $8 an hour at the **New York Table Tennis Club** (*35-26 Prince St*). Then, take a stroll around Flushing Meadows Corona Park, where $7 gets you into the **Queens Zoo** and $5 grants access to the famed **Queens Museum of Art**. If you still have energy and cash to burn, dive into one of Flushing's labyrinthine mini-malls: both **Flushing Mall** (*39th Ave at 138th St*) and **Golden Mall** (*Main St & 41st Road*) sell cheap stationary, jewelry, art, electronics, and Chinese knock-offs of movies at bargain prices—especially if you're prepared to haggle.

drop their choice of meats, seafood, and vegetables. For the adventurous, Little Lamb offers delicacies like fish

36-35 Main St
(near Northern Blvd)
718-358-6667
7 to Flushing-Main St
Hot pot for 4 $21,
Avg additional ingredient $6

stomach, chicken testicles, and beef penis, while those with more traditional tastes can select thin slices of various, more familiar meats.

Mirrors and light colors give the space an open, comfortable feel. And be sure to hit the condiment bar in the back of the dining room. Some lackluster service won't detract from the fun of this do-it-yourself adventure of a meal. Dining this way takes time, so come with friends and plan on making this the main event.

S&C Shaved Ice Stall *Dessert*

More than most places within the five boroughs, Flushing Mall feels like the suburbs, complete with a bustling food court that consists

Food Court, Flushing Mall,
133-31 39th Ave
718-888-1980
Mon-Tues 7am-3pm,
Wed-Fri 7am-10pm,
7 to Flushing-Main St
Average Bowl $4

of a row of fast food stalls surrounding a room of sterile white picnic tables and benches. If you find yourself stopping by for a quick, cheap lunch, head to S&C Shaved Ice for dessert, where a heaping bowl of shaved ice comes topped with your selection of fruit syrups (studded with candied fruit), tapioca, and gooey sweet beans. Those unfamiliar with Asian sweets may be reluctant, but the red beans are not to be missed. Their mild flavor combines with the super-sweet fruit syrups for a bracing contrast to the bitingly cold ice. One immense bowl is easily enough to share amongst four people, so make S&C the last stop on your Flushing Chinatown food tour.

PLAY

Kelly's Pub *Dive*

The last Irish dive left in Flushing, Kelly's offers everything you could hope for from a traditional neighborhood pub—

13611 41st Ave
718-359-9668
Mon-Sat 8am-4am,
Sun 12pm-4am
7 to Main St-Flushing
Average Drink $5

good service, a welcoming environment, and few frills. The drinks are strong and cheap, and the ice-cold beer is served by sociable Irish bartenders. Newcomers will stand out against the regulars but are sure to be graciously welcomed. Join the mass of locals who congregate here for drinks after work or stay late into the night chatting with your neighbors at the bar, watching ESPN on multiple TV screens, and listening to the Rolling Stones on the jukebox. Bring a group of friends or leave them behind—even solo you won't keep to yourself for long.

THE BRONX

THE BRONX

As you ride through The Bronx, the stylized decay art in the new Yankee Stadium subway station gives way to the real raw neglect of every other stop in this scarred but resilient borough. The Bronx provides comic-book contrasts of city life, from the rich suburbs of Riverdale to the slums of East Tremont.

Once a massive farm, and then a middle class county lined with fishing ports, the Bronx's divisions came quickly. While Manhattan escaped the dissecting knife of urban planner Robert Moses' highways, the Bronx was carved to pieces. The Cross-Bronx Expressway destroyed massive working-class apartment buildings, displacing many Jewish and Italian residents and leaving a stretch of blight, the effects of which are still reverberating.

The Bronx's regions are islands of low-rise buildings. Its best attractions lie in the center, away from the dismal stretches of highway. Some spots, like Yankee Stadium and a handful of green spaces, escape the dreary surroundings, but it's difficult to kick gloom around here. There are short waves of visitors to the Zoo or Botanical Gardens, but little sidewalk scene emerges. The Grand Concourse, South Bronx's art community, as well as Arthur Avenue and some other spots hold small pockets of commotion before 6pm. Lines of chains and discount stores on Fordham Road herd pedestrians inside, and City Island achieves an almost beach-town feel.

More than anywhere else in New York, the locals in The Bronx will talk to you, grumble about the new stadium, or boast about their devotion to the neighborhood. They will complain about the toxic sites that are only now being cleaned and describe a beautiful brick building that once stood nearby. But much like the bright murals and graffiti (an art born in this borough), The Bronx is very much alive. Whether you are visiting the hotspots or speeding through the busier streets, the Bronx provides a combination of rich and poor, a blend of nostalgia and constant change that is New York.

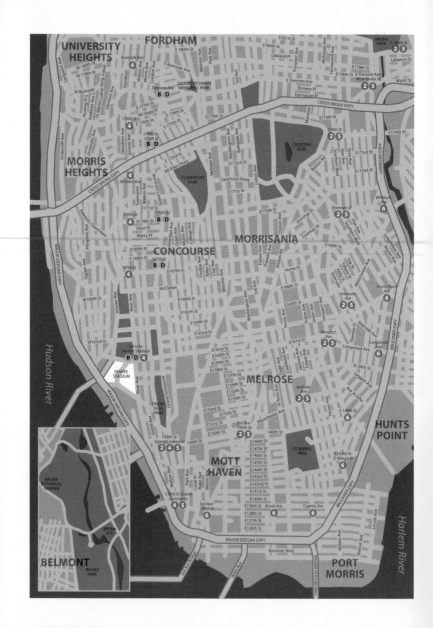

EXPLORE

Bronx Museum of the Arts

The Bronx Museum of the Arts combines cutting-edge aesthetic endeavors with an emphasis on social justice and community interaction. The result is something of a rarity: a major municipal museum that spends more time looking forward than backward. Its most distinctive program, Artists in the Marketplace (AIM), now in its 28th year, provides practical career advice, critical evaluation, and professional guidance to 36 young artists every year, culminating in a group show. A $19 million renovation, completed in 2006, has provided a major new gallery and events space, an outdoor terrace, and an entire floor dedicated

1040 Grand Concourse
(at 165th St)
718-681-6000
Mon, Thurs & Sun 12pm-6pm,
Fri-Sat 12pm-8pm
④⑧⓪ to 167th St
Adults $5, Students $3

DAY TO DAY

to classrooms and education programs. In the works is a plan to modernize the original structure and affix a residential co-op tower. More than other museums in the city, BxMA invests in its community.

Bronx Zoo

At the Bronx Zoo, 265 acres house over 4,000 animals, whose spacious trappings are thanks to the valiant efforts of the Wildlife Conservation Society. The grounds are pleasant and well organized (taxonomically and geographically), and the usual zoo favorites all put in an appearance: lions, tigers, bears, monkeys, aquatic mammals, birds, reptiles, rodents, and so on. Special attractions (which cost a bit extra) include camel rides, a butterfly garden, an Asia-themed monorail ride, an excellent children's zoo, the Skyfari (a two-mile elevated cable car ride), and, best of all, the Congo Gorilla Forest, a 6.5 acre mini-rainforest housing two families of our not-so-distant cousins.

2300 Southern Blvd.
718-367-1010
Hours vary seasonally,
Daily 10am-5pm
❷❺ to West Farms Sq–East
Tremont Ave
Adults $15, Seniors $13,
Children $11

New York Botanical Garden

Spanning over 250 acres (including 50 acres of uncut, native forest), the exceedingly tranquil, immaculately manicured grounds of New York Botanical Garden are home to a staggering 1 million living plants, 7 million herbarium specimens, and the world's most sophisticated botanical research center. This one is worth the visit for its many floral pleasures: a 4000-strong rose garden (in bloom in June and November), a meditative rock garden, and collections of lilies, orchids, daffodils, and magnolias, and the conservatory features a winter holiday train show. The native forest is the closest you're going to get to being alone with nature within the city limits. A constant stream of

2694 Dr Theodore Kazimiroff
Blvd (near E Fordham Rd)
718-817-8700
Tues-Sun 10am-6pm
❹❸❻ to Bedford Park Blvd,
Bx26 to Mosholu Gate
All-garden pass $20, Students
$18, Grounds-only pass $6,
Ground-only students $3

UNDER $20

THE BRONX

Take a morning stroll through the **Botanical Garden** (*Bronx River Parkway at Fordham Rd*) or the **Bronx Zoo** (*2300 Southern Blvd*)—on Wednesdays the zoo is pay what you can. Satisfy post-rambling fatigue with a slice at **Pugsley's** (*590 E 191st St*) or **Full Moon Pizzeria** (*600 E 187th St*). Don't want a pie? Grab miniburgers and potstickers for $1.50 at **Belmont Café** (*690 E 187th St*) or a $5 fish plate at **Kim's Fish Market** (*555 Morris Ave*). For some post-meal culture, head down the Art Deco-lined Grand Concourse to the **Bronx River Art Center Gallery** (*1087 East Tremont Ave*) or the **Bronx Museum of the Arts** (*1040 Grand Concourse*), free on Fridays. Check out the **Bronx Culture Trolley** (*450 Grand Concourse*) on the first Wednesday night of the month. Sponsored by the Bronx Council of Arts, this free ride stops at poetry readings, art exhibitions, and theater performances, granting visitors access to the "Gateway to the New Bronx." And if you're around in the summer, keep an eye out for **Bronx Week** in June. It features free events and concerts cool enough to attract even the stubbornist Manhattanites.

concerts, classes, and exhibits always ensure there's more to do than just look at plants.

Orchard Beach

Considered the Riviera of New York, this stretch of sand is a perfect spot to sunbathe on a sweltering dog day afternoon or to stroll on a chilly winter day. The beach is part of Pelham Bay Park, which offers a central pavilion of specialty shops and food stores, a playground, picnic areas, and 26 courts for volleyball, basketball, and handball. The 115-acre beach is actually man-made, and is often swarming with Fordham students and sun-loving families. Pack a lunch and head here—sunblock in tote—for a day at the beach.

nycgovparks.org/ parks/orchardbeach

Yankee Stadium

The New York Yankees' new home opened in 2009, replacing the stadium that had been been around since 1923. Angry locals deride the new ballpark's shrunken capacity and ballooned entry fares, but the elegant architecture of the Grand Hall and the widened cupholdered seats make it worth the visit. The Grandstand offers fantastic sightlines, but also pins you under loud, tinny speakers blasting Queen, Metallica, and clips from *300*. No pipe organs here, but you can still hear the old vendors' cries and fill up on $5 franks, fries, and Famiglia. But native New Yorkers know to bring their own or go for the classic meat sandwiches from the local vendors, Lobel's and Mike's Deli. For some Bronx Bombers history, check out the museum on the main level at Gate 6, and see if you can catch a glimpse of Derek Jeter speeding away right after the game.

1 East 161st St (at River Ave)
4 **B** **D** to 161st St, Metro North to 153rd St

SHOP

Casa Amadeo

Founded in 1927, the oldest Latin music store in New York has grown to become a hub for cultural exchange in the South Bronx.

ARTHUR AVENUE

Forget Mulberry Street. Arthur Avenue (also known as Bronx's Little Italy or Belmont) is where first- and second-generation Italian Americans know to find the best Italian bakeries, butchers, delis, markets, and coffee shops. **Arthur Avenue Retail Market** (*2344 Arthur Ave*), housed in a beautiful old structure with dark wood and skylights, is an intimate bazaar that might overwhelm first-time visitors with its smorgasbord of enticing produce. But the easygoing vendors at booths like **Casa Della Mozzarella** (*604 E 187th St*) and **Biancardi Meats** (*2350 Arthur Ave*), all of whom remember their patrons' names, are especially helpful at directing newcomers. Chefs flock here for the fresh meat from **Retail Market** (*2344 Arthur Ave*), fish from **Cosenza's Fish Market** (*2354 Arthur Ave*), and pasta from **Borgatti's** (*632 E 187th St*). And bakeries like **Madonia Brothers** (*2348 Arthur Ave*) and delis like **Mike's Deli** (*2344 Arthur Ave*) sell tantalizing munchies. Wandering Manhattanites will leave with overflowing bags of groceries, generous cooking advice, and a final tip from the smirking butcher behind the counter at Mike's: "You stay down there, except when you want to eat."

Current owner Miguel Amadeo bought his first record from the store in 1947 before returning 22 years later to buy the whole shop, creating this mecca of Latin music. A musician himself, he promotes lesser-known Latin musicians and local recording artists. Stop by here for rare and hard-to-find albums, as well as more popular tracks by musicians like Tito Puente and Juan Luis Guerra. Today the store is frequented by notables like Ray Baretto, the famous conga player, and Jose Serrano, the Bronx Congressman.

786 Prospect Ave
(at Mary Place)
212-328-6896
Mon-Sat 11am-7pm
2 5 to Prospect Ave

EAT

Bruckner Bar & Grill *American*

After an afternoon spent treading the sticky pavement of the South Bronx's broad thoroughfares, this combination art gallery/performance space/bar/restaurant, with its tasteful décor and gorgeous natural light, is a breath of fresh air. And the expansive and unusual beer selection complements the high quality bar grub. The Bruckner Salad, an enormous bowl of bitingly

1 Bruckner Blvd (at 3rd Ave)
718-665-2001
Sat-Thurs 11:30am-12am,
Fri 11:30am-2am
6 to 3rd Ave-138th St
Appetizers $4-9,
Entrees $11-17

fresh mesclun, bacon, blue cheese, and avocado, is an expert rendition of the traditional Cobb Salad, and the coarse ground burgers are meaty, juicy, and rich with herbs. Best of all, Bruckner uses its wall space to display the work of local artists. Patronizing Bruckner Bar & Grill is a great way to get to know a different part of New York, an area big on culture but low on spaces to showcase it.

The Feeding Tree *Jamaican*

There are no avant-garde plates or celebrity chefs at this tiny restaurant—just hot, filling, and delicious Jamaican dishes cooked by the people that know it best. A Pac-Man machine in the corner and a beach mural on the wall are the only decorations, but you're not there for the atmosphere. All dishes are $10 or less and come with rice, cabbage, plantains, and cornbread. While these generous sides and jaw-dropping prices will pique the interest of any bargain hunter, the real highlight here is the meat. Their curried goat slides right off the bone and the jerk chicken is flavored by wonderfully subtle spices. Those with a sweet tooth should skip desserts in favor of lemonade and fresh-squeezed juices, the perfect complement to a robust meal.

892 Gerard Avenue
(at 161st St)
718-293-5025
Mon-Sat 8am-10pm,
Sun 10am-8pm
4 B D to 161st-
Yankee Stadium
Appetizers $3-8,
Entrees $6-12
Cash only

GRAND CONCOURSE

Modeled after the Champs-Élysées in Paris, the Grand Concourse is easily the most famous street in the Bronx, a historically important thoroughfare that continues to abut some of the borough's most significant cultural landmarks. The ground floor of the **Bronx General Post Office** (at E 149th St) is covered with faded tempera murals painted during the Great Depression glorifying the nation's transformation into a modern industrial power. **The Mario Merola Building** (E 158th St), also known as the **Bronx County Courthouse**, houses more New Deal projects, including a sculptural frieze and two free-standing marble sculpture groups at each columned portico entrance. The north end of the courthouse leads into **Joyce Kilmer Park** (at E 161st St), named for a poet and soldier killed in action on the Western Front. The park is perhaps notable only, and bizarrely, for a fountain honoring Heinrich Heine, a 19th century German Romantic who has little in common with Kilmer. A block north is the **Bronx Museum of the Arts** (at W 165th). Further uptown, **Poe Park and Poe Cottage** (at 188th St) invite visitors to the last home of Edgar Allan Poe.

MOgridder's

BBQ

Attached to "Hunts Point Auto Sales and Service" is this barbecue stand that combats the smells of axle grease and engine smoke with pork fat and cherry wood. This may be one of the most oddly placed restaurants in town, but there's nothing odd about good old-fashioned barbecue. Smoked, shredded chicken has a musky flavor and supple texture, and mounds of meaty pulled pork are enlivened with welcome bits of crisp skin. All of the enormous portions are served with pillowy potato bread and Latin-inflected "BBQ rice," and when conquered with a plastic fork on one of their two sun-baked plastic picnic tables, it feels like lunch you wish you'd had in the middle school cafeteria.

565 Hunts Point Ave
(near Randall Ave)
718-991-3046
Mon-Tues 10am-4pm, Wed-Fri
10am-7pm, Sat 10am-2pm,
Sun closed
6 to Longwood Ave
Meals $9-16

STATEN ISLAND

STATEN ISLAND

The famous orange Staten Island Ferry started running in 1713, and the borough was incorporated into the City of Greater New York in 1898. Despite its potentially worrisome lack of subways, this safe, suburban isle is actually conveniently located, and many have chosen to settle here rather than in the borough's flashier cousins. The North Shore area is also becoming popular for artists and musicians who want reasonably priced housing near Manhattan. Still, today fewer than 500,000 people reside on this land that Henry Hudson named Staaten Eylandt in 1609.

The borough remained relatively undeveloped until the Verrazano-Narrows Bridge was finished in 1964. Since the burst of housing activity in the late 1960s, pitched battles have raged over the preservation of open space. Staten Island has the largest green spaces in the city, including dozens of small parks, a Greenbelt system that laces the borough with hiking trails, the fourth-largest boardwalk in the world, three 18-hole golf courses, enormous wildlife refuges, and the freshly constructed Fresh Kills Park. Three times the size of Central Park, this unimaginably vast landscape was created from a temporary landfill and originally opened in 1947.

Although it's hard to scoff at a park that large, most New Yorkers do alternately ignore and disparage the borough. Even still, the intensively protective and independent Staten Islanders are proud of their home. Starting in the 1980s, a movement for secession from the Greater New York system surfaced. The movement stemmed from the borough's drastic statistical differences with the rest of the city—Staten Island boasts highest percentage of Italian-Americans of any county in the country and a Republican majority in its public offices. The secession movement failed to gain traction, though, and Staten Island remains on as the suburban outlier of New York's five boroughs.

EXPLORE

Gerardi's Farmers Market and Nursery

For the freshest produce in Staten Island, Gerardi's is a must. Offering an assortment of both common and rare fruits, vegetables, herbs, plants, and trees, this farmer's market and nursery trumps your average grocery store and florist in selection and price. All of the produce is grown on farms in New Jersey, and it's damn cheap—a week's worth of fruit costs less than $20, while fresh-potted flowers and most trees run for under $50. If the prices don't sway you, the artful presentation will. You

561 Richmond Terrace (btwn
Franklin Ave & Lafayette Ave)
718-727-7787
Daily 8am-6pm
Staten Island Ferry to
Saint George Station,
S40/S90 to Richmond Terrace

won't complain about having to haul dozens of shopping bags (that, rest assured, you will have) back over the ferry.

Historic Richmond Town

This 25-acre area in the middle of the island houses an extensive complex of preserved historical buildings that form a living museum of early colonial life. Richmond Town, once the seat of government on Staten Island, remains the official legal name of the county. The buildings now contain a mill, carpenter shop, general store, bakery, smithy, and museums. Nature

441 Clarke Ave
(St Patrick's Place)
718-351-1611
Sept-June: Wed-Sun 1pm-
5pm, July-Aug: Thurs-Fri
11am-3pm, Sat-Sun 1pm-5pm
Staten Island Ferry to
Saint George Station,
S74 to Richmond Rd &
Saint Patrick's Pl
Adults $5

enthusiasts can enjoy the trails that crisscross the forested Bluebelt, or watch geese, ducks, and heron feed on the bracken and massive fish that swim in the mill creek. Come to check out one of the frequent community events or to immerse yourself in the daily activities of 300 years ago.

Jacques Marchais Museum of Tibetan Art

Most of the exhibits in this 62-year-old museum come from the vast private Tibetan art collection of Jacques Marchais, an American artist with a passion for studying the ancient cultures of the Himalayan regions. Its two buildings are modeled after a monastery, and are appropriately ensconced within the side of a hill that's swathed in serenity. Within, you'll discover a impressive array of sculptures, books, paintings, ritual artifacts, instruments, old photographs of Tibet, and a gallery that hosts rotating special exhibits. Every October, the museum hosts a two-day festival with mask making, Mongolian children's games, and Tibetan crafts. Before you leave, be sure to take a stroll through the terraced meditation gardens—they're so quiet you'll feel as if you're at the temple of the Dalai Lama himself.

338 Lighthouse Ave
(near Saint George Rd)
718-987-3500
Wed-Sun 1-5pm
Staten Island Ferry to
Saint George Station,
S74 to Lighthouse Ave
Adults $5, Students $3

Snug Harbor Cultural Center & Botanical Garden

In the past year, Snug Harbor—a former retirement center for sailors—and the Staten Island Botanical Garden combined forces to become the ultimate city getaway. The main complex features an impressive collection of Greek Revival architecture (picture tall white columns), with five interlinking temples at the center. Within these buildings lie the Snug Harbor Museum and Noble Maritime Collection. Behind the temples are a playhouse

1000 Richmond Terrace
(near Snug Harbor Rd)
718-448-2500
Dawn-Dusk
Tues-Sun 10am-4pm
Staten Island Ferry to St.
George Station, S40/S90 to
Richmond Terrace
Students $5

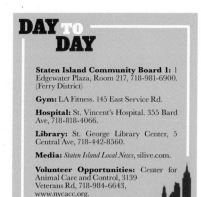

DAY TO DAY

Staten Island Community Board 1: 1 Edgewater Plaza, Room 217, 718-981-6900. (Ferry District)

Gym: LA Fitness. 145 East Service Rd.

Hospital: St. Vincent's Hospital. 355 Bard Ave, 718-818-4066.

Library: St. George Library Center, 5 Central Ave, 718-442-8560.

Media: *Staten Island Local News*, silive.com.

Volunteer Opportunities: Center for Animal Care and Control, 3139 Veterans Rd, 718-984-6643, www.nycacc.org.

STATEN ISLAND

and music halls, which showcase local talent on a daily basis. Galleries feature neighborhood artists and the center sponsors celebrated artists-in-residence who continue to beautify the grounds. If you're hungry, head to Café Botanica for a garden-inspired dish, and pack a picnic (basket provided!) when the weather is warm for a guided garden tour.

Staten Island Ferry

Join the over 80,000 passengers who take this ferry every day for the best free ride in the city. You'll pass some of New York's most spectacular views, including panoramas of the Statue of Liberty and Ellis Island. Bring a jacket along—even in summer months—if you intend to go out on one of the four open decks. If you plan your visit during the summer, be sure to check out the Whitehall Ferry Terminal's annual "Sitelines" event, sponsored by the Lower Manhattan Cultural Council. It features performances of world premiere dance, art, and theatrical shows—all for free.

1 Bay St (at Richmond Terrace)
718-876-8441
Daily 24 hours.
Runs on the half hour during the day, on the hour at night.
1 N R W to
South Ferry Terminal
Free

Staten Island Zoo

The smallest of New York area zoos, the Staten Island Zoo nonetheless features an internationally acclaimed reptile collection and several other exhibits which make it well worth a visit. The zoo houses a tropical forest exhibit, an aquarium, and an African Savannah exhibit that features a number of exotic animals native to the vast grasslands of central and southern Africa. Recent additions to the zoo include a Children's Center, complete with farm animals and educational programs, and an otter exhibit.

614 Broadway
(btwn Clove Rd & Forest Ave)
718-442-3100
Daily 10am-4:45pm
Staten Island Ferry to
Saint George Station,
S-48 Bus from the
Ferry Terminal
Admission $4-7

SHOP

Everything Goes Book Cafe & Neighborhood Stage

Flanked by nondescript storefronts, the bright yellow marquee of Everything Goes explodes from the its bland surroundings and beckons passersby inside. The largest used book collection in Staten Island also boasts an array of vinyl records, a gallery of local artists' works, and free WiFi. Curl up with a book on

208 Bay St (near Victory Blvd)
718-447-8256
Tues-Thurs 10:30am-6:30pm,
Fri & Sat 10:30 am-10pm,
Sun 12pm-5pm
Staten Island Ferry to
Saint George Station,
S40/S90 to Richmond Terrace

a chintzy armchair in the Reading Room, or move to the café's garden, where you can sip one of their organic coffees or teas and nibble on scrumptious vegan treats. Locals relax on the mismatched kitchen chairs of the café, open late on Friday and Saturday nights. Evenings and Sunday afternoons bring a variety of free events that from readings and book-signings to musical performances and open mic opportunities—where everyone's welcome and anything goes.

EAT

Café Botanica
American, Café

1000 Richmond Terrace (at Snug Harbor Rd)
718-720-9737
Breakfast $7-13, Lunch $9-14
Staten Island Ferry to Saint George Station,
$40 bus to Snug Harbor

Nestled in the midst of the Staten Island Botanical Gardens, on the historic and beautiful Cottage Row, this café satisfies ravenous garden-goers and others exploring the sprawling Snug Harbor. The breakfast, best taken on the cottage's porch, is standard but well-executed. Blueberry pancakes are perfectly fluffy and come paired with fresh fruit. The service is warm, and there's something distinctly anti-New York about the experience—sitting amongst sprawling vegetation, in a Victorian-era cottage, being doted on by servers who communicate in forms other than terse grunts and impatient stares—that can provide both a calm respite from the bustle of the neighboring boroughs.

Dosa Garden
South Indian, Sri Lankan

323 Victory Blvd
718-420-0919
Daily 11:30am-3pm, 5-11pm
Staten Island Ferry to Saint George Station,
then Walk or Cab it
Meals $7-20

Nestled in a cozy Sri Lankan neighborhood, Dosa Garden dresses up a plain, almost austere interior with eye-popping food. The savory bread basket or the fluffy vada are great to start, but their signature dosas are the culinary attraction. Made from either spiced lentil flour or semolina, these mammoth Indian crêpes require baking-sheet-sized trays. And their expertise extends well into other areas of sub-continent cuisine, as evidenced by the rich palak paneer. Malai chicken tikka, a succulent Tandoori dish, is the perfect accompaniment to the beautifully presented, aromatic biryani. Dozens of vegetarian and non-vegetarian curries, Indo-Chinese specialties, and soothing sweet or salty lassis complete the extensive menu. Room for dessert? Visit the traditional bakeshop across the way to sate your sweet tooth.

INDEX
BY CATEGORY

INDEX 417

INDEX
BY CATEGORY

DINING

INDEX BY NAME

INDEX BY NAME

INDEX BY NAME

INDEX BY NAME

INDEX BY NAME

NOTES

www.colorswirl.com
www.lifewithtigers.com

HANDMADE ART from 2 locals

brooklyn *in your house*

SUMMER IN NEW YORK CITY

The New School Summer Housing program offers all our guests a safe and convenient home base while taking classes, working, or completing an internship in New York City.

THE NEW SCHOOL SUMMER HOUSING

www.newschool.edu/studentservices/housing
summerhousing@newschool.edu
212.229.5459

SUMMER 2010 applications available starting January 2010
Housing Available in Greenwich Village and the Financial District